P9-EDQ-135

THE LIFE OF FRIEDRICH ENGELS

Other Works on Friedrich Engels by W. O. Henderson:

Engels: Selected Writings, edited by W. O. Henderson (Penguin Books, 1967)

Die Lage der arbeitenden Klasse in England, by Friedrich Engels, with an introduction by W. O. Henderson (Verlag J. H. W. Dietz, Hanover, 1965)

"Friedrich Engels in Manchester", by W. O. Henderson, in *Friedrich Engels 1820–1970* (Schriftenreihe des Forschungsinstituts der Friedrich-Ebert-Stiftung, 1971)

"The Firm of Ermen and Engels in Manchester", by W. O. Henderson in *Internationale Wissenschaftliche Korrespondez*, Heft 11/12, pp. 1–10, April, 1971

Books and Articles by Friedrich Engels translated and edited by W. O. Henderson and W. H. Chaloner:

Condition of the Working Class in England, by Friedrich Engels (Basil Blackwell, 1958; new edition 1970; Stanford University Press, 1968)

Friedrich Engels as Military Critic (Manchester University Press, 1959)

By W. O. Henderson and W. H. Chaloner:

"Friedrich Engels in Manchester" (*Memoirs and Proceedings of the Manchester Literary and Philosophical Society*, Vol. 98, Session 1956–7)

Friedrich Engels at the age of 25, 1845

The Life of Friedrich Engels

W. O. Henderson

In two volumes

VOLUME I

FRANK CASS: LONDON

First published 1976 *in Great Britain by*
FRANK CASS AND COMPANY LIMITED
67 Great Russell Street, London WC1B 3BT, England

and in United States of America by
FRANK CASS AND COMPANY LIMITED
c/o International Scholarly Book Services, Inc.
P.O. Box 4347, Portland, Oregon 97208

ISBN 0 7146 1320 7 (Case)
ISBN 0 7146 4002 6 (Paper)

Library of Congress Catalog Card No. 72–92963

Printed in Great Britain by
Clarke, Doble & Brendon Ltd.
Plymouth

**To
Fay
and
Joseph
Baggott**

Contents

Documents

Illustrations

Introduction

The year 1970 saw the 150th anniversary of the birth of Friedrich Engels who was Karl Marx's most intimate friend and collaborator. Today the disciples of Marx and Engels are numbered in millions and the way of life of great states is based upon their doctrines. An understanding of the career and work of Friedrich Engels is essential to an appreciation of the origin and development of the Marxist form of socialism in the nineteenth century. Since the publication of Gustav Mayer's biography of Engels in 1934 – only an abridged version is available in English – additional material on Engels's life has become available and many scholars have been engaged in research on various aspects of the early socialist movement. The studies of Auguste Cornu and Herwig Förder on Engels's career as a young revolutionary to 1848 are of particular value. Attention has also been paid to the activities of some of the disciples of Marx and Engels – such as Georg Weerth and Wilhelm Wolff – in the 1840s and 1850s. My own study of Engels's career endeavours to bring together for English readers the results of this recent research.

My interest in Engels began when Dr W. H. Chaloner and I made a new translation of Engels's *Condition of the Working Class in England* and also edited the military articles which he contributed to the *Volunteer Journal for Lancashire and Cheshire*. The task of preparing a new life of Engels has been facilitated by the University of Manchester which allowed me to have a term's leave of absence and the West German Government which gave me the opportunity of meeting various scholars interested in Marxist studies at a conference held in Trier in 1968. Among those who have helped me – but are in no way responsible for my errors – I should particularly like to mention Professor Ernst Hoffmann, Professor Helmut Hirsch, and Professor Wolfram Fischer. I should also like to thank Dr W. H. Chaloner and my wife for reading the proofs of this volume.

W. O. Henderson
1975

1

THE ROAD TO COMMUNISM 1820–1844[1]

I. Marx and Engels

Life in six cities in three countries helped to mould Karl Marx's closest friend and colleague into a communist. In Barmen, his birthplace, Friedrich Engels learned to hate the millowners and the Puritan way of life. In Bremen the life of a great seaport gave him his first glimpse of a wider world than that of a small provincial manufacturing town. In Berlin he gained his first experience of military affairs when he served for a year in the Prussian army while at the same time he received intellectual stimulus from his attendance at University lectures and from his contacts with the Young Hegelians. In London he met a group of exiled German workers who had become professional revolutionaries. In Manchester Engels became aware of the social evils brought about by the industrial revolution and he met Julian Harney, James Leach and other Chartists. And a brief visit to Paris in the autumn of 1844 saw the beginning of his collaboration with Karl Marx that lasted for nearly forty years.

Friedrich Engels became the junior partner of the most famous intellectual team of the nineteenth century. Marx and Engels formulated the doctrine of dialectical materialism and spent a lifetime in applying it to politics, to philosophy, to economics, to history, to literature, to art and to science. Together they founded the international socialist movement and gave it a programme in the Communist Manifesto. Together they started a political movement whose adherents accepted its principles with all the fervour of a new religion. The followers of Marx and Engels came to be counted by millions and fifty years after the establishment of the communist régime in Russia the influence of their ideas is more powerful than ever. Karl Marx gave his name to a new system of philosophical ideas and to a new political movement. His genius was recognised in his own day even by those who most detested his ideas and his political aims.

Yet without Engels the genius of Marx might have withered away. It was Engels who was largely responsible for stimulating

Marx to apply his philosophical doctrines to the study of economics. It was Engels who gave Marx the financial help that saved him from perishing miserably in his London lodgings. It was Engels who readily placed his facile pen at Marx's disposal so that the arid pages of *Das Kapital* sprang to life in *Anti Dühring* which enabled thousands of readers to understand the basic tenets of the Marxist doctrine. Ten years after Engels's death the German socialist historian Franz Mehring declared that there was "more danger of underestimating than of overestimating him".[2] Engels was far more than a mere assistant of Marx or an interpreter of Marx's ideas after his master's death. He worked with Marx as an independent collaborator and he made his own contributions to socialist doctrines.

II. Barmen 1820–38

The fact that Friedrich Engels was born in Barmen (November 29, 1820)[3] had an important influence upon his formative years. Barmen differed in two respects from many other German towns in the 1820s and 1830s. It was part of a manufacturing district in which the social evils of industrialisation could be seen some time before they became evident elsewhere[4] and it lay in one of the few regions in which most of the Protestant churches accepted the Pietist – or Puritan – doctrines and way of life. Engels's father was both a leading industrialist and a staunch Pietist and these two circumstances dominated Engels's boyhood.

The twin towns of Elberfeld and Barmen – with a population of over 40,000 after the Napoleonic wars – lay in the steep valley of the River Wupper, a tributary of the River Rhine. They formed part of the district of Berg and had been incorporated in the Prussian province of the Rhineland in 1815. In the later middle ages the lime-free waters of the Wupper were found to be suitable for bleaching linen yarn. At first the yarn came from the Low Countries but later some of it was spun and woven locally. By the eighteenth century silk and cotton had been added to the yarns that were bleached in the valley of the River Wupper. Barmen specialised in the production of cotton goods. The first cotton mill to be driven by water power in the valley of the Wupper was erected in 1785.[5] At the beginning of the nineteenth century the spinning process was largely mechanised but much weaving was still done on handlooms. In 1809 P. A. Nemnich described the Grand Duchy of Berg – which included the valleys of the Ruhr and the Wupper – as "a miniature England".[6] After the Napoleonic wars the collapse of the Continental System and the consequent revival of

English competition led to a depression in Elberfeld and Barmen and many of the handloom weavers were out of work.[7]

The fortunes of the Engels family had been founded in the second half of the eighteenth century by Johann Caspar Engels (the elder), who was Friedrich Engels's great-grandfather. This Johann Caspar began his career as a yarn merchant in a small way and in about 1770 he set up his own bleachworks and workshops for the manufacture of lace and ribbons. He became one of the leading citizens of Barmen and had the reputation of being a good employer who assisted his workers to buy their own cottages and gardens.[8]

In the next generation the firm was carried on by the two sons of the founder, one of whom was Johann Caspar (the younger), the grandfather of Friedrich Engels. He expanded the business and carried on the family tradition of social work by founding a school for the children of his operatives (1796) and by setting up a co-operative granary to provide cheap flour during the food shortage of 1816. On the death of Johann Caspar (the younger), his three sons – Engels's father Friedrich and two uncles – inherited the business. This partnership did not work smoothly and eventually Engels's father went into partnership with the brothers Godfrey and Peter Ermen to operate cotton spinning in Manchester,[9] Barmen and Engelskirchen[10] (1837–41). The German firm combined the manufacture of various kinds of cotton yarn and thread with the old established bleachworks. The English firm owned the Victoria Mills near Pendleton.[11] Engels's father is said to have been one of the first millowners in the Rhineland to install English machines in his factories.[12]

As a schoolboy Engels became familiar with the cotton trade since so many members of his family were engaged in it and he was sufficiently observant to appreciate something of the conditions under which the operatives and craftsmen of his native town lived and worked. At the age of nineteen he wrote an article in which he described the wretched lives of the lower classes in the Wupper valley and he pilloried the millowners whom he held responsible for this state of affairs. He declared that the weavers were robbed of their health by bending over their looms for excessively long hours, that the tanners were physical wrecks after only three years, that the carriers were "a crew of utterly demoralised fellows", and that over a thousand children of school age were employed in the factories.[13] Many workers suffered from consumption and syphilis because of bad working conditions and poor housing. At week-ends the inns were packed and disgraceful scenes were witnessed at closing time.[14] Many years later Engels recalled the evil consequences of the introduction of Prussian brandy into the Wupper valley in the late 1820s. He claimed that he could remember seeing crowds of drunken revellers staggering arm in arm along the streets and that quarrels and knifings were a common occurence.[15]

All this made a deep impression upon the young Engels. Already he recognised the gulf that separated the two social classes in his native town – the millowners on the one hand and the operatives and craftsmen on the other. He came to detest the millowners – the class to which his own father belonged – for he held them responsible for the wretched condition of the workers. He considered that the middle classes of the Wupper valley were to be condemned not only for the callous way in which they exploited their operatives but for their philistine way of life. "In Elberfeld and Barmen", he wrote in 1839, "a person is considered to be educated if he plays whist and billiards, talks a little about politics and has the knack of paying a compliment at the right time. These fellows lead an awful life and yet they are quite content. All day long they immerse themselves in figures in their offices and it is difficult to realise how zealously they throw themselves into their work. In the evening all of them regularly go to their clubs to smoke, play cards and talk politics. At the stroke of nine they all go home. One day is just like another without anything changing. And woe to anyone who interferes with this strict routine. The penalty would be to fall into disgrace with all the best families."[16]

Elberfeld and Barmen were not only industrial towns but they were also one of the main centres of the Pietist movement in Germany. There had been Puritan sects in Germany in the late seventeenth century and in the eighteenth century which subscribed to the Calvinist doctrine of predestination and ran their affairs on Presbyterian lines. Like the English Puritans they tried to regulate strictly the daily lives of their members. They wore sombre garments, they were strict Sabbatarians, and they frowned upon such worldly pleasures as reading novels, dancing, and visiting the theatre or the opera. Pietism had declined in the late eighteenth century with the rise of the rationalist ideas of the Enlightenment. But the movement revived in a new form in the early nineteenth century as a reaction against the excesses of the French Revolution. It was this type of Pietism – known as "Restoration Pietism" – that flourished in the Wupper valley in the 1820s. The Pietists believed in the literal truth of every word in the Bible and they were intolerant of those who views differed from their own. Their leader in Elberfeld and Barmen was Pastor F. W. Krummacher who eventually became court preacher to Frederick William IV of Prussia. Krummacher was a fiery preacher whose "narcotic sermons" (as Goethe called them) moved his congregation to tears when he described the fate that awaited evildoers in the next world.[17]

Since Engels's parents were Pietists he had a strict upbringing at home, in church and at school. Engels does not appear to have reacted against his religious instruction during his school days and when he was confirmed at the age of seventeen he was, at any rate outwardly, a believing Christian. But after he had left home for Bremen his attitude changed. In 1839 he wrote to his friend Friedrich Graeber that the Wupper valley was very properly criticised for its mysticism and obscurantism.[18] He claimed that he had never accepted the doctrines of the Pietists and that he was a "supernaturalist".[19] "If, at the age of 18, one has read Strauss,[20] the Rationalists and the *Kirchen Zeitung* one must either stop thinking for oneself or one must begin to doubt one's Wuppertal faith. I simply do not understand how the orthodox clergy can be as orthodox as they are in view of the fact that the Bible is so full of contradictions."[21]

Engels declared that he was "a wholehearted disciple of Strauss"[22] and that through Strauss he had taken "the road that leads straight to Hegelianism".[23] He dismissed the Calvinist doctrine of predestination as a patent absurdity[24] and he attacked Krummacher for being so silly as to expect his flock to believe that the sun revolves round the earth. "The fellow dares to shout this to all the world on April 21, 1839 and yet he argues that Pietism is not leading us all back to the middle ages. It really is a scandal!"[25] In the following year Engels wrote an article describing a lively controversy which had broken out in Bremen when Krummacher delivered two sermons there. Engels attacked "the Pope of the Wuppertal Calvinists and the St Michael of the doctrine of predestination" in no uncertain terms.[26] By this time he had taken the first step on the road from Pietism to atheism.[27]

If Barmen was exceptional because of its relatively early industrialisation and its fervent Pietism, it shared with many other Prussian towns a firm loyalty to the Hohenzollerns. Although the Wupper valley had only been joined to Prussia in 1815 the inhabitants quickly accepted their new rulers. Provided that they could keep the liberal *Code Napoléon* they were quite prepared to become loyal subjects of the King of Prussia.[28] And so Engels grew up in a household in which respect for the throne came second only to unqualified acceptance of Pietism doctrines. Here, too, there is ample evidence that soon after he left home for Bremen, Engels began to deviate from the political views of his parents and schoolmasters. In October 1839 he recommended Venedey's book *Preussen und Preussentum* to his friend Friedrich Graeber. He told Graeber that Venedey had shown that the rulers of Prussia favoured absolutism, suppressed political freedom, supported the rich at the expense of the poor, and aimed at keeping the majority of the people in a state of ignorance.[29] And in other letters and articles the young Engels left his readers in no doubt that he held the Hohenzollerns in the greatest contempt. Of Frederick William IV he wrote: "Compared with him Napoleon was an angel. If our monarch is to be regarded as a member of the human race then His Majesty of Hanover is a god indeed."[30]

Until the age of fourteen Engels was educated at the Town School in Barmen. This poorly-endowed school was controlled by a Pietist governing body which normally only appointed Pietist teachers. When he wrote about his old school in 1839 Engels commented favourably upon only two of his former teachers: Phillipp Schifflin, the French master, whom he regarded as "the best teacher in the school", and the young Heinrich Köser, a friend of the poet Freiligrath, who taught German literature. Engels's assessment of the intellectual attainments of the rest of the staff may be judged by his anecdote of the small boy who asked his teacher who Goethe was and received the answer: "A godless fellow". Engels was later sent to the grammar school at Elberfeld which enjoyed a high reputation for sound scholarship. It was run by a Pietist congregation but, according to Engels, the clergy generally left the governors to their own devices and interfered little in the running of the school. Engels commented favourably upon the classical scholarship of Dr Hantschke, the acting headmaster, in whose house he lodged since his home was too far away from the school for him to travel every day. His highest praise, however, was reserved for Dr Clausen who taught history and German literature. Engels's final school report showed that Dr Hantschke recognised the wide range of his pupil's interests. He paid tribute to Engels's unusual linguistic abilities.

When Engels left school Dr Hantschke in his final report (September 25, 1837) stated that he had originally intended to go to a university. But he left a year before he was due to take his final examination. It is not clear why Engels's father decided that his son should enter the family business at once. Engels may well have welcomed this arrangement. Had he studied at a university he might have been expected to enter the Prussian civil service and he had no ambitions in that direction. His real interests lay in literary work and in journalism, but his father would not have been prepared to accept this as a suitable profession for his son.

Engels may have felt that a career in business would give him time to achieve his literary ambitions. Perhaps he was influenced by the example of the poet Ferdinand Freiligrath who was able to carry on his literary work although he earned his living in an Elberfeld office. Engels worked in his father's office for twelve months (September 1837–August 1838) after leaving school but no information about his activities in this period has come to light.[31]

III. Bremen, 1838–41[32]

In the autumn of 1838 Engels left Barmen for Bremen to gain experience in the office of Heinrich Leupold who was the head of a firm of exporters. Engels's father probably sent his son to Bremen not only because he knew Leupold but because the Pietists were as strongly entrenched in Bremen as in Barmen. Engels lodged with a clergyman – Pastor Treviranus – and his father hoped that his son would continue to come under Pietist influences even after he had left home. But Treviranus[33] was no Krummacher. He was less interested in theology than in applying his faith to practical affairs and he founded societies to care for discharged prisoners and distressed Protestant emigrants. Engels's letters to his younger sister Marie and to his schoolfriends the Graeber brothers – and also his newspaper articles – record his impressions of Bremen and show how his ideas on literature and on politics were developing.

Engels was now in a quite different environment from that to which he had been accustomed at home. In the Treviranus household there was little of the intolerant Calvinist orthodoxy that he had known in Elberfeld and Barmen. He was given the front door key so that he could come home when he pleased.[34] And the free and easy atmosphere of the office of Consul Leupold[35] – whom Engels described as "a thoroughly decent chap"[36] – was a welcome change from his father's office where the clerks were expected to apply themselves strictly to their duties.

The Free Hanseatic City of Bremen had little in common with provincial Barmen. It was a sovereign state and a member of the German Confederation in its own right. It was one of Germany's largest ports, importing cotton, coffee, sugar and tobacco from the Americas and exporting linens and other manufactured goods from Westphalia and Silesia. It handled an ever-increasing volume of emigrant traffic from central Europe to the United States. In its streets, cafés, and bars traders and sailors from all over the world were to be found. Bremen was governed by a group of old families whose rule – old-fashioned though it might be – was less oppressive than that of the governments of the large north German states such as Prussia and Hanover. Despite the influence of an out-of-date patrician oligarchy and of the Pietist pastors, a young man of unorthodox views could enjoy a greater freedom in Bremen than in Elberfeld or Barmen.

In an article of 1840 Engels described the hierarchy of a small Bremen office of the type in which he worked. "The chief clerk already gives himself airs as a person of some importance for his next step will be to start up a business on his own account. He is the general factotum of the firm. He knows the business inside out. He is well-informed concerning the state of the market. When he visits the exchange he is surrounded by brokers. Below him is a senior clerk who flatters himself that he is very nearly as important a person as the chief clerk. Naturally he is not on the same footing as the chief clerk when it comes to discussing matters with the head of the firm but he certainly knows enough to be able to deal with a broker, a warehouseman or a boatman. If the head of the firm and the chief clerk are both away he represents the firm to the outside world and the good name of the firm depends on how he conducts himself. The junior clerk, on the other hand, is an unlucky fellow. He represents the firm only in relation to the packers and to the postman in whose round the office is situated. Not only must he copy out all the business letters and the bills of exchange but he has to make out the accounts and pay small bills. Moreover he has to act as a general errand boy. He goes to the post office to collect and to deliver letters. And he has to wrap up all the parcels and address the crates and packing cases."

Engels, however, found that the duty of copying Consul Leupold's business correspondence into a ledger was interspersed with more agreeable social activities. He occasionally complained of overwork,[37] but most of his references to the office in his letters suggest that life in Consul Leupold's somewhat unconventional establishment could be a very pleasant experience. He wrote to his sister: "There is a bar in our office. We have beer bottles under the table, behind the stove, and behind the cupboards – beer bottles all over the place. And if the old man is thirsty, he borrows one of our bottles and fills it up again afterwards. Our drinking is done quite openly and no one makes a secret of it. A bottle of beer and some glasses stand on the table all day. The empty bottles are in the corner on the right and the full bottles are on the left. I tell you Marie it is quite true that youth gets worse and worse. As Dr Hantschke says: 'Who would have thought 20 or 30 years ago of such goings on as beer drinking in an office?' "[38] A sketch in one of Engels's letters shows the writer reclining comfortably in a hammock after lunch enjoying a cigar.[39]

When the head of the firm and his son were away from the office the clerks left their ledgers to read, write and drink. Engels studied works on philosophy, theology, history and literature and improved his knowledge of modern languages. He carried on his private correspondence and he began to write for the press. In his free time he joined a choir and a fencing club[40] and he read the foreign papers in the Union Literary Institute.[41] He frequented bars, the theatre and the opera. At week-ends he indulged in horse riding, walking and swimming with his friend Richard Roth and he went on a steamship excursion on the River Weser.[42] He obviously enjoyed life to the full – even if he did get into debt.[43] His philosophy was summed up in a letter to Wilhelm Graeber: "To get the most out of life you must be active, you must live, and you must have the courage to taste the thrill of being young."[44]

In addition to his numerous other activities Engels found time to write for the press. His early articles either appeared anonymously or under the pen name 'Friedrich Oswald'.[45] They were influenced by the literary movement known as 'Young Germany'. In 1839 he told Friedrich Graeber that he was "a Young German with all his heart and soul".[46] The Young Germans were the angry young men of the 1830s. They rejected the fairy tale world of the romantic movement and wrote about live social issues. In politics they were radicals who supported parliamentary government, the right of public assembly, a free press, an independent judiciary and the emancipation of women. Their religious views were extremely liberal. They strongly opposed the narrow-minded orthodoxy of the Pietists. Their attitude towards social problems showed an awareness of the need to deal with the poverty and unemployment brought about by the first phase of the industrial revolution. These doctrines aroused the wrath of the reactionary rulers in Germany. An edict of the German Confederation of December 10, 1835 denounced 'Young Germany' for "attacking the Christian religion in a most impertinent manner, for denigrating the existing social order, and for flouting all standards of decency and morality". The edict named Heine, Gutzkow, Laube, Wienberg and Mundt as the leaders of the movement and ordered all members of the Confederation to ban the publication of the works of the Young Germans.

Carl Gutzkow, a leading Young German and editor of the Hamburg *Telegraph für Deutschland*, encouraged Engels's literary aspirations by publishing some of his early essays in 1839–41. Gutzkow, who had considerable experience in these matters, revised Engels's articles so that they passed the censor's scrutiny. Engels, however, soon found Gutzkow's tutelage to be irksome.

He objected to changes being made in his manuscripts and after 1841 he ceased to contribute to the *Telegraph*.[47] Gutzkow complained to Alexander Jung of this shabby treatment. "Nearly all these young authors (he wrote) are the same. We give them a chance to think and to write but as soon as they can stand on their own feet they indulge in intellectual patricide."[48]

At the same time Engels was acting as 'Bremen correspondent' for the *Morgenblatt für gebildete Leser* which was published in Stuttgart by the firm of Cotta.[49] Except for an ode to Immermann his essays were concerned with local events such as the theatre, the opera, military manœuvres, the Gutenberg festival, trade and commerce, and the controversy between the Pietists and the Rationalists.

These essays are important partly because they throw some light upon Engels's early life at home and in Bremen and partly because they contain evidence of the writer's progress towards intellectual maturity. In some of the articles – such as "Letters from the Wupper Valley", "A Trip to Bremerhafen" and "Landscapes" – Engels wrote about his home town or about excursions that he had made from Bremen. In these essays the young author showed both remarkable powers of observation and the ability to describe what he had seen in vivid phrases which held the reader's attention. Many years later Wilhelm Liebknecht wrote that Engels "had a clear bright mind, free from any romantic or sentimental haze". "He never saw men or things through coloured spectacles or a misty atmosphere but always in clear bright air. His clear bright vision pierced the surface to the bottom of things. . . . That perspicacity which Mother Nature so rarely bestows at birth was an essential feature of Engels and I was immediately struck by it when we met for the first time."[50] These qualities of keen observation and brilliant descriptive writing were characteristics of Engels's literary work throughout his life. His accounts of the Baden rising of 1849 and of the review of the volunteers on Newton Heath in 1860 can still be read with pleasure as descriptive pieces of unusual merit. And his vivid account of the English slums raised his book on *The Condition of the Working Class in England* far above the level of other works written about industrial England in the 1840s.

It has been seen that Engels's first contribution to the *Telegraph* – the "Letters from the Wupper Valley" – was a bitter attack upon the millowners and Pietists of Elberfeld and Barmen. Engels declared that the manufacturers were responsible for the wretched condition of the factory operatives and the domestic workers and that the Pietist pastors were responsible for keeping their flocks in ignorance of all modern thought and progress. These articles infuriated the pious citizens of Elberfeld and Barmen. According to Wilhelm Blank copies of the journal were quickly sold and there was much speculation concerning the identity of the author. Some thought that the poet Freiligrath had written the articles but no one seems to have guessed that they came from the pen of the nineteen-year-old son of one of the most respected Pietist millowners in the district. Engels himself was delighted at having thrown the cat among the pigeons in his home town. "Ha! ha! ha," he wrote to Friedrich Graeber, "Do you know who wrote the article in the *Telegraph*? I wrote it myself but I beg you not to say anything about it. If the authorship were known I would be in hot water with a vengeance."[51] So strong were the protests from Elberfeld and Barmen that Gutzkow felt it necessary to print a reply to Engels's articles from an anonymous correspondent.[52]

Engels's article on "Landscapes" gave a brief account of a journey to Holland and England in 1840.[53] His impressions of the Dutch countryside are of interest because of his suggestion that there might be a link between the physical environment of a people and its religious practices. The essay contains a hint of the materialist doctrine which later formed the basis of his philosophy. His description of a railway journey from London to Liverpool was Engels's first reference to a visit to the country in which so much of his life was to be spent. Engels's lively account of a river trip to Bremerhaven in the summer of 1840 was another early essay which gave the young author full scope for exercising his powers of observation.[54] He began by describing some of the passengers who boarded the *Roland* steamship – the office clerks, the craftsmen, the peasants, the prospective emigrants and a sprinkling of merchants who held themselves aloof from the common herd. When he reached Bremerhaven Engels visited an emigrant ship which was lying at anchor. He criticised the unsatisfactory accommodation of the steerage passengers, but consoled them with the reflection that they were better off than those who sailed from Le Havre.

While Engels's essays on life in the Wupper valley and in Bremen show the flowering of his style as a descriptive writer, his early efforts to establish himself as a literary critic are significant because they illustrate the speed with which the disciple of 'Young Germany' outgrew his enthusiasm for the writings of Gutzkow and Beck and became absorbed in the study of Hegel's philosophy, which proved to be the key to his future intellectual development. In July 1839 Engels still regarded the Young German poet Karl Beck as a genius[55] yet only six months later he curtly dismissed Beck's most recent verses as "utterly and childishly naive."[56] Soon afterwards he condemned the reactionary tendencies and the lack of originality in contemporary German literature but he saw a ray of hope for the future in the increasing influence of Hegel's system of philosophy on German writers and artists.[57] A brief note in April 1840 on August Platen's poems on Poland showed that Engels was already taking an interest in international affairs and that he was strongly opposed to the reactionary Tsarist régime in Russia.[58]

Engels's stay in Bremen enabled him to escape from the stifling restrictions of a Pietist home and at first he appreciated his good fortune in being able to live with the Treviranus family and to work in Consul Leupold's easy going office. And for a young man from provincial Barmen there were new experiences to be gained in a great seaport like Bremen. But Engels never really settled down in Bremen. He made a number of acquaintances but few friends. Adolf Torstrick and Richard Roth were the only new companions mentioned in his correspondence. Engels had a restless disposition and less than a year after going to Bremen he was already discussing with his father the possibility of leaving. But on January 20, 1840 he wrote to Friedrich Graeber: "I have delayed writing to you until I knew for certain if I am going to stay here or to leave. Now at last I can tell you that, for the time being, I shall remain in Bremen."[59] Early in 1841 Engels's father agreed that his son should come home. In a letter of March 8, 1841 Engels wrote to his sister: "Thank God I will soon be getting out of this boring hole where no one does anything except fence, eat, drink, sleep and work – and that's the lot."[60] By April he was back in Barmen.

IV. Berlin, 1841–2

Little is known of Engels's activities between his departure from Bremen in April 1841 and his arrival in Berlin in September or October of the same year. Only four letters, written to his sister Marie in these months, have survived.[61] Engels appears to have spent his time in private study and in enjoying himself. On April 5 he wrote that he was reading Italian books, that he had been fencing and that he had recently met a number of his old school friends. He declared that Barmen was as dull as ever and he complained of a boring visit to friends of the family.

Early in May he told his sister that he expected to be in Milan in a week's time. His visit to Switzerland and Italy is described in two essays which appeared in the *Athenäum* in December 1841.[62] By August he was home again and he told his sister that no decision had yet been reached concerning his departure for Berlin. "I do not worry about anything at all," he wrote, "and I am content to let others do the worrying." On September 9 he wrote to his sister that he expected to leave for Berlin in a week or a fortnight to perform his military service.[63]

The long interval between Engels's return to Barmen and his departure for Berlin was probably due to differences between his father and himself concerning his future career. There is no suggestion in his letters that he worked in his father's office at this time. And this would have been the obvious course to adopt if he intended to continue his training in the cotton business. It may be assumed that his father was pressing him to join the family firm while Engels was hoping to make a name for himself as a writer or a journalist. Eventually Engels went to Berlin for a year to perform his national service. Since he detested the Prussian army and all that it stood for one might have expected that he would have evaded conscription which was quite possible in those days for a young man with wealthy parents. Engels may well have been influenced by two considerations. While he was serving in the forces a final decision concerning his future career could be postponed. Moreover by going to Berlin he would have the opportunity both to attend lectures (as a visiting student) at one of the greatest universities in Germany and to make contact with a group of Young Hegelians with whose views he sympathised.

Engels went to Berlin in the autumn of 1841 as a "one year volunteer" in the Guards Foot Artillery.[64] In later years he became a recognised authority upon military affairs and his friends called him "the General".[65] But there is no evidence to suggest that he took his military training very seriously. He grumbled to his sister Marie about the "accursed shooting range" and the parade ground where men sank up to their knees in sand.[66] He complained about church parades but appears to have experienced little difficulty in avoiding them.[67] He boasted of his success in dodging a night route march by feigning toothache.[68] Although he performed his duties well enough to earn promotion to the rank of bombardier[69] and to secure a satisfactory certificate of discharge[70] his brief spell of duty under Captain von Wedell "did not increase his admiration of the Prussian military system or the Prussian government".[71] But Engels's experience of the parade ground seems to have left its mark upon him. Friedrich Lessner, who met him in London in 1847, described him as one who looked "more like a smart young lieutenant than a scholar".[72]

What Berlin had to offer Engels was not exercises with the artillery but lectures at the university, discussions with Young Hegelians, and a very agreeable social life. He did not have to live in barracks but was able to rent a private room in the Dorotheenstrasse. He wrote to his sister Marie about his visits to the theatre and the opera and the café which specialised in Rhenish dishes. He was fond of music and enjoyed a choral festival which was held in the spring of 1842.[73] Engels despised the officers, civil servants, courtiers and aristocrats who dominated Berlin society and the petty tradesmen and workers[74] whose way of life Glassbrenner described in countless sketches.[75] Yet Engels probably agreed with Michael Bakunin that the Prussian capital in those days was "a good town to live in". "It has excellent wine, cheap living, a very good theatre, and many newspapers in the cafés."[76]

As a contributor to the *Telegraph* Engels naturally made contact with the Young Hegelians in Berlin. They were a lively group of atheists, republicans and revolutionaries.[77] A little later – in July 1842 – they established a society called 'the Free'. The leaders of the group were not in Berlin when Engels arrived. Bruno Bauer[78] was teaching at Bonn University while Arnold Ruge[79] was lecturing at Halle University. Engels's closest friend among the Young Hegelians was Edgar Bauer[80] – Bruno's younger brother – and he also met Max Stirner,[81] Köppen,[82] and Nauwerck.[83]

Engels attended courses at the university including those of Schelling, Marheineke, Werder and Henning.[84] He wrote that "the fame of Berlin University is due to the fact that – more than any other seat of learning – it stands in the very forefront of modern intellectual movements. It is the arena in which the great controversies of our time are fought out. Many universities – Bonn, Jena, Giessen, Greifswald and even Leipzig, Breslau and Heidelberg – have sunk into intellectual apathy because they have ignored these controversies. Unfortunately for many years such a withdrawal has been the hallmark of scholarship at German universities. But in Berlin professors and lecturers have been appointed who hold very different opinions and they indulge in lively controversies which give their students an admirably clear picture of modern intellectual trends."[85] Engels's contacts with the Young Hegelians and with the university greatly stimulated his intellectual development and soon involved him in philosophical and political controversies that reverberated throughout Germany.

Engels's arrival in Berlin coincided with the publication of Feuerbach's book on *The Essence of Christianity*.[86] In later life Engels declared that only those who had "experienced the liberating effects of this book" could appreciate the impact upon the Young Hegelians of Feuerbach's attack upon revealed religion. "Enthusiasm was universal and we all immediately became disciples of Feuerbach." For Engels the significance of the book was that it "enthroned materialism once more" and showed that "nothing exists outside Nature and Man".[87] Feuerbach's ideas – a halfway house between idealism and materialism – profoundly influenced Marx and Engels in their years of "storm and stress". By analysing and criticising Feuerbach's views they came to realise how the doctrine of dialectical materialism could be derived from the Hegelian system of philosophy.

When he was in Berlin Engels wrote several articles and pamphlets which helped to establish the reputation of 'Oswald' as a political commentator. A new era for writers and journalists opened in 1840 when Frederick William IV came to the throne of Prussia. This brilliant but unstable monarch was conservative and autocratic in outlook. Yet his accession was marked by the cautious introduction of various reforms. In December 1841 the censorship authorities were told to interpret the regulations in a liberal spirit. At the same time, however, newspaper editors were warned not to abuse their new freedom. In 1842 books and caricatures – but not pamphlets – were freed from the censorship. This encouraged radical journalists to express their views with greater freedom than before. Engels took advantage of the new situation to contribute to left-wing journals such as the *Rheinische Zeitung* and the *Deutsche Jahrbücher*. He wrote a little later that during the "temporary relaxation of the censorship of the press . . . papers, published under the authorisation of a government censor, contained things which, even in France, would have been punished as high treason, and other things which could not have been pronounced in England, without a trial for blasphemy being the consequence of it."[88] But the royal honeymoon with the press was of short duration. In February 1843 caricatures were again censored and soon afterwards the *Deutsche Jahrbücher* and the *Rheinische Zeitung* were banned.[89]

The most important of Engels's writings while he was in Berlin dealt with the controversy concerning Schelling's attack upon the Hegelian system of philosophy. When Frederick William IV ascended the throne he persuaded Schelling to exchange his chair at Munich for one at Berlin in the hope that the new professor would counteract the influence of the existing lecturers in philosophy. The King abhorred the rationalist and freethinking tendencies shown by these teachers whose influence upon the students he considered to be wholly pernicious. Schelling's lectures were held in the winter term of 1841–2. Engels attended the course and gave a vivid description of the scene when the inaugural lecture was delivered.[90] Men of all nations, professions and religious beliefs filled the *auditorium maximum*. Grave scholars and clergymen who had matriculated fifty years before and grey-haired staff officers sat next to students and young army volunteers. It was a great occasion in the academic world for it was understood that the venerable Schelling – he was 67 years old – would reveal a new philosophical system on which he had been working for many years. And this system would sound the death knell of Hegel's influence upon the learned world in Germany.

Hegel had endeavoured to prove the existence of the Absolute scientifically by historical facts. Schelling now argued that the Absolute could be shown to exist by a process of reasoning. But he went further when he developed his own "philosophy of revelation" and claimed that "revelation must include within itself something more than reason – yet something that can be attained only by exercising one's reason". And as Schelling's lectures proceeded and his arguments were unfolded the philosopher moved into a private world of mystical phantasies into which few of his listeners could follow him. Engels was first in the field to defend the views of the Young Hegelians. In March 1842 – before Schelling had completed his lectures – his pamphlet on *Schelling und die Offenbarung* was published anonymously in Leipzig.[91]

In this pamphlet Engels discussed the development of Hegelian philosophy after Hegel's death in 1830. Hegel's followers had split into two groups – the orthodox disciples and the Young Hegelians. The latter accepted Hegel's principles but not his conclusions. They used Hegel's technique to undermine revealed religion and monarchical principles. Engels argued that the Young Hegelians were the most faithful followers of their master since they had pursued Hegel's ideas to a logical conclusion. He had no difficulty in disposing of Schelling's criticisms of Hegel but – since he dealt only with Schelling's first three lectures – had little to say about Schelling's own "philosophy of revelation". Engels's pamphlet aroused considerable interest. Ruge reviewed it favourably in the *Deutsche Jahrbücher* while Marheineke and Paulus made use of it in their own defence of Hegel.[92]

In a second pamphlet called *Schelling der Philosoph in Christo* Engels denounced the "philosophy of revelation". It appeared to be the work of a devout Christian who was arguing that the new philosophy demolished Hegelianism and supported the Pietist point of view. In fact it was a clever – if cruel – parody of the Pietist style of writing and it showed Engels's contempt for the faith in which he had been raised. This pamphlet fanned the flames of the controversy between Schelling and the Hegelians.[93] At first the Young Hegelians, tongue in cheek, pretended to accept the pamphlet at its face value but before long the *Rheinische Zeitung* admitted that it was a parody.[94] The conservative *Augsburg Allgemeine Zeitung* on the other hand declared that the parody was not a matter for levity. It was an exceedingly offensive attack upon the truths of revealed religion.[95]

The controversy between Schelling and his opponents soon came to a dramatic end. Professor Paulus of Heidelberg published Schelling's lectures with highly critical footnotes of his own. Schelling appealed to the courts for protection since his lectures had been printed without his permission. He lost his case and resigned his chair in disgust. Thus the King failed to stifle the new trends in the teaching of philosophy and theology at Berlin. Next – through his Minister of Education, Eichhorn – he tried to suppress revolutionary and rationalist ideas by dismissing radical teachers and by banning their journals. In 1842 the poet Hoffmann von Fallersleben lost his professorship at Breslau, while Bruno Bauer's licence to teach theology at Bonn was withdrawn. Soon afterwards Nauwerck was dismissed from the staff of Berlin University. Engels – in collaboration with Edgar Bauer[96] – sprang to Bruno Bauer's defence in a satirical poem entitled *Der Triumph des Glaubens*.[97] The verses proved to be of more than ephemeral interest since the authors named all the Young Hegelians who had recently formed the society known as "the Free" in Berlin.

In 1842 Engels wrote regularly for the *Rheinische Zeitung* which had recently been established by leading businessmen in Cologne as the principal organ of Rhenish liberalism. When Karl Marx became its editor in October 1842 the tone of the paper became much more radical than before. The most interesting of Engels's contributions was his article on Liberalism in north and south Germany. He observed that for many years Baden, Württemberg and the Bavarian Palatinate had been in the forefront of progressive political thought in Germany. He argued that "the new German philosophy" – the doctrines of the Young Hegelians – had given an impetus to a new and more powerful radical movement in north Germany which would one day sweep aside the forces of conservatism and reaction.[98] At this time, too, Engels wrote an essay on Alexander Jung for Arnold Ruge's *Deutsche Jahrbücher* – the leading journal of the Young Hegelians[99] – and an article on Frederick William IV for Georg Herwegh's *Einundzwanzig Bogen aus der Schweiz*.[100] He dismissed Frederick William's ideal of a medieval feudal Christian monarchy as quite impracticable in the 1840s and argued that the King would soon be forced to concede both a free press[101] and representative government to his subjects. In the summer of 1842 Engels told Ruge that he did not propose to write anything further for the *Deutsche Jahrbücher* as he wished to devote more time to his studies.

A year later, in an article published in Robert Owen's *New Moral*

World, Engels gave his own view of the astonishing progress of the radical and socialist agitation in Germany in 1842 under the stimulus of the Young Hegelians. He wrote:

> "The Young Hegelians of 1842 were declared Atheists and Republicans; the periodical of the party, the *German Annals*,[102] was more radical and open than ever before; a political paper was established, and very soon the whole of the German liberal press was entirely in our hands. We had friends in almost every considerable town in Germany; we provided all the liberal papers with the necessary matter, and by this means made them our organs; we inundated the country with pamphlets, and soon governed public opinion upon every question. A temporary relaxation of the censorship of the press added a great deal to the energy of this movement, quite novel to a considerable part of the German public. Papers, published under the authorisation of a government censor, contained things which, even in France, would have been punished as high treason, and other things which could not have been pronounced in England. without a trial for blasphemy being the consequence of it. The movement was so sudden, so rapid, so energetically pursued, that the government as well as the public were dragged along with it for some time. But this violent character of the agitation proved that it was not founded upon a strong party among the public, and that its power was produced by the surprise and consternation only of its opponents. The governments, recovering their senses, put a stop to it by a most despotic denial of the liberty of speech . . . the princes and rulers of Germany at the very moment when they believed to have put down republicanism for ever, saw the rise of communism from the ashes of political agitation; and this new doctrine appears to them even more dangerous and formidable than that in whose apparent destruction they rejoiced."[103]

Engels left Berlin in the middle of October 1842.[104] He went to Cologne to meet members of the staff of the *Rheinische Zeitung*. He saw Moses Hess, one of the editors, whom he later described as "the first communist" of the Young Hegelian party.[105] Hess, a leading supporter of utopian socialism in Germany,[106] believed that world revolution was inevitable and that France, Germany and England each had a special *rôle* to play in its accomplishment. From France would come the revolutionary spirit of 1789 and from Germany the intellectual stimulus of the Young Hegelian philosophy. But England, where the Chartists were on the march, would be the first country actually to achieve a social revolution.[107] Engels became one of Hess's disciples. Moses Hess wrote that "Engels was a revolutionary to the core before we met but when he left me he was a passionate communist."[108] Engels, who had been studying English social conditions,[109] accepted Hess's view of

England's *rôle* in the revolution of the future. He now proposed to go to England to examine the situation on the spot.

For once, Engels's plans coincided with those of his father. The elder Engels had become alarmed at the dubious company that his son had been keeping in Berlin and was horrified at his son's attitude towards politics and religion. His concern for his son was shown in a letter which he wrote to his brother-in-law, Karl Snethlage, in October 1842. He declared that he would not quarrel with his son. "A dispute would only make him more obstinate and more embittered. His salvation must come from above. I know that at his confirmation he had genuine religious feelings and I am certain that anyone who has once felt the power of God's Word in his heart can never be permanently satisfied with new beliefs. He may have to travel a hard road before he descends from his proud heights and realises that he must bow his head humbly before the mighty hand of the Almighty." "It is a heavy cross to bear that I have a son at home who is like a scabby sheep in a flock and openly opposes the beliefs of his forefathers. I hope however to give him plenty of work to do and – wherever he may be – I will arrange for him to be very carefully watched so that he does not do anything to endanger his future career." The elder Engels hoped that his son could be kept out of mischief in England where he could complete his training in the cotton trade. And where better could this be done than in the offices of Ermen and Engels in Manchester?

From Cologne Engels went home to Barmen to prepare for his forthcoming journey to England. On the way to London towards the end of November 1842 he again called at the offices of the *Rheinische Zeitung* and on this occasion he met Karl Marx. Many years later he recalled his first talk with the man who was to become his closest friend. He had a decidedly cool reception. This was because Marx "had taken a stand against Bruno and Edgar Bauer and has announced his opposition to the view that the *Rheinische Zeitung* should be mainly a vehicle for theological propaganda, atheism, etc. rather than for political discussion and action." Marx was also opposed to Edgar Bauer's "windy communism". Marx was also well aware of Engels's friendship with Edgar Bauer and he assumed that Engels shared Edgar's views. Consequently Marx regarded Engels's visit with some suspicion. Despite his somewhat unfriendly reception Engels seems to have been invited to continue to write for the *Rheinische Zeitung* during his forthcoming visit to England.[110]

V. London and Manchester 1842–4

Engels lived in England from November 1842 to August 1844. Since his correspondence for that period has not survived, his activities can be traced only by piecing together scattered items of information which appeared in his published works. There are also a few references to Engels's visits to England in 1842–4 in the writings of Harney, Weerth and Herwegh.

For most of the time Engels lived in Manchester but he was in London on at least two occasions. The evidence for the visit of 1842 is the fact that an article by Engels in the *Rheinische Zeitung* was headed "London, November 30" (1842). The fact that articles written towards the end of the year were headed "from Lancashire" suggests that Engels was in London for about three weeks. There is evidence for the visit to London in 1843 in Engels's account of the origins of the Communist League, written in 1885. Here he stated that he had met the German refugees Karl Schapper, Heinrich Bauer and Josef Moll in London in 1843. Although they made a deep impression upon him – they were "the first proletarian revolutionaries" he had met[111] – he declined their invitation to join the secret society (the League of the Just) to which they belonged. There is evidence that Engels visited Ostend in September 1843[112] and it is possible that he broke his journey in London. Moreover the vivid descriptions given by Engels in *The Condition of the Working Class in England* of the shipping in the Thames and the slums of St Giles suggest that he wrote from personal observation.[113]

In the first two articles which he wrote in England, dated November 30, 1842, Engels asked: "Is a revolution in England possible or even probable?" And he gave an affirmative answer to his question. He declared that the English stoutly denied that a revolution was imminent. They might admit that there was a social crisis but they considered that England's "wealth, industry and institutions would enable ways and means to be found to overcome the crisis before a catastrophe occurred". Engels considered that the English were deceiving themselves and would soon face a rude awakening. He argued that since the English economy was based entirely upon commerce, shipping and industry, the survival of the country depended upon a continual growth of its output of manufactured goods. But England's industry could not expand indefinitely. The sale of English goods abroad was being checked by hostile tariffs since other countries wished to foster their own industries. And the home market was stagnant since prohibitive import duties led to high prices which the poorer customers could not afford.

Engels argued that this situation had precipitated the crisis of 1842. Faced with a trade depression some northern manufacturers had attempted to reduce wages. The workers had gone on strike and had resorted to violence but the Plug Plot riots[114] had failed through lack of "preparation, organisation and leadership". Engels thought that the workers now realised that an improvement of their condition could be achieved only by overthrowing the nobility and the manufacturers by force. He asserted that hunger would soon drive the workers to new acts of violence.[115]

This article is of interest for two reasons. First, its date shows that it was written within a few days of Engels's arrival in England. The opinions expressed could not have been based upon an investigation of the condition of the factory workers. They were preconceived ideas similar to those held by Moses Hess. Shortly before – in June 1842 – Moses Hess had written an article in which he declared. "England, where distress has reached frightful proportions, is heading for a catastrophe sooner than had been expected. And no one can foretell the consequences that this catastrophe will have not only for Great Britain but also for the Continent."[116] Secondly, Engels's article illustrates his belief that he could predict the course of political events in England. As early as the autumn of 1842 he asserted that a workers' revolution in England was inevitable. Events proved him to be wrong. For years Engels waited for the fulfilment of his gloomy prophecy and for years he waited in vain.

In December 1842 Engels arrived in Manchester and stayed until 1844, working as a clerk in the office of the cotton firm of Ermen and Engels[117] of which his father had recently become a partner. His spare time was spent in free-lance journalism and in examining the life and work of the factory operatives in the industrial districts of the north. In an address to the English workers, written on his return home, he declared that he had come to England:

> "to see you in your homes, to observe you in your everyday life, to chat with you on your condition and grievances, to witness your struggles against the social and political power of your oppressors." "I have done so: I forsook the company and the dinner parties, the port-wine and champagne of the middle classes, and devoted my leisure hours almost exclusively to the intercourse with plain Working Men; I am both glad and proud to have done so. Glad, because thus I was induced to spend many a happy hour in obtaining a knowledge of the realities of life – many an hour, which else would

have been wasted in fashionable talk and tiresome etiquette; proud, because thus I got an opportunity of doing justice to an oppressed and calumniated class of men who with all their faults and under all the disadvantages of their situation, yet command the respect of every one but an English money-monger; proud, too, because thus I was placed in a position to save the English people from the growing contempt which on the Continent has been the necessary consequence of the brutally selfish policy and general behaviour of your ruling classes".[118]

Engels came into contact with various working class leaders, trade unionists, Chartists, and Socialists. He went to Leeds to see George Julian Harney,[119] the editor of the *Northern Star*,[120] which Engels regarded as one of the best newspapers in Europe. Harney later recalled a visit from "a slender young man with a look of almost boyish immaturity, who spoke remarkably pure English and said that he was keenly interested in the Chartist movement."[121] In Manchester Engels attended Chartist meetings in the Carpenters' Hall and met James Leach,[122] who was the author of a pamphlet on *Stubborn Facts from the Factories*. Leach was a member of the committee of the National Charter Association and Engels regarded him as a "good friend".[123] Engels also attended some of the Sunday lectures given by the Owenite secularist John Watts[124] in the Hall of Science in Campfield. At that time he regarded Watts as an "important person" and an able pamphleteer but in later years he took a less favourable view of Watts's activities.[125] Engels's companions on his tours of Manchester and other industrial towns included his girl friend the Irish millgirl Mary Burns and Georg Weerth, a young German friend who was then living in Bradford.[126]

Soon after he arrived in Manchester in December 1842 Engels wrote two further articles for the *Rheinische Zeitung*. In the first he argued that the situation of the British workers was becoming "more precarious every day". It was true that the excitement of the Plug Plot riots had subsided in Manchester where nine out of ten operatives were now in employment. Workers on the Continent would envy their standard of living since they could afford meat every day and drank tea, porter and brandy. But there was unrest among the English coalminers and ironworkers while in Scotland there was unemployment in the Glasgow district. Engels declared that when the next commercial crisis came – and it was due within the next few years – hunger would drive the English workers to revolt.

The second article discussed the Corn Laws. Engels believed that the bread tax would be swept away not so much by the efforts of the Anti-Corn Law League as by the fury of the "embittered masses". But he thought that the great landowners would fight to the last to defend their privileges. He considered that the propaganda of the Anti-Corn Law League had converted the tenant farmers to Free Trade and that they would now defy their Tory landlords and vote for the Whigs.[127]

In the summer of 1843 Engels contributed four articles on English affairs to a Swiss journal. The first described the English political parties and discussed the agitation concerning the education clauses of Sir James Graham's Factory Bill. The Dissenters bitterly opposed these clauses which appeared to hand over religious instruction in the factory schools to the Church of England. Supported by the Whigs, the Dissenters organised many public meetings to protest against the Bill. Engels attended such a meeting in Salford which ended in disorder when Chartists in the audience tried to propose an amendment to the resolution put forward from the platform.[128] The second article denounced the London correspondent of the *Augsburg Allgemeine Zeitung* who had informed his readers that the Anti-Corn Law League was "a power in the land". Engels declared that the League had no influence over the ministry or parliament and that its propaganda was overshadowed by that of the Chartists.

The third article discussed the socialist movement in England and described Sunday meetings addressed by men like Dr Watts in the Hall of Science in Manchester. The fourth article examined O'Connell's agitation for the repeal of the Union. Engels considered that only egoism, vanity and lack of judgment prevented O'Connell from making himself master of Ireland. "Give me two thousand Irish", he wrote, "and I will destroy the British monarchy once and for all." It was characteristic of Engels that in these articles he should have confidently forecast the future course of events in England. His confidence was sometimes misplaced. Contrary to his expectations the Anti-Corn Law League achieved its aims while the Chartist movement failed.[129]

Engels also wrote two articles for Robert Owen's *New Moral World* in 1843 in which he gave English readers a brief outline of the spread of communist ideas on the Continent.[130] While paying a tribute to the communist propaganda of Wilhelm Weitling among the Swiss and German workers Engels emphasised the importance of Marx, Ruge, Hess and Herwegh as leaders of a new communist movement in Germany. In a short third article, which appeared on February 3, 1844, Engels drew attention to the forthcoming publication of the *Deutsch-Französische Jahrbücher* to be edited by Ruge and Marx.

The first and only number of this journal appeared in Paris in February 1844.[131] Its youngest contributor was Engels whose "Outlines of a Critique of Political Economy" was his first essay on economics.[132] It is a significant article because it showed the progress that Engels had made on the road to communism before the commencement of his long period of collaboration with Marx. And Marx had a high opinion of the article since he referred to it as "a brilliant outline criticism of economic categories".[133]

In addition to criticising some of the contradictions inherent in the theories of the English classical economists, Engels attacked the entire capitalist system in no uncertain terms. He denounced the factory system because it undermined family life. "It is a common practice for children as soon as they are able to work – that is to say when they reach the age of nine – to spend their wages themselves and to look upon their parental home as a mere boarding house." Engels argued that the exchange of goods under the capitalist system lacked any moral basis and was no better than legalised robbery. "In commerce one is allowed to take the utmost advantage of the ignorance and the trust of the opposing party. One may bestow fictitious qualities on a commodity that one wishes to sell."

In a capitalist society the production and consumption of goods is regulated by supply and demand. In practice, according to Engels, "supply is always either a little too big or a little too small and never corresponds exactly to demand." This leads to "a state of continual fluctuation which never achieves equilibrium" with the result that "we now have a slump every five to seven years". Engels believed that "every new crisis must be more serious and more universal than the last". He warned his readers that eventually "commercial crises will lead to a social revolution far beyond the comprehension of the economists with their scholastic wisdom." The uncertain future of the economy fostered gambling in shares on the stock exchange. "The speculator always gambles on disasters – particularly bad harvests. He tries to profit from every disaster – such as the New York fire."[134] Engels argued that only the national planning of production – based upon a rational forecast of demand in the future – could cure the chronic evil of periodic slumps.

Although Engels had asserted that supply "never corresponds exactly to demand" a little later he described a situation in which "a state of equilibrium is reached between supply and demand and between production and consumption." When this happened "people starve from sheer abundance. England has been in this crazy position for some considerable time." So Engels was arguing that capitalism failed to work satisfactorily whether supply equalled demand or not.

Engels next criticised Malthus's population theory. He observed that "according to this theory population always presses upon the means of subsistence. . . . The inherent tendency of population to expand in excess of the available food is the root of all misery and vice. . . . Since it is the poor who are the surplus population nothing should be done for them except to make their starvation as easy as possible." Engels argued that there was a simple solution to the problem posed by Malthus. On the one hand there appeared to be a "surplus population". On the other hand there was "surplus wealth". Mankind had enormous productive powers. There was no limit to the potential increase in the productivity of land and factories. "Every day new scientific knowledge increasingly subjects the power of nature to mankind's needs." If human resources were intelligently planned the problem of a "surplus population" would vanish. Industrial societies were perfectly capable of producing all the goods and services required to maintain a decent standard of living for a growing population.

Engels regarded capitalism as inefficient, unfair, cruel and immoral. It was inefficient because of its chronic instability. It was cruel because its slumps condemned hundreds of thousands of workers to unemployment and distress. It was unfair because it tolerated great wealth side by side with grinding poverty. It was immoral because in a capitalist society men's actions were dictated solely by selfish motives of profit. Engels argued that private property – the root evil of capitalism – must be abolished and that uncontrolled competition must be replaced by central planning on rational principles. The essay was a remarkable one because it discussed issues with which we are quite familiar today but were still largely ignored by many of Engels's contemporaries. He examined factors of economic growth, the paradox of poverty in the midst of plenty, the phenomenon of the trade cycle, the tendency for free competition to lead to monopoly, the expansion of large businesses and estates at the expense of small firms and peasant holdings. It will be seen that Engels elaborated some of these points in his book on the English workers which was written in the following year.

It was with this book in mind that Engels gathered material on the political and economic history of England at the same time that he was engaged in the study of economics. He wrote two articles in *Vorwärts*, the radical organ of German emigrants in Paris with which Marx was associated. These articles may be regarded as a preliminary survey of the historical background of his forthcoming account of the condition of the English workers.[135] Engels described the course of the industrial revolution and the creation of a proletariat of wage-earners living in great manufacturing towns. He considered the emergence of a new kind of working class to be the most significant factor in the history of England in the eighteenth century. In his view there were now three social classes in the country – the landed aristocracy, the financial aristocracy, and the wage-earners. The first two shared the effective control of the state while the proletariat had no political power. Such a situation could not last for long. There would be a struggle between the propertied middle class and the oppressed workers. "In England the clash between aristocracy and democracy is the struggle between the rich and the poor." Engels concluded: "Democracy itself is incapable of curing social evils. Democratic equality is a chimera. The struggle between rich and poor cannot be fought on the basis of democracy – or indeed on the basis of politics. A political struggle between the rich and the poor is merely a transitional phase. It is simply a last attempt to solve the problem by purely political means. Out of this struggle will emerge a new principle overriding political conflicts. This is the principle of socialism."

Many years later Engels summed up the way in which his intellectual development had been furthered by his stay in England in 1842–4: "In Manchester it was forcibly brought to my notice that economic factors, hitherto ignored or at least underestimated by historians, play a decisive role in the development of the modern world. I learned that economic factors were the basic cause of the clash between different classes in society. And I realised that in a highly industrialised country like England the clash of social classes lay at the very root of the rivalry between parties and were of fundamental significance in tracing the course of modern political history."[136]

Twenty months in Manchester and London had turned Engels from an inexperienced youth to a young man who had found a purpose in life. Dr Julius Waldeck, a Berlin doctor, wrote in May 1844: "Engels has wrought a miracle in himself. His views and his style are more mature and more manly than they were a year ago."[137]

VI. Paris, 1844

In August 1844 Engels left Manchester and returned to Barmen. On the way he paid his first visit to Paris where he stayed for about ten days. At this time Paris was the centre of revolutionary movements in Europe and many observers considered that the fall of the July Monarchy would be the signal for the collapse of reactionary régimes in Austria, Germany and Italy. In July 1842 Heinrich Heine wrote that "the middle classes in Paris are obsessed by a nightmare apprehension of disaster. It is not fear of a republic but an instinctive dread of communism – of those sinister fellows who would swarm like rats from the ruin of the present régime." He added that the shopkeepers of Paris "sense instinctively that today a republic might no longer represent the principles of the 1790s. It might become the instrument through which a new unacknowledged power would seize control – a proletarian party preaching community of goods."[138]

It was in a city where the thunder clouds of social upheaval were already looming on the horizon that Engels met a group of exiles – Bakunin,[139] Bernays,[140] Ewerbeck[141] and Marx. And it was Paris that saw the beginning of the lifelong friendship between Marx and Engels.

Engels subsequently wrote: "When I visited Marx in Paris in the summer of 1844 we found ourselves in complete agreement on questions of theory and our collaboration began at that time." Engels had already met Marx on one occasion – when he had not been very warmly received – and had been in touch with Marx as a contributor to the *Deutsch-Französische Jahrbücher* and *Vorwärts*. With all the enthusiasm of young messiahs they proposed to overthrow the existing political and social order. Capitalism was to be replaced by a new kind of socialism. Established religions and philosophies were to be swept aside in favour of a new materialist ideology. The boldness of their plans was matched only by the astonishing successes that they eventually achieved.

Marx and Engels were well-matched collaborators. As Auguste Cornu has observed: "Since Engels had practical experience in the world of commerce and was always in contact with people in various walks of life he was an ideal partner for Marx who was applying theoretical principles to economic and social problems. On the other hand Marx had made greater advances in working out the basis of dialectical historical materialism and scientific socialism and he was able to help Engels to broaden his outlook on these matters. Marx was the leader in the partnership for he achieved, as Engels later admitted, what Engels could not have achieved by himself."[142]

After Marx's death Engels's verdict upon the years during which they had worked together was as follows: "I cannot deny that both before and during my forty years' partnership with Marx I had a certain independent share in working out the theory (of scientific socialism). But Marx was responsible for most of the leading basic ideas – particularly as far as economics and history were concerned – and he put those ideas into their final classic form. What I achieved – apart from work in a few specialised fields of study – Marx could have achieved without me. But what Marx achieved I could not have achieved."[143]

Karl Marx, two years older than Engels, was born in Trier in the Rhineland on May 5, 1818, of Jewish parents. On both sides of the family he was descended from rabbis who were highly respected in the Jewish community for their scholarship. Among his ancestors were several rabbis of Trier, but Heinrich Marx – Karl's father – was a lawyer. When Napoleon's empire collapsed Prussia secured substantial territories on the left bank of the Rhine, including Trier. Jews were not treated so liberally in Prussia as they had been under French rule. In 1815 they were not allowed to hold public office and in the following year they were excluded from various professions. In order to be able to continue to earn his living as a lawyer Heinrich Marx became a Christian. But he did not join the Catholic Church to which the vast majority of his neighbours belonged. He was baptised by the army chaplain Mühlenhoff and became a member of the tiny Protestant community.

These circumstances had a profound influence upon Karl Marx. At an early age he felt that he was different from his fellows. The fact that he had been baptised did not change the blood that ran in his veins. He was still a Jew and he suffered from the anti-semitism that was prevalent in Germany in his day. Yet he was outside the Jewish community. He reacted to the situation by conceiving an irrational hatred for his own race and he condemned the Jews as usurers and capitalists whose only purpose in life was to make money. Marx's anti-semitism was one of the less agreeable aspects of his character. If Marx could not escape from being classed with the despised Jewish minority he could derive little comfort from his membership of the Protestant Church. The Protestant congregation of Trier was a very small one, so that Marx was again a member of a minority group. While his father was a patriotic Prussian, Marx detested Prussian absolutism and militarism and eventually gave up his Prussian nationality.

As a young man he felt that he was different from his fellows in another way. He realised that his intellectual ability and will-power were greater than those of his contemporaries at school and at the university. In an essay, written for his school leaving examination, he discussed the choice of a profession. He argued that a professional career should not be adopted because it promised material rewards or honours. The only good reasons for adopting a profession were a sense of dedication and a desire to serve humanity. A profession should be a calling. But he realised that a young man might be restricted in selecting a profession because "his position in society has to some extent already been fixed before he can make his choice." And a time came when Marx believed that he was destined for higher things than a normal occupation. He was to be a philosopher who would show the world a new way of life. Like his rabbi ancestors he saw himself as a prophet and a teacher though his message to humanity was no religious faith but a doctrine of materialism. A messiah was no ordinary mortal and Marx felt that he was not bound by ordinary conventions of society. He had, for example, no need to concern himself with such mundane problems as earning a living, supporting a family, or even balancing a budget.

Marx secured his school leaving certificate at the early age of seventeen and went to the University of Bonn in the autumn of 1835 to read law. He did not devote himself very assiduously to his studies and in 1836 became secretly engaged to Jenny von Westphalen, the daughter of a titled senior official who was an old friend of the Marx family.[144] Marx's father now decided that Karl should go to the University of Berlin. At this time Berlin had a reputation for hard work. Feuerbach declared that Berlin was an intellectual factory compared with other German seats of learning which were little more than glorified taverns. Moreover Berlin was far from Trier and Karl would have fewer opportunities of seeing Jenny.

In Berlin Karl Marx enrolled for a few courses in jurisprudence but most of his time was spent in private study. In a letter to his father of November 10, 1837 he explained how he had spent his first year in Berlin. Apart from writing romantic verses for Jenny's edification he had studied philosophy and history so intensively that his health had suffered and on the advice of his doctor he had moved for a time to the village of Stralau. Karl explained that the purpose of his studies was to construct an entirely new system of metaphysics. No wonder that Heinrich Marx became alarmed at his son's conduct and that relations between father and son deteriorated. Heinrich Marx had discovered – as Engels found out later to his cost – that Karl was incapable of living within his allowance. More serious was Karl's neglect of his legal studies. Heinrich Marx warned his son that his engagement imposed responsibilities which should not be neglected. If he seriously intended to marry Jenny he should complete his studies and earn his living so that he could support a wife. Philosophy and poetry were no substitute for bread and butter. Instead of following his father's advice Karl continued to bury himself in his books. Although he had decided to give up law in preference for an academic career he postponed the writing of his doctoral thesis which would have been the first step to securing a university post.

The intellectual stimulus which Marx received in Berlin came not from his university teachers but from his membership of the Doctors Club, the forerunner of the group known as 'the Free' with which Engels was in contact shortly afterwards. The leading members of the Doctors Club – the theologian Bruno Bauer, the historian Karl Friedrich Köppen and the teacher Adolf Rutenberg – accepted the twenty year old student Marx as their intellectual equal and before long he came to dominate their discussions. In 1840 Köppen dedicated his book on Frederick the Great to "his friend Karl Heinrich Marx of Trier". The Doctors Club supported the Young Hegelian movement which emphasised the dialectical aspect of Hegel's teaching – the idea of change and progress – while rejecting the conservative aspect of Hegel's philosophy which regarded the existing Prussian State as the perfect culmination of a process of evolution. The radical ideas of the Young Hegelians found expression in the *Hallische* (later *Deutsche*) *Jahrbücher*, a periodical founded by Arnold Ruge and Theodor Echtermeyer in 1838.

In the autumn of 1839 Bruno Bauer was appointed to the post of lecturer in theology at the University of Bonn and he urged Marx to join him so that they could found a new radical periodical. But first he must procrastinate no longer. He should complete his doctoral thesis without delay. Marx however refused to be hurried. Bruno Bauer was waiting in Bonn to start his journal while Jenny was waiting in Trier to get married. But Marx continued to work on his manuscript until the early months of 1841. It was typical of Marx that his analysis and criticism of the philosophies of Democritus and Epicurus should have been only part of a more comprehensive survey of the Greek natural philosophers which he planned to write. His attitude towards the Prussian universities at which he had studied was shown by the fact that he submitted his thesis to the University of Jena in Thuringia although he had never been enrolled there. It took the philosophical faculty only nine days to award Marx his doctorate.

Any hopes that Marx may have had of securing a post at the University of Bonn through Bruno Bauer's influence were shattered when Bauer's licence to teach was withdrawn in 1842.[145] Marx's extreme radical views were such that it was unlikely that he would obtain a university post and he now turned to journalism as a career. He began to contribute to the *Rheinische Zeitung*, a newspaper established in Cologne on January 1, 1842 by a group of liberal businessmen in the Rhineland to challenge the powerful *Kölnische Zeitung*. Two young men – Georg Jung and Dagobert Oppenheim – soon secured for themselves an influential position on the editorial staff. They were Young Hegelians and they were influenced by the socialist writer Moses Hess. Jung and Oppenheim tried to secure contributions from fellow Young Hegelians and Marx was one of the first to be approached. Marx wrote a series of highly critical articles on the proceedings of the Rhenish Provincial Assembly which had met for nine weeks in Düsseldorf in the previous year. In October 1842 Marx was appointed editor in chief of the *Rheinische Zeitung*. He resigned in the following March owing to continual difficulties with the Prussian censorship. Soon afterwards the publication of the newspaper was forbidden by the government. His brief experience as a newspaper editor forced Marx for the first time to concern himself with the social problems of the day.

Arnold Ruge now suggested that Marx should join him in establishing a new left-wing periodical in Paris where they would be free from the exasperating restrictions of the Prussian censorship. Marx accepted this proposal. Although his income had ceased – and he had to accept the disagreeable fact that there was no chance of getting any money from his father's estate so long as his mother was alive – Marx was in no hurry to go to Paris. He married Jenny von Westphalen in June 1843 and afterwards Karl and Jenny lived for five months with Jenny's mother at Kreuznach. Leaving his bride to her own devices Marx spent his days in the study immersed in philosophy and French history in preparation for his future work as joint editor of the *Deutsch-Französische Jahrbücher*. Not until November 1843 did Marx and his wife move to Paris and it was not until February 1844 that the first – and only – number of the *Jahrbücher* appeared. Arnold Ruge, in a letter to Feuerbach, gave a sketch of Marx as he knew him in Paris. He considered that Marx was a born scholar and writer. But he would never be a successful journalist. He was an omnivorous reader and was capable of working with great intensity when the spirit moved him. Yet he rarely finished anything that he had begun. Half way through a project he would break off to throw himself wholeheartedly into some new plan.

In Paris Marx was soon in touch with French and German radicals and socialists such as Proudhon and Moses Hess. He also met the exiled German romantic poet Heinrich Heine whose work he greatly admired. The failure of the *Deutsch-Französische*

Jahrbücher meant that Marx was again in financial difficulties. He had no regular source of income and he now had a wife to support. Fortunately some of his friends in Cologne raised 4,400 francs to enable him to continue to live in Paris. And early in 1845 he secured 1,500 francs advance royalties from a German publisher for a book that he never wrote.

The economic manuscripts on which Marx worked at this time and his criticism of Hegel's philosophy of law in the *Deutsch-Französische Jahrbücher* show how closely Marx's views now corresponded with those of Engels. The Paris manuscripts of 1844, which were not published in his lifetime, included Marx's detailed notes on the works of the English classical economists and his comments on their views.[146] It is easy to appreciate how warmly Engels would be welcomed by Marx when they met in the autumn of 1844. They agreed to collaborate in the future and they decided that their first task would be to write a criticism of Bruno Bauer and his fellow Young Hegelians. There was a time when both Marx and Engels had regarded Bruno Bauer as their mentor. Now, as convinced communists, they were opposed to their former friend.

NOTES

1 For Engels's early life see G. Mayer, *Friedrich Engels in seiner Frühzeit* (1920); A. Conradi, "Friedrich Engels in seinen deutschen Jugendjahren" (in *Neue Zeit*, Vol. 38, 1920, p. 270 *et seq*); O. Jenssen, "Der junge Engels" (in *Sozialist*, Vol. 6, No. 17, 1920); E. Bernstein, "Vom Werden und Wirken des jungen Engels" (in *Archiv für Sozialwissenschaft und Sozialpolitik*, Vol. 42, 1922, p. 212 *et seq*); W. Andreas, "Der junge Engels" (in *Historische Porträts*, 1922, p. 159 *et seq*); R. Sieger, *Friedrich Engels. Die religiöse Entwicklung des Spätpietisten und Frühsozialisten* (1935).

2 Franz Mehring, "Friedrich Engels" in *Die Neue Zeit*, Vol. 2, 1904–5, translated in *Reminiscences of Marx and Engels* (Foreign Languages Publishing House, Moscow), pp. 361–4.

3 Engels's mother had a difficult labour: see F. Engels (senior) to Karl Wilhelm Moritz Snethlage, December 1, 1820 in *Stadt-Anzeiger-Bergische Wochenpost*, Friday–Saturday, April 18–19, 1969 ("Aus der Geschichte unserer Heimat").

4 For Elberfeld and Barmen in the 1840s see Klara Wittgenstein, "Die Entwicklung der sozialen Frage und Bewegung in Wuppertal in den vierziger Jahren des 19en Jahrhunderts und ihre wirtschaftlichen Grundlagen" in *Zeitschrift des Bergischen Geschichtsvereins*, Vol. 54, 1923–4, pp. 118–87.

5 It was "managed by some English spinners". See T. C. Banfield, *Industry of the Rhine*, Series II, *Manufacturers* (1848), p. 123. If Banfield's information is correct this is an earlier water mill for spinning cotton yarn than Brügelmann's at Ratingen, near Düsseldorf (1794).

6 N. J. G. Pounds, *The Ruhr* (1952), p. 41.

7 See F. O. Dilthey, *Geschichte der Baumwollenindustrie im niederrheinischen Industriebezirk* (1904).

8 See Gustav Kühne, "Das deutsche Manchester" in *Europa*, October 2 and 9, 1847.

9 For the Manchester firm, see W. O. Henderson, "The Firm of Ermen and Engels" in *Internationale Wissenschaftliche Korrespondenz*, Heft 11–12, April 1971, pp. 1–10.

10 For the German firm of Ermen and Engels see P. Steller, *Führende Männer des rheinisch-westfälischen Wirtschaftslebens* (Berlin 1830) and H. Watzmer, "Die Herkunft der industriellen Bourgeoisie Preussens in den vierziger Jahren des 19en Jahrhunderts" in Hans Motteck (ed), *Studien zur Geschichte der industriellen Revolution in Deutschland* (1960), p. 147. See also *100 Jahre Zinn*, Engels & Co. (Wuppertal).

11 See W. O. Henderson and W. H. Chaloner, "Friedrich Engels in Manchester" in *Memoirs and Proceedings of the Manchester Literary and Philosophical Society*, Session 1956–7, p. 2.

12 Edmund Wilson, *To the Finland Station* (Fontana Library, 1960), p. 133.

13 Shortly after the enactment of Prussia's first Factory Law in 1839 a foreman in a Barmen spinning mill was sentenced to five years penal servitude for offences against thirteen factory girls aged between 10 and 14. See G. A. Anton, *Geschichte der preussischen Fabrikgesetzgebung bis zu ihrer Aufnahme durch die Reichsgewerbeordnung* (1891; new edition 1953), p. 78. August von der Heydt (the future Minister of Commerce who was then a magistrate in Elberfeld) sent 2,000 letters of admonition and notices of penalty to parents who had failed to send their children to school in 1846. See T. C. Banfield *Industry of the Rhine*, Series II, *Manufactures* (1848), p. 134.

14 F. Engels, "Briefe aus dem Wuppertal" in *Gesamtausgabe*, Part I, Vol. 2, pp. 23–41.

15 F. Engels, "Preussischer Schnaps" in *Volksstaat*, 1876, No. 23–35.

16 F. Engels, "Briefe aus dem Wuppertal" in *Gesamtausgabe*, Part I, Vol. 2, p. 37.

17 For Engels's religious views in 1837–47 see R. Sieger, *Friedrich Engels, Die religiöse Entwicklung des Spätpietisten und Frühsozialisten* (Halle an der Saale, 1935). For Pietism see C. Marklin, *Darstellung und Kritik des modernen Pietismus* (Stuttgart, 1839) and L. Hüffel, *Der Pietismus geschichtlich und kirchlich beleuchtet* (Heidelberg, 1846).

18 F. Engels to Friedrich Graeber, February 19, 1839 in *Gesamtausgabe*, Part I, Vol. 2, p. 500.

19 *Ibid.*, April 8, 1839, p. 504.

20 i.e. David Friedrich Strauss who in his *Leben Jesu* (1835) had tried to prove that the gospel history was a collection of myths.

21 F. Engels to Friedrich Graeber, April 23–May 1, 1839 in *Gesamtausgabe*, Part I, Vol. 2, p. 505.

22 F. Engels to Wilhelm Graeber, October 8, 1839, in *Gesamtausgabe*, Part I, Vol. 2, p. 538.

23 F. Engels to Wilhelm Graeber, December 12, 1839; *ibid.*, p. 554.

24 "According to your sort of Christianity nine tenths of humanity are condemned to eternal damnation and one tenth is saved. Come, Fritz, is that really what you call the immeasurable love of God?" (F. Engels to Friedrich Graeber, July 27, 1839 in *Gesamtausgabe*, Part I, Vol. 2, p. 531).

25 *Ibid.*, April 27–30, 1839, p. 519.

26 F. Engels, "Rationalismus und Pietismus" in *Morgenblatt für gebildete Stände*, October 17, 1840 and in *Gesamtausgabe*, Part I, Vol. 2, pp. 128–30.

27 But in an emotional passage in a letter to Friedrich Graeber (July 12, 1839) Engels declared that he felt that he would "find his way to God" (*ibid.*, p. 531).

28 For Engels's comments on the political views of the younger generation in Elberfeld and Barmen see his "Briefe aus dem Wuppertal" (April 1839) in *Gesamtausgabe*, Part I, Vol. 2, p. 37.

29 F. Engels to Friedrich Graeber, October 29, 1839: *ibid.*, p. 547.

30 F. Engels to Friedrich Graeber, December 9, 1839–February 5, 1840: *ibid.*, p. 558. But on another occasion he referred to the king of Hanover as "a lousy old goat".

31 After leaving home Engels mentioned in his letters the names of some of his friends at school. They included Peter Jonghans, Friedrich Plümacher, Gustav Wurm, Gustav Heuser, Wilhelm Blank, Friedrich Graeber, Wilhelm Graeber, Hermann Graeber, and Strücher. Several of them were either sons of the manse or candidates for the Protestant ministry or both.

32 For Engels's stay in Bremen see his letters to his sister Marie, to Friedrich Graeber and to Wilhelm Graeber and his articles in the *Telegraph für Deutschland* (edited by Carl Gutzkow) and the *Morgenblatt für gebildete Leser* in *Gesamtausgabe*, Part I, Vol. 2.

33 For Treviranus see an article in *Bremer Biographien des 19en Jahrhunderts* (1912) and Tiesmeyer, *Georg Gottfried Treviranus* (1879).

34 From Engels's letter of October 29, 1840 to his sister (in *Gesamtausgabe*, Part I, Vol. 2, pp. 600–2) it is clear that some of Engels's friends in Bremen – clerks and apprentices who lodged in the homes of their masters – did not have front door keys. Describing a party he wrote: ". . . and then we drank another toast. So it went on until 10 p.m. when those who had no front door keys had to go home but we lucky ones who had keys stayed on and ate oysters. . . ."

35 Since Leupold was Consul for the Kingdom of Saxony in Bremen he was addressed as 'Consul Leupold'.

36 Engels wrote that Leupold was "ein schrecklich guter Kerl, o so gut, Du kannst Dir gar nicht denken" (F. Engels to Friedrich and Wilhelm Graeber, September 1, 1838 in *Gesamtausgabe*, Part I, Vol. 2, p. 486) and "ein köstlicher Kerl" (*ibid.*, p. 490).

37 F. Engels to W. Graeber, October 20–21, 1839: "I have had an excessively boring day. The work in the office nearly killed me" (*Gesamtausgabe*, Part I, Vol. 2, p. 542).

38 F. Engels to his sister Marie, July 7–9, 1840 (*Gesamtausgabe*, Part I, Vol. 2, p. 590).

39 F. Engels to his sister Marie, August 20–25, 1840 (*Gesamtausgabe*, Part I, Vol. 2, p. 595).

40 In a letter of February 22, 1841 to F. Graeber there is a reference to a duel fought by Engels. He boasted that he had given his opponent "a marvellous slash on the forehead – right from top to bottom – a real beauty" (*Gesamtausgabe*, Part I, Vol. 2, p. 564).

41 In a letter to his sister, Engels wrote that the Union subscribed to Dutch, English, American, French, Turkish and Japanese newspapers. "I have taken the opportunity to learn Turkish and Japanese and I can understand 25 languages" (September 28, 1839: *ibid.*, p. 588). In

another letter he offered to teach his sister Danish, Spanish or Portuguese (*ibid.*, p. 595).

42 F. Engels, "Eine Fahrt nach Bremerhaven" in *Morgenblatt für gebildete Leser*, August 17, 1841 (*Gesamtausgabe*, Part I, Vol. 2, pp. 147–8.

43 F. Engels to his sister Marie, August 4, 1840 (*ibid.*, p. 592): "It is a sad business. I have hardly a copper in my pocket and I have plenty of debts".

44 F. Engels to W. Graeber, November 20, 1840 (*ibid.*, p. 560) "*Tätigkeit, Leben, Jugendmut, das ist der wahre Witz.*"

45 Gustav Mayer, "Ein Pseudonym von Friedrich Engels" in *Archiv für die Geschichte des Sozialismus und Arbeiterbewegung*, Vol. 4, 1914.

46 F. Engels to Friedrich Graeber, April 9, 1839 in *Gesamtausgabe*, Part I, Vol. 2, p. 504. See R. Sieger, *Friedrich Engels als junger Deutscher* (University of Halle–Wittenberg dissertation, 1935).

47 Engels's last article in the *Telegraph* was in the number dated November 1841 and appeared in the middle of December 1841.

48 See *Gesamtausgabe*, Part I, Vol. 2, pp. xxv–xxvi (Rjazanov's introduction).

49 July 1840 to August 1841.

50 From an article by Wilhelm Liebknecht on Friedrich Engels in the *Illustrierte Neue Welt: Kalender für das Jahr 1897*. See also *Reminiscences of Marx & Engels* (Foreign Languages Publishing House, Moscow), pp. 137–48.

51 F. Engels to F. Graeber, April 23, 1839 (*Gesamtausgabe*, Part I, Vol. 2, pp. 505–6). In this letter Engels declared that the style of the article was shocking (*hundeschlecht*), yet a few months later (July 30, 1839) he wrote to W. Graeber: "I have recently read it again and I am astonished at the style. Since then I have not by any means managed to reach that standard of writing" (*Gesamtausgabe*, Part I, Vol. 2, p. 536).

52 "Einige Berichtigungen der Briefe aus dem Wuppertal" in the *Telegraph für Deutschland*, May 1839, No. 8, pp. 635–8 (summarised by D. Rjazanov in the introduction to *Gesamtausgabe*, Part I, Vol. 2, p. xxviii).

53 *Telegraph für Deutschland*, July 1840, reprinted in *Gesamtausgabe*, Part I, Vol. 2, pp. 76–82.

54 The excursion was first described in a letter to his sister on July 7–9, 1840 (*Gesamtausgabe*, Part I, Vol. 2, pp. 589–91). The article appeared a year later in the *Morgenblatt für gebildete Leser*, August 1841 (*Gesamtausgabe*, Part I, Vol. 2, pp. 147–54).

55 F. Engels to W. Graeber, July 30, 1839 (*Gesamtausgabe*, Part I, Vol. 2, p. 536).

56 F. Engels (F. Oswald), "Karl Beck" in *Telegraph für Deutschland*, November and December 1839 (*Gesamtausgabe*, Part I, Vol. 2, pp. 57–61).

57 F. Engels (F. Oswald), "Retrograde Zeichen der Zeit" in *Telegraph für Deutschland*, February 1840 (*Gesamtausgabe*, Part I, Vol. 2, pp. 62–6). On February 21, 1840 Engels wrote to Friedrich Graeber: "Through Strauss I have taken the road that leads straight to Hegelianism. Of course I will not become so fanatical a Hegelian as Hinrichs etc. but I must make some important aspects of Hegel's colossal system of philosophy part of my own intellectual heritage" (*Gesamtausgabe*, Part I, Vol. 2, pp. 554–5).

58 F. Engels's essay on Platen in *Telegraph für Deutschland*, February 1840 (*Gesamtausgabe*, Part I, Vol. 2, pp. 67–8).
59 F. Engels to Friedrich Graeber, January 20, 1840 (*Gesamtausgabe*, Part I, Vol. 2, p. 554).
60 F. Engels to his sister Marie, March 8, 1840 (*Gesamtausgabe*, Part I, Vol. 2, p. 611).
61 Engels to his sister Marie on April 5, early May, the end of August, and September 9, 1841 in *Gesamtausgabe*, Part I, Vol. 2, pp. 613–16.
62 "Lombardische Streifzüge" in *Athenäum*, December 4 and 11, 1841 in *Gesamtausgabe*, Part I, Vol. 2, pp. 159–68.
63 Engels to his sister Marie, September 9, 1841 in *Gesamtausgabe*, Part I, Vol. 2, pp. 615–16.
64 The photograph of a small painting of the head and shoulders of a young man in uniform reproduced in Horst Ullrich, *Der junge Engels* (two volumes, 1961), Vol. 1, p. 248 is stated to be a picture of Friedrich Engels in 1842. In fact it is a picture of Engels's father. In his will dated July 29, 1893 Engels left this painting of his father to his brother Hermann.
65 Gehard Zirke, *Der General: Friedrich Engels, der erste Militär Theoretiker der Arbeiterklasse* (Leipzig and Jena, 1957).
66 Engels to his sister Marie, April 14–16, 1842 in *Gesamtausgabe*, Part I, Vol. 2, p. 620.
67 *Ibid.*, p. 619.
68 *Ibid.*, p. 624.
69 *Ibid.*, p. 617.
70 The certificate is printed in *Gesamtausgabe*, Part I, Vol. 2, p. 365.
71 George Julian Harney in the *Newcastle Weekly Chronicle*, August 17, 1895.
72 F. Lessner in *Reminiscences of Marx and Engels* (Foreign Languages Publishing House, Moscow), p. 153.
73 F. Engels, "Rheinische Feste" in the *Rhenische Zeitung*, May 14, 1842 (*Gesamtausgabe*, Part I, Vol. 2, pp. 293–5).
74 F. Engels, *"Marx und die Neue Rheinische Zeitung"* in Karl Marx–Friedrich Engels, *Die Revolution von 1848* (selected articles from the *Neue Rheinische Zeitung:* Dietz Verlag, Berlin 1955), p. 32. Engels regarded the shopkeepers and craftsmen of Berlin as "loud-mouthed cowardly toadies".
75 Adolf Glassbrenner, *Berliner Volksleben* (1847).
76 Michael Bakunin to Alexander Herzen, October 23, 1840 in T. Klein (ed.), *Der Vorkampf deutscher Einheit und Freiheit* (edition of 1925), pp. 67–68.
77 R. Sieger, Friedrich Engels. *Die religiöse Entwicklung des Spätpietisten und Frühsozialisten* (Halle a.S., 1935).
78 Bruno Bauer (1809–82): Young Hegelian and biblical critic.
79 Dr Arnold Ruge (1802–80) edited the *Hallische* (later *Deutsche*) *Jahrbücher* (1841–3) and, with Marx, the *Deutsch-Französische Jahrbücher* (one double issue, February 1844). See Paul Nerrlich (ed.), *Arnold Ruges Briefewechsel und Tagebücher aus den Jahren 1825–1880* (two volumes, 1886).
80 Edgar Bauer (1809–86).
81 Pen name of Kaspar Schmidt (1806–56) whose book *Der Einzige und sein Eigentum* appeared in 1845.
82 Karl Friedrich Köppen (1808–63), radical historian and contributor to the *Rheinische Zeitung.*

83 Karl Ludwig Theodor Nauwerck was dismissed from his lectureship at the University of Berlin. The King told his Minister Thile in November 1843 that this "well-known revolutionary" should not be allowed to teach in a Prussian university. See Heinrich von Treitschke, *Deutsche Geschichte im neunzehnten Jahrhundert*, Vol. 5, (edition of 1927), p. 233.

84 F. W. von Schelling (1775–1854), P. K. Marheineke (1780–1846) and K. F. Werder (1806–93) lectured on philosophy while L. von Henning (1791–1866) lectured on public finance. On January 5, 1842 Engels wrote to his sister Marie (*Gesamtausgabe*, Part I, Vol. 2, p. 617) that he had attended a lecture given by the poet and orientalist Friedrich Rückert (1788–1866).

85 F. Engels, "Tagebuch eines Hospitanten" in the *Rheinische Zeitung*, May 10, 1842 (*Gesamtausgabe*, Part I, Vol. 2, p. 290).

86 Ludwig Feuerbach, *Das Wesen des Christentums* (Leipzig, 1841).

87 See F. Engels, *Ludwig Feuerbach and the End of German Classical Philosophy* (1888: English translation – Foreign Languages Publishing House, Moscow, 1950). Engels's pamphlet on Feuerbach first appeared in *Neue Zeit* in 1886 as a review of K. N. Stark, *Ludwig Feuerbach* (1885).

88 F. Engels, "Progress of Social Reform on the Continent: II Germany and Switzerland" in *The New Moral World*, November 18, 1843 (*Gesamtausgabe*, Part I, Vol. 2, pp. 447).

89 For Engels's views on the censorship see "Zur Kritik der Preussischen Pressgesetze" in the *Rheinische Zeitung*, July 14, 1842 (*Gesamtausgabe*, Part I, Vol. 2, pp. 310–17) and "Friedrich Wilhelm IV, König von Preussen" in *Einundzwanzig Bogen aus der Schweiz*, 1843, pp. 189–96 (*Gesamtausgabe*, Part I, Vol. 2, pp. 339–46).

90 Friedrich Oswald (F. Engels), "Schelling über Hegel" in the *Telegraph*, December 1841, pp. 825–7 and pp. 830–2. (*Gesamtausgabe*, Part I, Vol. 2, pp. 173–80).

91 *Gesamtausgabe*, Part I, Vol. 2, pp. 181–227. The pamphlet was long attributed to Bakunin. A letter from Engels to Ruge, June 15, 1842, proves that Engels was the author (*Gesamtausgabe*, Part I, Vol. 2, p. 631).

92 P. K. Marheineke, *Kritik der Schellingschen Offenbarungsphilosophie* (1843) and H. E. G. Paulus, *Die . . . positive Philosophie der Offenbarung . . .* (Darmstadt, 1843). For Marheineke's criticism of Schelling in his course of lectures at the University of Berlin see F. Engels, "Tagebuch eines Hospitanten" in the *Rheinische Zeitung*, May 10, 1842, (*Gesamtausgabe*, Part I, Vol. 2, pp. 290–2).

93 *Gesamtausgabe*, Part I, Vol. 2, pp. 229–49.

94 *Rheinische Zeitung*, May 18, 1842: see D. Rjazanov's introduction to *Gesamtausgabe*, Part I, Vol. 2, p. l.

95 *Augsburg Allgemeine Zeitung*, May 19, 1842: see D. Rjazanov's introduction to *Gesamtausgabe*, Part I, Vol. 2, p. l.

96 Contemporary references to Friedrich Engels and Edgar Bauer as joint authors of this poem are to be found in W. Koner, *Gelehrtes Berlin im Jahre 1845 . . .* (1846), p. 15 and *Wigands Conversations-Lexikonus* (1847), p. 81. See also D. Rjazanov, *op. cit.*, p. liv. The pamphlet was written in June or July 1842 and was published in Zürich in December 1842.

97 *Gesamtausgabe*, Part I, Vol. 2, pp. 253–81.

98 F. Engels, "Nord-und süddeutscher Liberalismus" in the *Rheinische*

Zeitung, April 12, 1842 (*Gesamtausgabe*, Part I, Vol. 2, pp. 287–9).

99 F. Engels, "Alexander Jung, Vorlesungen über die moderne Literatur der Deutschen" in *Deutsche Jahrbücher*, July 7, 8 and 9, 1842 (*Gesamtausgabe*, Part I, Vol. 2, pp. 323–35).

100 F. Engels, "Friedrich Wilhelm IV, König von Preussen" in *Einundzwanzig Bogen aus der Schweiz*, Part I, 1842 (*Gesamtausgabe*, Part I, Vol. 2, pp. 339–46).

101 For Engels's criticism of the press censorship in Prussia at this time see his article in the *Rheinische Zeitung*, July 14, 1842 (*Gesamtausgabe*, Part I, Vol. 2, pp. 310–17).

102 *Hallische Jahrbücher für deutsche Wissenschaft und Kunst* (edited by Arnold Ruge and Theodor Echtermeyer, January 1838–June 1841) continued as *Deutsche Jahrbücher für Wissenschaft und Kunst* (July 1841–January 1843).

103 F. Engels, "Progress of Social Reform on the Continent: II Germany and Switzerland" in *New Moral World*, November 18, 1843 (*Gesamtausgabe*, Part I, Vol. 2, p. 447).

104 Engels's military discharge was dated October 8, 1842 (*Gesamtausgabe*, Part I, Vol. 2, p. 635).

105 F. Engels, "Progress of Social Reform on the Continent: II Germany and Switzerland" in the *New Moral World*, November 18, 1843 (*Gesamtausgabe*, Part 1, Vol. 2, p. 448).

106 See Moses Hess, *Sozialistische Aufsätze* (1921); Auguste Cornu, *Karl Marx und Friedrich Engels* (1954), Vol. 1, pp. 213–23, 286–9, and 372–8; and H. Förder, *Marx und Engels am Vorabend der Revolution* (1960), pp. 25–6.

107 See Moses Hess, *Die europäische Triarchie* (Leipzig, 1841) reprinted in Moses Hess, *Philosophische und Sozialistische Schriften 1837–1850* (ed. by A. Cornu and W. Mönke, 1961), pp. 77–166.

108 Moses Hess to B. Auerbach, June 19, 1843 quoted by D. Rjazanov in the introduction to *Gesamtausgabe*, Part I, Vol. 2, p. lix. The letter appears in E. Silberner and W. Blumenberg (ed.) *Moses Hess: Briefwechsel* (The Hague, 1959), p. 103.

109 F. Engels in the *Rheinische Zeitung*, December 8, 1842 (*Gesamtausgabe*, Part I, Vol. 2, p. 356).

110 For Engels's account of his first meeting with Karl Marx in 1842 see D. Rjazanov's introduction to *Gesamtausgabe*, Part I, Vol. 2, p. lx.

111 Engels's introduction of 1885 to Karl Marx, *Enthüllungen über den Kommunistenprozess zu Köln*, 1853 (edition of 1952), p. 11 and p. 17.

112 Marcel Herwegh (ed.), *1848 Briefe von und an Herwegh* (Munich, 1896), p. 88 and D. Rjazanov's introduction to *Gesamtausgabe*, Part I, Vol. 2, p. lxxi.

113 F. Engels, *The Condition of the Working Class in England* (1945: translated by W. O. Henderson and W. H. Chaloner, 1958), p. 30 and pp. 33–4.

114 For the Plug Plot riots see A. G. Rose, "The Plug Riots of 1842 in Lancashire and Cheshire" in the *Transactions of the Lancashire and Cheshire Antiquarian Society*, Vol. 68, 1957, pp. 75–112.

115 F. Engels, "Die innern Krisen" (London, November 30, 1842) in the *Rheinische Zeitung*, December 9 and 10, 1842 (*Gesamtausgabe*, Part I, Vol. 2, pp. 351–5). A third short article by Engels dated December

3, 1842 appeared in the *Rheinische Zeitung* on December 8, 1842 (*Gesamtausgabe*, Part I, Vol. 2, pp. 456–7.

116 Moses Hess, "Über eine in England bevorstehende Katastrophe" in the *Rheinische Zeitung*, No. 177, June 26, 1842 (reprinted in Moses Hess, *Philosophische und Sozialistische Schriften 1837–1850* (1961), pp. 183–5). Hess argued that the fundamental causes of distress in England were of a social – not political – nature. He wrote: "Industry has passed from the hands of the people to the machines of the capitalists. Commerce – formerly operated on a modest scale by many small merchants – is now concentrated more and more in the hands of capitalists and adventurers (i.e. swindlers). The land has fallen into the grasp of a few aristocratic families owing to the working of the laws of inheritance. In fact a few great families expand and control ever greater amounts of capital."

117 Brief accounts of the firm appear in H. E. Blyth, *Through the Eye of a Needle. The Story of the English Sewing Cotton Company* (1947), p. 11 and 100 Jahre Zinn, Engels & Co. (Wuppertal). Peter Ermen, the founder, was of Dutch origin and came to England in 1825. He was listed as a merchant in Pigot's *Manchester and Salford Directory for 1832* (p. 96). In 1834 he took his brother Anthony into partnership. By 1837 another brother named Gottfried (Godfrey) and the elder Friedrich Engels had joined the firm. The local directory for 1838 (p. 26 and p. 118) described Peter Ermen as a "sewing and knitting manufacturer". In an advertisement in the *Manchester Guardian* on August 27, 1842 Ermen and Engels thanked the police for protecting their property during the Plug Plot riots. Slater's *Directory of Manchester and Salford* for 1845 listed Ermen & Engels as "cotton spinners and manufacturers of knitting and sewing cotton" (p. 112) with an office at 2 South Gate, St Mary's (off Deansgate), Manchester. The firm operated the Victoria Mills, Eccles New Road, Pendleton.

118 Dedication (in English) "to the working class of Great Britain" which appeared in F. Engels, *Die Lage der arbeitenden Klasse in England* (1845): English translation by W. O. Henderson and W. H. Chaloner (1958), p. 7.

119 See E. Aveling, "George Julian Harney . . ." in *The Social Democrat*, No. 1, January 1897 reprinted in *Reminiscences of Marx and Engels* (Foreign Languages Publishing House, Moscow, pp. 192–3); G. D. H. Cole, *Chartist Portraits* (second edition, 1965); A. R. Schoyen, *The Chartist Challenge: a Portrait of George Julian Harney* (1958); P. Cadogan, "Harney and Engels" in the *International Review of Social History*, Vol. 10, 1964). For Engels's view of Harney see F. Engels, "Das Fest der Nationen in London" in the *Rheinische Jahrbücher zur gesellschaftlichen Reform*, Vol. 2, 1846, pp. 1–19 reprinted in *Gesamtausgabe*, Part I, Vol. 4, pp. 457–71.

120 Harney edited the *Northern Star* in Leeds in 1843–4. The place of publication was changed to London in November 1844. See E. L. H. Glasgow, "The Establishment of the *Northern Star* newspaper" in *History*, February–June 1954, pp. 61–2 and p. 66.

121 See *Reminiscences of Marx and Engels* (Foreign Languages Publishing House, Moscow), pp. 175 and pp. 192–3.

122 James Leach, a factory worker who became a printer, was a leading Manchester Chartist. He helped to set up the National Charter Association in Manchester (1841) and he was vice-chairman of the

Chartist National Convention in London (1842). He was an ardent protectionist and a vigorous opponent of the Anti-Corn Law League.

123 Engels refers to Leach as his "good friend" in an article in *Das Westfälische Dampfboot* in 1846 reprinted as Appendix I (p. 342) of F. Engels, *The Condition of the Working Class in England* (translated and edited by W. O. Henderson and W. H. Chaloner, 1958).

124. For John Watts (1818–87) see the *Dictionary of National Biography*, Vol. 20, pp. 982–3. Watts played a leading part in the public life of Manchester and was associated with the establishment of the public library and Owens College. He was the author of *The Facts of the Cotton Famine* (1866).

125 Engels refers to Watts as "an important person" in his "Briefe aus London", No. 3 in the *Schweizerischer Republikaner*, June 9, 1843 (*Gesamtausgabe*), Part I, Vol. 2, p. 371.

126 For Georg Weerth see an article by Friedrich Engels in *Der Sozialdemokrat*, July 7, 1883 reprinted in F. Engels, *Biographische Skizzen* (1967), pp. 107–14 and Georg Weerth, *Sämtliche Werke*, Vol. 1 (1956), pp. 11–15. Engels wrote: "When I stayed in Manchester in 1843 Weerth came to Bradford as a clerk in his German firm and we spent many happy Sundays together." (In fact Weerth worked in Bradford for the Manchester firm of S. Passavant & Co.) In a letter to his mother, dated July 6, 1844 Weerth mentioned that he had been in Manchester over Whitsun and had been in Engels's company for much of his visit. (Georg Weerth, *Sämtliche Werke*, Vol. 5, p. 128).

127 F. Engels, "Lage der arbeitenden Klasse in England" in the *Rheinische Zeitung*, December 25, 1842 (dated December 20 "from Lancashire") and December 27, 1842 (dated December 22 "from Lancashire") (*Gesamtausgabe*, Part I, Vol. 2, pp. 361–4).

128 Sir James Graham's Factory Bill of 1843 was withdrawn because of the opposition of Nonconformists and Roman Catholics to the clauses concerning religious education.

129 F. Engels, "Briefe aus London" in the *Schweizerischer Republikaner*, May 16 and 23 and June 9 and 27, 1843 (*Gesamtausgabe*, Part I, Vol. 2, pp. 465–76).

130 F. Engels, "The Progress of Social Reform on the Continent" in the *New Moral World*, November 4 and 18, 1843 and "Continental Movements" (*ibid.*, February 3, 1844): reprinted in *Gesamtausgabe*, Part I, Vol. 2, pp. 435–55. See also *Northern Star* November 11 and 25, 1843.

131 The journal was banned in Prussia and 300 copies were seized at the frontier. See Franz Mehring, *Karl Marx* (edition of 1967), p. 72.

132 F. Engels "Umrisse zu einer Kritik der Nationalökonomie" in the *Deutsch-Französische Jahrbücher* 1844, reprinted in *Karl Marx-Friedrich Engels Werke*, Vol. 1 (1964), pp. 499–524. English translation in W. O. Henderson (ed.), *Engels: Selected Writings* (Penguin Books, 1967), pp. 148–77. The *Deutsch-Französische Jahrbücher* also published a review by Engels of Thomas Carlyle, *Past and Present*, 1843. See *Karl Marx-Friedrich Engels Werke*, Vol. 1 (1964), pp. 525–49.

133 Karl Marx's introduction to his *Zur Kritik der politischen Ökonomie* (1859). Karl Marx also mentioned Engels's essay in the first volume of *Das Kapital*, 1867: see Karl Marx, *Capital* (Everyman edition, 1930), Vol. 1, p. 49.

134 The New York fire of December 1835 destroyed nearly 700 buildings and caused damage estimated at about twenty million dollars.

135 F. Engels, "Die Lage Englands", I "Das achtzehnte Jahrhundert", II "Die englische Konstitution" in *Vorwärts* between August 31 and October 19, 1844, reprinted in *Werke*, Vol. 1, pp. 550–92.

136 F. Engels's introduction of 1885 to Karl Marx, *Enthüllungen über den Kommunistenprozess zu Köln* (edition of 1952), pp. 15–16.

137 J. Waldeck to Johann Jacoby, May 9, 1844 in Gustav Mayer, *Friedrich Engels*, Vol. 1 (second edition, 1934), p. 171.

138 Heinrich Heine, *Sämtliche Werke* (edited by O. J. Lachmann, four volumes, Leipzig 1887), Vol. 4, p. 296.

139 Michael Bakunin (1814–76) was the Russian revolutionary who later became the leader of the anarchist movement.

140 Karl Ludwig Bernays (1815–79) was at this time a member of the editorial board of *Vorwärts* to which Engels had contributed.

141 Dr August Hermann Ewerbeck (1816–80) was the leader of the Paris branch of the League of the Just, a secret revolutionary society of German emigrants. Engels had met the leaders of the London branch of the league.

142 Auguste Cornu, *Karl Marx und Friedrich Engels* (two volumes, 1954 and 1962), Vol. 2, pp. 270–1.

143 Friedrich Engels, *Ludwig Feuerbach und der Ausgang der klassischen deutschen Philosophie* (Stuttgart, 1888): English translation *Ludwig Feuerbach and the End of Classical German Philosophy* (Foreign Languages Publishing House, Moscow, 1950).

144 Ludwig von Westphalen was the son of Philipp Westphalen, secretary of Duke Ferdinand of Brunswick. During the Seven Years' War Philipp Westphalen acted in fact (though not in name) as chief of staff of the Duke's army and was ennobled for his services. Ludwig von Westphalen's son, Ferdinand Otto Wilhelm, (by his first wife) was Minister of the Interior in Prussia between 1850 and 1858 (Manteuffel ministry).

145 Friedrich Engels and Edgar Bauer (Bruno Bauer's brother) collaborated to write a satirical poem criticising Bruno Bauer's dismissal.

146 Karl Marx, *Economic and Philosophical Manuscripts of 1844* (second impression, Foreign Language Publishing House, Moscow, 1961). The first German edition of these manuscripts appeared in 1932. See also H. P. Adams, *Karl Marx in his earlier Writings* (1940; new edition, 1965).

2

THE CONDITION OF THE WORKING CLASS IN ENGLAND IN 1844

I. The Genesis of Engels's Book

Engels returned to Barmen in September 1844 and lived with his family until April 1845 when he joined Marx in Brussels.[1] It was during this period that he wrote his book on *The Condition of the Working Class in England*. A letter to Marx, written early in October 1844, began a correspondence which lasted for thirty-eight years. In this correspondence – as Lenin observed – the two friends applied materialist dialectics "to the reshaping of all political economy from its foundations up – to history, natural science, philosophy and to the policy and tactics of the working class".[2] In his letter of October 8–10 Engels was unable to report any progress on his book and explained that he could not get down to work as the entire household was in a state of turmoil over the engagement of his sister Marie to Emil Blank.

Engels also told Marx that he had recently been in touch with communist groups in Cologne, Düsseldorf, Elberfeld and Barmen.[3] He declared that in his absence "the Wupper valley has made more progress than in the last 50 years. The social tone of the district has become more civilised. Everyone is interested in politics and in resisting authority. Industry has made spectacular advances. New suburbs have sprung up and entire woodlands have been cut down. It can now be said that – as a civilised district – Elberfeld and Barmen are above, rather than below, the average in Germany". Engels hoped that the workers of the Wupper valley – "our wild hot-blooded dyers and bleachers" – would be converted to communism.[4]

In November 1844 Engels visited communist sympathisers in Cologne and Bonn and called upon Otto Lüning in Rheda.[5] Dr Lüning edited first *Das Weser-Dampfboot* and then *Das Westphälische Dampfboot*[6] and Engels hoped that communist articles might be placed in the latter periodical. Despite these activities and despite the distraction of a love affair Engels was able to assure Marx on November 19 that he was buried in English newspapers and books and that he was writing his account of the condition of the English workers. He indicated clearly the spirit in which the book was being written when he declared: "I shall present the English with a fine bill of indictment. At the bar of world opinion I charge the English middle classes with mass murder, wholesale robbery, and all the other crimes in the calendar. I am writing a preface in English which I shall have printed separately for distribution to the leaders of the English political parties, to men of letters, and to Members of Parliament." Engels assured Marx that he was attacking the German as well as the English middle classes. He would tell the German bourgeoisie plainly that "they are just as bad as the English middle classes – only more cowardly, more flabby and more stupid in their cruel oppression of the workers." Engels added that in writing his book he had escaped from the study of abstract philosophical problems and he was glad to be "actively concerned with real live issues – with historical developments and their consequences."[7]

In January 1845 Engels wrote that his parents had raised the question of his business career. Since his training in Bremen and Manchester had been completed they naturally expected him to take his place in the family firm. "In view of the glum faces of my parents I took the advice of my brother-in-law and had another shot at a business career by working for a few weeks in the office. Circumstances connected with my love affair have also influenced my decision. But I disliked the prospect from the start. Petty trade is too horrible, Barmen is too horrible, and the waste of time is too horrible. Above all it is too horrible to belong to the middle classes and actually to be associated with factory owners. It is too horrible to play the part of a member of the bourgeoisie and to be actively engaged in opposing the interests of the workers. A few days in my old man's factory were enough to remind me forcibly of the horrors that I have been in danger of forgetting." "I suppose that it is possible for a communist to behave like a bourgeois and to engage in petty trade so long as he is not actually writing. But it is quite impossible to be actively engaged in communist agitation and at the same time to be involved in the world of business."[8]

Engels also mentioned in this letter that Moses Hess, whom he had first met in 1842, was in Barmen. Engels and Hess planned to edit a new monthly socialist journal to be called the *Gesellschaftsspiegel*.[9] Engels hoped that this periodical would reveal the condition of the working class in Germany just as his own book would expose the sufferings of the working class in England. A month later Engels reported to Marx that the first number of the new journal was ready for publication.[10] When Engels joined Marx in

Brussels Hess became the sole editor of the *Gesellschaftsspiegel* until his own departure from Germany.[11]

At this time Engels acknowledged the receipt of a brochure announcing the publication of Marx's *The Holy Family* which was an attack upon Bruno Bauer and other Young Hegelians. Engels's name appeared before that of Marx on the title page although he had contributed only a few pages to the book. He had written a criticism of Faucher's views on English affairs. He told Marx that "the new title *The Holy Family* will only lead to family upsets with my pious father, who is now highly annoyed with me, but of course you could not be expected to know this." When the book was published Engels complained of its inordinate length but praised the brilliance of Marx's writing.[12]

In February 1845 Engels wrote enthusiastically to Marx about the success of three communist meetings recently held in Elberfeld. "At the first we had an attendance of 40, at the second 130, and at the third at least 200. All Elberfeld and Barmen were there from the wealthy aristocrats to the grocers – but no workers turned up."[13] Engels described the meetings in an article in the *New Moral World*[14] and printed his own speeches in the *Rheinische Jahrbücher*.[15]

The first meeting, held on February 15, was attended by "representatives of almost all the leading commercial and manufacturing firms" in the town as well as "the attorney-general of the district and other members of the courts of law". Moses Hess opened the proceedings by demanding the abolition of "the old system of competition which he called a system of downright robbery".[16]

Engels, who spoke next, was careful to present the middle classes of Elberfeld and Barmen with a moderate statement of his views. He summarised some of the arguments which he had put forward in the previous year in his article on "Outlines of a Critique of Political Economy" in the *Deutsch-Französische Jahrbücher*.[17] He suggested that an economic system which allowed unfettered competition was bound to cause grave social distress. The "small middle class", once the backbone of society, was being ruined by the "great capitalists". "There are universal complaints that wealth is being concentrated in fewer and fewer hands while the vast majority of the nation sinks into ever greater poverty." Engels denounced the capitalist system for its inefficiency. Manufacturers were continually misjudging the requirements of the market. Overproduction led to regular slumps during which factories were closed and workers were unemployed. In a communist society this would not happen because by state planning of the economy, industrial output would be accurately geared to meet a demand that had been previously ascertained.

Engels denounced the wastefulness of the capitalist system. He criticised the rich for spending too much on the employment of far more servants than they really needed. He attacked the activities of middlemen and speculators whose profits raised the price of goods to the public. He asserted that capitalism fostered crime. Offences against the person were declining while offences against property were increasing. Engels believed that in a communist society poverty would be abolished and crime would disappear. In his utopia "the police, the law courts and public administration" would be largely superfluous. No standing army would be needed since no communist state would dream of attacking its neighbours. A well-trained popular militia would be adequate to defend the country against attack. Engels also described the socialist communities advocated by Robert Owen and praised them for their efficiency. He argued, for example, that the central heating of several houses had great advantages over a multiplicity of small fires. And he recommended communal feeding in a canteen in place of the cooking of individual meals by housewives in their own kitchens. Engels had himself, however, no experience of life in such a community.[18]

A week later, on February 22, 1845, Engels spoke at a second meeting in Elberfeld. He endeavoured to answer the criticism that in his first address he had illustrated his arguments from the experiences of foreign countries, particularly England, and that he had failed to show that the establishment of a communist society was an inevitable and necessary development in Germany. He drew attention to the widespread distress in various parts of Germany both in rural districts – the Eifel, the Senne, the Mosel valley, the Erzgebirge, Silesia and Bohemia – and in manufacturing regions. In his view the continued growth of the proletariat was bound to lead to the collapse of the existing social order and the establishment of a communist society. Engels then discussed the controversy concerning the fiscal policy of the German customs union and argued that neither free trade nor protection would save the capitalist system from collapse. He finally assured his audience that – if preventive action to solve the social question were taken in time – a violent revolution could be avoided.

A third meeting was held in the following week when Moses Hess gave a lecture. The authorities became alarmed at the situation in Elberfeld and they forbade the holding of further communist assemblies. When another meeting was held the police turned up in force. Engels wrote: "Of course, under such circumstances, no public addresses were delivered; the meeting occupied themselves with beef-steaks and wine, and gave the police no handle for interference."[19] On May 18, 1845 Count von Arnim, the Prussian Minister of the Interior, congratulated Freiherr von Spiegel, President of the Rhineland province, on the measures that he had taken to suppress communist assemblies in Elberfeld.[20]

On March 17 Engels told Marx that he had finished writing his book and that the manuscript had been sent to the publisher. Engels promised to let Marx have the 100 thalers due to him when the manuscript was delivered.[21] He had already raised a subscription of 150 francs from German sympathisers to help Marx when he had settled in Brussels in the previous month after being expelled from France. Even at this early stage of their collaboration Engels was already helping Marx financially and this was to become a permanent feature of their relationship.

In the same letter Engels complained bitterly of his situation at home. "I am indeed living a dog's life here. All the religious fanaticism of my old man has been aroused by the communist meetings and by the 'dissolute character' of several of our local communists with whom I am of course in close contact. And the old man's wrath has been increased by my firm refusal to go into petty trading. Finally my appearance in public as an avowed communist has aroused in him a truly middle-class fury. Now try to put yourself in my place. Since I want to leave in a fortnight or so, I cannot afford to have a row. So I simply ignore all the criticisms of the family. They are not used to that and so they get even angrier." "You can have no notion of the sheer malice that lies behind this wild Christian hunt after my 'soul'." "I have a great affection for my mother who has a fine and noble character. It is only in relation to my father that she has no spirit of independence at all. Were it not for my mother I would not hesitate for one moment to refuse to make even the most trifling concession to my fanatical and despotic old man."[22]

The circumstances under which Engels wrote his account of the English workers were not favourable to literary work. He had other things on his mind besides his book. And, as he explained in his preface, he had hoped to write "a more comprehensive work on English social history". Two years later Engels was reported to be still engaged upon this larger work but it was never completed.[23] While he was writing his book Engels was also contributing articles to the *New Moral World* and the *Deutsches Bürgerbuch*. He was deeply involved, with Moses Hess, in political agitation in the Rhineland and Westphalia and also in founding a new socialist journal. Engels's activities had attracted the attention of the police and he feared that at any time he might be expelled from Prussia. Moreover, despite the success of the Elberfeld meetings, Engels was disappointed at the divisions among the German communists. He could not persuade Hess to give up his support of Christian Socialism in favour of materialism and he could not convince Georg Jung that Karl Marx held very different views from those of Arnold Ruge.

Engels was also working under a considerable emotional strain. He was extricating himself from a love affair. It is safe to assume that he looked forward to resuming his association with Mary Burns and was not prepared to allow any other friendship to stand in his way. At the same time his relations with his family were rapidly deteriorating. Engels's father had every reason to be displeased. Although Engels was now twenty-four years of age and had completed his commercial training he refused to enter the family business. Instead he persisted in engaging in communist propaganda. The whole family would be disgraced if his behaviour led to his arrest or his expulsion from the country. The rift between father and son widened. Mounting tension at home made the completion of Engels's book no easy task. Despite all difficulties, however, the work was finished in March 1845 and was published in Leipzig by Otto Wigand in the following May.[24] By this time Engels had left Barmen and was living in Brussels.[25]

II. Engels on the English Workers[26]

In an address to the British workers, written in English, which appeared as a preface to *The Condition of the Working Class in England*, Engels explained that he had studied their way of life by personal observation and by reading the relevant literature on the subject. "I wanted to see you in your own homes, to observe you in your everyday life, to chat with you on your condition and grievances, to witness your struggles against the social and political power of your oppressors." Engels had seen how the middle classes "enrich themselves by your labour while they can sell its produce" only to "abandon you to starvation as soon as they cannot make a profit by this indirect trade in human flesh". Engels was surprised that there was no "readable book from which everybody might easily get some information on the condition of the great majority of 'free born Britons' ". It had been left "to a foreigner to inform the civilised world of the degrading situation you have to live in". Engels made it clear that he was no impartial observer but that he had assembled evidence with the intention of condemning the

English middle classes at the bar of world public opinion for the way in which they had treated the workers.[27]

In his first chapter Engels examined the organisation of the English textile industries in the eighteenth century. He suggested that in those days the workers had led an idyllic existence. They were fully employed since a gradual growth of population provided them with a steadily expanding market. They were generally small-holders as well as textile workers and therefore had two sources of income. They lived far from cities in healthy surroundings and could arrange their hours of work as they pleased. Engels considered that these workers had "enjoyed a comfortable and peaceful existence", their standard of living being higher than that of the urban factory proletariat of the 1840s. This situation had been dramatically changed by the inventions of the eighteenth century – the new textile machines and the steam engine – and by the development of the factory system and the growth of great manufacturing towns. Rural textile workers became factory operatives in urban areas. "The industrial workers no longer owned any of the means of production and they lost all security of employment. This led to the demoralisation of the workers and to political unrest." Engels described the course of the industrial and agrarian revolutions which had "no parallel in the annals of mankind". Echoing the views of Moses Hess he declared: "The industrial revolution has been as important for England as the political revolution for France and the philosophical revolution for Germany." Engels considered that since the passing of the Reform Bill of 1832 English politics had been dominated by the social problems created by the industrial revolution – problems which, unless they were solved, would threaten the very existence of society. The middle classes, now dominant in parliament, were sitting on a powder keg which might explode at any moment.

As in his "Outlines of a Critique of Political Economy" Engels asserted that the intensification of competition between different classes and between individuals in the same social group had been major factors determining the character of the new industrial age. He argued that "competition is the most extreme expression of that war of all against all which dominates modern middle class society". "Everybody competes in some way against everybody else and consequently each individual tries to push aside anyone whose existence is a barrier to his own advancement." The middle classes competed among themselves for the profits of industry. When trade was booming the competition for labour would benefit some workers who could demand higher wages. But wage increases would be checked by competition among the workers themselves for the available jobs. "This explains the rise of trade unions which represent an attempt to eliminate such fratricidal conflict between the workers themselves." Engels thought that competition was the basic cause of the trade cycle – the rhythmic movement of trade from slump to boom and from boom to slump which was such a characteristic feature of the industrial age. He argued that only planned industrial output and the planned sharing out of manufactured products would eliminate the trade cycle and the need for a reserve of unemployed labour.

His description of the great manufacturing towns created by the industrial revolution was one of the finest pieces that Engels ever wrote. As an author Engels was at his best when describing his own experiences – in a merchant's office or on a military campaign – and when he was recalling his travels, whether they were in the wine growing districts of France or the urban industrial regions in England. He had not only acute powers of observation but the ability to convey his impressions in compelling prose. Engels observed that in the English industrial towns the poor were segregated from the rich and lived in "unplanned wildernesses of one or two storied houses, built of brick". "Wherever possible these have cellars which are also used as dwellings." "The streets themselves are usually unpaved and full of holes. They are filthy and strewn with animal and vegetable refuse. Since they have neither gutters nor drains the refuse accumulates in stagnant, stinking puddles."

Engels described some of the London slums – St Giles, Whitechapel and Bethnal Green – and drew attention to the tragic fate of the destitute homeless. His account of the working class districts of the manufacturing towns of Lancashire and the West Riding was based upon personal observation. He had lived in Manchester which was within easy reach of numerous cotton towns; he had visited Leeds to see Julian Harney, and Bradford to see Georg Weerth. He contrasted the pleasant greystone villages of the Pennine valleys with the sordid brick cottages of the nearby factory towns which were black with soot. In Bradford he shared Weerth's disgust at what he saw. He found that "the workers' houses at the bottom of the valley are packed between high factory buildings and are among the worst-built and filthiest in the whole city". He observed that the factory towns around Manchester were virtually "huge working class communities", consisting of factories and operatives' cottages with few shops or amenities of any kind. He described Bolton as "a gloomy unattractive hole" while Stockport, on the Cheshire side of the River Mersey, presented "a truly revolting picture" when viewed from the great viaduct which carried the

Manchester and Birmingham railway across the ravine in which the town was situated. Stockport had an unusually high proportion of inhabited cellars in relation to the total number of houses.

Ashton under Lyne, on the other hand, having been built within the last fifty years, struck Engels as being "comparatively well planned". The factories had been built on the banks of the River Tame, while the workers' dwellings were situated on the slopes above. "Owing to the way in which it has been built, Ashton has a much more agreeable appearance than most of the other manufacturing towns." Yet even in Ashton there were streets in which "the cottages are becoming old and dilapidated". From Ashton Engels climbed a hill from which he could see the fine villas of the factory owners. On the other side of the hill lay Stalybridge where the streets ran "in wild confusion up, down and across the hillsides". Here Engels saw "congested rows of old grimy and dilapidated cottages". He condemned the "wholly unplanned method of building" which had produced "a vast number of courts, back passages, and blind alleys".

Manchester, "the most important factory town in the world" and the English city that Engels knew best, was described in greater detail. Engels observed that the Manchester–Salford conurbation had three quite distinct regions – a central district of offices, warehouses and shops; an inner ring of factories, workshops and overcrowded slums; and a pleasant outer ring of middle and upper class suburban residences. "To such an extent has the convenience of the rich been considered in the planning of Manchester that these plutocrats can travel from their homes to their places of business in the centre of the town by the shortest routes, which run entirely through working class districts, without ever realising how close they are to the misery and filth which lie on both sides of the roads". Engels considered that "Manchester is unique in the systematic way in which the working classes have been barred from the main streets. Nowhere else has such care been taken to avoid offending the tender susceptibilities of the eyes and nerves of the middle classes. Yet Manchester is the very town in which building has taken place in a haphazard manner with little or no planning or interference from the authorities."

Next Engels gave an account of various working class districts which he had visited in Manchester and Salford. The first was the Old Town lying between the commercial centre and the River Irk. The district near the river was a slum of the most depressing character. "The worst courts are those leading down to the Irk, which contain unquestionably the most dreadful dwellings I have ever seen." The dilapidated cottages were packed closely together, the alleys were full of refuse and the river was simply an open sewer. In the maze of courts off Long Millgate conditions were no better. Between St Michael's Church and Withy Grove the houses were rather newer and there was some evidence of planning in the layout of the built-up area. Engels summed up his description of the Old Town by condemning the whole district as being "quite unfit for human habitation". "The shameful lay-out of the Old Town has made it impossible for the wretched inhabitants to enjoy cleanliness, fresh air or good health. And such a district of at least twenty to thirty thousand inhabitants lies in the very centre of the second city in England."

The New Town – or Irish Town – lying between the River Irk and St George's Road was no better than the Old Town. The wretched inhabitants were tightly packed in a small area which lacked drainage or facilities for the disposal of refuse. To make matters worse the district was "infested with small herds of pigs". Little Ireland – in a bend of the River Medlock south west of Oxford Road – was a dreadful district inhabited by some 4,000 people, mostly Irish immigrants. "This horrid little slum affords as hateful and repulsive a spectacle as the worst courts to be found on the banks of the Irk. The inhabitants live in dilapidated cottages, the windows of which are broken and patched with oilskin. The doors and the door posts are broken and rotten. The creatures who inhabit these dwellings and even their dark wet cellars, and who live confined amidst all this filth and foul air . . . must surely have sunk to the lowest level of humanity." The slum dwellings of Little Ireland consisted of two rooms, a cellar and an attic. Each was inhabited by about 20 people and a single privy was shared by 120 people. Small wonder that cholera had raged in Little Ireland in 1831. Yet the condition of the district had changed very little since that date. Engels added that the working class districts of Hulme and Salford were little better than those which he had already described.

Engels argued that speculative builders were largely responsible for the scandalous condition of the workers' houses in Manchester and Salford. They were determined to make a quick profit in a short time and so they put up as many cottages as could possibly be squeezed onto each site. Since the land upon which they built was normally leased, there was a strong incentive to erect jerry-built houses which would be unlikely to outlive the period of the lease. Not only were workers' cottages built as cheaply as possible but very little was spent by the landlords upon the maintenance of their property.

If the condition of those who lived in the working class quarters of Manchester and Salford was one of utter wretchedness that of the inhabitants of cellars was even worse. Engels estimated that between 40,000 and 50,000 workers lived in cellars in the built-up area of Manchester and Salford. For the homeless – those who could not afford a cottage or even a cellar – there remained the common lodging house. Engels stated that each of these houses accommodated between 20 and 30 persons. "In every room five or seven beds are made up on the floor and human beings of both sexes are packed into them indiscriminately." "Every one of these houses is a breeding ground of crime and also the scene of much conduct of an unnatural and revolting character."

Having described the housing of the workers Engels discussed their general standard of living. The Manchester operatives wore clothes of the poorest quality and subsisted upon a very inadequate diet. Although the better paid factory workers enjoyed good food when they had a job, the lower paid workers had to manage on a diet of bread and potatoes. To make matters worse the poor were cheated by unscrupulous shopkeepers who sold unwholesome and adulterated food and gave short weight. "The potatoes purchased by the workers are generally bad, the vegetables shrivelled, the cheese stale and of poor quality, the bacon rancid."

Engels concluded his chapter on the great towns by summing up his views on the condition of the workers. They had no security of employment and if they lost their jobs they suffered great hardships. They lived in jerry-built, damp, unhealthy and overcrowded cottages. They wore shabby clothes and ate poor food. "In favourable circumstances some of them enjoy, at least temporarily, a modest prosperity." "In bad times, however, the unlucky worker may sink into the deepest poverty, actually culminating in homelessness and death from starvation."

The health and morals of the workers – which Engels discussed in his chapter on the results of industrialisation – suffered as a result of the conditions under which they lived and worked. In London Engels had seen many consumptives – "pale, emaciated, narrow-chested and hollow-eyed ghosts". In the manufacturing districts fever was endemic in overcrowded insanitary slums and typhus regularly took its toll of the workers. Digestive complaints, skin infections and bone diseases were rife in the factory towns and were caused by the poor quality of the workers' diet. Other factors contributing to the poor health of the factory population were lack of suitable winter clothing, reliance upon quack medicines, and excessive consumption of beer and spirits. The factory districts had a high death rate owing largely to the heavy mortality among babies and young children. In Manchester over half of the workers' children died before they were five years old. Engels considered that this was due not only to bad housing and poor food but also to the neglect of children by their parents. When husband and wife both worked in a factory their children were "locked in the house or handed over to someone else's care" and consequently there were numerous fatal accidents among babies and young children.

Engels stated that the level of culture and education attained by the workers was as low as their physical condition. In the elementary schools "a narrow sectarianism and a fanatical bigotry are awakened in the children . . . to the serious neglect of any reasonable instruction in religion and morals." This was because education was controlled by rival churches. Engels added that many factory children were illiterate.

The English workers had their failings – which were due to poor housing, inadequate food, bad health, and lack of education. Engels considered that their most serious failings were addiction to spirits, sexual immorality, and lawlessness. "It is particularly on Saturday evenings that intoxication can be seen in all its bestiality, for it is then that the workers have just received their wages and go out for enjoyment at rather earlier hours than on other days of the week." "On such an evening in Manchester I have seldom gone home without seeing many drunkards staggering in the road or lying helpless in the gutter." Engels considered that gross immorality – like excessive drinking – was inevitable owing to the conditions under which the workers lived. "All the failings of the workers may be traced to the same sort of origin – an unbridled thirst for pleasure, to lack of foresight, inability to adjust themselves to the disciplines of the social order, and above all, the inability to sacrifice immediate pleasure to a future advantage." Moreover the English workers had little respect for the law. Engels declared that "the incidence of crime has increased with the growth of the working class population and there is more crime in Britain than in any other country in the world". He considered the situation to be so serious that "already we see society in the process of dissolution". Social strife was developing into open class warfare between the bourgeois capitalists and the oppressed proletariat. Engels was puzzled at what appeared to him to be a great complacency on the part of the middle classes when faced with a grave threat to their security. "Meanwhile national affairs take their course, whether the middle classes realise what is happening or not, and one fine day the property-holding class will be overwhelmed by events far beyond their comprehension and quite outside their expectations."

Having given an account of the homes and living conditions of the working classes Engels proceeded to describe the factories and mines in which they worked. He argued that in the textile industries the introduction of new and more efficient machines enabled employers to reduce their labour force and to replace men by women and young people. As more men became redundant, and as more married women went to work, the wife became the breadwinner while the husband stayed at home to look after the children. The conditions under which women and children worked in the factories were an incentive to immorality. "The factory owner wields complete power over the persons and charms of the girls working for him." Operatives suffered from numerous occupational diseases and physical deformities. Whenever Engels went for a walk in Manchester he saw people who suffered from spinal injuries. He quoted a remark of a Manchester millowner that the local operatives would soon degenerate into a race of pigmies. Workers in the mills were often unfit for work at forty years of age. Certain tasks in textile mills were particularly unhealthy. Those engaged in carding and combing as well as the flax wet-spinners suffered from chest and bronchial complaints. Accidents at work were common, particularly when machinery was being cleaned. "In Manchester one sees not only numerous cripples, but also plenty of workers who have lost the whole or part of an arm, leg or foot." Moreover since mill operatives were often engaged upon purely routine repetitive tasks they tended to suffer from excessive boredom.

Engels condemned the tyranny exercised by the millowners over their workers. The operatives had to obey their masters without question and they were fined for any breach of factory regulations. They were punished for unpunctuality, for talking or whistling, for bad work, or for leaving a machine without the foreman's consent. The workers were subject to harsh discipline. "Their slavery is more abject than that of the negroes in America because they are more strictly supervised." The power of the millowners over their operatives was strengthened by the truck system and by the tied cottage system. The payment of wages in kind – in goods purchased at inflated prices at the employer's 'tommy shop' – was illegal but the practice survived in some rural and colliery districts. The system whereby certain workers rented cottages from their employer was open to serious abuses. "The injustices of the tied cottage system become infamous when the manufacturer . . . forces his operatives, on pain of dismissal, to occupy one of his houses, to pay a higher rent than is normal, or even to rent houses which they do not occupy."

The description which Engels gave of the textile mills was based upon his own observations – he was working in the offices of a cotton firm – and upon talks with people like James Leach and his girl friend Mary Burns who had personal experience of life in the cotton mills. But when Engels discussed working conditions in other branches of industry or in farming he relied upon pamphlets, newspapers and parliamentary reports. Engels declared that the framework knitters and lace workers of the east Midlands were exceptionally badly paid and suffered from eyestrain, digestive troubles, scrofula and spinal defects. Calico printing was an industry which was changing from hand work to machine production. Engels wrote:

> "There was a calico printworks not far from my lodgings in Manchester, where work sometimes went on far into the night. When I got home the building was still lit up and I have been told that the children working in this establishment sometimes had to work such long hours that they snatched a few minutes of rest and slept on the stone steps of the factory and in corners of the outbuildings."

In the metal industries of Sheffield and the Black Country small workshops survived side by side with large factories. In both of them the condition of the workers was deplorable. The apprentice was exploited by the master craftsman in much the same way as the factory worker was exploited by the factory owner. Engels condemned the conditions that existed in the small metal workshops of the Black Country where apprentices and children were overworked, badly treated, and inadequately fed. The nail makers in the Sedgeley smithies lived and worked in wretched hovels. "In this industrial district the standard of education is incredibly low." In Sheffield, on the other hand, the cutlers enjoyed rather higher living standards, though some of them – such as the filers and grinders – suffered from asthma. In the Staffordshire potteries the factory children were "thin, pale, small and stunted". Any worker unlucky enough to have to handle chinaware which had been dipped in lead-arsenic glaze was certain to suffer from poisoning.

In London the dressmakers, milliners and needlewomen – whether they worked at home or on their employer's premises – were grossly exploited. At the height of the social season they worked long hours for low wages.

> "Poverty stricken needlewomen usually live in little attics, where as many herd together as space will permit. . . . Their health is ruined in a few years and they sink into an early grave, without having been able to earn the barest necessities of life. In the streets below, the gleaming carriages of the wealthy middle classes rattle

past, and close at hand some wretched dandy is gambling away at faro in a single evening as much money as a needlewoman could hope to earn in a year."

Engels's description of the English miners was based upon reports issued by the Children's Employment Commission in 1842–3. Miners suffered from many occupational diseases. In Cornwall the lives of tin and copper miners were shortened by galloping consumption and by physical deformities caused by climbing long ladders in mine shafts. At Alston Moor the lead miners had "a stunted physique and nearly all of them suffer from diseases of the chest." In coal mines and iron ore mines women and children were exhausted after a day's work and often stayed in bed on Sundays to recover from the exertions of the previous week's work. Since miners generally worked in a cramped position they suffered from spinal deformities, lung diseases and digestive complaints. Coal hewers and loaders were ready for retirement at the age of forty. In mines with thin seams of coal conditions were even worse as "the miner had to lie on his side, use his elbow as a lever and hack away at the coal with his pick." Fatal accidents were common. In 1844 over 90 miners were killed in an explosion at Haswell colliery in County Durham. Engels declared that in mining districts the illegal truck system was "the rule and not the exception" while the tied cottage system was universal. Moreover miners were paid by the weight of coal which they produced and Engels alleged that the owners repeatedly defrauded their workers of money that they had earned. He also criticised the annual contract which bound the miner to a particular colliery but often failed to guarantee him a year's work. Engels was able to record some improvement in the condition of the miners in 1844 as a result of a great strike in the Northumberland and Durham coalfield and of legal actions brought against colliery owners by the solicitor W. P. Roberts. But the Durham miners were eventually defeated. Roberts then agreed to represent the Lancashire miners. Engels wrote that before long "the gap between the factory workers and the miners – the former being more intelligent and energetic than the latter – will be closed. In the future they will stand shoulder to shoulder with the factory workers on a basis of complete equality. Thus one stone after another of the fortress of the middle classes is being knocked away."

Farm labourers, too, had their grievances. It is true that they worked in the open under relatively healthy conditions and did not suffer from the sort of occupational diseases that affected many industrial workers but they were exploited by the landed gentry and the farmers as much as factory operatives were exploited by the manufacturers. Engels summarised the gloomy accounts of their condition which had recently appeared in the *Morning Chronicle*[28] and *The Times*.[29] "Their food is meagre and poor in quality. Their clothes are in rags and their dwellings are small and poorly furnished. They inhabit wretched little cottages which have no home comforts." "If they are out of work even for a few days in a month the farm workers are in a desperate situation. . . . If one of their number refuses to work for the very low wages that are offered them there are dozens of unemployed farm labourers – or paupers from the workhouse – who would be happy to work for any wage, however miserable it might be." Farm workers were so poor that they were strongly tempted to indulge in poaching for which harsh penalties were inflicted. "It is the severity of the punishment that accounts for the frequency of bloody encounters with gamekeepers." Still more serious were the recurrent outbreaks of incendiarism in the rural districts. There had been widespread fire-raising in the winter of 1830–1 and when Engels was in Manchester numerous cases were reported in the columns of the *Northern Star*.

In Wales the decline of the small tenant farmers – owing to competition from more efficient English farms – had led to grave rural unrest which found expression early in 1843 in the Rebecca riots. In Ireland the peasants who leased tiny plots of land had sunk into a condition of abject poverty. They lived in "miserable mud huts which are hardly fit for animals". "They are as poor as church mice; they go about in rags; their educational attainments are negligible." And over a quarter of the Irish population received some form of public or private relief. In the circumstances it was hardly surprising that crime was endemic in rural Ireland. "Not a day passes without the perpetration of some serious breach of the law." "Nor do the Irish hesitate to kill their oppressors – the agents and other faithful henchmen of the landlords, the Protestant intruders, and the substantial tenants whose farms have been established by evicting hundreds of Irish peasants from their tiny potato patches."

Engels discussed the reaction of the workers to harsh discipline, long hours and low wages. So long as the Combination Laws had been in force the workers had resorted to violence to resist oppression. Domestic craftsmen, like the Luddites, had destroyed machines which threatened to deprive them of work. But the repeal of the Combination Laws had been followed by the establishment of new trade unions. They, too, had sometimes adopted violent methods when faced with recalcitrant employers and with fellow workers who had refused to support a strike. A notorious trial in Glasgow in 1838 had revealed the existence in that city of a union of cotton spinners which had resorted to murder and incendiarism to intimidate millowners and blacklegs. In 1843 a strike at Pauling and Henfrey's brickworks in Manchester had culminated in violence. The strikers first demolished the brickyard and then "broke into the house of the manager, beat up his wife, and destroyed the furniture". In February 1844 the Soho Grinding Works in Sheffield had been set on fire and completely gutted. But trade unions generally tried to achieve their aims by strikes rather than by violent action. Engels commented upon "the incredible frequency of strikes" in England in the early 1840s. "Not a week passes – indeed hardly a day passes – without a strike occurring somewhere." "They may be only minor engagements but they prove conclusively that the decisive battle between the proletariat and the bourgeoisie is approaching." "These stoppages of work are a training ground for the industrial proletariat and a preparation for the next campaign which draws inevitably nearer."

Through the trade union movement the workers fought their employers for better conditions and higher pay. Through the Chartist movement they tried to gain political power by reforming parliament. A House of Commons dominated by a workers' party could secure reforms that neither Whigs nor Tories would be prepared to grant. Engels described the fortunes of the Chartists since their programme – including the demand for manhood suffrage – had been adopted in 1838. At that time Chartism had been a radical movement supported both by workers and by the lower middle classes. Engels suggested that the northern manufacturers – interested in securing the repeal of the Corn Laws – had used social discontent in the early 1840s for their own ends. The factory owners had picked a quarrel with their workers in 1842 by threatening wage reductions so that when the men resisted they could be locked out. And then the unemployed "would leave the towns and swarm into the countryside over the estates of the landed aristocracy". Social unrest would force the Tory majority in parliament to abolish the Corn Laws. But the Plug Plot riots of 1842 were put down by the police and the military. The Chartists – who had played a relatively minor role in the affair – were discredited. "Chartism became a purely working class movement and was free from the trammels of bourgeois influence." Engels concluded by observing that "it is the factory workers, particularly in the Lancashire cotton districts, who form the solid core of the working class movement. Manchester is the headquarters of the most powerful trade unions, the focal point of Chartism, and the stronghold of the Socialist movement."

Finally Engels discussed the character of the English middle classes and their behaviour towards the workers. He considered the middle classes to be utterly demoralised. "They are so degraded by selfishness and moral depravity as to be quite incapable of salvation." Engels praised the vivid picture of the "revolting greed for money" of the middle classes given by Thomas Carlyle in *Past and Present*.[30] The middle classes were not only greedy but hypocritical as well. They claimed that, far from neglecting the poor, they had "subscribed to the erection of more institutions for the relief of poverty than are to be found anywhere in the world." Engels argued that "the vampire middle classes first suck the wretched workers dry so that afterwards they can, with consummate hypocrisy, throw a few miserable crumbs at their feet". "It never occurs to these pharisees that they are only returning a hundredth part of that which they have previously taken away from the broken-down workers whom they have ruthlessly exploited."

The attitude of the middle classes towards the Corn Laws was, in Engels's view, another example of their hypocrisy. The middle classes poured their subscriptions into the coffers of the Anti-Corn Law League in the hope of securing the abolition of the import duties upon cereals. They claimed that they were acting in an altruistic manner to secure cheap bread for the workers. In fact – according to Engels – the factory owners wanted cheap bread simply to be able to reduce wages. The way in which the law was administered was – according to Engels – another example of middle class hypocrisy. In theory all citizens were equal before the law but in practice the English legal system was used by the middle classes as a means to oppress the workers. "At the root of all laws lies the idea that the proletariat is an enemy which must be defeated." The police and the justices of the peace were hostile and prejudiced in their dealings with the workers. Offences against property – such as theft or poaching – were punished with the utmost severity.

Engels attacked the Poor Law as a glaring example of the inhumanity of the middle classes. They accepted Malthus's view that if a man could not find work and provide for his family then "at nature's mighty feast there is no vacant cover for him." If the middle classes were not prepared to let the poor starve to death they were prepared to treat the poor as if they were criminals. The workhouses – the hated bastilles – were no better than prisons and the paupers in them were treated with revolting cruelty. Engels quoted from the press numerous cases of brutality in workhouses. Moreover "in death as in life the poor in England are treated in an utterly shameless manner. Their corpses have no better fate than the carcases of animals." In the circumstances it was not surprising that there was strong resistance to the administration of the Poor Law by the workers. "No other Act passed by the capitalists has so incensed the workers as this."

Engels concluded his book with a declaration of faith in communism as the only possible solution to the social problems of the industrial age. He believed that the existing industrial society of England would soon collapse and that it would be replaced by a communist society. Under communism competition would vanish and the rivalry between the capitalists and the proletariat would disappear.

An examination of Engels's account of the condition of the English workers shows that in 1845 Engels was in close agreement with Marx's philosophical views. Engels, like Marx, had come to the conclusion that "the course of world history was determined by definite laws and that – in any society – the social and political structure of the state was determined by economic factors – by the way in which goods were produced."[31]

III. Engels's Book in Germany[32]

The weavers' rising in Silesia in 1844[33] alarmed the authorities and the middle classes in Germany who realised that the country was on the threshold of an industrial revolution and that new social problems must now be faced. Newspapers and periodicals were suddenly full of articles on the distress of the workers and the problem of pauperism and societies were founded to ameliorate the condition of the poor. Engels's book was published at a time when the effects of industrialisation upon the workers were a live issue in the press and in public discussions. It was the most important socialist work to be published in Germany between the weavers' rising and the appearance of the Communist Manifesto. It was widely reviewed, widely read, and widely quoted. The first edition of 1845 was reprinted three years later. The book made a greater impact upon the public than any other work on social conditions in England that appeared at this time.[34]

Engels's work soon attracted the attention of German governments and their ministers and civil servants. Some official commentators argued that Engels was concerned only with English affairs and not with conditions in Germany. Circumstances in the two countries were entirely different and the problems which Engels discussed were of no practical concern to the German reader. Other official commentators took a more realistic view and admitted that one day the German workers might – unless something were done about it – find themselves in the same unhappy position as the English workers of 1844. They suggested that Engels's book was a timely warning to the German authorities to take action in time to prevent German factory workers from being exploited as the English factory workers had been oppressed by their employers. They were confident that the monarchical régimes in Germany would have the will and the strength to protect industrial workers in the future. In Prussia official commentators used Engels's book as ammunition in their resistance to the demands of the liberals for constitutional reforms and parliamentary government. In the Rhineland and Westphalia some leading manufacturers were behind the liberal movement. Supporters of the monarchy argued that Engels's book was a warning of the fate that would overtake the factory workers if the manufacturers should weaken the traditional authority of the monarchy and gain political power in Germany.

In Prussia reports on Engels's book were prepared in the Ministries of Foreign Affairs and of the Interior. The distinguished statistician Dr Freiherr von Reden of the Foreign Office wrote a memorandum on the book for his Minister.[35] He praised the accuracy of Engels's description of the condition of the English workers and declared that the author had presented "an obviously truthful picture of the attitude of the middle classes to the proletariat". "I am glad that a German author should have been the first to make a thorough comprehensive investigation into the condition of the English workers." Von Reden hoped that a similar book on the German workers would soon be written. A report by an official named Seebode to the Minister of the Interior also praised Engels's book.[36] Seebode argued that the work dealt only with English affairs and that Engels's criticisms could not be applied to conditions in Germany. But Alfred, Freiherr von Bibra, an official in the little Duchy of Meiningen in Thuringia took a different point of view. In a report on the book he suggested that social conditions in England should be carefully examined so that the authorities could take action in time to prevent a situation arising in Germany similar to that described by Engels.[37]

The Prussian authorities feared that some readers of Engels's book might think that Engels's criticism of the treatment meted out to the workers by the middle classes applied to Germany as well as to England. To counteract such a possibility the newspapers which were subsidised by the Prussian government argued that the condition of the English workers, as described by Engels, was due to defects in the British constitution and political system. A similar situation could not exist under the authoritarian but benevolent rule of the Prussian kings.

This point of view was adopted by the *Allgemeine Preussische Staats-Zeitung*.[38] The reviewer of Engels's book was confident that the welfare services of the German states would shield the workers from the evils from which the English factory operatives suffered. He hoped that Prussia would develop into an industrialised country but that the monarchy would be strong enough to prevent the middle classes from dominating society as they did in England. The Prussian crown would defend the factory workers from exploitation by the capitalists. It would not allow the doctrine of *laissez faire* to triumph but would insist that industrialists should subordinate their own interests to the welfare of the whole community. By such arguments the writer hoped to show that the social evils described by Engels would not spread to Germany. A somewhat similar point of view was taken by Victor Aimé Huber in the journal *Janus* which was subsidised by the Prussian government.[39] Huber confirmed Engels's description of the condition of the industrial proletariat in England from his own observations but criticised Engels for lack of impartiality and for giving a biased view of the relations between workers and their employers.

The conservative press in Prussia generally adopted a point of view similar to that taken by official commentators. On the great estates east of the river Elbe the landowners encouraged the King to resist the demands of the manufacturers of the Rhine and Westphalia for liberal reforms. Political antagonism between the junkers and the industrialists was intensified by a clash of economic interests. The junkers favoured Free Trade while many manufacturers were protectionists. Friedrich von Farenheid, a conservative landowner in the eastern provinces, reviewed Engels's book in a Königsberg journal.[40] He did not doubt the existence of the social evils described by Engels but he did doubt whether they were caused entirely by industrialisation. He asserted that a number of these evils existed in rural societies which had few if any factories. For example, child labour was a social problem on the great estates of East Prussia just as it was a problem in the English industrial districts. Farenheid stated that he knew of three Prussian parishes in which 72 children were habitually absent from school, 33 attended irregularly, while 235 attended only during the winter. Farenheid thought that overpopulation was the root cause of social distress and pauperism.

The journals which represented the views of the business world were strongly opposed to Engels's political aims. They saw that Engels's criticisms of English capitalists could be applied with equal force to German industrialists. If German millowners, like Engels's father, read *The Condition of the Working Class in England* they realised that they had been pilloried as severely as the Manchester manufacturers. That Engels advocated the destruction of capitalism and the establishment of a communist society made it inevitable that middle class liberals in Germany would reject his views. Mönke observes that they instinctively recognised the threat to their own class if Engels's propaganda achieved any success. "The proletariat could change from an oppressed class to an aggressive revolutionary class and could become the most dangerous enemy of the middle classes."[41]

It doubtless caused Engels no surprise that a newspaper in his home town – the *Barmer Zeitung* which was subsidised by the Prussian government – should have given him an unfavourable review.[42] Again, a reviewer in the literary supplement of the influential *Augsburg Allgemeine Zeitung*[43] criticised Engels for assuming that there was already open warfare in England between the workers and the middle classes, and rebuked him for insisting that "the present sufferings of the proletariat are caused entirely by the greed of the bourgeoisie whom he loathes with a burning hatred." The reviewer thought that "every educated impartial reader must be shocked a hundred times by the wrong-headed views expressed by the author, whose lack of all moral sense can be seen in his foolish and unjustifiable hatred of the middle classes."[44]

One of the longest and severest contemporary criticisms of Engels's book came from the pen of Professor Bruno Hildebrand of Marburg.[45] In a work on the principles of economics the professor devoted over 70 pages to Engels's book. Hildebrand conceded that Engels was "the most gifted and knowledgeable German writer on social problems" and that his book was based upon independent research and personal observation. But he argued at some length that although his facts might be right, Engels's interpretations of the facts were wrong and his comments were extremely biased. Hildebrand endeavoured to show, for example, that Engels had failed to understand English criminal statistics correctly and had been wrong in his assertion that English factory workers were worse off in the 1840s than the domestic craftsmen had been in the eighteenth century. Although Hildebrand was one of the leading German academic economists of his day his detailed criticisms of Engels's book seem to have been hardly noticed and not answered.

Writers in radical journals did not share Engels's political opinions but found in his book ample material to use in their attacks upon German manufacturers. Professor Karl Biedermann – who was later Vice President of the National Assembly at Frankfurt – was no communist but he played an important part in bringing Engels's book to public notice. In the periodical *Unsere Gegenwart und Zukunft*[46] and in popular lectures held in Dresden and Leipzig[47] Biedermann discussed the rise of socialism in Germany and frequently referred to Engels's account of the condition of the English workers. M. Fleischer, another radical reviewer, declared that Engels's horrifying description of the miseries of the English factory workers was a warning of the gravity of the social evils that followed industrialisation if the State failed to curb the avarice of the capitalists.[48] Professor Weinlig of Erlangen, a radical publicist, reviewed Engels's book at some length in 1846. He was particularly interested in Engels's analysis of the economic and social factors which had brought about an industrial revolution in England. He praised Engels for explaining clearly how the social evils of a highly industrialised society had been brought about by "the tendency of the factory system to bring about great concentrations of capital, to promote a clash of interests between the factory owners and their workers and to reduce the industrial proletariat to a position of subjection to the employers".[49]

The socialist press and left wing journals which opened their columns to socialist writers were loud in their praises of Engels's book. They not only gave the book very favourable reviews but they often printed long extracts from it.[50] Moses Hess in the *Gesellschaftsspiegel*,[51] Dr Otto Lüning in the *Deutsches Bürgerbuch*,[52] Rudolph Matthi in the *Bote aus dem Katzenbachthal*,[53] Josef Weydemeyer in *Dies Buch gehört dem Volk*,[54] Hermann Semming in the *Constitutionelle Staatsbürger-Zeitung*,[55] and Dr Hermann Ewerbeck in the *Blätter der Zukunft*,[56] were among the socialists, of various shades of opinion, who wrote about Engels's account of the condition of the English workers. The *Westphälisches Dampfboot*,[57] the *Breslauer Volkspiegel*, and the *Trier'sche Zeitung*[58] also reviewed the book. Although some of these newspapers and journals had small sales and a short life – and were harassed by censorship regulations – they helped to establish Engels's reputation as a leading German socialist thinker.

IV. Engels's Book in England

Although Engels's book on the condition of the English workers made a considerable stir in Germany when it first appeared it was soon forgotten except by Karl Marx and his disciples. After the failures of the revolutions in 1848–9 reactionary governments in Germany and Austria suppressed workers' associations and drove the socialist movement underground until it was revived by Ferdinand Lassalle in the early 1860s. Marx regarded Engels's book as a brilliant survey of the way in which modern capitalism had developed and a classic description of the social consequences of an industrial revolution. In 1862 he wrote to Engels:

> "I have read your book again and I have realised that I am not getting any younger. What power, what incisiveness and what passion drove you to work in those days. That was a time when you were never worried by academic scholarly reservations! Those were the days when you made the reader feel that your theories would become hard facts if not tomorrow then at any rate on the day after. Yet that very illusion gave the whole work a human warmth and a touch of humour that makes our later writings – where 'black and white' have become 'grey and grey' – seem positively distasteful."[59]

In 1867 in the first volume of *Das Kapital* Karl Marx observed that "the fulness of Engels's insight into the nature of the capitalist method of production has been shown by the factory reports, the reports on mines etc., that have appeared since the publication of his book."[60] A few years later Marx could give no higher praise to a book on the Russian workers by N. Flerowski[61] than to say that it was the best book on the proletariat since Engels's *The Condition of the Working Class in England*.[62] By this time Engels's work had long been out of print.

It was not until the 1880s that interest in Engels's early book revived. The rise and fall of the First International, the establishment of socialist parties on the Continent and the growth of trade unions in Britain and the United States fostered an interest in early socialist works and there were now demands for a new German edition and for an English translation. In 1885 Engels wrote: "My friends in Germany say that the book is important to them just now because it describes a state of things which is almost exactly reproduced at the present moment in Germany."[63] At this time Mrs Florence Kelley Wischnewetzky undertook the translation of the book into English for an American edition. Engels revised the text, and the book appeared in New York in 1887. Engels complained that Mrs Wischnewetzky "translates like a factory, leaving the real work to me".[64] He was exasperated by her inefficiency. Instead of approaching a publisher herself she left this to Miss Rachel Foster-Avery (the secretary of the National Women's Suffrage Association)[65] who turned the manuscript over to the executive of the Socialist Labour Party in New York. Engels objected to this arrangement and strongly criticised Mrs Wischnewetzky for having "bungled everything that she has handled; I shall never give her anything again."[66]

Mrs Wischnewetzky's translation appeared in England in 1892. In a new preface[67] Engels, now aged seventy-two, asked for the indulgence of his readers for a book that had been written when he was only twenty-four. "His production bears the stamp of his youth with its good and faulty features, of neither of which he feels ashamed." Engels observed that in certain respects the book was now out of date. In some ways England had changed for the better since 1844. "The petty devices of swindling and pilfering", characteristic of early capitalism, were no longer practised in 1892. Since Engels had written his book England's output of manufactured goods had grown by leaps and bounds and the progress that had been achieved by 1844 "now appears to us as comparatively primitive and insignificant". Consequently "the competition of manufacturer against manufacturer by means of petty thefts upon the workpeople no longer pays." The truck system had been abolished, the Ten Hours Act had long been the law of the land, while the existence of trade unions had been accepted by many of the great industrialists. Indeed "the largest manufacturers . . . were now the foremost to preach peace and harmony" between employers and workers. Engels argued that the reason for this was the desire of powerful industrialists to crush their smaller competitors and so "to accelerate the concentration of capital in the hands of the few". Nevertheless Engels considered that capitalism was just as evil a system in 1892 as it had been in 1844. The growth of capitalism had divided society "into a few Rothschilds and Vanderbilts, the owners of all the means of production and subsistence, on the one hand, and an immense number of wage earners, the owners of nothing but their labour force, on the other".

Engels admitted that the environment of the workers had improved somewhat since 1844. The middle classes had been forced, in their own interests, to clean up the manufacturing towns. Alarmed by serious epidemics, they had improved public sanitation and had cleared away some of the worst slums such as Manchester's Little Ireland. "Accordingly, the most crying abuses described in this book have either disappeared or have been made less conspicuous." But as recently as 1885 the report of a Royal Commission had shown that the problem of providing adequate housing for the workers was still far from being solved. Another change that had occurred since Engels wrote his book was that while in 1844 Britain had been the workshop of the world her industrial monopoly was now being successfully challenged by the United States and Germany.

Engels blamed his "youthful ardour" for the erroneous prophecies which he had made in 1845. "The wonder is, not that a good many of them proved wrong, but that so many of them have proved right." He had correctly foretold that Britain's competitive position, as a manufacturing country, would be undermined by the growth of great industries in America and on the Continent. To show in greater detail how this prophecy had come true Engels reprinted an article which he had written a few years previously on "England in 1845 and 1885".[68]

Engels concluded his preface of 1892 with a caustic reference to a "momentary fashion among bourgeois circles of affecting a mild dilution of socialism" and with a comment upon changes that had taken place in the East End of London since his article of 1885 had been written. "That immense haunt of misery is no longer the stagnant pool it was six years ago. It has shaken off its torpid despair, has returned to life, and has become the home of what is called the 'New Unionism', that is to say, of the organisation of the great mass of unskilled workers." "And for all the faults committed in past, present and future, the revival of the East End of London remains one of the greatest and most fruitful facts of this *fin de siècle*, and glad and proud I am to have lived to see it."

The English translation of Engels's book received a warm welcome not only from socialists – who accepted it as a classic account of the evils brought about by an industrial revolution – but from historians who regarded it as a valuable source of information concerning social conditions in the English manufacturing towns in 1844.[69] Early accounts of the industrial workers and their environment had long been out of print. Not only was Engels's book available but it was written in a vigorous style which kept the attention of the reader. Many discussions of social problems written in the 1840s had been limited to particular industries or to special regions whereas Engels had attempted to give a fairly comprehensive survey of the condition of all types of workers in 1844. Economic historians – Archdeacon Cunningham,[70] Professor Brentano[71] and others – accepted Engels's book as an accurate account of industrial England in an age which had seen the country nearing a peak of manufacturing activity. Engels was an eye-witness who had described what he had seen and heard. His references to contemporary official reports and private investigations gave readers the impression that he was not only an acute observer but also one who had mastered the literature of the subject. The English translation of 1892 was reprinted in 1920[72] and a new translation appeared in 1958.

V. The Significance of Engels's Book[73]

Engels's *The Condition of the Working Class in England* has had a curious fate since its purpose has to some extent been misunderstood and it has been praised for the wrong reasons. The claims of the socialists on behalf of the book merit further examination. Socialists considered that Engels's account of the condition of the English workers had two unique features. First, by using a new intellectual tool – the doctrine of dialectical materialism – Engels was able to show how the state of the English workers in the 1840s was an inevitable consequence of a struggle between social classes. Secondly, he was in a position to forecast the doom of the existing capitalist system and the forthcoming triumph of the proletariat over its bourgeois oppressors. His sociological approach to the problem revealed that industrial capitalism carried within it the seeds of its own decay.

It may be doubted whether either of these propositions can be substantiated. Engels's historical introduction, far from having any claim to originality, was little more than a summary of Peter Gaskell's book on *The Manufacturing Population of England* (1833).[74] Gaskell had thought that in the eighteenth century the yeomen, the peasants and the craftsmen had led a happy idyllic existence and that the degradation of the workers in the manufacturing districts had been brought about entirely by the introduction of the factory system. No modern economic historian would repeat this myth. Many of the evils of the factory system – low earnings, long hours, unhealthy working conditions and the exploitation of the labour of women and children – were to be found in the domestic system of the eighteenth century. The small size and the scattered nature of the units of production at that time tended to hide social evils which came to light later when many workers were gathered together in large factories and mines. Even in Engels's day some of the worst conditions were to be found not in the great cotton mills, the ironworks or the mines but in such occupations as dressmaking in the East End of London and nail-making in the Black Country which were still largely organised on a domestic basis.

Engels's earliest attempt to forecast the future of a capitalist society was as unsuccessful as his first attempt to explain existing conditions by studying their history. He believed that his examination of the origins of the factory system, coupled with his analysis of the structure of English economic and social conditions in 1844 had enabled him to identify certain trends of historical development. If these trends were projected into the future the collapse of the capitalist system, the downfall of the middle classes and the future triumph of the proletariat could be predicted with certainty. But Engels was not a very successful tipster. His assertion that the Chartists were on the verge of success in 1844 was soon proved to be wrong since the Chartist movement collapsed in 1848. His confident belief that the cotton lords whom he detested would be swept away by a great rising of the oppressed workers was equally mistaken. All his life Engels waited patiently for the English revolution that he had so confidently predicted but it never occurred.[75] He was wrong in supposing that socialism would first triumph in highly industrialised societies. In fact it was established in the twentieth century in backward underdeveloped countries. Engels was mistaken in thinking that in an industrial society the labour force would be increasingly composed of women and children.[76] His assertion that under the capitalist system the gulf between rich and poor would widen as time went on was also erroneous.[77] To those who drew attention to his blunders Engels replied either by claiming that a faulty prediction was due to the appearance of some new – and unforeseen – factor or by asserting that the prediction was correct and would still come true at some future date.

Nor can it be claimed that Engels gave a well-balanced and entirely accurate account of social conditions in England in 1844. It is true that many of the facts reported by Engels can be readily confirmed from the writings of other observers – such as Léon Faucher – who visited the northern industrial towns in the 1840s. It is in the selection and interpretation of the facts that Engels was at fault. He never made a secret of the fact that his book had been written not to give an objective account of the manufacturing districts, but to attack social evils and to pillory the class which he considered to be responsible for their existence. He saw himself as an advocate prosecuting a criminal, not a judge giving an impartial summing-up. Engels's knowledge of England in the 1840s was less extensive than is sometimes supposed. In twenty months he became well acquainted with Lancashire and the West Riding but his visits to London were brief and there were many manufacturing regions – the Black Country, South Wales, Tyneside, Clydeside – of which he had little if any first hand knowledge. His reading was highly selective since he relied to a great extent upon a small number of books, pamphlets and parliamentary papers. He made considerable use of the Chartist newspaper, the *Northern Star*, which was an extremely biased left-wing journal.

Another criticism concerns the way in which Engels used the

material at his disposal. He sometimes exercised little judgement in evaluating evidence since evidence taken on oath appeared cheek by jowl with extracts from newspapers. Any statements, whatever their origin, were grist to Engels's mill so long as they could be used to attack the millowners. For example, Sir Archibald Alison estimated in 1840 that there were between 30,000 and 40,000 prostitutes in London. Engels naturally took the higher rather than the lower figure and then left his readers with the impression that the existence of 40,000 prostitutes in London was a known fact. Actually Alison had made it clear that he was only guessing and there are of course no accurate statistics of prostitution in England in the 1840s. Again, Engels claimed to describe social conditions in the 1840s, yet some of his evidence came from an earlier date. Thus he made use of an article by John Hennen on the insanitary state of Edinburgh, which had been written as early as 1818. He quoted from Kay's pamphlet of 1832 on the Manchester cotton operatives and from the official Factories Enquiry Commission of 1833–4 as if nothing had changed in the last ten years.

Engels's interpretation of evidence and his attribution of motives to the factory owners were often unsatisfactory. He confidently asserted – as if no other explanation were possible – that the Plug Plot riots in the northern industrial districts had been deliberately fomented by the factory owners who cut wages in the hope that the workers would strike and so force the government to repeal the Corn Laws. This view of the origin of the industrial unrest in 1842 was shared by such strange bedfellows as the Tory J. W. Croker and the Chartist Feargus O'Connor, but was hotly denied by the Anti-Corn Law League. Engels gave one side of the story without even suggesting that any other explanation was worthy of consideration.[78]

Engels also asserted that under the capitalist system the condition of the workers continually declined. He believed that when he was in England in the 1840s the sufferings of the proletariat were greater than they had ever been before. Socialist historians subsequently agreed with him. But other – no less competent – scholars have argued that during the so-called 'Hungry Forties' the workers as a whole were probably no worse off – and some of them may have been better off – than they had been in the 1830s or the 1820s.[79] Engels, however, put forward his point of view as an accepted fact which could not be contradicted.

Engels persisted in portraying the English capitalists as men dedicated to making money at whatever cost in suffering to their workers. So he argued that if hours of work in factories or mines were long and if heavy physical labour were involved, the entrepreneur was ruining the health of the workers to make large profits for himself. But if improved machines were installed which enabled hours to be reduced and lighter work to be undertaken the factory owner was still at fault. This time he was forcing his employees to work faster to keep pace with new machinery or he was making men redundant and replacing them by women. The capitalist who ignored the social problems of his day was condemned as a heartless monster. Yet the enlightened employer who built model cottages for his workers and provided them with a canteen and a reading room was still criticised and was supposed to have acted from the lowest motives. The model dwellings were tied cottages which meant that the loss of a job also meant the loss of a home while the reading rooms contained only periodicals approved by the employer. Engels's attitude towards the employers made it impossible for him to write a really impartial account of social conditions in England in 1844.

The merits of Engels's book were different from those sometimes attributed to it. Engels had not written an impartial survey of the social scene in industrial England. What he had done was to write a brilliant hard-hitting political tract. The forceful language with which social evils were denounced eventually gave the book a place in German political literature comparable with Thomas Carlyle's pamphlet on Chartism in England. Engels had denounced the social evils of an industrial society in the middle of the nineteenth century more effectively than they had ever been attacked before by a German writer. His book had a powerful impact upon public opinion in Germany between 1845 and 1848 and it helped to generate a feeling of responsibility towards the victims of industrial changes.

Moreover Engels went to the heart of various economic and social problems which were still being treated somewhat superficially by many of his contemporaries. While orthodox economists were discussing problems of rent, prices and the rational use of scarce resources, Engels drew attention to the fundamental problems of economic growth. He was one of the first to discuss the trade cycle and the existence of a pool of unemployed workers and to offer explanations for these phenomena. He saw the significance of the growth of big business at the expense of small undertakings. These topics were later discussed more thoroughly by Karl Marx, but to deal with them at all in 1845 was no mean achievement. Engels's chapter on the great towns – one of the best in the book – showed an insight into problems of urban geography and urban growth which was far ahead of his time.[80] And his discussion of the significance of class antagonism – based upon a clash of economic interests – in an industrial society anticipated much that Karl Marx and other later writers had to say on the subject. It is because Engels appreciated better than so many of his contemporaries the real significance of the factors which were changing the industrial society of his day that his book went on being read while the writings of so many authors who were at work at the same time have fallen into oblivion.

Engels's book was of vital significance in Marx's intellectual development. In the preface to his first major work on economics – the *Critique of Political Economy* (1859) – Marx explained that as a young man he had studied jurisprudence, philosophy and history but he had eventually realised that to get to the heart of legal forms and political institutions one had to examine the material conditions of life. "The method of production in material life determines the general character of the social, political and spiritual processes of life." Engels's early essay on economic theory in the *Deutsch-Französische Jahrbücher* and his book on *The Condition of the Working Class in England* played an important part in turning Marx's attention from law and philosophy to economics. A comparison between Engels's book and certain sections of the first volume of *Das Kapital* – for example Marx's discussion of 'the working day' – shows how much Marx owed to his friend's book. It was from Engels that Marx learned how to make effective use of evidence collected by parliamentary commissions, by the Registrar General, and by factory inspectors to gain a real insight into the workings of the industrial economy. In later years Engels influenced the writing of *Das Kapital* at every stage of its production but the initial impulse which attracted Marx to a study of economics came largely from Engels and was one of his important contributions to the development of a theory of 'scientific socialism'.

NOTES

1 See Horst Ullrich, *Der junge Engels* (1966), Vol. 2, Ch. 6.

2 W. O. Henderson (ed.), *Engels: Selected Writings* (1967), p. 387.

3 Engels wrote in the *New Moral World* (December 13, 1844): "I am just returning from a trip to some neighbouring towns, and there was not a single place where I did not find at least half a dozen or a dozen of out-and-out socialists. . . . We have partisans among all sorts of men – commercial men, manufacturers, lawyers, officers of the government and of the army, physicians, editors of newspapers, farmers etc.; a great many of our publications are in the press, though hardly three or four have as yet appeared; and if we make as much progress during the next four or five years as we have done in the past twelvemonth, we shall be able to erect forthwith a Com-

munity. You see, we German theorists are getting practical men of business. . . ." (*Gesamtausgabe*, Part I, Vol. 4, p. 341).

4 F. Engels to K. Marx, October 8–10, 1844 in *Gesamtausgabe*, Part III, Vol. 1, pp. 1–4.

5 Rheda is in Westphalia and lies between Münster and Bielefeld.

6 The *Weser-Dampfboot* survived for only one year (1844). In 1845 Dr Lüning brought out another periodical called *Das Westphälische Dampfboot*.

7 F. Engels to K. Marx, November 19, 1844 in *Gesamtausgabe*, Part III, Vol. 1, pp. 4–8.

8 F. Engels to K. Marx, January 20, 1845 in *Gesamtausgabe*, Part III, Vol. 1, pp. 9–13.

9 *Ibid.*, p. 9.

10 F. Engels to K. Marx, February 22–March 7, 1845 in *Gesamtausgabe*, Part III, Vol. 1, p. 16. The journal was published in Elberfeld.

11 For the *Gesellschaftsspiegel* see the introduction by Auguste Cornu and Wolfgang Mönke to Moses Hess, *Philosophische und Sozialistische Schriften* (1961).

12 F. Engels to K. Marx, January 20, 1845; February 22–March 7, 1845 and March 17, 1845 in *Gesamtausgabe*, Part III, Vol. 1, pp. 11, 16 and 19.

13 F. Engels to K. Marx, February 22–March 7, 1845 in *Gesamtausgabe*, Part III, Vol. 1, pp. 14–15.

14 *New Moral World*, third series, May 10, 1845, pp. 371–2 and *Gesamtausgabe*, Part I, Vol. 4, pp. 344–8.

15 *Rheinische Zeitung*, Vol. I, 1845, pp. 45–62 and pp. 71–81 and *Gesamtausgabe*, Part I, Vol. 4, pp. 369–90.

16 *New Moral World*, third series, May 10, 1845, pp. 371–2 and *Gesamtausgabe*, Part I, Vol. 4, pp. 344–8. For Hess's speeches at the communist meetings in Elberfeld see Moses Hess, *Philosophische und sozialistische Schriften 1837–1850* (1961), pp. 348–59.

17 W. O. Henderson (ed.), *Engels; Selected Writings* (1967), pp. 148–71.

18 Engels discussed communist settlements at greater length in an article entitled "Beschreibung der in neuerer Zeit entstanden und noch bestehenden kommunistischen Ansiedlungen" which appeared anonymously in the *Deutsches Bürgerbuch für 1845* (Darmstadt, 1845), pp. 326–40. The article has been reprinted in *Gesamtausgabe*, Part I, Vol. 4, pp. 351–66.

19 F. Engels in the *New Moral World*, third series, Vol. 6, May 10, 1845 and in *Gesamtausgabe*, Part I, Vol. 4, p. 346.

20 H. Hirsch, *Friedrich Engels* (1968), p. 53.

21 F. Engels to K. Marx, March 7, 1845 in *Gesamtausgabe*, Part III, Vol. 1, p. 17.

22 *Gesamtausgabe*, Part III, Vol. 1, pp. 19–20 and W. O. Henderson (ed.), *Engels: Selected Writings* (1967), p. 388.

23 The *Deutsche-Brüsseler Zeitung*, No. 91, November 14, 1847 reported that "F. Engels, who is living in Paris at present, is writing a comprehensive work in several volumes on the history of the English middle class." In 1845 the radical Darmstadt publisher C. W. Leske twice asked Karl Marx to approach Engels concerning his projected history. Leske wished to publish the book. See Wolfgang Mönke, *Das literarische Echo in Deutschland auf Friedrich Engels' Werk "Die Lage der arbeitenden Klasse in England"* (1965), p. 94.

24 For the relations between the radical Leipzig publisher Otto Wigand

and Marx and Engels see K. Wiegel, "Otto Wigand. Ein fortschrittlicher Drucker und Verleger des 19en Jahrhunderts" in *Marginalien Blätter der Pirckheimer-Gesellschaft*, March 1963, Heft 13, pp. 33–44.

25 In July 1845 Georg Weerth wrote to his mother: "My very dear friend Friedrich Engels of Barmen . . . has written a book in defence of the English workers and has fearfully but justly scourged the manufacturers. His own father has factories in England and Germany. He is now at terrible variance with his family; he is considered godless and impious, and the rich father will not give his son another penny for his keep". (Georg Weerth, *Sämtliche Werke*, Vol. 5, p. 172).

26 F. Engels, *Die Lage der arbeitenden Klasse in England. Nach eigener Anschauung und authentischen Quellen* (first German edition, Otto Wigand, Leipzig, 1845; second German edition, J. H. W. Dietz, Stuttgart with new introduction by the author, 1892; new German edition with introduction by W. O. Henderson, J. H. W. Dietz Nachfolger, 1965). The first German edition was reprinted in *Gesamtausgabe*, Part I, Vol. 4, 1932. The first English translation by Mrs Florence Kelley Wischnewetzky appeared in the United States in 1887 and in England in 1892. Engels wrote new introductions for these editions. A second English translation by W. O. Henderson and W. H. Chaloner was published by Basil Blackwell in 1958 and by the Stanford University Press in 1968. This edition includes a translation of Engels's article on "The Postscript of 1846. An English Strike" which appeared in *Das Westphälische Dampfboot*, January and February 1846 and was reprinted in *Gesamtausgabe*, Part I, Vol. 4, pp. 393–405.

27 F. Engels, *The Condition of the Working Class in England* (translated and edited by W. O. Henderson and W. H. Chaloner, 1958), pp. 7–8. All references are to this edition.

28 *Morning Chronicle*, July 6, 1843, p. 3, col. 2–4 (article by Alexander Somerville).

29 *The Times*, June 7, 1844, p. 6, col. 1–2; June 10, 1844, p. 7, col. 1–2; and June 21, 1844, p. 5, col. 1 and p. 6, col. 1.

30 See also Engels's review of Thomas Carlyle, *Past and Present* in the *Deutsch Französische Jahrbücher*, 1844 (in *Gesamtausgabe*, Part I, Vol. 2, pp. 379–404. English translation in appendix to Karl Marx, *Economic and Philosophical Manuscripts of 1844*, Foreign Languages Publishing House, Moscow, 1961).

31 Auguste Cornu, *Karl Marx und Friedrich Engels*, Vol. 2 (1962), p. 269.

32 Wolfgang Mönke, *Das literarische Echo in Deutschland auf Friedrich Engels's Werk "Die Lage der arbeitenden Klasse in England"* (1965), pp. 23–60: an excellent monograph on the reception of Engels's book in Germany.

33 For socialist views on the rising of the Silesian weavers in 1844 see F. W. Wolff, "Das Elend und der Aufruhr in Schlesien" in *Deutsches Bürgerbuch* (edited by H. Püttmann, 1845 and reprinted in C. Jantke and D. Hilger, *Die Eigentumlosen*, 1965, pp. 157–78) and Karl Marx, "Kritische Randglossen zu dem Artikel 'Der König von Preussen und die Sozialreform, von einem Preussen'" in *Gesamtausgabe*, Part I, Vol. 3 (1932).

34 See Eugène Buret, *De la misère des classes laborieuses en Angleterre et en France* (two volumes, 1844); Gustav Mevissen, "Englische Zustände" (*Rheinische Zeitung*, September 13, 18, and 20, 1842); Léon Faucher, *Manchester in 1844; its Present Condition and Future Pros-*

pects (translated anonymously with additional notes by J. P. Culverwell: new edition 1969) and *Etudes sur l'Angleterre* (two volumes, 1845; new edition 1969; German translation, 1846); C. G. Carus, *England und Schottland im Jahre 1844* (1845); C. T. Kleinschrod, *Der Pauperismus in England* (1845); J. Venedy, *England* (three volumes, 1845); G. Höfken, *Englands Zustände, Politik und Machtentwicklung mit Beziehung auf Deutschland* (two volumes, 1846).

35 H. Welsch, "Ein Urteil des preussischen Statistikers Friedrich Wilhelm Otto Ludwig von Reden über das Werk von Friedrich Engels, 'Die Lage der arbeitenden Klasse in England' aus dem Jahre 1845" (*Zeitschrift für Geschichtswissenschaft*, 1958, Vol. 6, Heft 4, pp. 821–4). The report has been reprinted in J. Kuczynski, *Die Geschichte der Lage der Arbeiter unter dem Kapitalismus*, Vol. 8 (1960), p. 168 *et seq*. Dr Freiherr von Reden (1804–57) subsequently edited the *Zeitschrift des Vereins für deutsche Statistik*, the first volume of which appeared in 1847.

36 K. Obermann, "Urteile über das Werk von Friedrich Engels 'Die Lage der arbeitenden Klasse in England' aus den Jahren 1845–1846" (*Zeitschrift für Geschichtswissenschaft*, 1959, Vol. 7, Heft 5, p. 1065 *et seq*).

37 Freiherr Bibra's report is printed in J. Kuczynski, *Die Geschichte der Lage der Arbeiter unter dem Kapitalismus*, Vol. 8, 1960, pp. 165–7.

38 *Allgemeine Preussische Zeitung*, October 31, November 1 and 7, 1845; reprinted in J. Kuczyniski, *op. cit.*, Vol. 8, pp. 170–85 and in Carl Jantke and Dietrich Hilger, *Die Eigentumlosen* (1965), pp. 406–25.

39 V. A. Huber, "Zur neuesten Literatur" in *Janus*, 1845, pp. 387–9. For Huber see the *Allgemeine Deutsche Biographie*, Vol. 8, pp. 249–58.

40 Friedrich H. J. von Farenheid in the *Neue Preussische Provinzial-Blätter*, Vol. 3, Königsber 1847. The review is not mentioned in W. Mönke's monograph on the reception of Engels's book in Germany. See Kurt Forstreuter, "Eine Stimme zu der Schrift von Friedrich Engels über 'Die Lage der arbeitenden Klasse in England'" (*Vierteljahrschrift für Sozial- und Wirtschaftsgeschichte*, Vol. 53, 1966, pp. 366–9.

41 W. Mönke, *op. cit.*, p. 59.

42 *Barmer Zeitung*, 1845, No. 291. A long criticism of this review appeared in the socialist journal *Gesellschaftsspiegel*, 1845, Heft 6, pp. 86–9.

43 Article on "Einige neueste Schriften auf dem Gebiete des Pauperismus, Socialismus und Communismus" in the *Monatsblätter zur Ergänzung der Allgemeinen Zeitung*, February 1846. Engels's book was also discussed in a later article entitled "Acht Monate der deutschen Litteratur" (*Monatsblätter* . . . , March 1846, p. 142).

44 Quoted by W. Mönke, *op. cit.*, p. 31.

45 Bruno Hildebrand, *Nationalökonomie der Gegenwart und Zukunft* (1848), Vol. I, pp. 155–241; a new edition edited by Hans Gehrig was published in 1922; extracts in J. Kuczynski, *op cit.*, Vol. 8, pp. 186–9.

46 K. Biedermann, "Sozialistische Brestrebungen in Deutschland" in *Unsre Gegenwart und Zukunft*, 1846, Vol. 1 and 4: see also W. Mönke, *op cit.*, pp. 33–5.

47 K. Biedermann, *Vorlesungen über Sozialismus und soziale Fragen* (1847).

48 M. Fleischer in the *Allgemeine Literatur-Zeitung*, December 1846.

A similar point of view was expressed by an anonymous reviewer in the *Blätter für literarische Unterhaltung*, 1846, Vol. 1.

49 Weinlig in *Archiv der politischen Ökonomie und Polizeiwissenschaft* new series, Vol. 4, 1846, pp. 74–98: extracts in W. Mönke, *op cit.*, pp. 116–18.

50 See W. Mönke, *op cit.*, pp. 43–58.

51 *Gesellschaftsspiegel* (Elberfeld and Iserlohn), Vol. 1 (1846) and Vol. 2 (1847). This journal was founded by Friedrich Engels and Moses Hess. It was edited by Moses Hess.

52 *Deutsches Bürgerbuch* (Mannheim), Vol. 2, 1846, pp. 222–45. Dr Otto Lüning was the editor of this publication.

55 *Constitutionelle Staatsbürger-Zeitung* (Grimma), October 1845, pp. 513–15 and November 1845, pp. 521–4.

56 W. Mönke, *op cit.*, p. 57, states that Dr Hermann Ewerbeck was probably the author of the review of Engels's book that appeared in *Blätter der Zukunft* (Paris), 1845–6, pp. 97–128.

57 Dr Otto Lüning did not himself review Engels's book in *Das Westphälische Dampfboot*, which he edited – probably because of difficulties with the censor. But he did reprint a review by R. Rempel which had appeared in the *Öffentliche Anzeigen der Grafschaft Ravensberg*. See *Das Westphälische Dampfboot*, 1845, Heft 11, 12, pp. 552–67.

58 For discussions of reviews of Engels's book in the *Trier'sche Zeitung* see articles by K. Obermann and B. Andreas in *Annali* (Milan), Vol. 6, 1963.

59 Karl Marx to F. Engels, April 9, 1863 in *Gesamtausgabe*, Part III, Vol. 3, p. 138.

60 Karl Marx, *Capital*, Vol. 1 (Everyman edition, 1930), pp. 240–1(n).

61 Pen name of Vasily Vasiljevitsch Bervy, 1829–1918.

62 Karl Marx to F. Engels, February 10, 1870 in *Gesamtausgabe*, Part III, Vol. 4, p. 275.

63 F. Engels to Mrs Florence Kelley Wischnewetzky, February 10, 1885 in K. Marx and F. Engels, *Letters to Americans 1848–1895* (1963), p. 145.

64 F. Engels to F. A. Sorge, April 9, 1887, *ibid.*, p. 182.

65 The inscription in Engels's own copy of the English translation of *The Condition of the Working Class in England* published in New York in 1887 was "Frederick Engels with the compliments of the publisher, R. G. Foster, Phila. June 7th, 1887" (*Ex Libris Karl Marx und Friedrich Engels*, 1967, p. 63).

66 F. Engels to F. A. Sorge, May 4, 1887 in K. Marx and F. Engels, *Letters to Americans 1848–1895* (1963), p. 185. Laura Lafargue wrote to Engels on July 22, 1887: "I have read the preface and appendix of your book with the greatest interest and the sight of the book itself has been an infinite delight . . . I was about 15, I think, when, a self-imposed task, I did the whole or part of your book . . . into English. . . ." (*F. Engels – Paul and Laura Lafargue Correspondence*, Vol. 2, p. 53).

67 F. Engels, *The Condition of the Working Class in England* (translated and edited by W. O. Henderson and W. H. Chaloner, 1958), pp. 360–71. The preface was dated January 11, 1892. A few days previously Engels had written to Laura Lafargue that he was working on the "proof sheets and new preface of (the) new English edition of *(Die) Lage der arbeitenden Klasse in England*". (F. Engels to Laura

Lafargue, January 6, 1892 in *F. Engels–Paul and Laura Lafargue Correspondence*, Vol. 3, p. 156).

68 F. Engels, "England in 1845 and 1885" in *Commonwealth* (London), March 1, 1885.

69 In 1895 the writer of an obituary notice of Friedrich Engels in the *Economic Journal* referred to *The Condition of the Working Class in England* as "this remarkable book" (*Economic Journal*, Vol. 5, 1895, pp. 490–2).

70 Dr Cunningham wrote: "Friedrich Engels's painstaking description of the housing of the Manchester poor is well worth perusal" (W. Cunningham, *The Growth of English Industry and Commerce in Modern Times*, edition of 1925, p. 807).

71 See L. Brentano, *Eine Geschichte der wirtschaftlichen Entwicklung Englands*, Vol. 3, Part I, 1928, p. 140.

72 Mrs Wischnewetzky's translation was also reprinted in Karl Marx and Friedrich Engels, *On Britain* (Foreign Languages Publishing House, Moscow, 1953).

73 This section is based upon my introduction to F. Engels, *Die Lage der arbeitenden Klasse in England* (new edition 1965: Verlag J. H. W. Dietz Nachfolger, Hanover). See also the introduction by W. O. Henderson and W. H. Chaloner to F. Engels, *The Condition of the Working Class in England* (new translation 1958: Basil Blackwell, Oxford).

74 An enlarged and revised edition appeared in 1836 under the title *Artisans and Machinery*.

75 J. M. Baernreither wrote that "the violent revolution which in 1844 Engels deemed inevitable never came to pass, and anyone who today, after a lapse of forty years, examines carefully the condition of the working class in England, will be convinced that it never will" (*English Associations of Working Men*, 1889, p. 5).

76 G. von Schulze-Gaevernitz, *Social Peace* (1895), p. 84.

77 *Ibid.*, p. 282.

78 See anonymous article by J. W. Croker on "Anti-Corn Law Agitation" in the *Quarterly Review*, Vol. 71, No. 141, December 1842 and G. Kitson Clark, "Hunger and Politics in 1842" in the *Journal of Modern History*, Vol. 15, No. 4, December 1953, pp. 355–74. For the point of view of the Anti-Corn Law League see Archibald Prentice, *History of the Anti-Corn Law League* (1853; new edition with introduction by W. H. Chaloner, 1969). For the Plug Plot riots of 1842 see A. G. Rose, "The Plug Plot Riots of 1842 in Lancashire and Cheshire" in the *Transactions of the Lancashire and Cheshire Antiquarian Society*, Vol. 68, 1957, pp. 75–112.

79 See, for example, W. H. Chaloner, *The Hungry Forties: a Re-examination* (Historical Association pamphlet, 1957).

80 See *Current Sociology:* "Urban Sociology (Research in Great Britain . . .) trend reports and bibliography", UNESCO, Paris, Vol. 4, 1955, No. 4, p. 30 where it is stated that Engels's description of the English factory towns in 1844 "should be studied as a model by those social scientists who talk so much nowadays about the need to introduce a 'conceptual framework' and 'hypotheses' into empirical research. . . . His description of Manchester is a masterpiece of ecological analysis. And he was the only one of the Victorians who understood the significance of urbanism – for better and for worse – also the reasons for anti-urbanism."

3

THE YOUNG REVOLUTIONARY 1845–1850

I. The German Ideology, 1845–7

Engels's happiest years were probably those which he spent as a revolutionary agitator between 1845 and 1850.[1] In those days – according to the German worker Friedrich Lessner – Engels was "tall and slim, his movements were quick and vigorous, his manner of speaking brief and decisive, his carriage erect, giving a soldierly touch. He was of a very lively nature; his wit was to the point. Everybody who associated with him inevitably got the impression that he was dealing with a man of great intelligence." Marx's Russian friend Annenkov later wrote that he remembered Engels in 1846 as being "tall and erect, and as dignified and serious as an Englishman".[2] He was a striking figure in any company – slim, tall, blond, short-sighted. He spoke very quickly and he stuttered from time to time, especially when he was excited.[3] He had a surprisingly youthful appearance for a man of over twenty-five. In 1847 he hesitated to accept office as Vice-President of the Democratic Association of Brussels because – as he wrote to Marx – "I look so dreadfully young."[4]

Between 1845 and 1850 Engels escaped from the drudgery of working in an office and spent his days in writing and in revolutionary agitation. Intriguing against his enemies and dodging the police gave an added spice to life. The close association with Karl Marx which began when they lived next door to each other in Brussels gave Engels the feeling of security that he needed. In the past he had been disillusioned by successive idols – Hegel, Strauss, Feuerbach – but now he had found a dynamic leader to whom he was faithful for the rest of his life.

Long afterwards – when Marx had died – he told his friend J. P. Becker that he believed his mission in life had been to play second fiddle to Marx. "I think that I played reasonably well and I was delighted to have such a wonderful first violin as Marx."[5]

In 1845–6 Marx and Engels collaborated in working out the doctrines of a new materialist philosophy. In 1847–8 Engels helped Marx to draw up the Communist Manifesto and – when the revolution broke out in Germany – to edit the *Neue Rheinische Zeitung*. When a warrant for his arrest was issued he fled to France and Switzerland. Back in Germany in 1849 he appeared briefly in Elberfeld as military adviser to the insurgents in the Wupper valley and then – when the revolutionary movement was collapsing – he acted as Willich's adjutant in a rising in Baden. In 1850 he shared Marx's exile in London for a few months before settling down to a business career in Manchester. Now thirty years of age he had found a philosophy of life, a leader to follow, and he had gained a unique experience as a revolutionary agitator.

How did Engels finance his five years of revolutionary activity? Georg Weerth stated in July 1845 that Engels's father had cut off his son's allowance.[6] Yet in the previous month he would have been welcomed home to his sister Marie's marriage to Emil Blank. Engels wrote to his sister that he could not come to Barmen for her wedding as his emigration passport was valid to leave Prussia but not to return.[7] Instead of going to Barmen Engels went to England with Marx and it appears likely that Engels's father paid his expenses. Possibly Engels was charged with some duties in connection with his father's business interests in Manchester.

Since Engels joined members of his family for a holiday in Ostend in the summer of 1846 it appears that there had then been a reconciliation between father and son. Engels was planning a visit to Paris and he hoped that his father would pay his fare.[8] He did go to Paris and there in 1847 – according to Stephan Born – Engels was receiving a monthly allowance.[9] It is possible that Engels's father sent his son a regular remittance to ensure his absence from Barmen. Had Engels returned to Prussia he might have been imprisoned or deported and this would have tarnished the reputation of the Engels family which prided itself upon its loyalty to church and state. Engels's allowance presumably ceased when he was able to support himself as an editor of the *Neue Rheinische Zeitung*.

Engels's only other sources of income in this period were his salary as an editor of the *Neue Rheinische Zeitung* (June 1848–May 1849) and occasional earnings as a free-lance journalist. When he was in Paris in 1846 he complained that the publishers of the *Deutsches Bürgerbuch* and the *Rheinisches Jahrbuch* still owed him money.[10] He was often short of money. In August 1846 he was not even able to prepay his letters to Marx and in October he wrote: "For God's sake don't send me unfranked letters that I will have to pay for!"[11] He was again in financial straits in Brussels in March 1848. Karl Marx – then in Paris – told him to collect for his own use 250 francs due to him from various people in Brussels.[12] Engels was still without funds later in that year when he fled to Belgium, France, and Switzerland to avoid arrest in Cologne. In his description of his travels he wrote: "I was short of money and so I travelled on foot."[13] On one occasion a farmer gave him a meal in return for some sketches which he made of leading French politicians.[14] In a letter of November 10, 1848 Marx wrote to the fugitive that he had already sent him 130 thalers to Lausanne.[15] Shortly afterwards Marx devised a shabby scheme – which he regarded as a brilliant idea – to raise money from Engels's family. "Since we are both broke", he wrote, "I have thought of a fool-proof plan to screw something out of your old man. Write to me saying that you are desperately hard up and I will arrange for your mother to see the letter. Your old man is beginning to get the wind up."[16] In January 1849 Engels told Marx that he was still short of money. "For several days I have not had a sou in my pocket and in this lousy hole there is no one from whom I can borrow money."[17]

When Engels went to Brussels in the spring of 1845[18] he became a leading member of a small group of young German radicals and revolutionaries who acknowledged Marx as the messiah of a new political philosophy. Some – like Wilhelm Wolff and Georg Weerth – were associated with Marx and Engels for the rest of their lives. Others – Hess, Weitling, Kriege, Born – sooner or later failed to give unquestioning support to Marx's doctrines and ceased to accept his leadership. The senior member of the group was the tailor Wilhelm Weitling. He was twelve years older than Engels and was an experienced revolutionary. He was an exponent of utopian socialism and believed that the principles of communism could be derived from a study of the New Testament. In 1843 Engels had regarded Weitling as the founder of communism in Germany[19] and in the following year Marx had declared that Weitling had a sounder grasp of socialist theory than Proudhon.[20] Weitling's *Garantien der Harmonie und Freiheit* (1842) was praised both by Karl Marx and Heinrich Heine. The former hailed it as "the brilliant début of the German workers" while the latter declared that it was "the catechism of the communists".[21] Weitling had been a prominent member of the League of the Just in Paris in the 1830s and he had established communist groups among German workers in Switzerland. He had suffered imprisonment for his activities.[22]

Moses Hess soon followed Engels to Brussels. He was a "true socialist" who claimed to have converted Engels to communism. He had recently been associated with Engels in spreading communist ideas in Westphalia and the Rhineland and in establishing a socialist periodical in Elberfeld. Wilhelm Wolff[23] was a revolutionary agitator from Breslau who had been in prison for his radical views. He was well known as a journalist for his exposure of the grievances of the Silesian handloom weavers. Ferdinand Freiligrath and Georg Weerth[24] were the poets of the new movement. Freiligrath had given up a royal pension to secure the freedom he needed to express his revolutionary views. Weerth had worked as a clerk in Bradford and was familiar with the condition of the factory operatives in the north of England. Joseph Weydemeyer, formerly a lieutenant in the Prussian army and now an active socialist journalist in Westphalia, was Marx's guest in Brussels for the first four months of 1846.[25] Other members of the group were Sebastian Seiler (who ran a press agency), Edgar von Westphalen (Jenny Marx's brother), Ernst Dronke (a writer from Berlin), Ferdinand Wolff (known as Red Wolff) and the typesetters Stephan Born and Karl Wallau. The Belgian librarian Philippe Gigot was one of the few foreigners to be admitted to the inner circle of Marx's friends at this time. In addition to those who stayed in Brussels for some time in Marx's company there were others who came for short visits. These included Karl Heinzen and Hermann Kriege – Marx failed to convert either to his way of thinking – and friends from Cologne (Heinrich Bürgers, Dr Roland Daniels, and Georg Jung) with whom Marx had been associated when he edited the *Rheinische Zeitung*.[26]

When Engels joined Marx in Brussels in 1845 the young revolutionaries set themselves three tasks. The first was "self-clarification" – the definition of their attitude to Hegel's philosophy as developed by his successors, and the working out of their own materialist doctrines. The second task was to show the superiority of Marxian communism (based upon these doctrines) over other forms of socialism. This involved criticising in some detail the views of various thinkers and revolutionary agitators such as Proudhon, Feuerbach, Bruno Bauer, Max Stirner, Wilhelm Weitling, Moses Hess, Karl Grün and Hermann Kriege. These objectives were attained by writing *The German Ideology*, *Misère de la Philosophie* and articles in various journals such as the *Deutsche-Brüsseler-Zeitung*. Marx did not allow his literary activities to be restricted by his promise to the Belgian authorities to refrain from publishing anything concerning "the politics of the day".[27]

The third task was stated in Marx's theses on Feuerbach in 1845: "The philosophers have only *interpreted* the world in various ways; the time has come to *change* it." To attain this object the Communist Correspondence Committee was established as a link between revolutionary groups in various countries. And the League of the

Just in London was persuaded to turn itself into the Communist League and to accept the principles laid down by Marx and Engels in the Communist Manifesto. Forty years later Engels wrote that in 1845 he and Marx had "felt that it was our duty to justify our convictions in a scholarly scientific fashion but it was equally important for us to win over first the German – and eventually the European – proletariat to our point of view".[28] And when the revolution broke out in Europe in 1848 Marx and Engels could feel that they had succeeded in laying the foundations of a new political movement.

Marx and Engels did not decide to write *The German Ideology* immediately after they settled down together in Brussels. Both had other plans. Marx was working on his critique of political economy – having already received an advance of royalties of 1,500 francs from the Darmstadt publisher C. W. Leske – while Engels had declared his intention of writing a book on "English history and English socialism".[29] The two friends went to England in the summer of 1845 and visited Manchester where Engels saw Mary Burns again. He took Marx to Chetham's Library to study the works of some of the older English economists. Many years later Engels wrote to Marx: "During the last few days I have again spent a good deal of time sitting at the four sided desk in the alcove where we sat together 24 years ago. I am very fond of the place. The stained glass window ensures that the weather is always fine there."[30] Engels also got in touch with Julian Harney again and on his return to the Continent he became a regular contributor to the *Northern Star* for five years.[31] Among the earliest articles from 'Your German correspondent' were three letters on the state of Germany. Engels gave his English readers a somewhat unconventional sketch of the history of Germany from the decline of the Holy Roman Empire to 1830. These articles showed "Engels's conviction that political and religious developments were brought about by economic changes."[32]

Soon after they were back in Brussels the appearance of a new number of *Wigands Vierteljahrschrift* caused Marx and Engels to drop their existing projects in order to mount a full scale attack upon the opinions expressed in this periodical by Bruno Bauer and Max Stirner. Bruno Bauer had defended himself against Karl Marx's attack in *The Holy Family* and had equated the communist views of Marx and Engels with those of Ludwig Feuerbach. Max Stirner had replied to criticisms by Ludwig Feuerbach and Moses Hess of his book *Der Einzige und sein Eigentum*. Marx and Engels considered that Feuerbach and Hess were not capable of demolishing the doctrines advanced by Bruno Bauer and his associates. So they undertook the task themselves. And then Marx and Engels decided to expand *The German Ideology* to include an attack upon the 'true socialists', whose doctrines – like those of French socialists such as Fourier and Cabet from which they were derived – appeared to be directed to the petty bourgeoisie rather than to the workers. Between 1845 and 1848 these views gained currency in Germany and were put forward in several periodicals such as the *Deutsches Bürgerbuch*, the *Rheinische Jahrbücher*, *Das Westphälische Dampfboot* and the *Trier'sche Zeitung*. Karl Grün in Paris and Hermann Kriege in London had been spreading the doctrines of 'true socialism' among German workers living abroad.[33]

In August 1846 Karl Marx wrote to C. W. Leske to explain why he had stopped working on his critique of political economy for a time. "It seemed to me a matter of great importance that I should write a polemical work directed against both present day German philosophy and present day German socialism and to make a *positive* statement of my own philosophical position." Such a book, he declared, would prepare the public for his forthcoming volume on economic theory.[34]

The German Ideology[35] was written in the spring of 1846. The correspondence between Karl Marx and Joseph Weydemeyer shows that the first part of the manuscript was finished at the end of April and the second part was ready by the end of May. The authors then decided that the first chapter of Part I on Feuerbach required revision and some progress in rewriting this chapter was made in 1846. But the task was never completed and the first chapter remained unfinished. Many years later – in the 1880s – when Engels was writing a book on Ludwig Feuerbach's philosophy he unearthed the old manuscript of *The German Ideology*. "The section on Feuerbach," he wrote, "is not complete." "What we had written was an explanation of our materialist view of history – an explanation which only shows how deficient was our knowledge of economic history in those days."[36] Early in 1847 Engels began to write a postscript to *The German Ideology* called "The True Socialists" but this too was never finished.[37] All efforts to find a publisher for *The German Ideology* failed. In view of the length of the book and its highly controversial nature this is hardly surprising. And the censorship laws of the German states in the 1840s gave little encouragement to publishers to accept manuscripts from socialist authors.[38] Marx complained to a Russian friend, Pavel Annenkov: "You would never believe the difficulties which a publication of this kind comes up against in Germany, from the police on the one hand and from the booksellers (who are themselves the interested representatives of all the tendencies that I am attacking) on the other."[39] In the end, as Marx later explained, the authors "abandoned the manuscript to the gnawing criticism of the mice".

The German Ideology is no easy book to read. Even in its incomplete form – for neither the first chapter nor the postscript were ever finished – it ran to over 500 pages. The first chapter was planned as a critical assessment of the doctrines of Ludwig Feuerbach but the part that was actually written was a statement of the materialist view of history. Marx and Engels acknowledged Feuerbach's distinction as a philosopher and treated him with respect even though they did not agree with him. But their criticisms of Bruno Bauer and Max Stirner were not at all respectful. Anyone who imagined that Marx had exhausted the language of vituperation when he castigated Bruno Bauer in *The Holy Family* was very much mistaken. Page after page of even more vigorous criticisms of Marx's former friend appeared in *The German Ideology*. Marx and Engels heaped sarcasm, invective, and sheer vulgar abuse upon Bruno Bauer, Max Stirner and their followers. Some 350 pages were devoted to a devastating onslaught upon Max Stirner's *Der Einzige und sein Eigentum*. Marx and Engels had an unerring eye for any weakness in their opponents' writings. Any error of fact or any defect in the logic of an argument was pounced upon and derided with savage enthusiasm. Marx and Engels were obviously deriving the greatest pleasure in denouncing what they regarded as the errors of their opponents. No wonder that the publishers to whom the manuscript was submitted rejected it. They recognised that very few readers could be expected to have the stamina required to read the whole of this lengthy philosophical diatribe from beginning to end.

Yet embedded in all the abuse of Bruno Bauer and Max Stirner there were passages in which Marx and Engels laid down doctrines which later appeared in the Communist Manifesto and became integral parts of the communist ideology. They stated the principles upon which their own materialist philosophy was based.

> In direct contrast to German philosophy which descends from heaven to earth, here we ascend from earth to heaven. That is to say, we do not set out from what men say, imagine, conceive, nor from men as narrated, thought of, imagined, conceived in order to arrive at men in the flesh. We set out from real active men, and on the basis of their real life-process we demonstrate the development of the ideological reflexes and echoes of this life-process.[40]

Marx and Engels proceeded to discuss their materialist conception of history. They believed that the way in which men produced what they needed in order to live – food, houses, goods – determined the social, legal, political and religious aspects of their society. Marx and Engels saw human development as a record of conflict between different social classes each fighting for its own economic interests. The climax would be a struggle between the proletariat and the middle classes – and the final triumph of the workers would not be achieved without violence. In a passage crossed out in the manuscript – perhaps deleted because it gave too much away – Marx and Engels wrote that Bruno Bauer would be "greatly surprised when judgment day overtakes him – a day when the reflection in the sky of burning cities will mark the dawn, when together with the 'celestial harmonies' the tunes of the *Marsellaise* and *Carmagnole* will echo in his ears, accompanied by the requisite roar of cannon, with the guillotine beating time; when the infamous 'masses' will shout *ça ira, ça ira* and suspend 'self-consciousness' by means of the lamp-post".[41] The fate that Marx and Engels had in store for any capitalists who survived the guillotine or the lamp-post was indicated by the threat that "just as after the Revolution the French aristocrats became the dancing instructors of the whole of Europe, so the English lords will soon find their true place in the civilised world as stable hands and kennel-men".[42] Marx and Engels proclaimed that a successful communist revolution would not merely sweep away "the muck of ages" and establish an entirely new society but that it would bring about a radical change in human nature itself. They argued that while previous revolutions had merely replaced one ruling class by another a communist revolution would produce both a classless society and a universal "communist consciousness" – which implied the radical "alteration of men on a mass scale".[43] Towards the end of his life Engels recognised a weakness in *The German Ideology* and other early writings by Marx and himself. In 1893 he admitted in a letter to Franz Mehring: "We all laid and were bound to lay the main emphasis at first on the derivation of political, juridical and other ideological notions, and of the actions arising through the medium of these notions, from basic economic facts. But in doing so we neglected the formal side – the way in which these notions came about – for the sake of the content."[44]

Bruno Bauer and Max Stirner were saved from a public castigation of their doctrines by the failure of Marx and Engels to find a publisher for *The German Ideology*. Proudhon was not so fortunate. He was one of the leading socialist writers in France and had made his name by his book *Qu'est-ce que la Propriété?* (1840) in which he had denounced landlords who exploited peasants, bankers who exploited borrowers and manufacturers who exploited artisans.

Marx had hailed Proudhon's essay on property in the *Rheinische Zeitung* as a "supremely penetrating book". And in *The Holy Family* Marx had praised Proudhon for making "the first resolute, pitiless, and at the same time scientific investigation of the foundation of political economy, *private property*. This is the great scientific progress he made, a progress which revolutionises political economy and first makes a real science of political economy possible. Proudhon's *Qu'est-ce que la Propriété?* is as important for modern political economy as Sièyes's work *Qu'est-ce que la tiers état?* for modern politics."[45] Marx met Proudhon in Paris in 1844 but was unable to teach him much about Hegel's philosophy since Proudhon could not read German. And Marx was unable to convert Proudhon to his own doctrines.[46]

About a year after moving to Brussels Marx wrote to Proudhon on May 5, 1846 inviting him to co-operate with the correspondence committee that he had recently formed. Engels added a postscript assuring Proudhon "of the profound respect which your writings have inspired in me". But Proudhon's suspicions were aroused by Marx's suggestion that "at the moment of action it is certainly of great interest to everyone to be informed about the state of affairs abroad as well as in his own country".[47] Proudhon realised that "the moment of action" would be the moment of revolution. So he declined to be associated with the Brussels Correspondence Committee and explained that he would "prefer to burn Property by a slow fire rather than to give it new strength by making a St Bartholomew's night of the proprietors".[48] Marx was determined to be avenged for this rebuff for he regarded those who would not collaborate with him as enemies to be destroyed. The opportunity came when Proudhon's new book – *Philosophie de la Misère*[49] – appeared at the end of 1846. It was translated into German by Karl Grün with an introduction which gave the work the highest praise.[50] The theme of Proudhon's book was the paradoxes of capitalism. "Society has provoked the consumption of goods by the abundance of products, while encouraging a shortage by the low level of wages."[51]

On September 16, 1846 Engels wrote from Paris to the Communist Correspondence Committee in Brussels that a new book by Proudhon would soon be published. Engels had attended a lecture by a German carpenter named Eisermann – one of Karl Grün's disciples – who had revealed some of the proposals contained in the book. Proudhon was advocating the establishment of "labour bazaars" or "labour markets" on the English model. Engels ridiculed the project – which in his view had already failed in England – and added contemptuously that "although Proudhon criticises the economists he is making every effort to secure recognition as an economist himself".[52] Two days later Engels wrote to Marx that he had now secured further details concerning Proudhon's proposals. He thought that "Proudhon's latest stupidity is indeed a piece of quite limitless folly."[53]

No sooner had Marx read Proudhon's book than he again stopped working on his critique of political economy so as to refute Proudhon's doctrines. In a letter to Annenkov he went much further than Engels in attacking Proudhon. He declared that although Proudhon professed to be a socialist he had in fact been guilty of making a damaging attack upon the whole conception of revolutionary communism. "M. Proudhon," he wrote, "mainly because he lacks the historical knowledge has not perceived that as men develop their productive faculties – that is, as they live – they develop certain relations with one another, and that the nature of these relations must necessarily change with the change and growth of the productive faculties."[54]

Karl Marx's reply to Proudhon – a pamphlet written in French entitled *Misère de la Philosophie* – was published in July 1847 at the author's expense. He "set upon Proudhon's new book with a ferocity entirely inconsonant with the opinion of the value of Proudhon's earlier work which he had expressed and which he was to reiterate later."[55] Marx vigorously criticised Proudhon's arguments and also indulged in a savage attack upon Proudhon's character and abilities. He could not forgive Proudhon for taking Karl Grün (a leading 'true socialist') under his wing. Marx denounced Proudhon as an ignoramus and a charlatan – one who had made himself a laughing stock by posing as a philosopher and an economist who was entitled to be taken seriously. The significance of Marx's pamphlet lay not in the coarse abuse of Proudhon but in the light which it shed upon the doctrines of Marx and Engels on philosophy, history and politics. Franz Mehring considered that here Marx "clearly enunciated the doctrine of historical materialism and, for the first time, decisively argued the merits of his theory in a scholarly fashion."[56] Marx's pamphlet, however, had little practical effect and Proudhon's ideas continued to represent a challenge to Marx's doctrines. Twenty years later, at the time of the First International, Proudhon's followers were still stoutly resisting the spread of Marxism in France.[57]

While Marx was attacking Proudhon, Engels was trying to ruin the reputation of Moses Hess. In 1845 Engels and Hess had worked together to spread communism in the Wupper district but Engels had been unable to convert his former mentor to the Marxist doctrine. By 1846 Marx and Engels were determined to destroy

Hess's influence in the socialist movement. The method which Engels employed was that which has since become known as 'character assassination'. Engels used Hess's relationship with Sybille Pesch to brand him as an individual unworthy of the support of the workers. Moses Hess and Sybille Pesch had been living together as man and wife, though they were not married until 1851. Presumably because her passport was not in order Hess asked Engels in 1846 to smuggle Sybille Pesch across the frontier from Belgium to France and this Engels was able to do. Once in Paris her conduct was such as to bring Hess into discredit. Engels wrote to Marx that "Madame Hess longs for a husband and pokes fun at Hess". Later he declared that the lady had made amorous overtures to him and had offered to reveal to him "the secrets of her bedchamber at dead of night". Hess was furious with Engels and wrote to Marx: "I do not want to have anything more to do with your party."[58] In September Hess tried to become reconciled with Engels but was rebuffed and Engels declared that he would "ignore the creature completely".[59] They met again in Paris in January 1847 but cordial relations were never re-established between them.[60] In March Engels was still ignoring Hess who, he declared, was "now utterly forgotten".[61] Engels's intrigues in Paris contributed to the decline of Hess as an influential figure in the socialist movement. There is, however, little substance in Franz Mehring's suggestion that Moses Hess ceased to accept the doctrines of the 'true socialists' and was converted to Marx's views. What happened was that Hess tried to resume his activities in the communist movement by paying lip service to Marx's doctrines without really giving up his own beliefs.

At this time Marx and Engels also sought to discredit Weitling as a socialist leader. The confrontation between Marx and Weitling – like the confrontation between Marx and Proudhon – was an early example of a clash in the socialist movement between intellectuals and workers. Marx and Engels were middle class intellectuals while Weitling was a tailor and Proudhon had been a compositor. Marx never forgot that he held a doctorate from a German university. Marx and Weitling had become socialists in different ways and for different reasons. Weitling passionately denounced the upper and middle classes for exploiting the workers and he advocated revolution as the only way by which the proletariat could free itself from the power of those who exploited its labour. Weitling did not need to study philosophy to know that only a revolution could change society so that tolerable conditions might be secured for the workers. He had been organising underground groups of workers in Switzerland and elsewhere for many years. He had advocated violent resistance to the capitalists and he was not interested in high-flown theories concerning the future of society. Marx and Engels, on the other hand, were intellectuals who had become communists by a process of reasoning from first principles. A study of philosophy, history and economics combined with an examination of contemporary society had convinced them that the next stage in the evolution of man would be the establishment of a communist society. Logical deductions from proven facts had revealed the truth to them.

Before his confrontation with Marx in Brussels in 1846 Weitling had been involved in a dispute with leading members of the League of the Just in London. He had arrived in England from Switzerland in September 1844 and had been welcomed by the League of the Just as an eminent exponent of utopian socialism and an experienced organiser of revolutionary groups among the workers. Between May and September 1845 Weitling took part in debates organised by the League.[62] He advocated an immediate rising of the workers – and he had the workers in Germany in mind – as the only method of sweeping the existing social order away and replacing it with a new communist society. But he soon found that his views were unacceptable to the members of the League. Indeed Hermann Kriege, one of the leaders of the 'true socialists' and a follower of Proudhon, was almost his only supporter in the debates. Weitling's strongest opponent was Karl Schapper who – in view of his own experience in Blanqui's abortive rising in Paris in 1839 – argued that it was premature to advocate an immediate rising of the workers. He favoured a policy of peaceful propaganda to educate the masses and to prepare them for a social revolution at some future date. This point of view had already been expressed by Karl Schapper, Josef Moll and Heinrich Bauer in a letter to Etienne Cabet on August 23, 1843 which stated that "the German communists . . . desire only to engage in peaceful propaganda and have never considered the use of physical force to secure the triumph of their principles".[63] And in September 1844 in a letter to the Hamburg *Telegraph für Deutschland* on the rising of the weavers in Silesia, Schapper and his colleagues had declared: "We are determined once and for all to raise ourselves out of the morass . . . not by violence but by educating ourselves and our children."[64]

Since his influence "continued to decline in London"[65] Weitling left England towards the end of 1845 or early in the following year. He settled in Brussels and attached himself to Marx and his disciples. Weitling, according to Engels, "could not get on with anybody" at that time. He saw himself as a misunderstood prophet who was surrounded by jealous rivals. Engels claimed that Karl and Jenny Marx put up with Weitling's eccentricities "with almost superhuman forebearance".[66] But there were limits to Marx's patience. On March 30, 1846 a meeting of the Brussels Correspondence Committee was held at which Marx, Engels, Weitling and others were present. Marx's Russian friend P. V. Annenkov was invited as a guest and he later described the meeting in his memoirs. It appears that Marx suddenly threw out a challenge to Weitling: "Tell us, Weitling, you who have made such a noise in Germany with your preaching: on what grounds do you justify your activity and what do you intend to base it on in the future?" Weitling replied that "his aim was not to create new economic theories but to adopt those that were most appropriate, as experience in France had shown, to open the eyes of the workers to the horrors of their condition." Marx interrupted him and in a "sarcastic speech" declared that "to rouse the population without giving them any firm, well thought out reasons for their activity would be simply deceiving them". He added that there was no hope of a successful communist revolution in the immediate future. "The middle class must first achieve power" – and only then would it be possible for the workers to think of achieving their aims.[67] Weitling replied that he could console himself "for the attacks of today by remembering the hundreds of letters and declarations of gratitude that he had received from all parts of his native land and by the thought that his modest spadework was perhaps of greater weight for the common cause than criticism and armchair analysis of doctrines far from the world of suffering and afflicted people". Annenkov described how the meeting ended. "Marx finally lost control of himself and thumped so hard with his fist on the table that the lamp on it rang and shook. He jumped up saying: 'Ignorance never yet helped anybody!' We followed his example and left the table."[68] The extent of the breach between Marx and Weitling was seen shortly afterwards when – at a meeting of leading communists in Brussels on May 16, 1846 – Weitling found himself in a position of complete isolation. He alone refused to denounce the policy of land reform that Hermann Kriege was advocating in the United States. Not long afterwards Weitling left Belgium to join Kriege in New York.

Karl Grün, a 'true socialist' and a follower of Proudhon was engaged in propaganda among German workers in Paris. One of them – the carpenter Eisermann – was his principal disciple. In August 1845 and again in April 1846 Karl Marx warned Dr A. H. Ewerbeck, the head of the Paris branch of the League of the Just, against Karl Grün. In the first postscript to Karl Marx's letter to

Proudhon of May 5, 1846 Karl Grün's activities were sharply criticised. The postscript was signed by Philippe Gigot but was obviously inspired by Karl Marx. The postscript asserted that Grün was "nothing more than a cavalier of the literary industry, a charlatan who wants to practise a trade in modern ideas. He attempts to conceal his ignorance in pompous phrases and arrogant sentences, and has so far only succeeded in making himself ridiculous with all this gibberish. . . . So beware of this parasite. . . ."[69] In August 1846 Engels went to Paris in order to destroy Grün's influence in the socialist movement.

Hermann Kriege, another 'true socialist' had enjoyed a certain influence among the workers in Bielefeld when he was stationed there during his period of service as a volunteer in the Prussian army. The military authorities arrested him when he made an inflammatory speech at an open air meeting. Armed with a letter of introduction from J. Meyer,[70] he went to Barmen to see Engels who passed him on to Marx in Brussels. Kriege soon went to London where he joined the League of the Just and supported Weitling in his controversy with Schapper. Next he emigrated to the United States where he edited a weekly journal called the *Volks-Tribun*. He now preached a form of utopian socialism very different from the communist doctrines of Marx and Engels. Kriege joined forces with a group of radical land reformers. He suggested that the land should first be nationalised and then leased – rent free – in plots of 150 acres to smallholders. On May 16, 1846 Marx, Engels and their closest associates (only Weitling dissenting) drew up a "Circular against Kriege" which was lithographed and sent to leading communists in Germany, England, France and the United States. Marx and his friends declared that Kriege's highly unorthodox views "gravely compromised the communist party in Europe and in the United States inasmuch as Kriege is regarded in New York as the literary representative of German communism".[71]

Another revolutionary agitator who not merely declined to accept Marx's doctrines but had the temerity to campaign against them was Karl Heinzen. Here was another opponent to be attacked and discredited. Heinzen had contributed articles to the *Rheinische Zeitung* and had visited Brussels in 1845 where he had long political discussions with Marx. But Marx failed to convert Heinzen to his own point of view. Heinzen then went to Switzerland where he collaborated with Arnold Ruge to bring together a collection of essays called *Die Opposition*. While Ruge criticised Moses Hess and the 'true socialists', Heinzen (without mentioning Marx by name) criticised the materialist doctrines of Marx and his followers.

When Heinzen carried his attack into the enemy camp by publishing his views in the *Deutsch-Brüsseler-Zeitung*[72] Engels promptly replied to Heinzen's criticisms in the same journal in an article entitled "The Communists and Karl Heinzen". Engels refuted Heinzen's argument that the German princes were responsible for social distress in Germany. He declared that views of this kind were typical of middle class radicals such as Karl Heinzen and Johann Jacoby. The sins of the princes were irrelevant to any discussion of Germany's political and social problems. The only solution to Germany's problems was to overthrow the entire existing social and political system and replace it by a classless communist society.[73]

By 1847 Marx and Engels had achieved some success in discrediting their opponents and in purging their movement of what they considered to be undesirable elements. The influence of Bruno Bauer, Weitling, Kriege, Grün, Hess and Heinzen was declining while the position of Marx and Engels was improving. Only the attack on Proudhon had misfired. Marx and Engels had failed to secure his allegiance and had failed to undermine his position as an acknowledged socialist leader in France.

II. The Communist Correspondence Committee 1846–8[74]

When they worked together in Brussels Marx and Engels were no mere armchair philosophers. They not only produced a new philosophy and a new political programme – abusing vehemently all who rejected their doctrines – but they believed (as Marx had declared in his *Theses on Feuerbach*) that philosophers should not only interpret society but should also change it.

Between 1846 and 1848 Marx and Engels spread their new gospel by establishing the Communist Correspondence Committee and the German Workers Association in Brussels and by infiltrating into various socialist and revolutionary groups such as the Paris and London branches of the League of the Just. They were engaged in propaganda through left-wing political organisations – such as the Brussels Democratic Association – and through journals in four different countries. The *Deutsch-Brüsseler Zeitung* (Brussels), the *Northern Star* (Leeds), *La Réforme* (Paris), and *Das Westphalische Dampfboot* (Bielefeld) all published articles by either Marx or Engels or both. Marx and Engels also maintained contact with leaders of workers abroad such as Julian Harney in England and Ferdinand Flocon in France. And they attempted, though without success, to set up a Communist Publishing Company.[75]

Several of the correspondents of the Brussels Committee were men whom Marx had known in Cologne and Paris or whom Engels had known in Elberfeld. Marx had not been forgotten in Cologne by those with whom he had been associated when he edited the *Rheinische Zeitung* while Engels had only recently been actively engaged in recruiting supporters for the communist cause in Elberfeld and Barmen. Socialists and radicals like Joseph Weydemeyer, Otto Lüning, G. A. Köttgen, Roland Daniels, Heinrich Bürgers and Karl d'Ester kept in touch with Marx and Engels in Brussels. In France and England there were branches of the secret revolutionary society called the League of the Just, the majority of whose members were German artisans. Marx and Engels had met some of the leaders of the League – Ewerbeck and Bernays in Paris; Schapper, Moll and Heinrich Bauer in London – and they hoped to turn the branches of the League into communist cells. Marx and Engels also corresponded with other foreign radical and revolutionary associations such as the Chartists – Engels had met Julian Harney in Leeds in 1843 – and international bodies such as the Fraternal Democrats of London.

Although most of the correspondence of the Brussels Committee no longer survives its policy may be gathered from the advice which it gave to the communists in Elberfeld and the Chartists in England as well as from Engels's reports on his efforts to gain control over the Paris branches of the League of the Just. A letter to G. A. Köttgen of Elberfeld dated June 15, 1846[76] – signed by Marx, Engels, Gigot and Ferdinand Wolff – welcomed the view "that the German communists should emerge from isolation and should be united by a regular mutual exchange of ideas". "We too appreciate the value of reading circles and discussion groups." Köttgen was warned against any premature political action on the part of the communists in Germany. Marx and Engels considered that it would be unwise at the moment to attempt to organise petitions or to hold a congress. "A petition would be effective only if it were a threat supported by a mass of compact organised public opinion." And "only when Germany is covered with a network of communist groups with adequate financial reserves would it be possible for representatives from these groups to hold a congress with any chance of success. This will not be possible before next year."

The postscript is more significant than the letter itself for the light it throws upon the way in which Marx and Engels expected to seize political power. Köttgen was told that since the German communists were powerless to take the political initiative they should support demonstrations organised by the liberals. "Behave like jesuits! Forget your German honour, candour and respectability! Support middle class petitions for freedom of the press, a constitution and so on. When these middle class demands have been achieved the ground will be prepared for communist propaganda. Then we shall have a better chance of getting our way since the rivalry between the middle classes and the proletariat have been accentuated. To aid the communist party you should support any policy which will be to our advantage in the long run. And do not be deterred by any stuffy moral scruples." Marx and Engels argued that the communists should first pose as allies of the middle class liberals in their struggle against the feudal aristocrats but as soon as the landed gentry had been crushed and the middle classes were in control of the government the communists should turn upon their former associates and seize power themselves.

In England, on the other hand, Marx and Engels held that the downfall of the landed interest as a political force was already assured by the triumph of the Anti-Corn Law League in 1846. There was no need, as in Germany, for the workers to support the middle classes against the aristocracy. Already the way was clear for the workers – organised in the Chartist movement – to overthrow the middle classes and gain power for themselves. A month after giving their machiavellian advice to the Elberfeld communists Marx, Engels, and Gigot wrote an open letter to Feargus O'Connor in which they declared that "the ground is cleared by the retreat of the landed aristocracy from the contest; middle class and working class are the only classes betwixt whom there can be a possible struggle. The contending parties have their respective battle cries forced upon them by their interests and mutual position – the middle classes: 'Extension of commerce by any means whatsoever, and a ministry of Lancashire cotton lords to carry this out;' the working class: 'A democratic reconstruction of the constitution upon the basis of the People's Charter,' by which the working class will become the ruling class of England."[77]

It was, however, to France rather than to England or Germany that Marx and Engels looked as the country which would first see the overthrow of the established order. Twice before – in 1789 and in 1830 – a French revolution had been a turning point in European history. By 1846 revolutionary groups throughout the Continent were looking to Paris for the sign that would herald the fall of reactionary governments in Germany, Austria and Italy. Marx and Engels considered that it was essential for his Correspondence Committee to be kept fully informed of the revolutionary movement in France. They hoped to "ally themselves with the Social-Democrats against the conservative and radical bourgeoisie, reserving, however, the right to take up a critical position in regard to phrases and illusions traditionally handed down from the great

Revolution."[78] Marx's attempt in May 1846 to enrol Proudhon as a correspondent of his committee had failed. In August, following a holiday in Ostend with members of his family,[79] Engels went to Paris as an emissary of the Brussels Committee. He had two main tasks to perform. The first was to establish contact with French socialists such as Etienne Cabet, Louis Blanc and Ferdinand Flocon, the editor of *La Réforme*. The second was to eradicate the influence of the 'true socialists' in the Paris branches of the League of the Just. Engels's reports to the Brussels Committee and his letters to Marx tell the story of his mission to Paris.

When he arrived in Paris in August 1846 Engels called upon Etienne Cabet whom he regarded as "the acknowledged spokesman of the vast mass of the French workers".[80] He wrote to Marx that he had been cordially received by the veteran socialist but advised Marx not to press Cabet to correspond with the Brussels Committee since "in the first place he is very busy and secondly he is too mistrustful".[81] Engels also met Dr A. H. Ewerbeck, one of the leaders of the revolutionary German artisans working in Paris and organised as a branch of the League of the Just. Marx had already warned Ewerbeck against the activities of the utopian and 'true socialists' – Proudhon, Weitling, Hess, Grün and their disciples. Now Engels made it clear that the object of his mission was to stamp out these heretical views. He found that a number of the workers were influenced more by the carpenters Adolph Junge and Eisermann than by Dr Ewerbeck. Engels contemptuously dismissed Eisermann as "a sheepshead",[82] "a windy old master carpenter and nothing more than one of Grün's lackeys" but he formed a higher opinion of Junge who had "ten times more sense than the rest of the gang put together – though he is very unstable and is always hatching out new schemes".[83] Engels regarded with the utmost contempt the bulk of the German artisans whom he met in Paris and he dismissed them as "blockheads" and "donkeys". He gained the confidence of Ewerbeck and Junge and felt sure that he could soon dispose of Eisermann. But the task proved to be more difficult than he had anticipated. The carpenters and tailors showed a greater interest in Proudhon's scheme for labour bazaars than in Engels's lectures on history and economics.

In October 1846 Engels reported his first success to his friends in Brussels. He wrote to Marx that his opponents among the German workers in Paris had been "barking loudly" at him. But he had got his way "with some patience and a certain amount of terrorism".[84] In a report to the Communist Correspondence Committee Engels stated that he had attended several meetings of the workers at which Proudhon's proposed labour bazaars had been discussed. Engels wrote that he had been "furious at the endless repetition of the same arguments of my opponents" and that he had goaded Eisermann into openly challenging the validity of communist doctrines.

Engels then submitted the following definition of communism to the German workers:

(1) To achieve the interests of the proletariat in opposition to those of the bourgeoisie.
(2) To do this through the abolition of private property and its replacement by community of goods.
(3) To recognise no means of carrying out these objectives other than a democratic revolutionary force.

By thirteen votes to two the meeting approved this definition of communist principles.[85] Engels's thirteen supporters would have been surprised if they could have known that Lenin would one day regard this meeting as the genesis of the German Socialist Party.

To recruit thirteen workers was a small reward for several weeks of propaganda and intrigue among the German workers in Paris. The Correspondence Committee in Brussels had hoped for something better than this from their emissary. Engels had shown in Elberfeld that he had no difficulty in holding the attention of a middle class audience but he was no demagogue who could arouse the enthusiasm of a working class audience. Stephan Born's comments upon Engels's activities in the early months of 1847 are relevant in this connection. Born was a twenty-three-year-old compositor who came to Paris in January of that year and soon made friends with Engels. In his memoirs Born wrote: "We spent most of our evenings together and frequently made excursions on Sundays in the districts around Paris." Born observed that Engels "must himself have realised that he had failed to exercise any influence over the real working classes." "After all he came from a rich middle class family and was quite well off. He received a monthly remittance from his father who owned a large mill in Barmen."[86]

There was another reason for Engels's lack of success in Paris. Towards the end of December 1846 he informed Marx that he had been denounced to the police by his enemies. Fearing expulsion from France he dropped his agitation among the German workers for some months, excusing himself with the reflection that he had achieved the main object of his mission – "the triumph over Grün". He indulged in the pleasures available to a young man in Paris with a private income. He frequented the cafés[87] and the Palais

Royal music hall[88] and he enjoyed "some very agreeable friendships with *grisettes*".[89] In one letter to Marx he declared that "but for the French girls, life would be insupportable here"[90] and in another he referred to his "mistresses, past, present and future".[91]

Events in Germany and England, however, soon led to a resumption of Engels's political activities. Early in 1847 Joseph Moll, having visited Marx in Brussels, came to Paris to invite Engels to join the London League of the Just and to co-operate in its reorganisation. And on February 3 the King of Prussia announced that he proposed to summon a United Diet of representatives from all the provincial assemblies. Engels hoped that the calling of the United Diet would herald the rise to power of the middle class liberals in Prussia and other German states and so pave the way for the eventual triumph of the workers under communist leadership. In March and April he wrote a pamphlet on the political situation in Germany which he called "a brochure on the constitution".[92] He sent the manuscript to Marx who wrote in May 1847 that he was very pleased with the first part but felt that the second and third parts needed revision. The pamphlet was not printed owing to the arrest in Aachen of C. G. Vogler, the Brussels bookseller who intended to publish it.[93] Part of the manuscript was lost and it was many years after Engels's death before what survived was published under the title *The Status Quo in Germany*.[94] Iring Fetscher regards it as "one of the most brilliant criticisms of the (German) bureaucracy and political backwardness to be written by a revolutionary intellectual in the nineteenth century.[95]

The purpose of Engels's pamphlet was to discuss the possible courses of action open to the communists in Prussia and other German states in the light of the forthcoming meeting of the United Diet.[96] The communist party, he wrote, "must make up its mind and adopt a definite policy and a definite plan of campaign." It "must assess the actual means at its disposal to achieve its aims." Engels recommended that the communist party should "wash its hands of any connection with the reactionary 'true socialists' ". He argued that in Germany in 1847 effective political power lay in the hands of the old landed aristocracy and a social group which he called the 'petty bourgeoisie'. By 'petty bourgeoisie' Engels seems to have meant the small manufacturers, traders, shopkeepers and independent craftsmen. The landed gentry were the dominant partner, the 'petty bourgeoisie' the junior partner. These two social classes had "handed over administration to a third social group – the bureaucracy".

Engels considered that "the main cause of Germany's wretched condition today is that so far no social class has been strong enough to raise its economic activity to one of such overwhelming national importance that it can come forward as the undisputed leader of the whole country." The great landowners were declining – many were head over heels in debt – while the 'petty bourgeoisie' operated on too small a scale to become powerful either from an economic or a political point of view. The only class which was capable of wresting political power from the landed aristocracy and the petty bourgeoisie was the middle class. This class, wrote Engels, "is the only one in Germany which knows exactly what it wants to put in the place of the *Status Quo*. It is the only party which does not have a policy based upon abstract principle and historical deductions. Its platform has definite and clearly formulated aims capable of immediate realisation. It is the only party which – at any rate on a local or provincial basis – has some sort of organisation and some sort of plan of action. In short it is the party which has taken the lead in fighting the *Status Quo* and is directly concerned with bringing it to a speedy end. The middle class party is therefore the only party which has any serious chance of success in the struggle against the *Status Quo*." "At this very moment it is essential that the middle class should gain political supremacy in Germany and it is not to be destroyed." Unfortunately Engels's manuscript is incomplete and it breaks off before he discusses the future political *rôle* of the communists in Germany. His views on this question were soon to be given in his "Principles of Communism" and in the Communist Manifesto itself.

Having expressed his views on the political situation in Germany Engels turned his attention to the affairs of the League of the Just in England. As a result of Moll's mission to Brussels and Paris early in 1847 Marx and Engels had agreed to co-operate in the proposed re-organisation of the League. Arrangements were made to call a conference of League delegates in the summer. Engels was anxious to gain some influence over the largest and most important of the groups of revolutionary German workers living abroad. He wished to attend the conference as the accredited representative of the Paris branch of the League. But there was some opposition to Engels's candidature. The way in which Engels was selected was recounted by Stephan Born in his memoirs. Born wrote: "A meeting of the League of the Just was held to elect a representative to the Central Committee in London and I was asked to take the chair. Engels wished to be elected but I realised that it would not be easy to accomplish this as he had to face a great deal of opposition. I secured his election by breaking the usual rules of procedure. Instead of asking those who favoured Engels's election to raise their hands I called upon those who opposed his election to put up their hands. Today I look back with horror upon this masterpiece of chairmanship. On our way home Engels said to me: 'You made a good job of that!' "[97]

The conference of the League of the Just was held in London in June 1847. In Marx's absence Engels was the leading representative of the Marxist point of view – with Wilhelm Wolff as an able colleague. He achieved a considerable measure of success in persuading the delegates to accept the new Marxian philosophy and to re-organise the League – now renamed the Communist League – on lines acceptable to Marx and himself. New statutes were adopted and it was decided to circularise them to branches of the League and to hold a second conference later in the year to ratify the decisions of the first conference.

When Engels left London in the middle of August he did not return to Paris but went to Brussels. At that time Marx was in Holland visiting his relations – the Philips family – from whom he hoped to raise some money. So, as at the recent conference of the League of the Just, Engels again had to act as Marx's representative and assume responsibility for the policy of the communist group in Brussels. He had to deal with the affairs of the Brussels German Workers Association and the *Deutsch-Brüsseler Zeitung*.

The German Workers Association had been established in Brussels (as a branch of the new Communist League) on August 5, 1847 and it provided both educational and recreational facilities for its members most of whom were craftsmen, factory workers or clerks. It soon enrolled over 100 members. The association was virtually controlled by Marx and his friends. Moses Hess and Karl Wallau[98] were the presidents of the Association while Wilhelm Wolff was the secretary. Wilhelm Wolff's talks on current affairs on Sunday evenings and Wallau's renderings of German ballads in a fine baritone voice were popular features of the Association's weekly programme. Marx, too, lectured to members of the Association on his theory of surplus value.[99]

The hold of the communists over the German Workers Association was challenged by Adalbert Bornstedt. In public he was a radical journalist; in private he was almost certainly a Prussian spy. A former Prussian army officer, he had edited the journal *Vorwärts* in Paris in 1844 and Marx had been one of his contributors. Between January 1847 and February 1848 he edited the *Deutsch-Brüsseler Zeitung* which, in Engels's words, "mercilessly exposed the blessing of the police régime in the Fatherland".[100] Marx and Engels tried to capture this paper as an organ for the propagation of their views. Bornstedt was a member of the Communist League until his expulsion in March 1848. He had been in the pay of the Austrian[101] and Prussian governments in the past and it is reasonable to assume that he was still plying his unsavoury trade and was reporting to the Prussian authorities on the activities of the German political exiles in Brussels.[102] Freiligrath had written in 1845: "Adalbert von Bornstedt, who has been ostensibly expelled from France at the request of the Prussian authorities, is really here to spy on us emigrées and only incidentally to edit a newspaper which furthers the cause of the German customs union. He is indeed a queer character."[103] The occasion chosen by Bornstedt to launch his campaign against Marx and Engels was the holding of a banquet in Brussels attended by democrats from a number of countries. The purpose of the banquet was to found a new international Democratic Association. Marx and Engels hoped to dominate this organisation as they already dominated the local German Workers Association. Bornstedt, on the other hand, wished to exclude Marx and his friends from holding office in the Democratic Association.

Engels wrote to Marx towards the end of September 1847 that advantage was being taken of his absence from Brussels to plan a coup which would lead to the establishment of "a much larger and more universal society than our poor little Workers Association".[104] Although Engels heard of Bornstedt's intrigue only at the last moment he was able to scotch it. The banquet was held on September 27 and was attended by 120 guests. Engels himself – though he had protested that he looked too young for the part – was elected one of the vice-presidents of the new Democratic Association.[105] This society was modelled on the Fraternal Democrats which had been established in London in 1845. Engels told Marx that "this affair has greatly raised – and will continue to raise – the morale of the [German Workers] Association both in its internal affairs and in its relations with outside bodies. Chaps who formerly kept their traps shut have now come forward and attacked Bornstedt . . . Bartels said to me this morning: 'German democracy is getting very strong in Brussels'."[106]

The growing strength of Marx and his followers had just been illustrated by another incident in September 1847. An international Free Trade congress had been held in Brussels at which Georg Weerth – a close associate of Marx and Engels – had made a striking speech denouncing Free Traders who argued that their policy would benefit the workers. Weerth claimed that Free Trade would do nothing to alleviate the distress of the proletariat and he warned the employers: "If you do not take care you will have to fear an erruption of your own workmen, and they will be more terrible to you than all the Cossacks in the world." Weerth's attack on the

Free Traders was widely reported in the press in many countries – Engels wrote about it in the *Northern Star*[107] – and the communists in Brussels could feel that they were emerging from obscurity and were making their influence felt.

At the same time that Engels was involved in a dispute with Bornstedt over the founding of the Brussels Democratic Association, he also crossed swords with Bornstedt in connection with his controversy with Heinzen. As editor of the *Deutsch-Brüsseler Zeitung* Bornstedt had given certain undertakings to Marx concerning the opening of his paper to articles written by Marx and his friends. But when Heinzen attacked the communists in the columns of the *Deutsch-Brüsseler Zeitung* on September 26, 1847 Bornstedt made various excuses to avoid printing a reply by Engels. Only a strong protest by Engels secured the publication of his reply to Heinzen on October 3 and October 7.[108]

In October 1847 Engels was back in Paris. This time he was determined to get into touch with the leaders of the working class movement in France in the hope of securing their co-operation with the Brussels Communist Correspondence Committee. It was also his intention to represent the German workers in Paris at the forthcoming second conference of the Communist League in London. And he wished to ensure that any proposals from the Paris branch of the Communist League to this conference should be in accordance with Marx's doctrines and not those of the 'true socialists'. The first objective of Engels's mission to Paris was accomplished when he had an interview with Louis Blanc. He introduced himself as Marx's personal representative and as one authorised to speak on behalf of the democrats of London, Brussels and the Rhineland. He also claimed to be an agent of the Chartists. Louis Blanc assured Engels that a very active underground movement among the workers existed in France. He declared: "The workers are more revolutionary than ever before but they have learned by experience to bide their time. They are not going to waste their energies in minor risings but they will wait until a major revolt promises certain success."[109]

At this time Engels also visited Ferdinand Flocon, the editor of *La Réforme*. He did not disclose his true identity but pretended to be an Englishman representing the Chartist leader Julian Harney. Engels complained to Flocon that *La Réforme* had ignored the *Northern Star*. When Flocon explained that no member of his staff could read English, Engels declared that he was "a correspondent of the *Northern Star*" and would be prepared to contribute regularly to *La Réforme*. Engels reported to Marx that he hoped "to imprison Flocon still more tightly in our net". He proposed to tell

Flocon that he was in touch with the workers' newspaper *l'Atelier* but would reject any offer from *l'Atelier* if Flocon would agree to print his articles in *La Réforme.* The stratagem appears to have worked since Engels contributed nine articles on English affairs to *La Réforme* between October 1847 and March 1848.[110]

Towards the end of October 1847 Engels gave Marx particulars not only of his conversations with Louis Blanc and Flocon but also of his activities among the German workers in Paris. He declared that everything was in "hellish confusion". "A few days before I arrived the last of the followers of Grün were expelled. This represented an entire cell (*Gemeinde*) but half of them have returned. The cell has now only 30 members." Engels wrote that he hoped to increase the membership in the near future. Writing "in the strictest confidence" he told Marx that he had "played a devilish trick on Hess". At this time Hess was attempting to advance the cause of 'true socialism' within the framework of Marx's doctrines – by no means an easy task. He was putting forward his ideas in a series of articles in the *Deutsch-Brüsseler Zeitung* and he hoped to exercise some influence upon the forthcoming deliberations of the Communist League in London. He drew up a declaration of communist principles in the form of a catechism and on October 22 he submitted it to one of the cells of the League in Paris. The meeting began to go through Hess's catechism question by question but before this detailed examination was completed the members declared that they were satisfied. Engels wrote: "At this point *without encountering any opposition* I persuaded the meeting to authorise me to draw up a new catechism and this will be discussed at group (*Kreis*) level and will be sent to London *behind the backs of the cells.*" "Obviously no one must know about this or there will be a frightful scandal and we shall all be turned out."[111] Engels thereupon produced his own catechism which in due course became the basis upon which Marx wrote the Communist Manifesto.

In the middle of November 1847 Engels was elected to represent the Paris branch of the Communist League at the forthcoming conference of the League in London. On November 27 Engels met Marx in Ostend. They crossed to England to attend a banquet of the Fraternal Democrats on November 29 – the anniversary of the Polish rising of 1830[112] – and to address the German Workers Education Society on the following day. Above all they took a leading part at the conference of the Communist League which was held between November 29 and December 10. Marx was asked to prepare for publication the final version of a statement of communist principles.

Engels was in Brussels over Christmas. Stephan Born has described in his memoirs an incident which occurred at this time at a party organised by the Brussels Workers Association. "Among those present were Marx who came with his wife and Engels who brought his – lady. The two couples were at either end of a large room. When I greeted Marx he indicated by a significant glance and a smile that his wife would in no circumstances meet Engels's companion. In matters of honour and morals the noble lady was quite intransigent." "Obviously Engels should not have brought his mistress to a gathering attended mainly by members of the working class. It was tactless of him to remind the workers that the sons of rich millowners had often been accused of using the daughters of their operatives to gratify their own pleasure.[113] Although Born mentioned no names it is generally assumed that Engels's companion was Mary Burns. Certainly in the previous summer Engels – according to Georg Weerth – had been living in Brussels with an English girl.[114] The incident reported by Born shows that even at an early stage in their friendship Engels's private life raised certain obstacles between them. Engels was always a welcome guest in Marx's home but – since Jenny Marx strongly disapproved of people living together as man and wife without being married – he was never able to bring Mary Burns with him.

In January 1848 Engels was back in Paris. He complained to Marx that he had been unable to see Louis Blanc, who appeared to be avoiding him. On the other hand he had no difficulty in meeting Flocon who was pleased that the *Northern Star* and the *Deutsch-Brüsseler Zeitung* had supported his journal *La Réforme* against its rival, the *National*. Flocon reminded Engels that since France has eleven million peasants French socialism was bound to be different from German socialism. Nevertheless Flocon declared that "our principles are too close to yours for us to be unable to march together shoulder to shoulder."[115]

At the same time Engels complained to Marx that he had made little progress in organising the German workers in Paris under the communist banner. He declared that the Paris branch of the Communist League was in a wretched state. "I have never met fellows who are so stupid and so prone to petty jealousies. The doctrines of Weitling and Proudhon are just right for these idiots and no one can make anything of them." "Workers of this sort – men who, like the Irish, live by depressing the level of wages in France – are quite useless for our purpose."[116] And the workers for their part had no very high opinion of Engels. When Marx came into contact with them in March 1848 he told Engels that the artisans – the *Straubinger* – "are all more or less furious with you".[117] But Engels hoped that once the London communists produced their manifesto – which Marx was then writing – it might be possible to revive the Paris branch of the League.

On this occasion Engels's stay in Paris was a short one for on January 29 the government ordered him to leave the country. It was officially stated that Engels's expulsion had nothing to do with his politics.[118] Stephan Born, writing many years later, gave the following account of Engels's enforced departure from Paris: "Engels had learned from his friend the painter Ritter that a certain French nobleman had cast off his mistress without making any provision for her. Engels threatened to make the whole affair public unless the Count decided to act fairly towards the lady. The Count complained to the Minister who issued an expulsion order against Engels and his friend Ritter."[119]

Engels just missed the fall of Louis Philippe and the outbreak of revolution in France. He returned to Brussels in time to join Marx in attending a meeting of the Democratic Association on February 22, 1848 to mark the second anniversary of the Austrian annexation of Cracow. In his speech on this occasion Engels declared that before 1846 it had been doubtful if a democratic revolution in Germany could count upon the support of the Poles. But after the revolution in Cracow and the loss of its independence the Germans and the Poles were destined to be allies because they were both being oppressed by the same three reactionary powers – Russia, Austria and Prussia. The future alliance of the German and Polish peoples was no longer merely a dream but it had become a practical necessity.[120]

A few days before his arrival in Belgium an article from Engels's pen appeared in the *Deutsch-Brüsseler Zeitung* which warned the middle class liberals in Germany of their fate in the revolution which could not be long delayed. Their *rôle* was merely to prepare the way for the triumph of the proletariat.

> "You may as well know beforehand", he wrote, "that you are working only in our interests. But you cannot on that account give up your struggle against the absolute monarchs, the nobles and the priests. This is a fight that you cannot lose if you are not to go under immediately. Before very long in Germany you will actually have to call upon us to help you. So fight on my worthy valorous capitalists! We need you. Indeed here and there it is, from our point of view, actually necessary that you should gain political power. You have a job to do for us. You must sweep away what is left of the middle ages. You must exterminate the absolute rulers. You must destroy all patriarchal forms of government. You must centralise authority. You must turn into a true proletariat all classes in society which own no property or very little property. You must

turn them into recruits for our movement. Through your factories and commercial interests you must provide us with the weapons which the workers need to gain their freedom. And your reward for doing all this for us will be that you will rule the country for a little while. Your laws will be in force. You can bathe in the sunshine of royal glory. You can dine like kings and you can court the daughters of kings. But remember – the executioner is waiting at the door!"[121]

III. The "Principles of Communism" and the Communist Manifesto, 1847–8

The climax of Engels's collaboration with Marx between 1845 and 1847 was the production of the "Principles of Communism" and the Communist Manifesto. In those years they hammered out their materialist philosophy in *The German Ideology* and drew up a political programme to translate their ideas into reality. Together they attacked capitalists, reactionaries and liberals as well as socialists and radicals who would not subscribe to their doctrines. On the eve of the revolution of 1848 they issued their declaration of faith in the Communist Manifesto enunciating the principles of a creed which eventually came to be accepted by millions of their disciples. To appreciate how Engels's first draft of the Communist Manifesto – the "Principles of Communism" – and the Manifesto itself came to be written it is necessary to examine the origin and to trace the development of the Communist League. Engels's account of the League, written in 1885, gives an excellent survey of its early history.[122]

In their account of the German revolutionary societies in the 1830s and 1840s two senior police officials – Dr Wermuth of Hanover and Dr W. Stieber of Berlin – traced their origin to associations set up by liberal reformers after the Napoleonic wars. Many who had fought in the War of Liberation were bitterly disappointed at their failure to achieve either the unification of their country or its political freedom. This led to the rise of revolutionary associations of students and artisans which were soon driven underground by the repressive measures of reactionary German governments.

Writing in 1860 Marx gave a description of the dual character of these societies. Each secret society had a public educational association as a front to disguise its real activities. "The programmes of these public workers' societies", wrote Marx, "were always the same. One day of the week was set aside for discussions and another for recreation, such as singing and reciting. Whenever possible the society maintained a library. Educational classes were organised for the artisans at an elementary level. Each workers' association acted as a cover for a secret 'league' (*Bund*). The open propaganda of the league was conducted through the public association. And the most promising workers of the public society were recruited as new members of the underground league. It was rarely necessary for the central committee of a league to send emissaries to local branches since German artisans were constantly on the move (and would carry messages from one place to another)."[123]

A group of German artisans working in Paris – some of whom had fled to France to avoid arrest at home – set up a Press Association in 1832 to agitate for the abolition of press censorship in Germany. This association developed into the German Popular Society (*Volksverein*) which sent J. H. Garnier to Germany to establish new branches there. When the Popular Society was banned by the French authorities in 1833 it became an underground organisation called the League of Exiles (*Bund der Geächteten*).[124] Its statutes were typical of the secret political societies of its day. An oath was taken on admission; the members were known by secret names; and those who divulged the affairs of the society were threatened with dire penalties. One of its most active emissaries – first in Germany and then in Switzerland – was J. C. B. von Bruhn.[125]

A schism occurred in the ranks of the League of Exiles in 1836. The more radical members broke away and founded a new secret society in Paris called the League of the Just (*Bund der Gerechten*) and efforts to reconcile the two factions failed. The League of Exiles led first by Jacob Venedey and then by Théodore Schuster survived for a time and some of its members returned to Germany to establish new branches of their society there. In 1840, however, the activities of the League of Exiles came to an end when several of its members were arrested in Germany.[126]

A different fate was in store for the League of the Just. From the beginning Karl Schapper and Heinrich Bauer gave the League an inspiring leadership which Venedey and Schuster had never been able to give in the past. As a student of forestry at Giessen, Schapper had supported Georg Büchner in spreading revolutionary doctrines among the peasants in Hesse. He had taken part in the attack upon the Frankfurt guardhouse in 1833 and had joined Mazzini in his abortive expedition to Savoy in 1834. In Paris he earned his living as a compositor. Engels declared that this "resolute and energetic giant" had developed into "an ideal professional revolutionary". Heinrich Bauer, a shoemaker, was described by Engels as "a lively, wide-awake, gay little fellow – small in stature but mighty in determination and cunning".[127]

While Schapper and Bauer were the leaders and organisers of the League of the Just, Wilhelm Weitling was the thinker who tried to convert its members to his doctrines of Christian Socialism. Hitherto the aim of the League had been to free Germany from its reactionary rulers and to secure the establishment of a united and democratic republic but some of its members now supported Weitling's plans which involved the overthrow of existing capitalist society and its replacement by a socialist utopia where private property would be abolished and goods would be communally owned. Weitling's propaganda was the first step on the road that led to the League of the Just becoming first a socialist and eventually a Marxist organisation.

Soon after its establishment the League of the Just became closely associated with the *Société des saisons,* a French revolutionary organisation led by Blanqui and Barbès. The *Société des saisons* engineered a rising against the government on May 12, 1839 and occupied the Town Hall in Paris. The insurgents were quickly suppressed and leading members of the League of the Just were involved in the debacle. Weitling went to Switzerland in 1841 where he established several new branches of the League. Karl Schapper and Heinrich Bauer – after being in custody for some time – were expelled from France and sought refuge in London. There was a colony of German artisans in London at this time so that Schapper and Bauer were soon able to form a new branch of the League of the Just.

The Paris section of the League of the Just survived the failure of the coup d'état of 1839[128] and the new Swiss and English branches recognised it as the leading branch of the association and the main centre for its propaganda activities. But it had lost its leaders and declined in importance. When Engels arrived in Paris in 1846 he found that the League, then led by Dr Hermann Ewerbeck, consisted of three small and rather quarrelsome groups of German workers, two of which consisted largely of tailors and one of carpenters. Many of them subscribed to the doctrines of Weitling or of Proudhon and Grün.

Meanwhile in London the League went from strength to strength. Engels wrote in December 1846 that the London branches had "a few hundred" members and that their activities had caused alarm in the German press.[129] In 1847 the League in London claimed a membership of about 500, divided between two branches.[130] Long before it took over the leadership of the whole League from the Paris branch, the London branch became a large and active group of revolutionary workers. In London its members were able to associate and to express their views with a freedom denied to them on the Continent except, to a limited extent, in Switzerland and Belgium. In London its membership could make common cause with other groups of exiles – such as Poles and Italians – who were agitating against the oppression of their native lands by foreign tyrants. In London members of the League of the Just could hope for support from left-wing Chartists who belonged to the most powerful working class movement in Europe. And probably only London could have seen in March 1846 the founding of the Fraternal Democrats, a society in which some of the Chartists co-operated with various groups of foreign refugees and with organisations of workers abroad to set up one of the earliest international labour associations ever to be founded.

The London branch of the League of the Just was served by able leaders. Karl Schapper and Heinrich Bauer were seasoned revolutionaries and skilful organisers. They had learned a lesson from the failure of the Blanqui coup d'état and now advised their followers to devote themselves to educational and propaganda activities rather than to preparations for an armed rising. They had the support of several competent lieutenants – Moll, Pfänder, Eccarius, and Schabelitz. Engels considered Josef Moll (a watch-maker from Cologne) to have greater intellectual gifts than Schapper and Bauer. "He was a born diplomat – witness the success of all his missions abroad on behalf of the league – and he was quite receptive to new political ideas."[131] Karl Pfänder was "a splendid thinker – witty, dialectical, ironical."[132] Johann Georg Eccarius was a tailor who played a leading *rôle* in the affairs of the League[133] and eventually became secretary of the First International. Jakob Lukas Schabelitz, a young radical from Switzerland, (though never a convinced Marxist) supported the cause of the revolutionary exiles by publishing articles expressing their point of view in the *Deutsche-Londoner Zeitung* which he edited. In 1851 Marx praised Schabelitz as one who "had been active here as our agent and had been most useful in that capacity since he enjoyed the confidence of all the respectable people in London".[134]

The progress of the League between 1840 and 1847 was also stimulated by the founding, in February 1840, of a German Workers Education Society (*Bildungsverein*) in Great Windmill Street in London. This association gave German-speaking artisans opportunities for cultural and social activities similar to those available to English workers in their clubs and mechanics institutes. Discussion groups on current affairs and on philosophical and political questions were formed to debate the meaning of their motto: "All men are brothers", the advantages and drawbacks to the workers of the introduction of machinery into factories, the security of employment in a capitalist society, Weitling's doctrine of Christian Socialism, and Feuerbach's materialist philosophy.[135] Engels considered that these educational activities met a very real need. He doubted whether in those days a single member of the League had ever read a book on economics. As far as they were concerned lofty catchphrases – 'equality', 'justice', 'brotherly love' – helped them over every hurdle in economics.[136]

The German Workers Education Society – and its offshoot the Sunday Club – were largely run by the leaders of the League of the Just who used an apparently innocuous organisation as a convenient cover for their activities. The society proved to be an excellent recruiting ground for new members of the League of the Just. And when Karl Schapper and his friends wished to express their views in public they generally did so as members of the German Workers Education Society rather than as members of the League of the Just.

Two significant developments occurred between 1840 and 1847. The first was that the League of the Just changed from a German to an international association. The second was that the League became increasingly a socialist – and eventually a Marxist – body. Initially the League of the Just and the German Workers Education Society had attracted only German-speaking members but in time they were joined by workers of other nationalities. The motto "All men are brothers" was printed in at least twenty different languages on the membership cards of the German Workers Education Society. As its membership became more cosmopolitan so its interests became more international. In June 1846 Karl Schapper accepted an invitation from Karl Marx to exchange information with the Brussels Correspondence Committee. The London branch of the League of the Just set up a special committee for this purpose and exchanged letters with Marx with greater regularity than any other group. The international outlook of Karl Schapper and his friends was shown by the interest which they took in other left-wing political movements. They supported the demands of the Polish and Italian exiles in London. They forged links with the Chartists and the Fraternal Democrats. The influential Chartist leader Julian Harney joined the League of the Just while Ernest Jones, who spoke German fluently, was a welcome visitor at meetings of the German Workers Education Society.

Moreover the leaders of the League of the Just in London openly expressed their views on the political issues of the day. In 1844 they wrote to the Hamburg *Telegraph für Deutschland*[137] expressing sympathy for the Silesian weavers who had risen in revolt. In 1846 they were largely responsible for producing a leaflet on the

Schleswig-Holstein question issued by the German Workers Education Society. And in 1846 Schapper and Moll supported a pacifist address of the Fraternal Democrats – drawn up by Julian Harney – on the Oregon dispute.[138]

But the most important aspect of the League's activities was its search for a philosophy and a programme of action. Karl Schapper and his friends realised that the violent overthrow of dynasties and reactionary governments was a programme of somewhat limited appeal. They also appreciated the need to devise a policy for the situation that would arise if existing governments disappeared. And their followers would have to be given some indication of what kind of new society would replace the old. In the early days of the League in Paris the only plans for the future that had been seriously discussed were those of Weitling. And in September 1844 Weitling himself appeared in London. At meetings organised by the Workers Education Society he preached his doctrine of brotherly love yet at the same time he advocated the violent overthrow of existing society. Karl Schapper, Heinrich Bauer, and Josef Moll rejected the idea that their aims could be quickly achieved by revolution in the near future. In a letter to Etienne Cabet in 1843 and in an address to the Hamburg *Telegraph* on the weavers' revolt in Silesia they had already declared that they were engaged in peaceful propaganda and were opposed to a policy of violence. Weitling was disappointed with his reception in London and early in 1846 he left to join Marx and his friends in Brussels.

Karl Schapper's rejection of Weitling's brand of utopian socialism mixed with violence encouraged Marx and Engels to try to win over the London branch of the League of the Just to their own doctrines. In June 1846 Schapper agreed to a regular exchange of information with the Communist Correspondence Committee in Brussels. But then Marx and Engels suffered a setback. When they appealed to their new colleagues for support against the 'true socialists' they were rebuffed. Far from welcoming Marx's "Circular against Kriege" of May 1846 Karl Schapper and his friends replied on July 17, 1846 that they were opposed to this attack upon a leading exponent of 'true socialism'. And in September 1846 a leaflet on the Schleswig-Holstein question – representing the views of the leaders of the League of the Just in London – echoed the doctrines of the 'true socialists' and was contemptuously dismissed by Engels as "utter rubbish".[139] In October 1846 Marx wrote a second circular against Kriege in the hope of convincing Karl Schapper and his friends of the error of their ways.

By the autumn of 1846 Marx and Engels had every reason to be disappointed at their failure to convert Schapper and his colleagues to their point of view. In November a new central executive committee of the League was elected and this body was in future to meet in London and not, as formerly, in Paris. The leaders of the London branch sat on the central executive committee and were in effective control of the affairs of the whole League.[140] Marx and Engels were now fighting for control not merely of the most active branch of the League but of the entire organisation. Engels complained to Marx that they were distrusted as 'intellectuals' by Schapper and his working class colleagues in London. He wrote, "The affair of the people in London is exasperating – first because of Harney, and secondly because they are the only group of artisans (*Straubinger*) to whom we can speak frankly without *arrière-pensée* and with whom co-operation is possible. But if the fellows do not want us, very well, let them go their own way!" "The whole affair has taught us that, so long as we have no properly organised movement in Germany, we cannot do anything with artisans – not even with the best of them."[141]

In November 1846, soon after assuming office, the new central executive committee of the League issued an address to all its branches.[142] The executive committee argued that throughout Europe all progressive groups were demanding the transformation of society. League members should infiltrate these groups and take the initiative as leaders in the struggle against reactionary governments. And, as a first step, the members of the League should co-operate with the radical petty bourgeoisie in their fight against the aristocracy and the middle classes.

But before any action of this kind could be taken the League would have to put its own house in order by agreeing to "a straightforward declaration of communist beliefs". A conference of delegates from all the branches should be held in May 1847 to draw up a declaration of faith and "to resolve differences of opinion", and a second conference should meet in 1848 "to which the supporters of the new doctrine should be openly invited from all parts of the world". Since Marx and Engels were the most prominent advocates of the 'new doctrine' it appears that the executive committee of the League was proposing to keep them at arm's length until agreement had been reached on the declaration of faith.

The League's address of November 1846 proceeded to attack the followers of Fourier. The severest criticism, however, was reserved for what the address called the "Christian-German-Prussian party". Schapper and his colleagues alleged that some German governments – through their officials, the police and the churches – were subsidising associations of German workers at home and abroad.

Through these clubs it was hoped to keep German artisans away from organisations controlled by the socialists. Freiherr von Bunsen, the Prussian ambassador in England, was attacked for giving his support to a German library (*Leseverein*) and for helping to set up two "Christian artisan clubs" in London. They received financial support from the ambassador, from members of the Prussian royal family, and from German pastors and bankers living in London. It was alleged that German workers on the Continent, proposing to come to London, were being advised to join the Christian clubs rather than the German Workers Education Society. The League appealed to its members to warn all newly arrived German workers of the machinations of the "Protestant Jesuits".

At the end of the address the leaders of the League of the Just suggested that all branches should discuss the following questions:

"1. What policy should the workers adopt in relation to the middle classes and the petty bourgeoisie? Would it be advisable for us to approach the petty – or radical – bourgeoisie (with a view to the conclusion of an alliance)?
2. What policy should the workers adopt in relation to the various religious parties? Is an approach to one or other of these groups possible and desirable and if so what is the simplest and surest way of making such an approach?
3. What should our attitude be towards the various socialist and communist parties? Would it be desirable – or possible – to bring about the union of all socialists? If so, what is the quickest and surest way of bringing this unification about?"

It is clear from the League's address that at the end of 1846 its leaders were still not prepared to accept Karl Marx's doctrines. They hoped that the forthcoming conference would produce an agreed statement of policy without the assistance of Marx and Engels. But soon afterwards there was a sudden and surprising change of heart. In February 1847 Josef Moll was sent to the Continent to interview Marx and Engels. He took with him the following letter in Schapper's handwriting, dated January 20 and addressed to the Communist Correspondence Committee in Brussels:

"The members of the Communist Correspondence Committee in London who have signed this letter hereby authorise and instruct Citizen Josef Moll to enter into negotiations with the Communist Correspondence Committee in Brussels and to make a verbal report concerning the state of affairs here (in London). At the same time we ask the Brussels Committee to give Citizen Moll – who is a member of the London Committee – full information about all important matters and to entrust to him any messages that are to be sent to the London Committee." (Karl Schapper, Henry Bauer, Karl Pfänder, Friedrich Doepel, Albert Lehmann, Charles Molly, Jos. Goebel).[143]

It is not clear why Schapper and his friends changed their minds. In November 1846 they still distrusted Marx. In the following month Engels saw little hope of reaching an agreement with Schapper. Yet in January 1847 Schapper was ready to open discussions with Marx and Engels. Perhaps there were differences of opinion on the League's central executive committee concerning co-operation with Marx and Engels, and Moll's mission may have represented a victory for those in favour of such co-operation.

Moll's talks with Marx in Brussels and Engels in Paris came to a satisfactory conclusion. Engels subsequently stated that Moll assured him that the leaders of the League of the Just "were just as convinced of the correctness of our doctrine as they were of the necessity of removing from the League its old conspiratorial forms and traditions". "If we joined the League we would have an opportunity to develop our ideas on critical communism in the form of a manifesto which would be published by the League as a statement of policy." "We could also express our views concerning the transformation of the antiquated organisation of the League into one which would be more efficient and more appropriate to modern conditions."[144] Marx observed that before agreeing to become a member he had insisted that the constitution of the League should be revised so that its leaders and officials would be elected in a democratic fashion. When they had been given the assurances that they required Marx and Engels joined the League. Marx founded a new branch of the League of the Just in Brussels which included the members of the existing Communist Correspondence Committee while Engels went ahead with his efforts to persuade the three branches of the League in Paris to accept Marx's doctrines.

On receiving a satisfactory report from Moll concerning his discussions with Marx and Engels the central executive committee of the League of the Just issued a second address to its branches in February 1847.[145] It opened with a complaint that many branches had failed to reply to the first address of November 1846. The central executive warned the branches of the League that Europe was on the verge of revolution and war. A Russian invasion of Germany was imminent. "Hundreds of thousands of Russian barbarians are camped on Germany's frontiers, ready at any moment to overrun central and western Europe. Our fathers and brothers will be sent to the slavery of the icefields of Siberia while our wives and sisters will be raped. Brothers! Shall we stand by unmoved when this takes place? Shall we reply with mere words and not with deeds? Shall we act like cowards and bow our necks beneath the Russian yoke?"

The address warned members of the League that a revolution might break out in the spring of 1847. "By standing in the front rank of the defenders of freedom you can show that we can fight with muskets as well as with words." "Wherever you may be you should preach the gospel of communism. Your listeners will welcome this wonderful doctrine which will, at long last, fulfil their hopes of freedom from oppression." "Should existing governments collapse it would be the duty of members of the League to work by word and by deed for the establishment of administrations run by men who believe in the principles of communism." It was, of course, an unrealistic assessment of the situation in Europe in 1847 to suppose that there was the remotest possibility of any new administration being dominated by men inspired by communist views. The only socialists who could hope for office were men like Louis Blanc or Flocon who were far from being communists. The address warned members of the League not to co-operate with middle class liberals who only want to replace the tyranny of princes with the "despotism of money bags".

The central executive committee of the League invited delegates from all branches to attend a conference to be held on June 1, 1847 in order to revise the constitution of the League; to formulate a declaration of policy; to establish a party journal; and to send emissaries to organise new branches, particularly in Germany and in the Scandinavian countries. The address admitted that, despite its large membership, the League lacked a strong organisation and – until this weakness was rectified – it could "never hope to exercise any decisive influence upon public affairs". Members of the League were urged to cease to support other political parties. The fact that a party might claim to be in favour of 'progress' did not excuse such co-operation. "It is we who are now standing in the forefront of the progressive movement and we should all rally under our own banner and not allow ourselves to be swallowed up in a vast army of philistines." The address suggested that the League should follow the example of the Chartists who had refused to compromise on the six points of their programme by co-operating with any other party.

Next the address surveyed the existing state of the League. The branches in Paris and Brussels were being re-organised. In Switzerland the rivalry between Weitling and his opponents had weakened the League, though hopeful reports had been received from branches in Bern and Lausanne. In Sweden new associations of workers were being established. In London a membership of 500 had been attained. The League could afford to ignore the opposition of the German pastors in London who had denounced the German Workers Education Society from their pulpits. A report on the Chartist movement was promised in a future address but in the meantime the League denounced Feargus O'Connor's land scheme as "disgusting nonsense".

The central committee of the League asked its branches to discuss certain questions and gave some guidance as to how they might be answered. The first two questions were: "What is communism? What are the aims of the communists?" The answers were: "Communism is a system by which all property is communally owned. Everybody is expected to produce according to his abilities and everybody is entitled to consume according to his needs. Communists will sweep away existing social institutions and replace them by an entirely new system."

The second two questions were: "What is socialism? What are the aims of the socialists?" The address asserted that socialism was not a new social system. Socialists closed their eyes to fundamental problems and tried to tinker with the existing capitalist system. The idea that communism and socialism were really the same must be decisively rejected.

The last question was: "What is the easiest and quickest way of introducing a system of communal property?" No answer was given but it was suggested that branches might discuss the desirability of having a period of transition before private property was nationalised. And they might also consider whether this change should be introduced by force or by peaceful means.

Finally the address again warned members of the League against the propaganda of the followers of Fourier and the supporters of "brotherly love socialism". Above all members were warned to "beware of revolts, conspiracies, the purchase of firearms, and similar follies". "Our enemies are plotting devilish schemes. After actually inciting the workers to support street demonstrations they will put the workers down by force and claim that they are restoring law and order."

The branches of the League proceeded to elect delegates to attend the first conference to be held in London in June 1847. The Brussels branch elected Karl Marx and Wilhelm Wolff while the Paris branches – stimulated by a little sharp practice on the part of Stephan Born – appointed Engels as their representative. Since Marx could not raise the fare to London, Engels and Wolff presented the Marxist point of view to the conference. No records of

Friedrich Engels at the age of 19, 1839

Karl Marx as a student, 1836

Georg Weerth, 1822–1856

Moses Hess, 1812–1875

the proceedings have survived but some of the results of the conference can be seen from the pages of the *Kommunistische Zeitschrift* and from the new constitution of the League. The conference approved the establishment of a communist journal in London and the first – and only – number appeared in September 1847. One of its main articles, entitled "The United Diet and the Proletariat in Prussia", was probably written by Wilhelm Wolff and reflected the views of the Brussels Correspondence Committee.[146] This was one indication of the influence which Marx and his followers were now able to exert over the League. An examination of the new constitution, drawn up by the conference in June 1847 also showed that the League was moving away from utopian and 'true' socialism and was drawing closer to Marx's doctrines. The name of the League was changed to the League of Communists while its motto was changed from "All men are brothers" to "Workers of the world, unite!"

The new constitution of the Communist League provided for the re-organisation of the former underground movement so that it became a society openly engaged in political propaganda. The League was now an international association divided into cells (three to twenty members), groups (two to ten cells), and senior groups (linking all groups in a region or country). Its affairs were to be controlled by a democratically elected central executive committee and by periodic delegate conferences. A few vestiges of the former secret society survived since members still had special 'League names' and promised not to divulge to outsiders anything concerning the affairs of the organisation. This provisional constitution was subsequently submitted to the branches of the Communist League and to a second delegate conference in December 1847 for final ratification.[147]

There was a spate of activity on the part of the leaders of the Communist League in the six months between the two conferences of June and December 1847. They founded a new journal in London – the *Kommunistische Zeitschrift* – and launched a recruiting drive to enrol new members. In October Stephan Born was sent to Lyons, Geneva, Chaux-de-Fonds and Bern to spread communism among the French and Swiss workers.[148] The leaders of the Communist League, no longer impressed by the utopian doctrines of Weitling or the 'true socialists', were more ready to accept advice from Marx and Engels. Cabet found that he had embarked upon a fruitless errand when he visited London in the autumn of 1847 in the hope of persuading the Workers Education Society to support his utopian emigration plan.[149] By this time the League's central committee had already prepared a draft statement of policy to serve as a basis for discussion at the second conference to be held in December.[150] It was probably written by Schapper and Moll and it was sent to branches of the League. It was discussed by the Workers Education Society in London, by the Brussels and Paris branches of the League, and presumably by branches in Germany as well. No copy of this draft now exists but it is possible to ascertain the policy that it advocated by examining the leading article in the *Kommunistische Zeitschrift* of September 1847.[151]

This article was probably written by Karl Schapper and was a commentary upon the recently issued draft manifesto. The writer discussed the future of the proletariat, a class which in his view included not only the workers but also intellectuals, artists, and the petty bourgeoisie. Formerly the workers had "sought freedom in death" by violent attacks upon their reactionary oppressors. Now they should aim at "establishing a society in which everyone could lead a free and happy life". The writer asked himself whether force would be needed to establish the ideal society of the future. While the address of the executive committee of February 1847 had rejected the use of violence the leading article in the *Kommunistische Zeitschrift* held that the workers would have to meet force with force if their enemies resorted to violence. "We communists are no advocates of eternal peace while our enemies are everywhere mobilising for war." In England and the United States a peaceful transition to socialism might be possible but elsewhere the workers would have to fight for their rights. The article warned the workers, however, that if they faced overwhelming odds it would be foolish to indulge in armed risings that had no possible chance of success.

The article rebuked Heinzen for attacking communism in *Der Deutsche Tribun* and discussed the extent to which communists should co-operate with other left-wing parties. Heinzen was criticised for supposing that a new society would be established if his proposed democratic reforms were adopted. These reforms were merely a programme suited to a period of transition which would pave the way for the establishment of a socialist society. But all democrats should unite to support Heinzen's programme as a first step towards achieving the ideal of a socialist society. That the *Kommunistische Zeitschrift's* leading article covered the main topics of the statement of policy of the League's executive committee is confirmed if one compares it with Moses Hess's articles – written at about the same time – in the *Deutsch-Brüsseler Zeitung*, which reflected the discussion of this draft manifesto by the Brussels branch of the Communist League.

Moses Hess had himself drawn up a draft communist programme

which he submitted to the German communist workers in Paris as an alternative to the proposals circulated by the League's executive committee in London. No copy of Hess's programme has survived but it is evident from his articles in the *Deutsch-Brüsseler Zeitung* in October and November 1847 that his programme was a forlorn attempt to reconcile Marx's doctrines with those of the 'true socialists'.

Since Engels had dismissed these articles as "rubbish" it is not surprising that when he arrived in Paris in October 1847 he should have persuaded one of the local cells of the League to reject Hess's proposals. Engels was asked to replace Hess's programme by a programme of his own as soon as possible. It has been seen that Engels failed to submit his draft to all the Paris cells and urged Marx to keep what he had done secret.[152] No more was now heard either of the draft probably prepared by Schapper or of the draft drawn up by Hess. Engels's draft – also in the form of a catechism – held the field. The copy of Engels's proposed manifesto – the "Principles of Communism" – which has survived is a revised version which includes amendments made to an earlier draft. Engels's "Principles of Communism" is incomplete since the answers to three questions are missing. Two of these questions are followed by the words "No change" thus indicating that the answers already given in an earlier draft were to be inserted in the revised version. Engels's "Principles of Communism" was the genesis of the Communist Manifesto of 1848.[153]

On Tuesday, November 23, 1847 Engels informed Marx that it had at last been decided that he should represent the Paris branch of the Communist League at the delegate conference to be held in London in the following week. He suggested that they should meet in Ostend on the next Saturday and travel to England on the Sunday. He declared that "this conference must be decisive, as this time we shall have it all our own way." In the second part of the letter, written on Wednesday, November 24, Engels asked Marx to read his draft catechism on communist policy which he enclosed. He continued: "It would be better to drop the idea of a catechism and call it the Communist Manifesto. Its present form is really unsuitable since some history, more or less, must be included. I will bring my copy with me – a straightforward narrative badly written in great haste." "My catechism is not yet quite finished but – except for a few unimportant changes – we shall be able to get it passed without having to agree to the inclusion of anything contrary to our doctrines."[154]

Engels's catechism – the "Principles of Communism" – soon fell into undeserved oblivion, being completely overshadowed by

Marx's more brilliant manifesto. Nearly seventy years elapsed before it was published by Eduard Bernstein and even then he – and later Gustav Mayer[155] – did not rate it very highly. Both dismissed it as a somewhat elementary exposition of communism written in simple language so that its meaning could easily be grasped by artisans who had little knowledge of history or economics. Only in 1954 did Hermann Bollnow take the "Principles of Communism" sufficiently seriously to subject the catechism to a careful analysis and to discuss Engels's conception of revolution and peaceful transition as means of establishing a socialist society.[156]

In his "Principles of Communism"[157] Engels defined communism not as a new social order – a classless society operating a planned nationalised economy – but simply as "the doctrine which explains how the proletariat can throw off its chains and gain its freedom". He explained that the proletariat was a class created first in England and later in other manufacturing countries by the industrial revolution and that it was "the social group which exists simply by selling its labour and which draws no profit from any kind of capital". A characteristic feature of the industrial revolution had been the invention of new machines and the introduction of the factory system which had led to the decline of domestic craftsmen and their transformation into a factory proletariat. Now only two social classes existed – the middle classes and the workers. The middle classes – the capitalists – monopolised "all the necessities of life and all the raw materials, factories and machinery required to produce them" while the proletariat was "forced to sell its labour to the bourgeoisie in order to secure the necessities of life". Moreover the middle classes enjoyed not only economic power but political power as well and they had been able to ride roughshod over the privileges once enjoyed by the nobles in the rural districts and by the gilds in the towns. Engels considered that since "the average price of an article always equals the cost of production" in a capitalist society in which there is unfettered competition, it was inevitable that the wages of the industrial workers should be "no more than the minimum required for the purchase of the necessities of life". In his view a factory worker was "worse off than a slave or a serf".

Engels observed that industrial societies suffered from the evil effects of periodic booms and slumps. "There has been a crisis every five or seven years and this state of affairs has been marked by great distress among the workers, by a general revolutionary fever, and by the most serious threat to the existing social order." Since the trade cycle was caused by unbridled competition among manufacturers the only way to get rid of it would be to abolish free competition. In the early days of the industrial revolution unrestricted competition might have acted as a spur to economic development but now competition had become a serious threat to the stability of the capitalist system. Engels proposed to solve the problem by the introduction of economic planning. He argued that competition between rival manufacturers would have to be stopped, leaving society to assume full responsibility for all industrial production "in accordance with a predetermined plan".

In a communist society with a planned economy the very aspect of capitalism which lay at the root of commercial crises – the production of more goods than the market could absorb – would be turned to advantage. With continued advances in scientific and technical knowledge there were no limits to man's ability to expand industrial output and – in a communist society – it would be possible to produce enough food and manufactured goods to abolish poverty. In Engels's utopia, where everybody would be able to "develop his potentialities to the full", private property would become communal property and all factories, mines and farms would be nationalised. Co-operation between nationalised factories would replace cut-throat competition between rival private firms. Society would control both the production and the distribution of food and manufactured goods. And distribution would be based upon social needs and not upon ability to pay.

Engels argued that it would seldom be possible to nationalise private property peaceably since although communists were opposed to violence their enemies would undoubtedly use force to protect their property. "If the oppressed proletariat is driven to revolt we communists will support the workers with deeds as vigorously as we now support them with words."[158] Moreover the state could not take over all property at once. This could be done "only when the economy is capable of producing the volume of goods needed to satisfy everybody's requirements."

A revolution, in Engels's view, should pave the way for the political supremacy of the proletariat under a democratic constitution. "In England the power of the proletariat will be established directly because the majority of the population already consists of the working classes," but in France and Germany the rule of the workers would be established indirectly since in those countries the population consisted mainly of peasants in the rural districts and middle classes in the towns.

Various measures – some already advocated by other reformers – would facilitate the transition from a capitalist to a communist economy. Engels proposed that the rights of owners of property should be limited in various ways – by progressive taxes, by high death duties, and by restrictions on the right of inheritance. Property should eventually be taken over by the state. By "property" Engels did not mean all kinds of property. He meant landed estates, farms, mines, factories, shipyards, transport facilities, public utilities, banks and other financial institutions. He favoured the "organisation of labour" on co-operative lines – advocated by Louis Blanc – and suggested that "competition as between workers" should be abolished at least as far as workers employed in nationalised industries were concerned. "In so far as private factory owners were allowed to survive they would have to pay the higher wages earned by workers in nationalised enterprises." Engels took over from Fourier the idea that large buildings should be constructed "on state farms as common dwelling houses for groups of citizens who would be engaged both in agriculture and in industry". "In this way the advantages of town life and country life could be united without having to put up with the drawbacks of either." Other reforms would be the demolition of slums, the introduction of free education, and granting of "full rights of inheritance to illegitimate children".

The revolution leading to the establishment of a communist society would, in Engels's view, not be confined to a single country. "Modern society had already created a world market. All countries in the world – certainly the civilised ones – are so closely linked together that every country is influenced by what happens elsewhere." The more industrialised a country had become the more quickly would it be able to adopt the communist system. "In Germany the revolution will take place more slowly and will be achieved with the greatest difficulty, while in England it will take place most rapidly and with the greatest ease."

Engels proceeded to describe the main features of a communist society. There would be no rivalry between classes since classes would disappear and there would be no rivalry between town and country since "farming and industrial work should be carried out by the same people and not by two different classes". Women would no longer be dependent upon their husbands while children would no longer be dependent upon their parents. In a communist state the responsibility for bringing up children would rest with society as a whole. The means of production and distribution would be owned, controlled and planned by the state. The expansion of the output of goods and services would no longer lead to slumps but would raise living standards for everybody. Engels admitted that the advantages of communism would be fully realised only if the behaviour and habits of human beings could be changed. "Just as the peasants and craftsmen of the eighteenth century had to alter their way of life and actually became quite different people when they were swallowed up by modern industry so the new method of production and the new society will require the services of a new type of human being and will, in fact, be responsible for creating such a type." In a communist society excessive specialisation on the part of the worker would give way to a new organisation of industrial production. "Education in the future will enable young people to appreciate the whole process of production and will give them the training necessary to exercise one skill after another according to the varying needs of society and their own inclinations."

Finally Engels discussed the differences between communism and socialism. He considered that there were three main groups of socialists. The first he described as members of the old feudal and patriarchal classes who wished to restore an obsolete way of life that was being destroyed by modern society. Their efforts to restore the powers of the nobles and the gilds were doomed to failure. The second group consisted of socialists who recognised the evils of modern industrial societies and supported various reforms designed to remove those evils. Engels dismissed these reformers as "middle class socialists" because they accepted the basic principles upon which capitalist society was organised. The third group of socialists were democrats – craftsmen, shopkeepers, tradesmen, and some factory workers – who supported some of the radical changes advocated by the communists. "But they advocate these changes not as a means of establishing a communist society but simply as measures which they regard as adequate to cope with the evils that exist in modern society." "It is clear that communists must be prepared to enter into discussions with these socialists so as to try to remove differences that may divide them." In England, France and Belgium where the middle classes were already in power the communists should co-operate with left-wing democratic parties such as the Chartists. But in Germany where "the decisive struggle between the bourgeoisie and the absolute monarchy has only just begun" the communists would have to adopt a different policy. Here they should help the liberal middle classes to overthrow the reactionary German governments as soon as possible.[159] And once the bourgeoisie have seized power "the communists can then turn them out again". In other words the decisive struggle between the communists and the bourgeoisie in Germany would have to be postponed until after the bourgeoisie had overthrown the feudal reactionaries.

The "Principles of Communism" was one of the most important

documents ever penned by Engels since it was the draft declaration of policy upon which both the deliberations of the second conference of the Communist League and the Communist Manifesto were based. A striking feature of Engels's catechism of November 1847 was that virtually everything in it had previously appeared in Engels's earlier writings. Indeed the discussion of such matters as the origins of the industrial revolution, the causes and consequences of the trade cycle, the clash of interests between the factory workers and their employers echoed views that Engels had already expressed in his "Critique of Political Economy" and in *The Condition of the Working Class in England*. And these ideas had been formulated before Engels had begun to collaborate with Karl Marx. Only the last section of the catechism on the differences between communism and various types of socialism had been influenced by his work with Karl Marx on *The German Ideology*. The "Principles of Communism" is also significant because it contained a clear statement concerning Engels's view on the vexed question as to whether a revolution would be necessary to secure the transfer of political and economic power from the middle classes to the workers. For this Engels attempted to lay the blame upon the bourgeoisie. He claimed that the communists did not want a revolution provided that they could get what they wanted without one. But he was confident that the capitalists would not surrender their property without a fight so that force would inevitably be needed to establish the communist system. Engels also believed that communism could not be established in one country only. He saw no possibility of peaceful co-existence between communist and capitalist societies. He considered that communism must eventually be established in all countries in the world. Marx and Engels wrote a great deal about the evils of the capitalist system and the way in which its destruction could be achieved. They were not so ready to discuss the new society that would arise from the ashes of capitalism. In the "Principles of Communism", however, Engels did attempt to indicate at any rate some aspects of the classless communist utopia which he hoped to see established in his own lifetime. And he admitted that in a communist society human nature would have to be changed. The ultimate success of a communist economy and a communist society lay in the hands of the communist schoolmaster of the future.

Engels met Karl Marx – and Victor Tedesco – in Ostend on November 27, 1847. They travelled to London on November 28 and on the following day they attended a meeting organised by the Fraternal Democrats to celebrate the seventeenth anniversary of the Polish insurrection of 1830.[160] Here Marx and Engels met leading left-wing Chartists such as Julian Harney and Ernest Jones as well as the young Swiss radical J. L. Schabelitz, the editor of the *Deutsche-Londoner Zeitung*. Marx and Engels both addressed the meeting. Marx, who represented the Brussels Democratic Association, asserted that Poland's only hope of freedom lay in the collapse of the reactionary autocratic governments of Europe. "Poland will not be liberated in Poland, but in England. You Chartists, therefore, do not have to offer pious wishes about the liberation of nations. Strike out at your enemies at home, and you will then have the proud knowledge that you have fought against all the old societies."[161] It was at this meeting that Schapper referred to Karl Marx as "the nightmare of the middle class in Germany".[162]

The fact that Marx suggested to the Fraternal Democrats that an international conference of democrats should be held in September 1848 – a proposal which the delegates accepted – shows that he was not relying entirely upon the Communist League as a vehicle for his political ambitions. If Marx and Engels failed to convert the League to their programme they could still hope to capture the Fraternal Democrats.

On the day after the meeting of the Fraternal Democrats on the premises of the German Workers Education Society the second conference of the Communist League opened in the same hall. In his old age the German tailor Friedrich Lessner recalled the impression that Marx and Engels had made upon him when he saw them for the first time at the conference in December 1847. "Marx was then still a young man, about 28 years old, but he greatly impressed us all. He was of medium height, broad-shouldered, powerful in build, and energetic in his deportment. His brow was high and finely shaped, his hair thick and pitch black, his gaze piercing. His mouth already had the sarcastic line that his opponents feared so much. Marx was a born leader of the people. His speech was brief, convincing, and compelling in its logic. He never said a superfluous word; every sentence was a thought and every thought a necessary link in his chain of demonstration."[163] "Engels was different from Marx in outward appearance. He was tall and slim, his movements were quick and vigorous, his manner of speaking brief and decisive, his carriage erect, giving a soldierly touch. He was of a very lively nature; his wit was to the point. Everybody associated with him inevitably got the impression that he was dealing with a man of great intelligence."[164]

Few details of the proceedings of the second conference of the Communist League have survived. Schapper presided over the deliberations while Engels acted as secretary. On December 8,

1847 both signed the new statutes of the League which had been drawn up at the first conference in the previous June and were now ratified. Many years later Engels wrote that the second conference lasted for at least ten days[165] and that Marx expounded his doctrines at some length. "At last all doubts were removed and all opposition was overcome. The new principles were unanimously accepted and Marx and I were entrusted with the task of drawing up the manifesto."[166] When Engels referred to the "new principles" he meant the doctrines enunciated in his own draft manifesto. One topic discussed by Engels in his "Principles of Communism" – the causes and results of the trade cycle – was elaborated by him in a lecture to the German Workers Education Association.[167] Lessner later remarked that the German workers in London were well satisfied with the conference. "Much was expected from this meeting and hopes were not frustrated but on the contrary, greatly exceeded."[168]

The second conference of the Communist League ended on about December 10, 1847. Marx and Engels returned to Brussels taking with them certain documents for use in the preparation of the manifesto which they had promised to write. The actual composition of this statement of communist doctrine was left to Marx. But instead of writing the manifesto he spent a good deal of his time in spreading his revolutionary doctrines among the workers in Brussels. He lectured to them on wages and capital[169] and also upon Free Trade. Marx had not completed the manifesto when Engels left for Paris early in 1848. Probably a date had been set by the Communist League for the delivery of the manuscript and Marx failed to meet the deadline. On January 26 the central executive committee of the League sent the following peremptory message to the Brussels branch: "The Central Committee hereby orders the local committee in Brussels to inform C. Marx that if the manifesto of the Communist Party, which he agreed to draw up at the last Congress, does not arrive in London before Tuesday, February 1 further measures will be taken against him. In the event that C. Marx does not write the manifesto, the Central Committee requests the immediate return of the documents turned over to him by the Congress. In the name of the Central Committee and by its orders – Schapper, Bauer, Moll."[170] The communist workers in London were clearly becoming impatient and they indicated their displeasure in no uncertain fashion.

Marx completed the manifesto early in 1848. In London Lessner delivered the manuscript to the printer[171] and later collected the proofs for Schapper to correct. *The Manifesto of the Communist Party* was published in February 1848 as a pamphlet and it also appeared in the columns of the *Deutsche-Londoner Zeitung*.[172] It was a brilliantly written tract – a clarion call to workers everywhere to overthrow their oppressors and to found a classless society in which private property would be transferred to the ownership of the state.[173] The first edition had only a limited circulation and does not appear to have been on sale in bookshops. Marx stated that six translations into foreign languages would be issued. In a letter of April 25, 1848 Engels told Marx that he was translating the manifesto into English – half of it was already finished – and that Dr Ewerbeck had arranged for translations to be made into Italian and Spanish.[174] In fact only a Swedish translation appeared in 1848. Consequently the manifesto was then known only to members of the Communist League who could read German and it had little influence upon events on the Continent in 1848. Marx's assertion that Europe was haunted by the spectre of communism – "let the ruling classes tremble at a communist revolution" – was mere wishful thinking. But in later years Marx's dreams became a reality and his manifesto, translated into many languages,[175] came to be accepted by tens of thousands of Marx's followers as the only authentic declaration of the communist faith.

It has been observed that the manifesto contained "nearly all the elements which were to make Marxism the last and most contemporary of the great religions. It provided both a system of historical development and a programme for political action. It demonstrated that capitalism would inevitably be overthrown by socialism and laid down, rather less clearly, how the proletariat could bring this overthrow about."[176] A few years after it first appeared Marx claimed that in three important respects the manifesto had contained original ideas. He declared: "Long before me, bourgeois historians had described the historical development of the class struggle in modern society, and bourgeois economists the anatomy of classes. What I did that was new was to prove (1) that the existence of classes is only bound up with *particular, historic phases in the development of production*; (2) that the class struggle necessarily leads *to the dictatorship of the proletariat*; (3) that this dictatorship itself only constitutes the transition to the *abolition of all classes* and to *classless* society."[177]

Although Marx and Engels were jointly responsible for the manifesto, Engels insisted that Marx alone was the original thinker who should have the sole credit for working out the fundamental doctrine which lay at the heart of the new communist creed. In his preface to the English edition of 1888 Engels wrote: "The Manifesto being our joint production, I consider myself bound to state that the fundamental proposition, which forms its nucleus, belongs to Marx. That proposition is: that in every historical epoch, the prevailing mode of economic production and exchange, and the social organisation necessarily following from it, form the basis upon which is built up, and from which alone can be explained, the political and intellectual history of mankind (since the dissolution of primitive tribal society, holding land in common ownership) has been a history of class struggles, contests between exploiting and exploited, ruling and oppressed classes; that the history of these class struggles forms a series of evolutions in which, nowadays, a stage has reached where the exploited and oppressed class – the proletariat – cannot attain its emancipation from the sway of the exploiting and ruling class – the bourgeoisie – without, at the same time and once and for all, emancipating society at large from all exploitation, oppression, class distinctions and class struggles." Engels added that, in his view, Marx's doctrine "is destined to do for history what Darwin's theory has done for biology".[178]

Engels was too modest. Marx was indeed the philosopher whose doctrines permeated the manifesto but it is also true that the development of Marx's ideology owed much to the collaboration of Marx and Engels between 1845 and 1847. It was Engels who encouraged Marx to turn his attention to the significance of economic changes as factors in the development of society. It was Engels who described the condition of the workers in England and emphasised the role of the class struggle in the most highly industrialised country in the world. It was Engels's economics and Marx's philosophy which together laid the foundations of the new Marxian form of socialism. And it was Engels's "Principles of Communism" which provided Marx with a framework around which he was able to construct his manifesto. The differences between Engels's draft of the manifesto and Marx's final version were differences of emphasis, style and presentation rather than differences of ideas or aims.

While Engels's catechism had begun with a description of the rise of the industrial working class Marx opened his manifesto with a wider discussion of the origin and development of capitalists and the proletariat and the conflict between them. Engels had emphasised the economic factors which fostered the industrial revolution and the creation of the working class but for Marx these changes were significant because they lay at the root of the clash between two new classes in society – the proletariat and the bourgeoisie. Marx argued that "the history of all hitherto existing society is the history of class struggles." In the ancient world the freemen had oppressed the slaves; in the middle ages the feudal lords had oppressed the serfs and the master craftsmen had exploited their journeymen and apprentices; and in the nineteenth century the middle class capitalists – the bourgeoisie – were oppressing the new industrial proletariat. The clash between oppressors and oppressed had in the past always led to the overthrow of one ruling class and the ascendancy of another. In the age of the industrial revolution the middle classes had overthrown the feudal lords and now dominated the economy and wielded effective political power. Marx acknowledged that the middle classes had been responsible for great economic advances. "The bourgeoisie, during its rule of scarce one hundred years, has created more massive and more colossal productive forces than have all preceding generations together. Subjection of Nature's forces to man, machinery, application of chemistry to industry and agriculture, steam navigation, railways, electric telegraphs, clearing of whole continents for cultivation, canalisation of rivers, whole populations conjured out of the ground. What earlier century had even a presentiment that such productive forces slumbered in the lap of social labour?"

Marx argued that the prosperity and power of the middle classes rested upon foundations of quicksands and were ready to collapse at any time. It was clear that either the workers would soon revolt and overthrow their oppressors or that a great slump would cause the capitalist system to collapse like a pack of cards. The wealth of the bourgeoisie had been amassed at the expense of the workers. "In proportion as the bourgeoisie, i.e. capital, is developed in the same proportion is the proletariat, the modern working class, developed – a class of labourers, who live only so long as they find work, and who find work only so long as their labour increases capital. These labourers, who must sell themselves piecemeal, are a commodity, like every other article of commerce, and are consequently exposed to all the vicissitudes of competition, to all the fluctuations of the market."

When he discussed the depressed condition of the workers Marx virtually repeated what Engels had already written in his catechism. He considered that "the cost of production of a workman is restricted, almost entirely, to the means of subsistence that he requires for his maintenance and for the propagation of his race." And as the machinery in the factories became more efficient so the position of the workers became more precarious. They might be replaced by cheap female labour and if they kept their jobs they might have to accept wage reductions. The proletariat was rapidly increasing in numbers and had become "concentrated in great masses". Consequently "its strength grows and it feels that strength more". The proletariat had become "a really revolutionary class" and was only waiting for the opportunity to overthrow the capitalists. In the past class rivalries had been "movements of minorities or in the interest of minorities" but now the workers were the immense majority of society and their triumph over their oppressors was assured.

Marx, like Engels, believed that capitalism carried within it the seeds of its own decay. He argued that modern bourgeois society "is like the sorcerer who is no longer able to control the powers of the nether regions whom he has called up by his spells". Recurrent slumps threatened its very existence. "In these crises a great part not only of the existing products, but also of the previously created productive forces, are periodically destroyed. In these crises there breaks out an epidemic that, in all earlier epochs, would have seemed an absurdity – the epidemic of overproduction." "The productive forces at the disposal of society no longer tend to further the development of the conditions of bourgeois prosperity; on the contrary, they have become too powerful for these conditions by which they are fettered, and so soon as they overcome these fetters, they bring disorder into the whole of bourgeois society, [and they] endanger the existence of bourgeois property." Indeed the bourgeoisie had "forged the weapons that bring death to itself." The proletariat alone – the only really revolutionary class in society – would bring about the fall of the middle classes. "The other classes decay and finally disappear in the face of modern industry; the proletariat is its special and essential product."

Having examined the rise of the modern industrial proletariat and its *rôle* in the forthcoming revolution Marx discussed the relations between the communists and the workers. He claimed that whereas other working class parties represented the interests of the proletariat in particular countries, the communists – "the most advanced and resolute section of the working class parties of every country" – were the representatives of a truly international movement. Moreover, the communists had a great advantage over the vast mass of the proletariat because they clearly understood "the line of march, the conditions, and the ultimate general results of the proletarian movement". Engels, in his catechism, had observed that "the abolition of private property is now not only possible but absolutely necessary". Marx, for his part, declared that the main object of the communists was to secure the "abolition of private property". He qualified this statement by explaining that what he meant by private property was "not the abolition of property generally, but the abolition of bourgeois property". Only about a tenth of the population – the middle classes – owned property and it was their property that Marx proposed to expropriate.

Marx observed that various objections had been raised by middle class critics to the establishment of a communist society. It was said that communism would lead to universal idleness, to the end of family life, to the disappearance of individual liberty, and to the loss of national identity. Marx brushed these criticisms aside; they were misinformed or irrelevant. They could be dismissed as the hostile reaction of capitalists faced with the prospect of losing their ill-gotten gains. But the vast majority of the people – the workers – had everything to gain and nothing to lose from the establishment of a communist society.

Looking to the future Marx declared that when the communists secured power "the proletariat will use its political supremacy to wrest, by degrees, all capital from the bourgeoisie, to centralise all instruments of production in the hands of the state, i.e. of the proletariat organised as the ruling class; and to increase the total of productive forces as rapidly as possible."

As an interim measure – in the period of transition between capitalism and communism – Marx demanded the introduction of the following reforms "in the most advanced countries":

"1. Abolition of property in land and application of all rents of land to public purposes.
2. A heavy progressive and graduated income tax.
3. Abolition of all rights of inheritance.
4. Confiscation of the property of all emigrants and rebels.
5. Centralisation of credit in the hands of the state, by means of a national bank with state capital and an exclusive monopoly.
6. Centralisation of the means of communication and transport in the hands of the state.
7. Extension of factories and instruments of production owned by the state; the bringing into cultivation of waste lands, and the improvement of the soil generally in accordance with a common plan.
8. Equal liability of all to labour. Establishment of industrial armies, especially for agriculture.
9. Combination of agriculture with manufacturing industries; gradual abolition of the distinction between town and country by a more equable distribution of the population over the country.
10. Free education of all children in public schools. Abolition of children's factory labour in its present form. Combination of education with industrial production etc."

This programme of immediate reforms was similar to the one proposed by Engels in his "Principles of Communism" except that Marx declined to make any concessions to the followers of Louis Blanc or Fourier. Marx summed up his view of the communist society of the future by declaring that "in place of the old bourgeois society, with its classes and class antagonisms, we shall have an association, in which the free development of each is the condition for the free development of all".

Marx's manifesto, like Engels's catechism, ended with a section criticising the various socialist groups which existed in 1848. Here Marx was on familiar ground and he summarised the attacks which he had already made upon Max Stirner, Bruno Bauer, Weitling, Kriege, Proudhon and others. He dealt in turn with three forms of socialism which he called, "reactionary", "conservative" and "utopian". Reactionary socialism, in his view, included "feudal socialism", "petty bourgeois socialism" and "true socialism". Feudal socialism represented an attempt of the landed aristocracy in England (Young England) and in France to secure support from the workers in their rear-guard action against the middle classes. Petty bourgeois socialism (as preached by Sismondi in France) supported the interests of the rural and urban craftsmen who were being driven out of business by the new factories with their power-driven machines. "True socialism" was the product of German writers who tried to combine French socialist ideas with German idealist philosophy. All these forms of feudal socialism were dismissed by Marx as "reactionary" because they aimed at restoring a way of life that had long been undermined by the growth of modern industry and was doomed to extinction. And they were reactionary because they were supported by reactionary groups and absolute governments who were not really interested in promoting socialism but merely borrowed the arguments of socialists in order to attack their middle class enemies.

"Conservative socialism", according to Marx, was a form of socialism advocated by middle class philanthropists and humanitarians who recognised the urgent need to remedy the social evils brought about by industrialisation. Proudhon's *Philosophie de la Misère* was a typical example of "conservative socialism". Marx criticised the type of socialism advocated by Proudhon because it expected the workers to "remain within the bounds of existing society, but should cast away all its hateful ideas concerning the bourgeoisie". Finally Marx discussed the views of utopian socialists such as Robert Owen and Charles Fourier. He praised their ruthless criticism of "every principle of existing society" and he agreed with many reforms that they had suggested – "such as the abolition of the distinction between town and country, of the family, of the carrying on of industries for the account of private individuals,

Stephan Born, 1824–1898

Godfrey Ermen, partner of Friedrich Engels, 1864–1869

Carl Schorlemmer, 1834–1892

Louis Borchardt, 1813–1883

and of the wage system . . .". But Marx had no sympathy with the attempts of these socialists to break away from the world – to contract out of existing society – and to found new isolated utopian societies of their own, such as Robert Owen's communist colonies (New Harmony), Fourier's *phalanstères* or Cabet's *Icaria*.

The Communist Manifesto concluded with a declaration that the "communists everywhere support every revolutionary movement against the existing social and political order of things". "They openly declare that their ends can be attained only by the forcible overthrow of all existing social conditions." Communists everywhere pledged themselves to demand the expropriation of private property and to seek co-operation with other left-wing political parties. "Let the ruling classes tremble at a communist revolution. The proletarians have nothing to lose but their chains. They have a world to win. Workers of the world, unite!"

The assessment of Marx and Engels of the political situation in 1848 and their forecasts of future developments were soon proved by events to be erroneous. They were unduly optimistic when they imagined that successful revolutions would quickly overthrow the reactionary régimes in Europe and replace them by democratic – or even by socialist – administrations. They failed to appreciate the strength of their opponents or the possibility of alliances between the aristocracy and the middle classes to crush the revolutionaries. If Marx and Engels had been right the revolution would have broken out first in England and Belgium because they were the most industrialised countries in Europe. But it was just in those countries that the social structure was the most stable while the rulers of the industrially underdeveloped Habsburg dominions were eventually saved only by Russian intervention. The Chartist demonstration in London was a fiasco and not a prelude to the fall of capitalism in England. The workers in Brussels – to whom Marx made a contribution towards their purchase of arms – proved to be singularly ineffective revolutionaries. In France the republicans and the socialists co-operated to topple the July Monarchy in February 1848 but their shortlived triumph ended in the following June when a rising of the Paris workers was put down with heavy loss of life by General Cavaignac. And Engels was soon to learn, by personal experience in Elberfeld and Baden, that Germany was not yet ready for a successful revolution of the proletariat.

IV. Revolution and Reaction, 1848–9

The climax of Engels's career as an active revolutionary came in 1848 and 1849 when, as a colleague of Marx on the editorial staff of the *Neue Rheinische Zeitung*, he was a leading radical journalist in a significant period of German history. In later years he looked back with satisfaction on the part that he had played in helping Marx to run an influential newspaper which expounded communist doctrines to a wide circle of readers. But these were also years of frustration. Nowhere – not in England, France, Belgium or Germany – did the workers behave as they should have behaved if Marx's theories on the fall of capitalism were correct. In England the Chartist movement collapsed after the abortive demonstration on Kennington Common; in Belgium the workers failed to rise in revolt; in France the rising of the Paris workers in June 1848 was ruthlessly suppressed by Cavaignac; while in Germany the workers failed to follow the advice so liberally offered by Marx and Engels in the columns of the *Neue Rheinische Zeitung*. Moreover, Engels's conduct in 1848 was not always that of a leader who inspires his followers. His flight from Germany to France in the autumn of 1848, when he was threatened with arrest, suggests that his nerve failed him at a critical moment. And in May 1849 when he appeared in Elberfeld to take part in a rising against the government he allowed himself to be somewhat unceremoniously ejected from the town within a few days. But he redeemed his reputation in the Baden rising in 1849 when – as Willich's adjutant – he bore himself well in several engagements. But the insurgents were soon put down by Prussian troops and Engels was fortunate to find refuge in Switzerland. The triumph of their enemies dashed the hopes of Marx and Engels that a successful revolution would sweep the reactionary rulers of Europe into well deserved oblivion. When new authoritarian régimes were established in France, Prussia and Austria, Marx and Engels had to admit that their plans had failed. Had Engels tried to return home he would have had to face a court martial since he had fought against the Prussians in Baden although he had once served in the Prussian army. So he fled to England which now became his permanent home. The days of cloak and dagger intrigues and open rebellion against bourgeois authority were over. Engels, back at his office stool in Manchester, sheathed his sword and turned to his pen to further the cause of communism.

The long-awaited revolution in France, which Marx and Engels hoped would herald the downfall of reactionary rulers all over Europe, broke out on February 23, 1848. Louis Philippe abdicated on the following day, fleeing to England disguised as 'Mr Smith' and a republic was proclaimed. Engels had been expelled from France three weeks previously and had gone to Brussels where Marx was putting the finishing touches to the Communist Manifesto.

He resumed his political activities through the local branch of the Communist League, the Democratic Association, and the *Deutsch-Brüsseler Zeitung*. On February 22 the Democratic Association celebrated the second anniversary of the Cracow rising of 1846 and Engels made a speech strongly supporting the cause of Polish independence. He declared that Germans and Poles were both equally interested in overthrowing the autocratic rulers of Prussia, Austria and Russia. Only their defeat would secure independence for Poland and freedom for Germany.[179]

Two days later – on February 24 – the trains from France failed to arrive in Brussels. Stephan Born and some of his friends waited hopefully at the main railway station for the latest news from Paris. At last a train from France arrived and the guard jumped out and exclaimed: "La république est proclamée!"[180] If Engels hoped that the establishment of a republic in France would soon be followed by a revolution in Belgium he was doomed to disappointment. Leopold I was a more adroit politician than his father-in-law and he had little difficulty in keeping his throne. Many years later – in a sketch of the life of his friend Wilhelm Wolff – Engels recalled what had happened in Brussels in February and March 1848. He wrote:

> "When the revolution broke out in February there was an immediate echo in Brussels. Crowds of people gathered every evening in the large market square in front of the Town Hall which was occupied by the police and the civil guard. The numerous bars and cafés were always packed. As the crowds grew larger there was much pushing and jostling to the strains of the Marseillaise and the chanting of 'Long live the republic'. In the capital the government was as quiet as a tiny mouse but in the provinces troops were recalled from leave and the reservists were summoned to the colours. The government privately informed M. Jottrand, the most respected of the Belgian republicans, that the king was prepared to abdicate if his people so desired. And Jottrand was assured that he could at any time secure confirmation of this offer from Leopold himself. The king told Jottrand that he was republican at heart and would never stand in the way of his people if they wished to set up a republic. All he asked was that his abdication should take place in an orderly fashion without bloodshed and that he should receive an adequate pension. The king's views were quickly made known to the Belgian people with the result that no armed rising was attempted. But the reserves were soon available and most of the troops were concentrated around Brussels. This could be done in three or four days in so small a country as Belgium. Now there was no more talk of abdication. Suddenly one evening the police attacked the crowd in the market place of Brussels with the flats of their

sword blades. People were flung into prison right and left. Wilhelm Wolff, while quietly making his way to his lodgings, was one of the first to be mishandled and cast into prison. Later he was again assaulted by angry drunken militiamen and after being locked up for several days he was packed off to France."[181]

Marx complained that Wilhelm Wolff had been treated in a disgraceful fashion by the police who "tore off his spectacles, spat in his face, kicked him, and cursed him".[182]

Wilhelm Wolff's arrest was the first indication that the Belgian government had decided to rid the country of the foreign – particularly the German – exiles who had turned Brussels into a notorious centre of revolutionary activity. On the outbreak of the revolution in France the central executive committee of the Communist League transferred its authority to its Brussels branch so that Marx and Engels were at last able to take over control of the League from Schapper and his colleagues. The Belgian authorities may not have known that on March 3 the new central executive committee had decided on a second move – this time to the safe haven of republican Paris. And while this was being done Karl Marx was authorised to exercise the powers invested in the committee.[183] But the Belgian authorities did know that Marx had broken his undertaking to refrain from political activities and that he had – as Jenny Marx later admitted – "willingly provided money" to the workers to pay for daggers and revolvers to be used in a rising in Brussels.[184]

On March 4 – on the day after the crucial meeting of the central executive committee of the Communist League in Brussels – Marx and his wife were arrested and, after being held briefly in custody, were given twenty-four hours to leave the country. Their departure was so sudden that Jenny Marx had to leave her silver plate and best linen behind. They went to Paris where Flocon, now a member of the republican government, had cancelled the expulsion order made against Marx in 1845. Marx's disciples in Brussels were soon dispersed. Weerth went to Paris from Rotterdam as soon as he heard that Louis Philippe had fallen, though he returned to Brussels for a time in March. It has been seen that Wilhelm Wolff was quickly expelled from Belgium. Tedesco – who had accompanied Marx to London in the previous November – was arrested.[185] Bornstedt fled to Paris and his *Deutsch-Brüsseler Zeitung* came to an end with a number which hailed the establishment of the second French Republic as the dawn of a new era.

Only Engels was left undisturbed. Shortage of funds kept him in Brussels for a few weeks. He believed that the authorities did not molest him because they had previously issued him with a passport.[186] In a letter of March 8–9, 1848 Engels told Marx that the

Democratic Association had protested against both his expulsion from Belgium and the rough handling that he and his wife had received at the hands of the police. Engels declared that "the petty bourgeoisie here are furious at what has happened". "The affair has really caused a stir and has contributed in no small measure to reducing anti-German feelings in Brussels." He had heard that the police commissioner responsible for Marx's arrest had been dismissed.

Engels wrote that all was quiet in Brussels. "The carnival was celebrated as usual yesterday evening and now hardly anyone even mentions the existence of the republic in France." This was a disappointment to Engels since – if Marx's theories were correct – so highly industrialised a country as Belgium should have been in the vanguard of the revolutionary movement. The contempt felt by Marx's friends for the Belgians who not only failed to set up a republic but actually locked Louis Blanc up when he fled from France was expressed by Georg Weerth in an article in the *Neue Rheinische Zeitung*.[187]

Engels was also disappointed by the turn of events in Cologne where popular disturbances had been quickly suppressed. But news from other parts of Germany was more hopeful, Engels was confident that a successful rising was certain in Prussia "if only the king holds firmly to his traditional feudal ideas". "But the devil only knows what mischief that insane and cunning rascal will be up to next."[188] A few days later Marx advised Engels to come to Paris.[189] Engels replied that he was still short of money.[190] On March 25 Engels informed the police that he was leaving Brussels and by the end of the month he had joined Marx in Paris. Two days later Georg Weerth wrote to his mother that all his friends had left Brussels.[191]

Most of the communist leaders had now assembled in Paris and the central executive committee of the Communist League had been reconstituted with Marx as president and Schapper as secretary. (At the recent conference in London Schapper had been president and Engels had been secretary.) The other members of the committee were Wallau, Wilhelm Wolff, Heinrich Bauer, Joseph Moll and Engels. They were in touch with Julian Harney and Ernest Jones who were in Paris in March 1848. Confident that the revolution would soon spread across the Rhine the committee – calling itself the "committee of the Communist Party of Germany"[192] – issued a political programme of seventeen points.

The main communist demands were that Germany should be united; that the monarchs should be dethroned; that a republic should be established; that manhood suffrage should be introduced and that feudal dues and services should be swept away. The state should nationalise royal and noble estates and mines as well as farm mortgages, ground rents, banks and transport. Rights of inheritance should be restricted; indirect taxes should be replaced by progressive direct taxes; and national workshops should be established. "The State guarantees full employment and takes responsibility for the welfare of workers who are unable to earn a living." Education should be universal and free, while Church and State should be separated. A number of these demands had already been made in the "Principles of Communism" and in the Communist Manifesto.[193] This programme showed that the communists were not prepared to co-operate with the middle class parties in the forthcoming revolution. The liberals would obviously be unwilling to have anything to do with a party which proposed to embark upon far-reaching schemes for nationalising private property on a large scale.

The seventeen-point programme, like the Communist Manifesto, had appealed to the workers of the world to unite but there were no signs that the German workers in Paris were prepared to unite. Even before Engels arrived in Paris, Marx had denounced Bornstedt and Herwegh as a couple of rogues who had had the effrontery to set up a rival party "*contre nous*". Bornstedt – suspected of spying for the Prussian authorities – was expelled from the Communist League.[194] Herwegh and his friends tried to persuade the German artisans in Paris – many of whom were now unemployed – to join a legion to fight for a republic in Germany. Lamartine, the French Foreign Minister, welcomed the scheme since – as Herwegh himself appreciated – "it promised to rid France of many thousand foreign artisans who were competing with French workmen for jobs".[195] Marx and Engels realised that the plan was doomed to failure and that Lamartine would betray the legion to the Prussian government. They appealed to the workers to return to Germany peaceably as individuals and not as members of an armed legion. They succeeded in persuading Flocon to give German workers who followed their advice the same assistance – free accommodation on their journey and a subsistence allowance of 50 centimes a day – as they would have received as members of the legion. "In this way", wrote Engels, "we organised the return to Germany of three or four hundred workers, including most of the members of the Communist League."[196]

In March 1848 the long awaited revolutions broke out in Germany and Austria. In the southern states – Bavaria, Württemberg and Baden – democratic reforms, such as the establishment of a representative parliament, a free press and a jury system were introduced but Hecker's attempt to set up a republic in Baden collapsed after the battle of Kandern. In Hesse-Darmstadt the Grand Duke abdicated and Heinrich von Gagern became head of a liberal ministry. In Hesse-Cassel the Elector was faced with a revolutionary movement and made many concessions – such as religious equality for Catholics and Protestants – to save his throne. In Saxony, too, the liberals – led by Ludwig Freiherr von der Pfordten – gained control of the administration and introduced various reforms. On March 18 there was a popular rising in Berlin. After indecisive street fighting Frederick William IV withdrew his troops and agreed that a citizens' militia should be set up to maintain order. By the end of March a liberal ministry under Ludolf Camphausen and David Hansemann was in office and shortly afterwards a Prussian national assembly was convened. Meanwhile in Austria a rising in Vienna had forced Metternich to resign. Thus within a few weeks progressive ministries had been installed in many German states and numerous democratic reforms had been introduced. At the same time the movement in favour of German unification was rapidly gaining momentum.

Marx and Engels believed that the revolution in Germany was following the course that they had predicted. Although the autocratic rulers had not been dethroned the middle classes seemed to have political power within their grasp. The next phase of the revolution – according to Marx – would be a rising of the masses. On March 16, two days before the rising in Berlin, General Joseph von Radowitz warned Frederick William IV that the socialist movement in Germany might develop into "a rising of the proletariat to secure the organisation of labour and the guarantee of full employment."[197] But at the very moment when the danger to the established order seemed greatest the Communist League disintegrated. Marx and Engels had worked hard to gain control over the League and just when they had succeeded it ceased to be of any value in their hands.

Engels later explained why this had happened. "Three quarters of the supporters of the League, who had been living in exile abroad, returned home so that most of the branches to which they had belonged lost most of their members and lost contact with the central executive committee. On reaching Germany some of the most ambitious members failed to resume contact with the League's central committee and to establish – each in his own locality – a little separatist movement of his own. Since conditions varied enormously in every petty German state, in every province, and in every town it would have been impossible for the central committee to have given members advice which would have been universally applicable. Advice to members could best be given through the press."[198] Marx could have had no illusions concerning the collapse of the League in the spring of 1848 in view of the information that he received from Wilhelm Wolff, Ernst Dronke and Stephan Born.[199]

Wilhelm Wolff, writing on April 18, drew a gloomy picture of the state of the League's branches in Cologne and Berlin.[200] He reported that the Cologne branch was "vegetating". In Berlin he saw Hätzel[201] – a notorious conspirator well known to the police – who admitted that the local branch of the League now consisted of only twenty members. Wolff asked Hätzel to call his supporters together so that he could address them "but this proved to be impracticable since at that time the Berlin workers were attending many public meetings and were debating the appointment of delegates to form deputations". Hätzel promised Wilhelm Wolff that he would revive the Berlin branch of the League but this proved to be an impossible task. Subsequently in a statement to the police Hätzel declared that "circumstances were not favourable in 1848 for the establishment of an association – or even for organising a meeting – of the workers who supported the communist cause". He added that "the will to act was lacking".[202] From Berlin Wilhelm Wolff went to his native province of Silesia. In Breslau – where he had once been the leader of a group of radical university students – he found that there was bitter enmity between the middle classes and the workers. He could find no trace of any communist movement. He tried to remedy the situation by intensive propaganda among the workers and was rewarded by being elected a "reserve deputy" to the Frankfurt National Assembly.[203]

Stephan Born, writing on May 11, 1848 told Marx that the Berlin branch of the League no longer existed. "No one has had time to revive the defunct organisation." But he thought that the workers in Berlin were thoroughly imbued with revolutionary ideas. Born claimed that he was "more or less the acknowledged leader of the working class movement" in Berlin. "I am the chairman of a sort of workers' parliament which consists of delegates from many factories and workshops."[204] What Born did not tell Marx was that since arriving in Berlin he had begun to doubt the value of communism as a doctrine which would inspire the workers. Many years later Born declared in his memoirs that communism offered no solution to the situation as he found it in Berlin in 1848.[205] But Born kept in touch with Marx and Engels – he was cordially received by them in Cologne early in 1849 – and there was no open breach between them at this time.

Ernst Dronke, a recent young recruit to the Communist League,[206] sent a report to the central committee on May 5, 1848. He explained that, as he was short of money, he had been able to visit only Frankfurt am Main, Coblenz and Mainz. In Frankfurt only two recruits had been secured for the League and this was hardly surprising since in that city "one almost runs the risk of being stoned if one admits to being a communist". In Coblenz Dronke had recruited only four new members while in Mainz he found that the local branch of the League was "in a state of utter anarchy". He hoped that Wallau might be persuaded to leave Wiesbaden for Mainz and revive the flagging fortunes of the branch. And a few days earlier Georg Weerth, writing to Marx from Cologne, used almost the same words as Dronke when describing the fear inspired by communist doctrines. In Cologne, he wrote, "the very word 'communism' inspires terror and anyone who openly declares that he is a communist would be stoned."[207]

Although the Communist League had virtually ceased to exist as a political force and its manifesto and seventeen demands made little impact upon events in 1848 Marx and his disciples were in the forefront of the revolutionary movement in Germany. Marx himself was editor in chief of the *Neue Rheinische Zeitung*; Engels and Wilhelm Wolff were his closest collaborators on this paper; Wilhelm Wolff actively supported the revolutionary cause in Breslau and Cologne; Schapper and Moll were engaged in propaganda among the workers in Cologne; Stephan Born organised the workers in Berlin, edited a newspaper there, and fought on the barricades in Dresden; Engels, Willich and Moll took part in the Baden insurrection in which Moll fell at the engagement on the River Murg.

It was not until the middle of April 1848 that Marx and Engels were ready to leave Paris for Germany. Since the Communist League was virtually defunct they had to consider how best to further the cause of revolution. Andreas Gottschalk, a leader of the workers in Cologne, suggested that they should stand for election to the new Prussian national assembly in their home towns – Marx in Trier and Engels in Barmen. Georg Weerth, on the other hand, wrote from Cologne that "it would be a good idea if you would come here instead of studying in Paris".[208] Political activity in Berlin – as envisaged by Gottschalk – had few attractions for Marx and Engels. They knew Berlin only too well – a city (in Engels's words) inhabited by "a virtually undeveloped middle class; a crawling cowardly petty bourgeoisie, a proletariat without class-consciousness; a pack of bureaucrats, aristocrats and lackeys at court." Marx and Engels agreed with Weerth and went to Cologne to set up a newspaper as a vehicle for their propaganda. They chose Cologne because the Code Napoléon was in force in the Rhineland and this gave greater freedom to the press than the Prussian civil code (*Landrecht*) which applied in Berlin. Engels boasted that they used this freedom "to the last drop".[209] Moreover, Cologne was the chief business and banking centre of the most progressive province in Prussia. And here Marx had once edited the *Rheinische Zeitung* and still had contacts among his old friends.

Marx and Engels, however, were not the first to think of establishing a new radical paper in Cologne. Towards the end of March 1848 Georg Weerth told Marx that Heinrich Bürgers and Karl d'Ester were talking about founding a paper but that it seemed doubtful if they would be able to raise the necessary capital.[210] Marx and Engels went to Cologne determined to push Bürgers aside and to take over his project. Engels later claimed that they succeeded in doing so within twenty-four hours of their arrival and that at the same time they frustrated an intrigue "to ban us to Berlin".[211]

On April 24, 1848 a prospectus, drawn up by Heinrich Bürgers, was issued announcing the forthcoming publication of the newspaper which was to be called the *Neue Rheinische Zeitung*. Now it was necessary to find the capital with which to start the new venture. Engels was already in Barmen – his first visit in four years – seeking financial support for the paper. Marx appealed to Engels to put pressure on his father to buy some shares.[212] Engels replied that he was having little success in raising money and that he would have none at all if a copy of the programme of seventeen points ever found its way to Elberfeld or Barmen. Engels's father – not unnaturally – firmly declined to have anything to do with a paper which was to be edited by avowed communists. Engels added that even the local radicals thought that one day the communists "would be their bitterest enemies". It was indeed hardly surprising that they would not support a project fostered by people who would very soon turn against them.[213] On May 9 Engels informed Marx that he had been able to sell only fourteen shares.[214] When the first number appeared Marx tried to reassure his middle-class readers by describing the newspaper as an "organ of democracy" rather than an organ of the Communist League. But a fierce attack upon the Frankfurt National Assembly showed the shareholders only too clearly how extreme were the editorial views of the paper and they lost no time in withdrawing their financial support. Engels later recalled that "immediately after the appearance of our first number half of them deserted us and by the end of the month [of June] the rest had also left us in the lurch."[215] Eventually Marx – who had only recently been giving financial support to the workers in Brussels – used what was left of his personal fortune to keep the paper alive.[216]

Marx solved the problem of securing good contributors more successfully than the problem of obtaining enough money to launch the new paper. When the first number appeared on the evening of May 31 – it was dated June 1, 1848 – it was announced that Marx was the editor in chief and that the other editors were Engels, Weerth, Dronke, Wilhelm Wolff, Ferdinand Wolff and Heinrich Bürgers. All belonged to the Communist League except Bürgers who appears to have been an editor in name only and to have written no more than a single leading article. Marx had considerable experience as a journalist and had edited the *Rheinische Zeitung* in 1842. Engels had written for newspapers in four countries while Wilhelm Wolff had made a name for himself as a journalist in Silesia before joining Marx in Brussels. Marx was all-powerful as editor in chief. Engels wrote that "a great daily newspaper that has to go to press regularly at a definite time cannot be run in any other way". "To us Marx's dictatorship was selfevident, acknowledged and unquestioned." "There can be no doubt that it was his clear vision and determination that made the *Neue Rheinische Zeitung* the most famous German newspaper in the years of revolution."[217] The paper was read both by middle-class radicals and by workers. Lessner later recalled that he read aloud articles from it to his fellow workers.[218]

Karl Marx was not only responsible for the newspaper as a whole but he also wrote many leading articles particularly upon German domestic affairs. And between April 5 and April 11, 1849 he printed in its columns some of his lectures on "Wages and Capital" which he had delivered to an audience of workers in Brussels in December 1847.[219] Engels's most important contributions were on foreign affairs (such as the workers' rising in Paris in June 1848) and on military operations (such as the campaign in Hungary).[220] In Frankfurt Dronke reported on the debates in the National Assembly. In Paris Dr Ewerbeck was Marx's main correspondent while Schabelitz reported on the proceedings of the French parliament.[221] In Vienna Eduard von Müller-Tellering was the correspondent of the *Neue Rheinische Zeitung*. Wilhelm Wolff wrote a series of striking articles on the heavy feudal burdens which the peasants in Silesia had to bear. Georg Weerth – and later Ferdinand Freiligrath – were responsible for the literary supplement. Weerth's satirical novel on *The Life and Deeds of the Famous Knight Schnapphahnski* – a savage attack upon the

Prussian junkers – first appeared as essays in the *Neue Rheinische Zeitung*. With such an array of talent to support him Marx was able to secure nearly 5,000 regular readers by September 1848 and when the paper ceased publication in May 1849 there were about 6,000 subscribers. Although it had such a short life Engels was able to claim that no German newspaper had ever exercised so great an influence upon public opinion as the *Neue Rheinische Zeitung* and that "no paper has been able to electrify the masses in the same way".[222]

The domestic policy for Germany advocated by the *Neue Rheinische Zeitung* was consistent with the Communist Manifesto and the seventeen points of the communist programme. Marx and his followers hoped that the German liberals would overthrow the reactionary governments and destroy the surviving feudal elements in society. They expected that – particularly in Prussia – the powers of the junkers, the army officers, the civil servants, and the churches would be eliminated. They believed that once this had been achieved the middle classes would soon fall before a rising of the masses which would in turn be followed by the establishment of a classless society in which private enterprise would give way to the state ownership of the means of production. They also expected the German states to be united and the dynasties to be replaced by a republic.

Accepting these principles the contributors of the paper attacked both the monarchical régimes and the liberals who opposed them. They ridiculed the King of Prussia and the Prussian nobles, officers, civil servants and clergy. In nine articles on "Die schlesische Milliarde" (March 22–April 5, 1849) Wilhelm Wolff pilloried the Silesian landowners for oppressing the peasants and there was a marked increase in the sale of the paper in the eastern provinces of Prussia immediately afterwards. Georg Weerth pilloried the Prussian junkers in his novel on the scandalous career of Schnapphahnski which was based upon lurid incidents in the life of Prince Felix Lichnowski. At the same time the *Neue Rheinische Zeitung* attacked the democrats – particularly the Prussian liberals – for failing to make a clean sweep of the reactionary administrations and the feudal institutions when they had the chance to do so. Ludolf von Camphausen and David Hansemann, the leaders of the liberal ministry in Prussia which took office at the end of March 1848, were criticised for handling the forces of reaction with kid gloves. The policy of the liberals in the Frankfurt National Assembly was denounced by Marx as "parliamentary cretinism".[223] Engels declared: "Our first number opened with an article which scoffed at the nullity of the Frankfurt National Assembly, the uselessness of the long-winded speeches delivered there, and the waste of time of its cowardly resolutions."[224] And when the supporters of reaction began to gain the upper hand Marx and Engels condemned their return to power with all the venom at their command.

At first the *Neue Rheinische Zeitung* supported the policy of the extreme radicals who advocated the establishment of a united German republic and the adoption of a policy of extreme nationalism – the founding of a "Greater Germany", the freeing of Schleswig and Holstein from Danish rule, and war against Russia. But by the spring of 1849 Marx and Engels had lost faith in the radicals and they now concentrated their propaganda on the working classes. The *Neue Rheinische Zeitung* incited unrest among the workers in the Rhineland and took a greater interest than before in Stephan Born's Committee of Workers in Berlin and the Brotherhood of Workers (*Arbeiterverbrüderung*) which had been set up in Leipzig.

Since the communists hoped for a successful revolution of the masses the *Neue Rheinische Zeitung* fanned the flames of popular discontent. They supported both passive resistance – by a refusal to pay taxes[225] – and armed revolt. But Marx and Engels condemned risings which they considered to be premature or lacking any chance of success. Thus in articles in the *Neue Rheinische Zeitung* on May 4 and May 6, 1849 Engels declared that the Prussian authorities in the Rhineland were deliberately trying to provoke a workers' rising so as to have an excuse to declare a state of siege and introduce military rule.[226] And the last number of the *Neue Rheinische Zeitung* (May 19, 1849) contained an appeal from the editors to the workers of Cologne to refrain from violence. "An armed revolt on your part at this time would simply provide the government with an excuse to declare a state of siege in Cologne and this would inevitably lead to the demoralisation of the workers throughout the Rhineland."[227]

But if Marx and Engels opposed risings which they felt were doomed to failure they believed that eventually only a revolution of the masses could finally sweep away the forces of reaction. On December 31, 1848 the *Neue Rheinische Zeitung* – reviewing the events of the past year – declared: "The history of the bourgeoisie in Prussia – and indeed in all Germany – between March and December 1848 proves that in this country there is no possibility of the middle classes carrying out a successful revolution and there is no prospect of the middle classes securing political power by establishing a constitutional monarchy. It is now clear that a social-republican revolution is the only practical alternative to a feudal-reactionary counter-revolution."[228]

The *Neue Rheinische Zeitung* favoured the establishment of a democratic German republic and strongly criticised two of the obstacles which barred the way to unification. The first was Prussia's insatiable ambition to dominate Germany. Engels later observed that "in Germany itself the one really serious opponent – the one enemy which the revolution ought to have destroyed – was the Prussian state with its dynasty, its traditions, and its apparatus of government." "Moreover Prussia could unite Germany only by dismembering her – by excluding the Germans in Austria."[229]

A second obstacle to unification was the existence of a number of small independent territories which clung tenaciously to their sovereignty. Marx and Engels regarded these insignificant principalities as survivors of a bygone age and argued that they should be swept aside so that national unity might be achieved. The *Neue Rheinische Zeitung* advocated the establishment of a unitary state and rejected all proposals for the establishment of a new federation.

Engels summed up the foreign policy of the *Neue Rheinische Zeitung* as follows: "Support for every popular revolution; support for a general war of revolutionary Europe against Russia, the backbone of European reaction."[230] Marx and Engels considered that the Romanov régime was the embodiment of reaction and a constant danger to a democratic Germany. Only Russia's defeat could guarantee the success of a German revolution. At the same time Russia's defeat would enable the Poles to regain their independence. Marx and Engels had supported the Polish cause for some years. Now they wrote a series of articles in the *Neue Rheinische Zeitung* on the debate in the Frankfurt National Assembly on the Polish question. They warned Poland's oppressors that the day of reckoning was at hand. "You may have swallowed the Poles but, by God, you will never digest them!"[231]

Marx and Engels denounced not only the Romanovs but also the Hohenzollerns and the Habsburgs for sharing in the spoils of the partitions of Poland. And the Habsburgs were ruling over other subject nationalities such as the Italians. The *Neue Rheinische Zeitung* appealed to the Germans to change their policy with regard to the Poles and the Italians. "Now that the Germans are throwing off their own chains, their foreign policy should be completely reversed. Otherwise the chains with which we bind others will strangle our own newly won liberties."[232] But the *Neue Rheinische Zeitung* did not follow a consistent policy with regard to the Slavs – the Czechs, Serbs, Croats and others – who were under Habsburg or Turkish rule. At first their claims to independence were supported but when a Pan–Slav movement developed with Russian support Engels attacked the Slavs as "counter-revolutionaries". Early in 1849 he described them as backward peoples who could hardly be regarded as civilised. Their fate would be to be wiped out in a future great European war.[233] Engels tried to justify his view of the Slavs by advancing a curious theory of "peoples without history". He argued that there were some peoples which lacked any capacity for self-government and were doomed to be ruled by more advanced nations. "They will never achieve national independence." "They are peoples who were either already under foreign rule when they entered into the first primitive phase of civilisation or who were actually *forced* into the earliest phase of civilisation by their foreign masters."[234] And the Slavs under Habsburg rule fell into this category. This was not one of Engels's happiest doctrines – though Engels himself did not live to see it disproved.

The attitude of Marx and Engels towards France was one of support for the republican revolutionaries and opposition to the upper and middle class reactionaries. The *Neue Rheinische Zeitung* declared that General Cavaignac's suppression of the workers rising in June 1848 had "divided France into two nations – the owners of property and the proletariat". Marx and Engels appealed for sympathy for the defeated insurgents and they watched with growing concern the return to power of the forces of reaction.[235]

While the editors of the *Neue Rheinische Zeitung* were confident that they could explain events in France to their readers satisfactorily they were faced with certain difficulties when discussing affairs in Britain. According to Marx the English workers should have been in the forefront of the revolutionary movement but the Chartist demonstration of April 10, 1848 had failed to shake the British government which proved to be the most stable in Europe. Writing in the *Neue Rheinische Zeitung* in May 1849 Georg Weerth tried to explain why the English workers had not lived up to Marx's expectations. Weerth argued that the Chartist fiasco had been due to Feargus O'Connor's poor leadership and to the fact that the unrest in the south of England had not been matched by equal revolutionary fervour in the manufacturing districts of the north where improved trade and increased wages had caused support for the Chartist cause to melt away. Weerth was confident, however, that the revolution in England had only been postponed. He thought that the recent abolition of the Corn Laws had already led to a depression in the agricultural districts. "Another industrial crisis now threatens the north of England and this time it will take place at the same time as an agricultural crisis and a great war." All this would lead to "the collapse of the traditional structure of English society". "The fall of Old England will herald the complete dissolution of modern middle class society." "The collapse of the power of the bourgeoisie will herald the triumph of the proletariat."[236]

The Prussian authorities replied to the attacks of the *Neue Rheinische Zeitung* by showering writs upon Marx and other editors alleging offences from "defamation of the administration" and "incitement to revolt" to high treason. But the Cologne juries refused to convict. Not content with using the *Neue Rheinische Zeitung* as a vehicle for their views the editors took an active part in stimulating revolutionary agitation among the workers of Cologne and the Rhineland. When they arrived in Cologne they realised that the local branch of the Communist League was too insignificant an organisation to be of any use to them. And they appreciated that avowed communists were unpopular in the Rhineland. So they tried to take over another left-wing organisation. This was a workers' association led by Andreas Gottschalk. They planned to oust Gottschalk from office just as they had once ousted Schapper from his leading position in the Communist League. At first Gottschalk stood his ground, relying upon the loyalty of the workers in Cologne who knew him not only as a political agitator but as a devoted medical practitioner. But when Gottschalk was in custody from July to December 1848 awaiting trial – he was eventually acquitted – Schapper and Moll were able to take his place as leaders of the workers' association. When Gottschalk was free again he tried to recover his former position but without success. Only a small number of workers followed him to form a splinter group. Some of the editors of the *Neue Rheinische Zeitung* also played an active part in the affairs of the Cologne Democratic Society to which Wilhelm Wolff lectured on current affairs.[237] In April 1849 however, Marx, Schapper and Wilhelm Wolff left this society and devoted their energies to organising the workers in the Rhineland against the reaction which threatened all that had been gained by the revolution.[238]

In August 1848 three left-wing political organisations in Cologne – the Workers Association, the Democratic Association, and the Union of Employers and Workers – joined to set up a committee in the Rhineland and Westphalia of the German democratic conference which had recently met in Frankfurt am Main. Marx was the life and soul of this committee and he strongly supported its activities in the *Neue Rheinische Zeitung*.

On September 13, 1848 Engels and some other editors of the

Neue Rheinische Zeitung took part in an open air demonstration (presided over by Heinrich Bürgers) which approved an address urging the Prussian National Assembly in Berlin to use force to resist any attempt to dissolve it. At Wilhelm Wolff's suggestion a committee of public safety was set up to represent those citizens in Cologne who had no vote at local elections. A few days later another demonstration was held in a meadow near Worringen on the Rhine (north of Cologne) and this time the red flag was flown.[239] The meeting was attended by deputations from Cologne, Düsseldorf and other towns in the Rhineland. On this occasion Engels and Lassalle – one of the leaders of the Düsseldorf delegates – met for the first time. In later years the rivalry between Marx and Lassalle was to cause deep divisions in the socialist movement in Germany. Elsewhere in the Rhineland – at Neuss and Crefeld for example – meetings demanding the establishment of a united democratic German republic were addressed by Engels, Wilhelm Wolff, Schapper and Lassalle.

On September 26, 1848 following unrest in Cologne, a state of siege was declared; the civil militia was disarmed; public meetings were forbidden; and the publication of the *Neue Rheinische Zeitung* was suspended.[240] Schapper and Moll were arrested while Wilhelm Wolff went to the Bavarian Palatinate and Georg Weerth went to Bingen in Hesse-Darmstadt. Engels seems to have lost his nerve. He first went into hiding in his parent's house in Barmen (the family being absent on a visit to Engelskirchen) and then fled to Brussels. The Belgian authorities, who had not molested him earlier in the year, now treated him as a vagabond – he had no passport, little money and little baggage – and put him on a train to the French frontier. By Thursday, October 12, when the *Neue Rheinische Zeitung* resumed publication,[241] he was in Paris. He dared not return to Cologne as there was a warrant out for his arrest. He decided to take a holiday and go on a walking tour across France.

It is not easy to account for Engels's decision to give up his political activities and to take a long vacation. Since Germany was in the throes of revolution one might have expected him to return to his editorial duties in Cologne as soon as possible. And if fear of prison kept him away, why did he not stay in Paris – or go to London – and continue to write for the *Neue Rheinische Zeitung*? He would have served his cause more effectively as a foreign correspondent than by tramping through the wine districts of France. He was admittedly short of money but if he had waited in Paris the *Neue Rheinische Zeitung* would have supplied him with funds.

Engels had other worries as well. There had been a new breach with his family. Early in October his mother wrote to him that she had seen a newspaper report that a warrant (*Steckbrief*) had been issued for his arrest. She begged him to take his father's advice and emigrate to America. A few days later she declared that she had reliable information that if he returned to Cologne there would be no place for him on the editorial board of the *Neue Rheinische Zeitung*. In a third letter she declared that his friends in Cologne "are a lot of rogues who will make use of you as long as they can get hold of your money and then they will throw you over". Engels feared that his mother might be right and that Marx might regard his continued absence from Cologne as an act of desertion. He probably realised too that Moses Hess and Dr Ewerbeck were intriguing against him. He expressed his anxiety about his future in a letter to Marx who replied with an emphatic assurance that "it is pure phantasy to imagine that I could leave you in the lurch". "You will always be my intimate friend and I hope that I will always be yours too."[242] Engels seems to have been depressed owing to his fears for the future. He was exhausted after four years of intense activity in the cause of world revolution. He appreciated that he needed a rest and he set off from Paris to throw aside the cares of politics for a few weeks.

Engels gave an account of his walking tour through France in one of the finest descriptive pieces that he ever wrote.[243] He was an enthusiastic admirer of France and the French. He praised Paris – "a city in which European civilisation reaches its greatest heights, a city in which all the strands of our history and culture are brought together, and a city from which at regular intervals are emited those electric impulses which rock the universe." "Here people combine a passion for a full life with a passion for making history." Engels declared, however, that the full flavour of life in Paris could be properly appreciated only if one knew the French provinces as well because the city expressed the creative genius of a whole people which had lavished its wealth and artistic skill to create a capital worthy of a great nation.

But in the autumn of 1848 Engels found that Paris was a very different place from the city that he had known in the twilight of the July Monarchy and the dawn of the Second Republic. In 1846 and 1847 Paris had been a city of "universal cheerfulness and care-free abandon" while in March and April 1848 the workers had rejoiced in their new freedom and had planted trees of liberty along the boulevards. Now – after the suppression of the workers' rising in June 1848 "in an ocean of blood" – the halcyon days of spring had vanished. Engels saw hungry, disarmed and disillusioned workers in the streets. "The balls and the theatres are deserted and the boulevards are frequented only by the bourgeoisie and the police spies." "In short we are back in the Paris of 1847 without the life, the spirit, the fire and the ferment that the workers had injected into the city in those days." To Engels Paris had become a city of the dead and he decided to leave it as soon as possible.

As he was short of money he travelled on foot and enjoyed the experience of a vagabond life. He ceased to worry about his own future and he was no longer concerned with the ever growing threat of reaction in Germany. His leisurely pilgrimage gave him an opportunity to appreciate all that rural France had to offer and – for the first time – he learned at first hand something of the way of life of a peasant society. He observed changes in the geology and topography of the districts through which he passed. He noticed differences in farm buildings, outhouses and cottages. He commented upon different types of farming and he noted local variations in the countryman's patois, dress, customs and outlook.

Engels tramped along the country lanes over the hills that divided the basin of the Seine from that of the Loire. He came across a group of itinerant basket weavers from Alsace who were delighted to meet someone who understood their German dialect. An overnight stop at the village inn at Dampierre gave him an opportunity of meeting members of a colony of workers from Paris who had formerly been employed by the National Workshops and were now engaged in constructing a dam. "There were all kinds of workers from goldsmiths, butchers, shoemakers and joiners to a rag and bone man from the Paris boulevards." "A lusty butcher, who had already established himself as a sort of foreman, was loud in his praises of the undertaking. He said that it was possible to earn from 30 to 100 sous a day depending upon how hard one worked. A fair day's work could easily bring in from 40 to 60 sous. He offered me an immediate job in his 'brigade' and declared that he was sure that I would soon settle down and earn 50 sous a day in my second week. He assured me that I would make good money as the work would last for at least another six months. I would not have minded exchanging my pen for a shovel for a month or two but as I had no papers I would soon have lost the job." Engels remarked that these exiles from Paris read no newspapers and had lost their interest in politics. "Hard work, reasonably good wages, and – above all – the move from Paris to a quiet remote corner of France has restricted their outlook in a remarkable way. They have been in Dampierre for only a couple of months but they are already half way to being turned into peasants."

And Engels had a very poor opinion of peasants. He declared that a peasant was an utterly stupid creature – "a barbarian in the midst of civilisation".

> "A peasant is isolated in a remote village, and lives as a member of a small social group which changes only as one generation follows another. Hard repetitive work ties him – as even serfdom would not tie him – to the same smallholding that passes unchanged from father to son. All aspects of his life are characterised by stability and uniformity. The family is vital to him for it is the most important factor in his life. All this restricts his vision to the narrowest limits that are possible in modern society. The great movements of history either pass him by or carry him along with them – but the peasant knows nothing of their origins, their aims, or the impetus behind them."

Engels's contemptuous dismissal of the French peasants as ignorant barbarians may have been due to the fact that there was obviously no hope of converting them to communism. They were passionately devoted to their little pieces of land and were determined to protect their property against all comers. They had been alarmed in the previous February when the revolution had brought to power men who – so they thought – might try to nationalise the land. Their fears appeared to be confirmed when the Provisional Government increased the land tax. The failure of the workers' rising in Paris in June had been welcomed by the peasants. Now they gave their support to Louis Napoleon whom they regarded as a protector of private property. Since two thirds of the voters were peasants Engels had no doubt that Louis Napoleon would be the next ruler of France. Engels's caustic criticisms of the French peasants was, however, modified by his appreciation of their friendliness, courtesy, and generous hospitality.

When he reached Briare Engels decided to go to Switzerland by way of Auxerre. He left the valley of the Loire and made for Burgundy. He described the inhabitants of this province as good-natured, naïve and witty "French Austrians". The peasants were so friendly and good hearted that Engels even forgave them their "abysmal ignorance of politics and their enthusiasm for Louis Napoleon". He reached Auxerre in time to enjoy a wine festival to celebrate the exceptionally good harvest of 1848. The quality of the wine was superior to that of 1834 and 1846. From far and near the peasants streamed into Auxerre to buy what was left of the vintage of 1847 at very low prices. Engels then crossed the River Yonne and tramped through the vineyards to Saint-Bris where he again saw a little market town given over to the buying and selling of wine. His next stop was at Vermenton. Here Engels's manuscript unfortunately breaks off. By the end of October he was in Switzerland where he stayed until January 1849 first in Geneva, then in Lausanne and finally in Bern.

While he was in Switzerland Engels received three letters from Marx. In the first – clearly a reply to an urgent appeal for money – Marx stated that he was enclosing 50 thalers and that a similar sum had already been sent to Paris. The *Neue Rheinische Zeitung* had resumed publication on October 12. Marx's colleagues – except Weerth – had not yet returned to Cologne. Marx asked Engels to send him some articles.[245] In his second letter Marx expressed great surprise that Engels had still not received any money from him since he had sent 61 thalers as well as 20 thalers to Gigot and 50 thalers to Dronke which should have been passed on to Engels. Apparently some of the shareholders of the *Neue Rheinische Zeitung* were trying to remove Engels from the editorial board but Marx assured Engels that – in the first issue of the paper after the resumption of publication – he had announced that no change in the membership of the editorial board was contemplated. Marx had also told the "reactionary shareholders" that although they could remove Engels from the editorial board they would save no money by doing so since Marx had the power to pay any fee that he pleased to his contributors. Marx concluded his letter by declaring: "Your old man is a dirty dog and we will write him a really rude letter."[246]

Marx's third letter advised Engels to stay in Switzerland until it was safe to return to Cologne. Marx suggested that Engels should write articles on Proudhon and on the Hungarian campaign ("Hungarian shit" as he elegantly put it). He declared that he had thought of a "fool-proof plan" to raise money from Engels's father. Engels should write to Marx saying that he was in dire financial straits and Marx would then pass this information on to Engels's mother. The *Neue Rheinische Zeitung*, Marx observed, was still advocating an armed rising (*émeute*) – "la révolution marche".[247]

At this time Engels also received letters from his mother and from Georg Weerth. At the end of February his mother wrote: "If you are earning something – but not enough for your needs – simply ask your father for a small remittance." And Weerth wrote that Engels had been summoned to appear before the magistrate in Cologne on December 20.[248]

At the end of December 1848 Engels wrote to Marx to enquire if he could return to Cologne. He declared that he would cheerfully face any jury but that he was not prepared to go to goal while awaiting trial because he would not be allowed to smoke.[249]

Early in January he sent Marx his article on the Hungarian campaign. He declared that he had no money and could not borrow any in "this lousy hole". He complained that he could no longer vegetate in idleness. "Soon I will decide to face prison in Cologne rather than endure freedom in Switzerland." "Let me know if there is the slightest chance of my case being dealt with as favourably as those of Bürgers and Becker."[250]

The manuscript which Engels sent to Marx was published on January 13, 1849 as a leading article entitled "The Magyar Struggle."[251] This – and later – reports by Engels on the war in Hungary were important for two reasons. First, they were the earliest essays in which Engels showed his gift for military criticism which later earned him the nickname of 'the General'. In 1852 in a letter to Marx he boasted that "we gave a wonderfully accurate account of the Hungarian war based upon *Austrian* reports and we gave a cautious but brilliantly accurate forecast of the way in which the campaign would end".[252] At the time Engels's articles were attributed to a high-ranking officer in the Hungarian army while a German journal praised the "very able reporter" who had written on the campaign in the *Neue Rheinische Zeitung*.[253]

Secondly, in this article Engels threw caution to the wind and advocated armed resistance against those who sought to deprive the people of the reforms that they had gained from the revolution. He declared that the Magyars had not yet been defeated and that even if they were defeated they would soon rise again. "One day the wild barbaric counter-revolution of the Slavs will overwhelm the Habsburg monarchy and then the camarilla in Vienna will come face to face with their allies in their true colours." "The first victorious rising of the French workers – which Louis Napoleon is doing his best to provoke – will free the German Austrians and the Magyars and will give them the opportunity to take a terrible revenge upon the Slav savages." "The universal war which will follow will crush the Slav alliance and will wipe out completely those obstinate peoples so that their very names will be forgotten." "The next world war will wipe out not only reactionary classes and dynasties but it will also destroy these utterly reactionary races." "And that will be a real step forward."[254]

In the middle of January 1849 Engels at last felt that it was safe for him to return to Cologne and shortly afterwards he was informed that no charges would be brought against him in connection with his activities during the unrest of the previous September. But on February 7 Engels appeared with Marx, Schapper and their publisher Korff, charged with libelling the police and the local attorney-general (*Oberprokurator*) in an article in the *Neue*

Rheinische Zeitung on July 5, 1848. Marx told the jury that "a new society cannot be founded upon obsolete laws". He argued that after the Berlin rising of March 1848 and the calling of the Prussian National Assembly the laws formerly in force must be considered to be in abeyance pending the promulgation of a new constitution. Engels also addressed the jury and the charges against the four accused were dismissed.

On the following day Marx, Schapper and their lawyer Schneider – but not Engels – were charged with inciting citizens to armed rebellion. They were alleged to have done this as members of the Rhenish-Westphalian committee of the conference of democratic societies which had been held in Frankfurt. Again Marx and his colleagues were found not guilty.[255] On February 24 Marx and Engels attended a dinner organised by the Workers Association of Cologne to celebrate the first anniversary of the founding of the Second Republic in France. Engels proposed a toast to the Roman Republic. At about the same time Moll – who had fled to England at the time of the disturbances in Cologne in the previous September – returned to Cologne as the envoy of the London branch of the Communist League to discuss with Marx and Engels the revival of the League.

Between April 20 and May 9, 1849 Engels acted as chief editor of the *Neue Rheinische Zeitung* while Marx was away from Cologne making a last effort to raise funds to keep the newspaper alive. On April 23 Marx wrote to Engels from Hamburg that he had not secured any money from Bremen. But he had not given up hope – "les choses marcheront".[256]

It was while he was in control of the paper that Engels printed an unusually violent attack upon Prussia. There had been a rumour that Russian troops were crossing Silesia on their way to Bohemia to assist the Habsburgs to restore order in their territories. Engels wrongly assumed that the rumour was correct and his fury knew no bounds. He declared that "we Rhinelanders became Prussian citizens – and remained Prussian citizens – only because our province was annexed by force. We have never really been Prussians. But now that we are moving against Hungary – now that hordes of Russian bandits are on Prussian soil – now we do feel that we are Prussians. We know full well the shame of being called Prussians."[257]

Early in May 1849 there were popular risings in Saxony, the Bavarian Palatinate and the Rhineland in support of the draft constitution drawn up by the Frankfurt National Assembly. Elberfeld was one of the centres involved and on May 10 – immediately after Marx's return from his fund-raising tour – Engels left Cologne to place his military training at the disposal of the insurgents. After five years of political journalism and revolutionary agitation he exchanged the pen for the sword and arrived in Elberfeld to help to man the barricades. He had stopped at Solingen on the way to gather recruits and to collect some ammunition which local workers had seized at the arsenal at Gräfrath. Soon afterwards Engels described his experiences in Elberfeld in an article in the *Neue Rheinische Zeitung.*[258]

When Engels reached Elberfeld on May 11, 1849 the military commission of the local Committee of Public Safety placed him in charge of the defence works of the town. On May 12 the artillery was put at Engels's disposal – although this consisted only of half a dozen small cannon which were normally used to fire loyal salutes on the King's birthday. Since Engels was known to be a communist he can hardly have been surprised that some of the bourgeois supporters of the rising regarded him with suspicion. As soon as Engels arrived in the town Herr Riotte, a member of the Committee of Public Safety, asked him point blank why he had come to Elberfeld. Engels replied "that he had come because he had been sent from Cologne and because he believed that he could perhaps make himself useful in a military capacity." "Moreover as he had been born in Berg, Engels considered that it was a matter of honour to stand shoulder to shoulder with the people of Berg on the first occasion that they had taken up arms." "Engels declared that he wanted to devote himself entirely to his military duties and to hold himself completely aloof from the political side of the movement." Riotte appears to have been satisfied with these assurances.

On May 14, however, Herr Höchster, another member of the Committee of Public Safety, told Engels that "although he himself had no criticism whatever to make of Engels's conduct, the middle classes in Elberfeld were greatly alarmed at Engels's presence in the town". "They feared that Engels might proclaim the red republic at any time and they all hoped that Engels would leave Elberfeld." Engels gave way, saying that he would not stay in Elberfeld if he was not wanted. But he declared that he would not leave unless he was asked to do so in writing by all the members of the Committee of Public Safety and by Mirbach, the commander in chief of the insurgents. This was done and Engels left Elberfeld on May 15. On his way back to Cologne he again stopped at Solingen, this time – pistol in hand – to lead a crowd of insurgents against the arsenal to requisition some uniforms.

In his account of these events – written immediately after they occurred – Engels declared that "the free corps and the armed workers were highly incensed at the decisions of the Committee of Public Safety". "They demanded that Engels should stay in Elberfeld and they declared that they were prepared to sacrifice their lives to protect him." "Engels went to the insurgents and calmed them down." Finally Engels assured the readers of the *Neue Rheinische Zeitung* that "the present movement is merely a curtain-raiser to a new and different movement". "And the new movement will be a thousand times more serious than the present movement because it will concern the real interests of the workers themselves." "The new revolutionary insurrection will be a direct consequence of the present movement and the workers may be certain that, as soon as it breaks out, Engels – as well as other editors of the *Neue Rheinische Zeitung* – will be on their side." Two days after this article appeared the *Neue Rheinische Zeitung* – in its last number on May 19, 1849 – again referred to the rising in Elberfeld. The paper declared that it was unfortunate that the workers there had failed to crush the perfidious middle classes but there could be no doubt that the proletariat would soon hurl "the infamous, hypocritical, cowardly, putrefying, and arrogant bourgeoisie" to the doom that it so richly deserved.

In a later account of the Elberfeld rising of May 1849 Engels sharply criticised the workers for their lack of revolutionary fervour. He declared that the proletariat of the Wupper valley had hardly had time to recover its self-respect after being doped for so many years by hard liquor and pietism. He thought that a recent improvement in trade had sapped their enthusiasm for insurrection. He wrote:

> "On May 11 when I reached Elberfeld at least 2,500 or 3,000 armed insurgents were available. But the only really reliable ones were a small number of Elberfeld workers and some supporters who had come from other towns. The territorials (*Landwehr*) hesitated to support us since most of them were panic-stricken at the mere thought of ending up in chains if the revolt failed. And the number of doubtful supporters increased when they were joined by members of other detachments who were undecided or fearful for the future. Finally the citizen's militia (*Bürgerwehr*) had – from its inception – been a reactionary body set up to suppress the workers. It declared its neutrality and its members concerned themselves only with protecting their own property. All this became clear in the next few days. Meanwhile we lost some of the workers while some of our supporters from neighbouring towns went home. The revolutionary movement was stagnant and our effective forces declined in numbers. The members of the militia, on the other hand, held together and every day they became bolder in supporting the counter-revolution.

Finally when we mustered our forces we found that we could rely only upon a mere 700 or 800 men. Neither the territorials nor the militia responded to this call to arms."[259]

It has often been stated that on the Sunday when he was in Elberfeld, Engels went to the River Wupper to inspect the defences of the Haspel bridge which linked the two towns of Elberfeld and Barmen. Here, it is said, Engels unexpectedly met his father who was returning from church. The elder Engels was horrified to see his son wearing a red sash and leading an insurrection.[260] The evidence for this alleged confrontation between Engels and his father is far from conclusive. Certainly Engels himself never mentioned the incident. Soon after Engels left Elberfeld a local newspaper denounced his followers as "gangs of unemployed, escaped jail-birds, and licentious thugs"[261] and a warrant (*Steckbrief*) was issued for his arrest.[262]

The days of the *Neue Rheinische Zeitung* were numbered. By the middle of May, as Engels later recalled, "the risings in Dresden and Elberfeld had been suppressed, the insurgents in Iserlohn had been surrounded, and the Rhineland and Westphalia bristled with bayonets. As soon as the reaction had triumphed in Westphalia and the Rhineland the Prussian troops were ready to advance upon the [Bavarian] Palatinate and Baden. Now at last the government dared to attack us openly. Warrants were issued against half of our editors while the other half were liable to expulsion as aliens because they were not Prussian subjects. Against such odds there was nothing that we could do."[263] Engels did not mention that, owing to its precarious financial position, the *Neue Rheinische Zeitung* would not have survived for long even if the authorities had left the paper and its editors in peace.

On May 16, 1849 Marx was served with a notice of expulsion from Prussia and since he had given up his Prussian citizenship he had no redress against such an order. Three days later the final number of the *Neue Rheinische Zeitung* appeared, printed in red ink, with a defiant farewell poem by Freiligrath. Marx's last message to the workers of Cologne was an appeal to them to refrain from violence since no armed rising could hope to succeed in a well-armed garrison town. Engels indulged in a final vitriolic attack upon the middle classes whom he so heartily detested. Fearing arrest for his part in the rising in Elberfeld Engels decided to accompany Marx when he left Cologne and to shake the dust of Prussia off his feet for ever. The rest of his life was spent in exile. But before leaving Germany for good Engels indulged in one last gesture of defiance against the Prussians. He joined the rebels in

Baden and fought against the Prussian army in which he had once served as a volunteer.

In the middle of May 1849 when Marx and Engels left Cologne they realised that they could no longer hope to foment insurrection in the Rhineland. Here, as Engels later admitted, "the actual fighting was of little importance. All the large towns being fortresses commanded by citadels, there could be only skirmishes on the part of the insurgents. As soon as a sufficient number of troops had been drawn together there was an end to armed opposition."[264] And now the only German territories in the hands of insurgents were Baden and the Bavarian Palatinate. This part of Germany was a predominantly agrarian region where the traditional – almost medieval – structure of rural society was breaking down. Loss of access to open commons and to woodlands was making is impossible for smallholders to survive. Poor harvests and the potato blight added to their distress. In the towns the craftsmen were feeling the first effects of competition from cheap factory goods produced in the more industrialised parts of Germany and conveyed by the newly built railways. Engels observed that the risings in Baden in 1848 and 1849 were supported by the petty bourgeoisie and the peasants and not – as in the Rhineland or Saxony – by the industrial proletariat. In 1848 the Grand Duke of Baden had been able to suppress risings led by Friedrich Hecker, Franz Sigel and Gustav Struve. But in 1849 there were fresh revolts both in Baden and in the Bavarian Palatinate and this time a number of military units mutinied and went over to the insurgents.

By May 1849 the Bavarian government had lost control over its isolated province of the Palatinate where the radicals had formed a provisional government at Kaiserslautern. This was no revolution of an embittered proletariat against its capitalist oppressors. It was a revolution of peasants, craftsmen and shopkeepers against the Bavarian bureaucracy and army. In his description of the rising in the Palatinate Engels wrote: "The dull, pedantic, old-Bavarian beer drinking officials were at last thrown out and replaced by the gay wine-bibbers of the Palatinate." "The abolition of police regulations on taverns was the first revolutionary act of the people of the Palatinate. The whole of the province was transformed into an immense wine tavern and the quantity of strong drinks consumed during those six weeks 'in the name of the people of the Palatinate' defied all accounting." "All the old uncongenial constraint seemed to have vanished with the old bureaucracy. People dressed in a free and easy way with a view to convenience, and with the difference in clothing every other difference in social relations instantly disappeared. All classes of society met in the same drinking houses and a socialist dreamer might have seen the dawn of universal brotherhood in that unconstrained intercourse." "The provisional government followed the example of the province. It consisted almost exclusively of genial wine-drinkers whom nothing astonished more than the fact that they were suddenly to form the provisional government of their native land which Bacchus had so favoured. And yet these jolly regents behaved much better than their Baden neighbours. . . . In good will and sober reason the government of the Palatinate was far above that of Baden."[265]

Meanwhile Baden was also in the throes of revolution. This rising however was different from that in the Palatinate. In Baden virtually the whole of the country rose in revolt whereas in the Palatinate there were significant royalist pockets of resistance to the new provisional government. In Baden the army went over to the insurgents but in the Palatinate only some of the troops supported the cause of revolution. In Baden the provisional government was a right-wing administration while that of the Bavarian Palatinate was a left-wing radical administration. Engels was much more in sympathy with Karl d'Ester – a former leader of the Cologne democrats and a member of the Frankfurt National Assembly – who tried to inject some revolutionary fervour into the Palatinate provisional government, than with Lorenz Brentano whose extreme caution and singularly inept leadership of the Baden insurrection filled him with contempt.

When his army mutinied the Grand Duke of Baden fled from Karlsruhe to Alsace and Lorenz Brentano set up a new provisional government on May 14, 1849. This bourgeois administration was sharply criticised by Marx and Engels for failing to pursue a resolute revolutionary policy. They held that "the defensive is the death of every armed rising"[266] and argued that the armies of Baden and the Bavarian Palatinate should immediately take the offensive, march on Frankfurt – the seat of the National Assembly – and act as the spearhead of a vigorous assault upon the supporters of the counter-revolution.

Engels later declared that there had never been "such a favourable position for a provincial and partial insurrection as this". "A revolution was expected in Paris; the Hungarians were at the gates of Vienna; in all the central states of Germany, not only the people, but even the troops, were strongly in favour of the insurrection, and only wanted an opportunity to join it openly." "And yet the movement, having once got into the hands of the petty bourgeoisie, was ruined from its very beginning. The petty bourgeoisie rulers, particularly of Baden – Herr Brentano at the head of them – never forgot that by usurping the place and prerogatives of the 'lawful' sovereign, the Grand Duke, they were committing high treason." "They sat down in their ministerial armchairs with the consciousness of criminality in their hearts. What can you expect of such cowards?" "They not only abandoned the insurrection to its own uncentralised – and therefore ineffective – spontaneity, they actually did everything in their power to take the sting out of the movement, to unman, to destroy it".[267]

On leaving Cologne Marx and Engels went to Frankfurt am Main (May 19–21) in the hope of persuading the more radical members of the National Assembly to call on the revolutionary armies of Baden and the Bavarian Palatinate to march upon Frankfurt. Wilhelm Wolff, the only communist representative in the Assembly, attacked his fellow members – and the *Reichsverweser* – for their cowardice when faced with the forces of reaction. On this visit to Frankfurt Marx took the opportunity to discuss with his friend Joseph Weydemeyer the possibility of using the *Neue Deutsche Zeitung* – edited by Otto Lüning – as a vehicle for his views now that the *Neue Rheinische Zeitung* had ceased publication.[268]

Marx and Engels went on to Baden where they pleaded with the leaders of the revolution in Mannheim, Ludwigshafen and Karlsruhe to march on Frankfurt. But they had no success. Next they went to Speyer and Kaiserslautern only to be disappointed at the failure of the provisional government of the Bavarian Palatinate to adopt a more positive policy of armed opposition to the German counter-revolution.

At the end of May 1849 Marx and Engels went to Bingen where they were arrested by the authorities of Hesse-Darmstadt on suspicion of being involved in the rising in the Palatinate. They were taken to Frankfurt but were released almost immediately and allowed to return to Bingen. Here they parted company. Marx went to Paris as the accredited representative of the democratic party of the Bavarian Palatinate while Engels went to Kaiserslautern. Here the provisional Palatinate government offered him various civilian and military posts which he declined. He was, however, persuaded by d'Ester to contribute to the newspaper *Der Bote für Stadt und Land*. In an article in this official organ of the provisional government Engels argued that "in a few weeks – perhaps in a few days – there will be a great clash on German soil between the massed armies of the republican West and the enslaved East." "All national issues will disappear for now only one question has to be answered: 'Do you want to be *free* or do you want to be Russian?'."[269] Once more Engels was confidently making a wildly inaccurate prophecy. This first article in *Der Bote für Stadt und Land* was also his last. Engels's second article was rejected as being "too inflamatory". And then Engels was actually arrested but he was freed within twenty-four hours owing to the protests of his supporters.

Early in June 1849 Engels received a letter from Karl Marx who had reached Paris safely but was in urgent need of money.[270] Engels replied to Marx but did not post the letter because he heard that Prussian troops had occupied Homburg and cut off communications with Paris. He later wrote to Jenny Marx: "So far I had held aloof from all connection with the so-called revolution but when I heard that the Prussians were coming I could not deny myself the pleasure of joining in the struggle." "Willich was the only officer who was any good so I went to him and became his adjutant."[271]

Engels did not join the insurgents because he believed in their cause but because he welcomed the opportunity – denied to him in Elberfeld – of fighting the Prussians. Moreover he thought that if none of the editors of the *Neue Rheinische Zeitung* took up arms their enemies would taunt them with cowardice.[272] He recognised that the rising had no chance of success. All hopes that the revolutionary movement in south west Germany would secure outside support faded away when the attempt to dislodge Louis Napoleon failed on June 13 and when Amand Goegg failed to march on Vienna. The Baden insurgents (placed under the command of Louis Mierowlawski on June 10) were completely isolated and could no longer take the offensive. They could only retreat in face of the overwhelmingly superior forces of Prussia and the German Federation massed against them under the Crown Prince of Prussia. The revolutionary army was a motley collection of trained troops and untrained volunteers. It included much of the Baden regular army, the Baden militia, some units of the army of the Bavarian Palatinate, and some groups of revolutionary supporters from other parts of Germany and from abroad. Among the more important of these free corps were workers' battalions from Mannheim, Karlsruhe and elsewhere and foreign units such as the Magyars and the Poles. Willich's corps of 700 to 800 men was made up of a company of Rhineland workers (including compositors from the *Neue Rheinische Zeitung*), a company of French workers from Besançon, four companies of volunteers from the Palatinate, and a company of students.[273]

The campaign lasted for only a few weeks – from June 12 when the Prussians left Homburg to advance on the Palatinate until July 23 when they captured Rastatt, the last stronghold of the insurgents. The three Prussian army corps had no difficulty in disposing of the ill-equipped and ill-disciplined forces of Baden and the Palatinate. Wedged in between France, Württemberg and Switzerland, the insurgents had little room in which to manœuvre and they could only retreat southwards through the Black Forest. Once the Crown Prince had crossed the River Neckar the only point at which a stand could be made was on the River Murg. Here Baden's territories narrow to a mere twelve or thirteen miles between the Rhine and the Württemberg frontier, with the fortress of Rastatt as a strong defensive position. The Prussians turned the enemy's flank by marching through Württemberg territory. The rebel front collapsed on June 29. Willich's corps then fought rear-guard actions to cover the retreat of a number of Baden troops. Willich and Engels crossed into Switzerland on July 12. Rastatt fell on July 23. Willich, Engels and Liebknecht were lucky to escape capture for the Prussians took a terrible revenge upon the revolutionaries who fell into their hands. According to Franz Mehring twenty-eight of the insurgents were shot and sixty-eight received long prison sentences.[274] No one knows how many died of typhus in the damp dungeons of Rastatt. For those who escaped, long years of exile lay ahead.

Engels had played an active part in the campaign. As soon as he joined Willich at Offenbach he was sent back to Kaiserslautern to secure supplies. When he reached Neustadt he learned that Kaiserslautern had been evacuated. He secured some ammunition, lead and powder and rejoined his corps. On June 17 and 18 Willich's force successfully covered the retreat of the Palatinate volunteers into Baden territory and accompanied them to the outskirts of Karlsruhe. On June 19, despite Brentano's protests, Willich and Engels marched their troops into Karlsruhe. They were inspecting the Grand Duke's collection of weapons when they learned that the Prussians were crossing the Rhine at Germersheim. Willich at once marched against them but – lacking support from the main Baden force – he was unable to check the advance of the Prussians. On June 21 the insurgents counter-attacked and recaptured Waghäusel but when Prussian reinforcements appeared they had to evacuate the town again. The failure of Sznayde's troops, stationed near Karlsruhe, to take part in this engagement contributed to the Prussian victory. Willich's corps retreated to Rastatt which was reached on June 26. Two days later it took part in the battle of the Murg, the last serious stand of the revolutionary army. Here Josef Moll fell in action. He had been an active revolutionary for over ten years – a leader first of the London branch of the Communist League and then of the Workers Association in Cologne. After the disturbances in Cologne in September 1848 Moll had fled to London but he had soon returned to Germany under an assumed name and – in Engels's words – had "carried out propaganda work in different districts and undertook missions the danger of which terrified everybody else". "I met him again in Kaiserslautern. There, too, he undertook missions to Prussia for which he would immediately have been shot if he had been found out. On his return from his second mission he succeeded in getting through all the enemy lines as far as Rastatt, where he immediately entered the Besançon Workers' Company of our corps. Three days later he was killed. In him I lost an old friend and the [Communist] Party lost one of its most indefatigable, fearless and most reliable soldiers."[275]

On reaching Switzerland Engels wrote to Jenny Marx for news of Karl Marx for he had heard a rumour that Marx was in prison. He told Jenny Marx that he had taken part in four engagements. "I discovered that the much vaunted courage of attack recklessly is a most ordinary accomplishment. The whistling of bullets is a trifling matter. I saw plenty of cowardice during the campaign but there were less than a dozen cases of cowardice *in the face of the enemy*. I did see plenty of courage that bordered on folly."[276] Marx replied early in August that he was still at liberty though the French government had ordered him to leave Paris for Morbihan – "the Pontine marshes of Brittany". He suggested that Engels should write an account of the revolution in Baden and the Palatinate. Marx added that he was planning to edit a new journal "most of which will have to be written by the two of us".[277] Engels took Marx's advice and wrote a lengthy account of the insurrection which was published in the following year in Marx's *Neue Rheinische Zeitung: Politisch-ökonomische Revue*. It was a brilliant piece of reporting on the circumstances leading to the rising and on the campaign itself. This "masterpiece of German descriptive prose"[278] helped to establish Engels's reputation in socialist circles as a military critic.

On August 23 Marx wrote that – rather than perish in Morbihan – he would leave Paris for London and he asked Engels to join him there. Marx reminded Engels that if he fell into the hands of the Prussians he would face two firing squads – "1. because of Baden, and 2. because of Elberfeld".[279] Shortly afterwards Engels received a letter from his mother in which she wrote that she prayed that he would reach London safely. Engels stayed in Switzerland – in Vevey, Geneva and Bern – from July until September 1849. In Bern he met Stephan Born and in Geneva he made the aquaintance of Wilhelm Liebknecht, who had fought in the Baden rising and was later to become one of the leaders of the German Social Democrat Party.[280]

Engels decided that London would be a safer refuge than Switzerland. He had an unpleasant experience there when walking in the Jura mountains for he was arrested since he had no papers with him. Having received money from his family in Barmen he sailed from Genoa to England for he had decided that it would be too risky to travel across the Continent overland. It was characteristic of Engels that he should have taken the opportunity of a sea voyage to improve his knowledge of navigation. He kept a diary in which he noted the position of the sun, the direction of the wind, and the nature of the waves at different times of the day.[281] He arrived in London on about November 10, 1849. His friend Georg Weerth, who was in England at this time, wrote to his mother on November 28, 1849: "Recently I also met my colleague Friedrich Engels who has reached London after a voyage of five weeks in a sailing vessel from Genoa."[282]

Since many members of the central committee of the Communist League and former editors of the *Neue Rheinische Zeitung* were now in London Engels was able to resume the activities of a revolutionary exile. With Marx he planned to infuse new life into the Communist League and to start a new political review. In December a contract was signed with a Hamburg firm for the publication of the *Neue Rheinische Zeitung: Politisch-ökonomische Revue*. But the future was dark. Since he had fought with the rebels in Elberfeld and Baden he could hardly expect his father to finance his career as a revolutionary agitator by making him a regular allowance. His mother made this crystal clear in a letter of December 2, 1849: "I must agree with your father when he says that you cannot expect us to support you so long as you pursue a way of life which, to put it mildly, does not meet with our approval." And the financial position of Marx, who had a family to support, also gave Engels cause for anxiety. After paying off the debts of the *Neue Rheinische Zeitung* Marx had completely exhausted the funds at his disposal. Five years of intensive work and study for the cause of communism had ended in disaster. On the Continent the revolution had collapsed and reactionary rulers were firmly in the saddle again. In 1850 it needed supreme faith in the ultimate success of their cause for Marx and Engels to plan a resumption of their researches into the capitalist system and a continuance of their communist propaganda and agitation.

V. Exile in London, 1849–50[283]

The phase of Engels's career as a revolutionary agitator which had begun when he left Barmen to join Marx in Brussels in April

1845 ended with a stay of twelve months as a refugee in London. He arrived by sea from Genoa in November 1849 and left again for Manchester in November 1850. When Engels reached London, Marx had already been there for three months.[284] Marx had taken his seat on the central committee of the revived Communist League, which he was determined should be a spearhead of revolution in Germany. Marx had refused to accept defeat and, despite the triumph of the forces of reaction on the Continent, he still believed that it would soon be possible for the revolutionary workers to mount a successful counter-attack against their oppressors. In December 1849 he assured his friend Weydemeyer that "a tremendous industrial, agricultural, and commercial crisis" was approaching in England. "If the Continent postpones its revolution until the crisis breaks out, England may turn out to be from the very start, even against its will, an ally of the revolutionary Continent."[285] And in July 1850 he declared that if the cabinet fell in England "then a real revolutionary movement will commence here".[286]

Meanwhile Marx had no money and was bombarding his friends in Germany with appeals for financial aid. His wife later recalled that small sums sent by her mother "often saved us from the bitterest privations".[287] Marx and his family were ejected from their Chelsea lodgings in April 1850[288] – "harassed on all sides and pursued by creditors"[289] – and found temporary accommodation for £5 a week in the German Hotel near Leicester Square[290] before moving to two rooms in the house of a Jewish lace dealer in Soho.[291] In May 1850 Jenny Marx wrote to Weydemeyer that her husband was "almost overwhelmed with the paltry worries of life in so revolting a form that it has taken all his energy, all his calm, clear, quiet sense of dignity to maintain him in that daily, hourly struggle".[292] In August 1850 Jenny Marx – although she was pregnant and in poor health – travelled to Holland in a vain attempt to raise some money from her husband's uncle Lion Philips and in November she lost her baby son Guido who died "from convulsions caused by pneumonia" a fortnight after his first birthday.[293] Despite his own financial worries, Marx did not forget the needs of his compatriots and he served on a relief committee which was set up by the German Workers Education Society to help penniless German refugees stranded in London. When his enemies accused Marx of feathering his own nest from the fund, Engels quickly sprang to his defence. He assured Weydemeyer that there was no truth in the allegation that the relief committee was "eating up the refugee funds itself". He asserted that no member of the committee had ever received a penny from the fund.[294]

When the *Cornish Diamond* completed its voyage of five weeks from Italy and sailed up the Thames with Engels on board, only two years had elapsed since Engels had last been in London to attend the conference of the Communist League at which Marx had been commissioned to draw up the Communist Manifesto. In those two years the Continent had been shaken to its foundations by revolution, war, and counter-revolution but England had escaped unscathed. The Chartist rising which Engels had hoped would instal Harney in Downing Street had petered out in the fiasco of the demonstration on Kennington Common in April 1848. Londoners were now looking forward to the Great Exhibition which was to be held in Hyde Park in 1851 and they gave little thought to the reaction on the Continent that had driven a thousand liberals, radicals, and socialists to seek refuge in London.[295]

It is true that in September 1850 the draymen of Barclay & Perkins' brewery showed their detestation of Habsburg tyranny by assaulting General Haynau with whips and sticks when he came to London and that in the following month there was a strong Protestant reaction when the Pope divided England into episcopal divisions for the purpose of Roman Catholic worship. But, for the most part, it was Lola Montez on a charge of bigamy, the Queen attacked by "a person respectably dressed", and the safe arrival of the Koh-i-Noor diamond that made the headlines in the London newspapers in 1850.[296]

While all this was happening, Marx and Engels were busy making their preparations for the revolution on the Continent that they were confident would soon break out. In April 1850, largely on Marx's initiative, the Universal Society of Revolutionary Communists was founded, following a meeting between Marx, Engels and Willich (Communist League), Adam and Jules Vidil (followers of Blanqui) and Julian Harney (representing the Chartists). The following statutes, drawn up by Marx and Engels, were adopted:

"1. The aim of the society is the overthrow of all the privileged classes, and to submit these classes to the dictatorship of the proletariat by maintaining the revolution in permanence until the realisation of communism, which will be the last organisational form of the human family.

2. For the attainment of this aim the society will form bonds of solidarity among all sections of the revolutionary communist party by breaking down the barriers of nationality in conformity with the principle of republican fraternity.

3. The founding committee of the society constitutes itself the Central Committee. Wherever it is necessary to carry out the

appointed tasks there will be established local committees in direct communication with the Central Committee.

4. There is no limit to the number of members in the society, but no one may be a member who is not elected by a unanimous vote. But on no account may the vote be secret.
5. All members of the society are obliged by oath to observe unconditionally the first article of the statutes. Any changes, which may conceivably have the effect of weakening a member's deliberate intention to follow the first article, releases the member of the society from his obligations.
6. Decisions of the society will always be arrived at by a two thirds majority of the votes."[297]

Although this society seems to have been still-born, Marx, for a moment, saw himself as the guiding hand behind a great conspiracy of revolutionary German, French, and English workers which was destined to overthrow governments and to establish communism. And the reactionary governments on the Continent took Marx seriously. Prussian agents kept a sharp eye upon German refugees in London[298] and in June 1850 Marx, Engels and Willich wrote to the *Spectator* to protest against this harassment of their fellow countrymen.

In the previous month Marx and Engels had already clearly laid down their policy for the immediate future. They had drawn up an address on behalf of the central committee of the Communist League (March 1850) which had been sent to all its branches. It was a sort of new Communist Manifesto – revised in the light of the events of 1848–9 – and it was a practical handbook for revolutionaries.

Marx and Engels began by claiming that the Communist League already had two achievements to its credit. First, its members had played an active part in the revolutions of 1848–9 "in the press, on the barricades, and on the battlefield". Secondly, the policy laid down in the Communist Manifesto had proved to be "the only correct policy for the proletariat to follow". But in 1850 the League had virtually collapsed. In the winter of 1848–9 Josef Moll had tried to reorganise the League in Germany but his mission had failed and he had fallen in the battle of the River Murg in the rising in Baden. It would now be necessary to send another emissary (Heinrich Bauer) to Germany.

Marx and Engels gave their version of what had happened during the recent revolution in Germany. They claimed that, on seizing power in March 1848, the bourgeoisie had "used its power to oppress the workers – their allies in the struggle – and to reduce them to their former state of servitude". Eventually the middle class had been forced "to abdicate its power in favour of the old authoritarian feudal elements in society".[300]

Looking into the future, Marx and Engels declared that a new revolution might be expected to break out at any time. "It may come through a rising of the French workers or it may come as a reaction to an invasion of the Holy Alliance." "The party of the proletariat must take its part in this revolution as a fully organised, completely united, and absolutely independent organisation." "If it fails to do this, history will repeat itself and – as in 1848 – the party of the proletariat will be exploited and taken in tow by the middle classes."

Next Marx and Engels analysed the social structure of the German middle classes in Germany in 1850. They classified the bourgeoisie in three groups – on the right "the prosperous section of the upper middle class", in the centre "the democratic constitutional petty bourgeoisie", and on the left the "republican petty bourgeoisie". The group in the centre – the democratic petty bourgeoisie – was, in their view, the most important, since it included most of the middle class urban population, the petty traders, and the master craftsmen. In addition many smallholders and farm-workers in the country districts supported this party.

Marx and Engels discussed the future relationship between the revolutionary workers and the petty bourgeois democrats. They urged the revolutionary workers to "support the petty bourgeois democrats against the groups which they both wish to overthrow". "But the revolutionary workers oppose the petty bourgeois democrats in any action which would benefit only the petty bourgeois democrats." Marx and Engels observed that socialists and democrats pursued quite different aims. The former wished to overthrow the existing social system and to replace it by a socialist society. The latter accepted the existing social system and merely demanded reforms to improve it. These reforms – all of which would benefit the democrats – included higher taxes on the rich; a restriction on the right of inheritance; an expansion of the nationalised sector of the economy; lower interest rates; and the abolition of all surviving feudal institutions. To achieve these aims the democrats favoured the establishment of democratic institutions in central and local government.

Marx and Engels went on to argue that the democrats "intend the workers to retain the status of wage-earners, though they would like the workers to enjoy higher wages and greater security". The democrats favoured a quick revolution to achieve the reforms that they desired. The proletariat, on the other hand, was urged by Marx and Engels "to further its own interests by promoting a permanent revolution". They summed up their own policy as follows: "The most important aspects of the economy should be concentrated in the hands of the workers. We are not interested in making changes in private property. We propose to destroy it." "We have no desire to hide class distinctions. We wish to remove them." "We do not propose to improve the existing structure of society: we seek to create a new society."

The problem of the attitude to be adopted by the revolutionary workers towards the petty bourgeoisie was the next topic to be examined in the address. Marx and Engels suggested that a revolution passed through three phases in each of which the proletariat should adopt a different policy. The phases were: "(1) the present position when petty bourgeois democrats are as much oppressed as the workers"; "(2) the next phase of the revolution when the petty bourgeois democrats will hold the upper hand"; "(3) after the completion of the revolution when the oppressed classes and the proletariat will be in power".

During the first phase of the revolution Marx and Engels advised the workers not to allow the middle classes to take the initiative. They should set up public and secret organisations of their own. Every branch of the Communist League should act as "a rallying point for the local workers' associations". When a common enemy had to be fought, the workers should co-operate with the democrats. But after the defeat of the forces of reaction by demonstrations and street fighting, the proletariat should firmly resist appeals to go home and return to work. The armed workers should see to it "that a victorious revolution is not immediately followed by a return to normality". "The workers should not be frightened of so-called 'excesses' – popular vengeance against detested individuals or buildings – which leave unpleasant memories in their wake." "On the contrary the workers should not merely accept the fact that 'excesses' occur, but they should try to control them." Marx and Engels suggested that "as soon as there are signs that the bourgeois revolution is achieving its aims, the workers should cease to attack the reactionary parties and should begin to oppose the middle classes with whom they have formerly been allied."

In the second phase of the revolution – immediately following initial successes – the democrats would try to betray the workers. Marx and Engels urged the workers to offer a firm resistance to their erstwhile allies. "The workers must be organised and they must be armed." "They will have to get hold of flintlocks, fowling pieces, cannon and ammunition." "They must, if possible, prevent the revival of the old middle class national guard which would oppose the proletariat. If this cannot be done, the workers should try to set up their own militia under elected officers and an elected general staff. This militia should not obey a bourgeois government but should take its orders from revolutionary workers' councils. . . . This militia should in no circumstances surrender its arms or ammunition. If the government should try to do this it should be opposed – if necessary by force. . . ."

In the third and final phase of the revolution the proletariat should establish a government of its own and take over the control of the administration. The central committee of the Communist League would move from London to Germany and would call a national assembly. This assembly would work in association with local workers' clubs. During the elections for the national assembly the workers should insist upon their right to vote and – in every constituency – they should put forward their own candidates (preferably members of the Communist League) in opposition to middle class candidates. The workers' candidates should advocate "a radical and revolutionary programme" of legislation. Marx and Engels warned the revolutionary proletariat "not to listen to the argument that to split the left wing vote by putting up working class candidates would allow reactionary candidates to be elected". "To fall for such arguments would be to prepare the way for the certain defeat of the workers." In Germany Marx and Engels urged the workers to insist upon the establishment of a powerful central authority.

Finally, Marx and Engels returned to the phase of the revolution during which the bourgeois democrats would be in control. They suggested that the revolutionary workers should demand the nationalisation – without compensation to the owners – of factories and railways because "such reforms would compromise the democrats in the eyes of the upper classes and the reactionaries". The workers should also demand the immediate abolition of the national debt. The address ended with an appeal to the German workers to "hold fast to the policy of organising a workers' political party". "Their battle cry must be: 'Forward to a victorious permanent revolution!' "[301]

Thirty-five years later Engels claimed that the arguments which he and Marx had put forward in 1850 were still valid. He argued that in 1885 as in 1850 a revolution on the Continent was due at any time and he thought that it would bring the petty bourgeois democrats into power "as the saviours of society from the communist workers". The advice which Marx and Engels had given to the German revolutionary workers in 1850 still held good in 1885.[302]

A second address of the central committee of the Communist League was issued in June 1850. It was not written by Marx and Engels, though they probably saw it before it was sent to branches of the League.[303] The address briefly surveyed the progress made by the League in the past three months. It was stated that the leading regional centre (*Kreis*) of the League was the London centre which had the largest membership and the largest financial resources. The London centre bore the expense of sending emissaries to the Continent. The London centre dominated the local German Workers Educational Society as well as the main fund-raising organisation for the relief of German refugees. In Germany the League's emissary – the shoemaker Heinrich Bauer – had completed a successful propaganda tour. The Communist League had several regional centres (*Kreise*) and branches (*Gemeinde*) in Germany which had forged links with numerous workers' associations and gymnastic clubs.[304] It was reported that the recent attempt of a Swiss democratic organisation to contact workers' associations in Germany had failed. One of its emissaries had stated that he had found that all the useful contacts were already in the hands of the Communist League. Brief references were made in the address to the League's activities in France and Belgium.[305] In Paris Dr. Ewerbeck had recently resigned his membership so that this branch was without a leader. The address of June 1850, like the address drawn up by Marx and Engels in the previous March, was confident that a new revolution would soon break out on the Continent.

In the summer of 1850 Marx and Engels changed their minds on the likelihood of a revolution breaking out within the next few months. In June Marx was assured by his friend Georg Weerth that he did not think that there would be a revolution in Germany.[306] In March when Marx and Engels had written their fiery call to the workers to rise in revolt and in April when they had helped to found the Universal Society of Revolutionary Communists they had confidently expected a rising of the workers at any time. But shortly afterwards they realised that they had been mistaken. Writing in November 1850 they declared:

> "There can be no question of a revolution breaking out just now in view of this universal prosperity, which has enabled the productive powers of the middle classes to develop as much as they can develop within the framework of a bourgeois society. A revolution of the kind that we have in mind can take place only when there is a clash between the modern powers of production and the bourgeois method of production. . . . A new revolution will be possible only as the aftermath of a new economic crisis. But the revolution is as certain as the crisis."[307]

When Engels quoted these words in 1885 he wrote that in 1850

"the commercial crisis of 1847, which had prepared the way for the revolution of 1848, had been overcome. A new period of prosperity, such as the world had never seen before, had begun. Anyone who had eyes to see – and was prepared to use them – was bound to appreciate that the storms of revolution that had broken out in 1848 were now gradually subsiding."[308]

As soon as he was satisfied that there was no likelihood of an immediate revolution in Europe, Marx retired from active politics for the time being. In June 1850 he obtained a ticket to the reading room of the British Museum, where he pursued his researches into the growth and structure of the capitalist system. By the following January he was immersed in the problems of theories of rent and of currency, but seventeen years elapsed before the first volume of *Das Kapital* was published.

Marx's withdrawal from revolutionary politics[309] was facilitated by a crisis in the affairs of the Communist League. In the autumn of 1850 Marx and Willich were involved in a series of disputes at meetings of the Communist League, the German Workers Education Society, and the refugee relief committee. So bitter was the quarrel that it led to a duel – held in Belgium – between Willich and Marx's supporter Konrad Schramm. On September 15, 1850 the Communist League in London split into two rival factions – the majority led by Marx and Engels and the minority led by Willich and Schapper. Marx persuaded the Communist League to move its central committee from London to Cologne, where Willich and Schapper were unlikely to secure any support. Marx was determined that no organisation to which he belonged should survive if he could not dominate it. He acted in exactly the same way in 1872 when he secured the expulsion of Bakunin from the First International and the transfer of its General Council from London to New York.

There were several reasons for the split in the Communist League. Personal animosities and rivalries played their part. There was a bitter struggle for leadership in the revolutionary movement. In 1847 Marx and Engels had ousted Schapper from his leading position in the administration of the League. Now Schapper sought to recover his former influence. Willich – who has been described as "a Prussian version of Garibaldi"[310] – believed that, as an experienced soldier he, rather than a bookworm like Marx, should lead the workers to victory when the next revolution broke out. Marx and Engels, however, were not prepared to step down in favour of Willich and Schapper, whom they regarded as "two old good-for-nothings".[311] And while Willich favoured co-operation between the communists and members of various democratic associations in London, Marx was strongly opposed to this. Again, Willich and his supporters were urging the workers to attack the strongholds of reaction on the Continent by "the power of the guillotine",[312] but Marx and Engels were convinced that, in a period of prosperity, any attempt at an armed rising was doomed to failure. Marx told Willich and Schapper:

> "You are insisting that sheer *will power* rather than the facts of the situation are the driving wheel of the revolution while we tell the workers: 'You have 15 or 20 or 50 years of bourgeois war to go through, not just to alter existing conditions but to alter yourselves and qualify for political power'. You, on the contrary, tell them: 'We must take over political power *at once* or else we may lie down and go to sleep'."[313]

The Communist League did not long survive the transfer of the powers of its central committee from the London centre to the Cologne centre. In May 1851 the leading communists in Germany were arrested and for practical purposes the League was at an end. The trial of the German communists in Cologne ended on November 12, 1852 and within a week – at Marx's suggestion – the London centre passed a resolution dissolving the League. The Willich–Schapper faction was dissolved shortly afterwards.

It is astonishing that in 1850 Marx should have been able to edit a new socialist review when so much of his time was devoted to revolutionary politics and to fending off importunate creditors. Five numbers of the *Neue Rheinische Zeitung: Politisch-ökonomische Revue*[314] were published in Hamburg between January and October. Here Marx and Engels applied their doctrine of historical materialism to an examination of various aspects of French and German history. Marx dealt with the recent revolution and reaction in France in 1848 and 1849 while Engels wrote an account of the peasants war in Germany in the sixteenth century. Engels laid the foundations of his future reputation as a military critic by writing a series of articles on the campaign in Baden in 1849 in which he had taken part. He also discussed the English Ten Hours Bill and reviewed Carlyle's *Latter-Day Pamphlets*. J. C. Eccarius contributed an article on the tailoring trade in London. In their writings in this review Marx and Engels showed that they were at the height of their powers as political journalists.

By November 1850 Marx's fortunes were at a low ebb. His political career seemed to have come to an abrupt end since the powers of the central committee of the Communist League had been transferred from London to Cologne and the last number of his review had appeared. He no longer had any facilities for influencing public opinion. His wife claimed that the journal had been "a great success" but blamed the publisher for being "so negligent and inefficient over the business side of it, that it was soon obvious that it could not go on for long."[315] Marx had no regular source of income and no prospects. Yet he made no effort to secure paid employment which would enable him to support his family. Instead he carried on with his researches in the reading room of the British Museum.

Engels, too, was in a difficult situation. He does not seem to have earned any money since arriving in England. He had no regular remittance from home, though his father and mother may have sent him money from time to time. His parents told him that they would not support him so long as he persisted in his existing way of life.[316] Although he would much rather have stayed in London so as to be near Marx, he reluctantly decided to submit to his father's wishes and to join the firm of Ermen and Engels in Manchester as a clerk at a salary of £200 a year. Engels left London in the middle of November 1850 – he was now 30 years of age – and he hoped to earn enough to be able to give Marx some financial assistance. Soon after taking up his post in Manchester he sent Marx a postal order for £2 – the first of many remittances. Engels hoped that his stay in Manchester would be short. He was convinced that there would soon be a trade depression which would be the signal for a rising of the proletariat in England and on the Continent. As soon as the revolution broke out, Engels was determined to leave Manchester at once and rejoin his friend in London. He waited in vain. Economic crises occurred – as in 1857 – but there was no revolution. It was not until 1869 that he was able to retire from business and it was not until 1870 that Marx and Engels were again united in London.

NOTES

1 For Engels between 1846 and 1848 see Herwig Förder, *Marx und Engels am Vorabend der Revolution* (1960).

2 See *Reminiscences of Marx and Engels* (Foreign Languages Publishing House, Moscow), p. 173 (Friedrich Lessner) and p. 270 (P. V. Annenkov).

3 See police description of Engels in 1849 in the *Kölnische Zeitung*, June 9, 1849: reproduced in H. Hirsch, *Engels* (1968), p. 62.

4 F. Engels to K. Marx, September 28–30, 1847 in *Gesamtausgabe*, Part III, Vol. 1, p. 73.

5 Quoted by A. Künzli, *Karl Marx. Eine Psychographie* (1966), p. 380.

6 Georg Weerth to his mother, July 19, 1845 in Georg Weerth, *Sämtliche Werke*, Vol. 5, 1957, p. 172.

7 F. Engels to his sister Marie, May 31, 1845 in F. Engels, *Zwischen 18 und 25* (1965), pp. 262–72.

8 F. Engels (Ostend) to Karl Marx (Brussels), July 27, 1846 in *Gesamtausgabe*, Part III, Vol. 1, p. 23.

9 Stephan Born, *Erinnerungen eines Achtundvierzigers* (1898), p. 49.

10 F. Engels (Paris) to K. Marx (Brussels), September 18, 1846 in *Gesamtausgabe*, Part III, Vol. 1, pp. 39–40 and October 23, 1846, *ibid.*, p. 54.

11 F. Engels to K. Marx, August 19, 1846, second postscript, *ibid.*, p. 29, and F. Engels to K. Marx, October 23, 1846, *ibid.*, p. 54.

12 F. Engels to K. Marx, March 12 and 16, 1848, *ibid.*, p. 96. Engels had little success in collecting money due to Marx (F. Engels to K. Marx, March 18, *ibid.*, p. 98).

13 F. Engels, "Von Paris nach Bern" in F. Engels *Auf Reisen* (1966), p. 129.

14 F. Engels, *Auf Reisen* (1966), pp. 134–5.

15 K. Marx (Cologne) to F. Engels (Lausanne), November 10, 1848, *ibid.*, p. 102.

16 K. Marx (Cologne) to F. Engels (Bern), November 28, 1848, *ibid.*, p. 104.

17 F. Engels (Bern) to K. Marx (Cologne), January 7–8, 1849, *ibid.*, p. 105.

18 Engels registered with the Brussels police on August 25, 1845. His address was 7 rue de l'Alliance, Saint Josse ten Noode. Marx lived next door at number 5 (Gustav Mayer, *Friedrich Engels*, Vol. 1, 1934, p. 389).

19 F. Engels, "Progress of Social Reform on the Continent" in *The New Moral World*, No. 19, November 4, 1843: extracts in the *Northern Star*, November 11 and 25, 1843.

20 K. Marx, "Kritische Randglossen zu dem Artikel: Der König von Preussen und die Sozial reform. Von einem Preussen" (second article: *Vorwärts*, August 10, 1844, reprinted in *Werke*, Vol. 1, pp. 404–5).

21 Quoted by W. Seidel-Höppner in postscript to Wilhelm Weitling, *Das Evangelicum des armen Sündners* (Reclam edition, 1967), p. 275.

22 For Weitling see W. Seidel-Höppner, *Wilhelm Weitling, der erste Theoretiker und Agitator des Kommunismus* (1961).

23 For Wilhelm Wolff see Ch. 4, section (ii).

24 For Georg Weerth see Ch. 4, section (ii).

25 The *Triersche Zeitung* and *Das Westphälische Dampfboot*. For Weydemeyer see Karl Obermann, *Joseph Weydemeyer. Pioneer of American Socialism* (New York, 1947).

26 Jenny Marx, "Short Sketch of an Eventful Life" in *Reminiscences of Marx and Engels* (Foreign Languages Publishing House, Moscow), p. 222.

27 Karl Marx was given permission to reside in Belgium on giving the following undertaking: "In order to obtain the authorisation to reside in Belgium I hereby declare on my honour that I will refrain while in Belgium from publishing any work concerned with the politics of the day" (signed: Dr Karl Marx, March 22, 1845). The original document is reproduced in R. Payne, *Marx* (1968), p. 153.

28 F. Engels's introduction of 1885 to K. Marx, *Enthüllungen über den*

Kommunistenprozess zu Köln (third edition, 1885: new edition, 1952), p. 17.

29 F. Engels to K. Marx, January 20, 1845 in *Gesamtausgabe*, Part III, Vol. 1, p. 10. In his preface to *The Condition of the Working Class in England* Engels had written that "this book was originally designed to form part of a more comprehensive work on English social history." He had contributed some articles on English history to *Vorwärts* (Paris) between August 31 and October 19, 1844 (*Gesamtausgabe*, Part I, Vol. 4, pp. 292–334).

30 F. Engels to Karl Marx, May 15, 1870 in *Gesamtausgabe*, Part III, Vol. 4, p. 328.

31 A list of 18 contributions by Engels to the *Northern Star* is printed in *Marx–Engels Verzeichnis* (1966), p. 308.

32 Gustav Mayer, *Friedrich Engels*, Vol. 1, p. 224.

33 Engels had criticised the 'true socialists' in the postscript of "Ein Fragment Fouriers über den Handel" in *Deutsches Bürgerbuch für 1846* (second year) and in *Werke*, Vol. 2, pp. 604–10.

34 Karl Marx to C. W. Leske, August 1, 1846 in *Marx–Engels Werke*, Vol. 27, p. 448: see also Arnold Künzli, *Karl Marx, Eine Psychographie* (1966), pp. 241–2.

35 The first chapter of *The German Ideology* was printed in a Russian translation in 1924 and in the original German in the *Marx–Engels Archiv* (edited by D. Rjazanov), Vol. 1, 1926. A new version of Chapter 1 appeared in the *Deutsche Zeitschrift für Philosophie*, Year 14, 1966, No. 10. *The German Ideology* was published in its entirety in German in *Gesamtausgabe*, Vol. 5, 1932 and in *Werke*, Vol. 3, 1958. There are two English editions of *The German Ideology*. The first, edited by R. Pascal in 1938, included only Parts I and III. The second included the whole of the book and also some pages missing from earlier editions and first printed in the *International Review of Social History*, Vol. 7, Part I, 1962. The original manuscript (apart from the preface) is in the possession of the International Institute of Social History in Amsterdam.

36 F. Engels, *Ludwig Feuerbach und der Ausgang der klassischen deutschen Philosophie* 1888 in *Werke*, Vol. 21, p. 264: see also "Neuveröffentlichung des Kapital I des I Bandes der 'Deutschen Ideologie' von Karl Marx und Friedrich Engels" in *Deutsche Zeitschrift für Philosophie*, Year 14, 1966. No. 10, p. 1196.

37 Karl Marx and F. Engels, *The German Ideology* (1965), pp. 597–642.

38 Engels assured the Hamburg publisher Julius Campe in a letter of October 14, 1845 that *The German Ideology* was in no danger of falling foul of the censor: see F. Engels, *Zwischen 18 und 25* (1965), pp. 272–3.

39 Karl Marx to P. V. Annenkov, December 28, 1846 in K. Marx and F. Engels, *Selected Correspondence* (Foreign Languages Publishing House), p. 51.

40 K. Marx and F. Engels, *The German Ideology* (edition of 1965), p. 37.

41 K. Marx and F. Engels, *The German Ideology* (edition of 1965, p. 86 (n).

42 *Ibid.*, p. 149 (deleted passage).

43 *Ibid.*, p. 86.

44 F. Engels to F. Mehring, July 14, 1893 in K. Marx and F. Engels, *Selected Correspondence* (Modern Languages Publishing House, Moscow), p. 540.

45 K. Marx and F. Engels, *The Holy Family* (Foreign Languages Publishing House, Moscow, 1956), p. 46.

46 K. Marx to S. M. von Schweitzer, January 24, 1865 in K. Marx, *Elend der Philosophie* (edition of 1952), p. 41.

47 K. Marx to P. J. Proudhon (postscripts by Gigot and Engels) in R. Payne, *Marx* (1968), p. 141 and (without the postscripts) in K. Marx and F. Engels, *Selected Correspondence* (Foreign Languages Publishing House, Moscow), pp. 32–3.

48 P. J. Proudhon to K. Marx, May 17, 1846 in Maxime Leroy *Les Précurseurs français du Socialism* (1948), pp. 439–42 and in English translation in R. Payne, *Marx*, (1968), pp. 143–4.

49 The full title was *Système des contradictions économiques ou Philosophie de la Misère* (two volumes, 1846): English translation – *The Poverty of Philosophy . . . with a preface by F. Engels* (translated by H. Quelch, 1900: new edition edited by C. P. Dutt and V. Chattopadhyaya, 1936 and 1956).

50 P. J. Proudhon, *Philosophie der Staatsökonomie oder Notwendigkeit des Elends* (translated by Karl Grün, two volumes, Darmstadt, 1847). Another German translation by Wilhelm Jordan was published in Leipzig in 1847.

51 Quoted by R. Payne, *Marx* (1968), p. 145.

52 F. Engels (Paris) to the Communist Correspondence Committee in Brussels, September 16, 1846 – Committee Letter, No. 2 (*Gesamtausgabe*, Part III, Vol. 1, pp. 34–5). Karl Marx agreed with Engels on the failure of the English labour bazaars. He wrote in *Misère de la Philosophie*: "They founded in London, Sheffield, Leeds and in many other towns in England equitable labour-exchange bazaars. These bazaars, after having absorbed considerable capitals have all scandalously gone bankrupt. They have lost the taste for them once for all – M. Proudhon take warning!" (H. P. Adams, *Karl Marx in his earlier Writings*) (edition of 1940, new edition, 1965), pp. 192–3.

53 F. Engels to K. Marx, September 18, 1846 in *Gesamtausgabe*, Part III, Vol. 1, p. 41.

54 K. Marx to P. V. Annenkov, December 28, 1846 in Marx and Engels, *Selected Correspondence* (Foreign Languages Publishing House, Moscow), pp. 39–51.

55 Edmund Wilson, *To the Finland Station* (Fontana Library, 1960), p. 157.

56 Franz Mehring, *Karl Marx* (edition of 1967), p. 13.

57 For the relations between Marx and Proudhon see Franz Mehring, *Karl Marx* (edition of 1967), pp. 129–39; G. Guy-Grand, *La pensée de Proudhon* (1947), p. 38 *et seq.*; Erich Thier, "Marx und Proudhon" in *Marxismusstudien*, Vol. 2, 1957, pp. 120–50; H. Förder, *Marx und Engels am Vorabend der Revolution* (1960), pp. 135–42; H. P. Adams, *Karl Marx in his earlier Writings* (1940: new edition, 1965), Ch. 11; and R. Payne, *Marx* (1968), pp. 138–48.

58 Moses Hess to Karl Marx, May 29, 1846 in M. Förder, *Marx und Engels am Vorabend der Revolution* (1960), p. 74.

59 F. Engels to Karl Marx, July 27, 1846 in *Gesamtausgabe*, Part III, Vol. 1, p. 23; August 19, 1846, *ibid.*, p. 29 and September 16, 1846, *ibid.*, pp. 36–7.

60 F. Engels to Karl Marx, January 15, 1847 in *Gesamtausgabe*, Part III.

61 F. Engels to Karl Marx, March 9, 1847 in *Gesamtausgabe*, Part III, Vol. 1, p. 70.

62 Max Nettlau, "Londoner deutsche kommunistische Diskussion 1845" in *Archiv für die Gaschichte des Sozialismus und der Arbeiterbewegung*, Vol. 10, 1922, pp. 366–8.

63 See Arthur Lehring, "Discussions à Londres sur le Communisme Icarien" in *Bulletin of the International Institute of Social History*, Vol. 7 (1952), pp.94–6 and H. Förder, *Marx und Engels am Vorabend der Revolution* (1960), p. 56.

64 *Telegraph für Deutschland* (Hamburg), No. 165, October 1844: reprinted in G. Winkler (ed.), *Dokumente zur Geschichte der Kommunisten* (1957), pp. 64–6.

65 Friedrich Lessner in *Reminiscences of Marx and Engels* (Foreign Languages Publishing House, Moscow), p. 151.

66 F. Engels, "Zur Geschichte des Bundes der Kommunisten" (1885), introduction to reprint of Karl Marx, *Enthüllungen über den Kommunistenprozess zu Köln*, 1853.

67 H. Förder compares this argument with similar arguments advanced by Engels in his article in the *Northern Star*, April 4, 1846.

68 For this stormy session of the Communist Correspondence Committee in Brussels see the extract from P. V. Annenkov's memoirs in *Reminiscences of Marx and Engels* (Foreign Languages Publishing House, Moscow), pp. 269–72; W. Weitling to Moses Hess, March 31, 1846 in E. Barnikol, *Weitling, der Gefangene und seine "Gerechtigheit"* (Kiel, 1929), pp. 269–71; and F. Engels to A. Bebel, October 25, 1888 (in F. Engels, *Briefe an Bebel*, Berlin 1958, pp. 155–7).

69 K. Marx to P. J. Proudhon, May 5, 1846 in R. Payne, *Marx* (1968), pp. 141–2.

70 K. Marx (Hanover) to F. Engels (Manchester), May 7, 1867: "Do you remember J. Meyer of Bielefeld who failed to print our manuscript on Stirner etc. and sent that young fellow to Kriege to be a millstone round our necks? A few weeks ago he went to Warsaw on business, fell out of a window and obligingly broke his neck" (*Gesamtausgabe*, Part III, Vol. 3, p. 390).

71 Published in *Gesamtausgabe*, Part I, Vol. 6, p. 3 *et seq.* and *Werke*, Vol. 4, pp. 3–17. Weydemeyer published the circular (or manifesto) in *Das Westphälische Dampfboot*. Kriege published it in the *Volks–Tribun* with a reply written by Weitling. The foreword to the circular is printed in G. Winkler (ed.) *Dokumente zur Geschichte des Bundes der Kommunisten* (1957), p. 70.

72 *Deutsch-Brüsseler Zeitung*, September 26, 1847.

73 F. Engels, "Die Kommunisten und Karl Heinzen" in the *Deutsche-Brüsseler Zeitung*, October 3 and October 7, 1847 (*Marx–Engels Werke*, Vol. 4, pp. 309–24). The article was delivered to the newspaper on September 27 but Bornstedt, the editor, hesitated to publish it. Engels protested and the article appeared in print. Karl Marx also attacked Karl Heinzen in a series of articles in the *Deutsch-Brüsseler Zeitung*, October 28, October 31, November 11, November 18, and November 25, 1847 (*Marx–Engels Werke*, Vol. 4, pp. 331–59). Marx's articles were entitled: "Die moralische Kritik und die Kritisierend Moral, Beitrag zur deutschen Kulturgeschichte. Gegen Karl Heinzen." Karl Heinzen carried on the controversy in his book *Die Helden der deutschen Kommunismus* (Bern, 1848). For the controversy with Heinzen see also H. Förder, *Marx und Engels am Vorabend der Revolution* (1960), pp. 217–38.

74 For the Brussels Communist Correspondence Committee see Franz

Mehring, *Karl Marx*, (edition of 1967), Ch. 5 and H. Förder, *Marx und Engels am Vorabend Der Revolution* (1960).

75 See a fragment of a memorandum, written by Engels when he was in Ostend in August 1846, on founding a Communist Publishing Company (*Gesamtausgabe*), Part III, Vol. 1, pp. 24–6.

76 G. Winkler (ed.), *Dokumente zur Geschichte des Bundes der Kommunisten* (1957), pp. 67–9.

77 *Northern Star*, July 25, 1846 (Address of the German Democratic Communists to Mr Feargus O'Connor).

78 K. Marx and F. Engels, *The Communist Manifesto*, 1848 (edited by A. J. P. Taylor: Penguin Books, 1967), p. 119.

79 F. Engels to K. Marx, July 27, 1846 in *Gesamtausgabe*, Part III, Vol. 1, pp. 22–4.

80 F. Engels, *The Status Quo in Germany*, 1847 in K. Marx, F. Engels, Vol. 4: *Geschichte und Politik* 2 (Fischer Bücherei, 1966), p. 18.

81 F. Engels to K. Marx, August 19, 1846 in *Gesamtausgabe*, Part III, Vol. 1, p. 27.

82 F. Engels to the Communist Correspondence Committee in Brussels, October 23, 1846 (Committee Letter, No. 3) in *Gesamtausgabe*, Part III, Vol. 1, p. 53.

83 F. Engels to the Communist Correspondence Committee in Brussels, September 16, 1846 (Committee Letter, No. 2) in *Gesamtausgabe*, Part III, Vol. 1, p. 33.

84 F. Engels to K. Marx, middle of October 1846, in *Gesamtausgabe*, Part III, Vol. 1, p. 48.

85 F. Engels to the Communist Correspondence Committee in Brussels, October 27, 1846 (Committee Letter, No. 3) in *Gesamtausgabe*, Part III, Vol. 1, pp. 49–53.

86 Stephan Born, *Erinnerungen eines Achtundvierzigers* (1898), p. 49.

87 "I was in Paris on March 20 and had breakfast with my friend Engels in the Rue Rivoli. We greatly enjoyed the new chablis of 1846 and the whole world seemed a good place to be in" (Georg Weerth to his mother, April 18, 1847 in Georg Weerth, *Sämtliche Werke*, Vol. 5 (1957), p. 252).

88 Stephan Born, *op. cit.*, p. 49.

89 F. Engels to Karl Marx, December 1846 in *Gesamtausgabe*, Part III, Vol. 1, pp. 58–9.

90 F. Engels to K. Marx, March 9, 1847 in *Gesamtausgabe*, Part III, Vol. 1, p. 69.

91 F. Engels to K. Marx, January 14, 1848 in *Gesamtausgabe*, Part III, Vol. 1, p. 92.

92 F. Engels to K. Marx, March 9, 1847 in *Gesamtausgabe*, Part III, Vol. 1, p. 68.

93 K. Marx to F. Engels, May 15, 1847, in *Gesamtausgabe*, Part III, Vol. 1, p. 70.

94 *Gesamtausgabe*, Part I, Vol. 6, 1932; *Marx–Engels Werke*, Vol. 4, pp. 40–57; and *K. Marx–F. Engels, Vol. 4: Geschichte und Politik* 2 (Fischer Bücherei, 1966), pp. 17–33.

95 Iring Fetscher's introduction to K. Marx–F. Engels, Vol. 4; *Geschichte und Politik* 2 (Fischer Bücherei, 1966), p. 13.

96 The United Diet met from April 11 to June 26, 1847.

97 Stephan Born, *Erinnerungen eines Achtundvierzigers* (1898), p. 49.

98 Karl Wallau and Stephan Born were compositors on the staff of the *Deutsch-Brüsseler Zeitung.*

99 Franz Mehring, *Karl Marx* (edition of 1967), pp. 149–56 and note 21 on page 555 and Stephan Born, *op. cit.*, pp. 73–4.

100 F. Engels, "Karl Marx" in the *Volkskalender* (Brunswick, 1877), translated in *Reminiscences of Marx and Engels* (Foreign Languages Publishing House, Moscow), p. 19.

101 In the Vienna *Haus, Hof-und Staatsarchiv* there are records of payments of 1,000 francs (November 1, 1835) and 300 francs (January 31, 1836) to Bornstedt from the secret funds of the Austrian Ambassador in Paris. See Tibor Dénes, "Lehr und Wanderjahre eines jungen Schweizers, 1845–1848" in *Schweizerische Zeitschrift für Geschichte*, Vol. 16 (1966) (i), p. 51 (note 39).

102 For Bornstedt see article by H. F. Schmitz op der Beek in the *Brüsseler Zeitung*, January 24, 1943.

103 Quoted by Gustav Mayer, *Friedrich Engels*, Vol. 1 (1934), p. 386.

104 F. Engels to K. Marx, September 28–30, 1847 in *Gesamtausgabe*, Part III, Vol. 1, p. 72.

105 Marx took Engels's place as a vice president of the (Brussels) Democratic Association when Engels left Brussels for Paris in October 1847.

106 F. Engels to K. Marx, September 28–30, 1847 in *Gesamtausgabe*, Part III, Vol. 1, p. 79. Bartels was either Adolphe Bartels (formerly editor of the *Débat Social*) or his brother Jules.

107 *Northern Star*, No. 520, October 9, 1847 (by F. Engels). Engels's own views on the fiscal controversy had appeared in an article in the *Deutsch-Brüsseler Zeitung*, No. 46, July 10, 1847 and in *Marx–Engels Werke*, Vol. 4, pp. 58–61.

108 H. Förder, *Marx und Engels am Vorabend der Revolution* (1906), p. 223.

109 F. Engels to K. Marx, October 25–26, 1847 in *Gesamtausgabe*, Part III, Vol. 1, pp. 79–80.

110 F. Engels to K. Marx, October 25–26 in *Gesamtausgabe*, Part III, Vol. 1, pp. 81–2. For a list of Engels's contributions to *La Réforme* see *Marx–Engels Verzeichnis: Werke, Schriften, Artikel* (Berlin, 1966), (p. 312 (column 1).

111 F. Engels to K. Marx, October 25–26, 1847 in *Gesamtausgabe*, Part III, Vol. 1, pp. 79–81. Moses Hess's four articles appeared in the *Deutsch-Brüsseler Zeitung* on October 14, October 31, November 7 and November 11, 1847 and are reprinted in Moses Hess, *Philosophische und Sozialistische Schriften, 1837–1850* (1961), pp. 427–44.

112 See Engels's article of this meeting of the Fraternal Democrats in the *Northern Star*, December 4, 1847.

113 Stephan Born, *Erinnerungen eines Achtundvierzigers* (1899), p. 71.

114 Georg Weerth to his mother, June 13, 1846 in Georg Weerth, *Sämtliche Werke*, Vol. 5 (1957), p. 215.

115 F. Engels to K. Marx, January 14, 1848 in *Gesamtausgabe*, Part III, Vol. 1, p. 91.

116 F. Engels to K. Marx, January 14, 1848 in *Gesamtausgabe*, Part III, Vol. 1, p. 92.

117 K. Marx to F. Engels, March 16, 1848 in *Gesamtausgabe*, Part III, Vol. 1, p. 96.

118 Gustav Mayer, *Friedrich Engels*, Vol. 1 (1934), p. 388 quotes the following passage from the *Moniteur*: "Deux seuls étrangers M. Engels, allemand et un de ses compatriots ont été récemment expulsés de France; mais les causes qui ont motivé cette mesure de la part de

l'autorité sont complètement étrangères à la politique." There are references to Engels's expulsion in the following French newspapers: *Moniteur*, February 15, 1847; *Le Constitutionnel*, February 6 and 8, 1847; *Patrie*, February 14, 1847; and *National*, February 9 and 14, 1847.

119 Stephan Born, *Erinnerungen eines Achtundvierzigers* (1898), pp. 70–1.

120 Friedrich Engels's speech to the Brussels Democratic Association (in French) on February 22, 1848 is printed in *Gesamtausgabe*, Part I, Vol. 6.

121 F. Engels, "Die Bewegung von 1847" in the *Deutsch-Brüsseler Zeitung*, January 23, 1848; Gustav Mayer, *Friedrich Engels*, Vol. 1 (1934), p. 290.

122 For the Communist League see Dr Wermuth and Dr W. Stieber, *Die Communisten-Verschwörungen des neunzehnten Jahrhunderts* (two volumes, 1853–4; new edition, 1969); F. Engels, "Zur Geschichte des Bundes der Kommunisten" (introduction of 1885 to a new edition of Karl Marx, *Enthüllungen über den Kommunisten-Prozess zu Köln*, 1853); Franz Mehring's introduction of 1914 to Karl Marx, *Enthüllungen über den Kommunisten-Prozess zu Köln*, 1853); Karl Obermann, *Zur Geschichte des Bundes der Kommunisten 1849–52* (1953); Gerhard Winkler (ed.) *Dokumente zur Geschichte des Bundes der Kommunisten* (1957), Herwig Förder, *Marx und Engels am Vorabend der Revolution* (1960), pp. 128–35 and pp. 266–78; E. P. Kandel, *Marx and Engels – the Organisers of the Communist League* (Moscow, 1953: in Russian); S. Na'aman, "Zur Geschichte des Bundes der Kommunisten in Deutschland in der zweiten Phase seines Bestehens" in *Archiv für Sozialgeschichte*, Vol. 5, 1965.

123 E. Engelberg (ed.), *Die Klassiker des wissenschaftlichen Kommunismus zur deutschen Abeiterbewegung* (1958), p. 17.

124 For the League of Exiles see H. Schmidt, "Ein Beitrag zur Geschichte des Bundes der Geächteten" in *Neue Zeit*, Vol. 16, No. 1, p. 150 *et seq*.

125 For J. C. B. von Bruhn see Wermuth and Stieber, *Die Communisten-Verschwörungen des neunzehnten Jahrunderts*, Vol. 3 (1853) (reprinted 1969), pp. 32–3.

126 According to Wermuth and Stieber (*op. cit.*, Vol 1, p. 10) sixteen separate police departments were involved in the enquiries concerning the activities of members of the League of Exiles in Germany.

127 F. Engels, "Zur Geschichte des Bundes der Kommunisten" (introduction to edition of 1885 of Karl Marx, *Enthüllungen über den Kommunisten-Prozess zu Köln*, 1853) (edition of 1952), p. 11. For Karl Schapper see Wermuth and Stieber, *op. cit.*, Vol. 2, pp. 108–9; A. W. Fehling, *Karl Schapper und die Aufänge der Arbeiterbewegung bis zur Revolution von 1848* (University of Rostock dissertation, 1922); and Wolfgang Schieder, *Aufänge der deutschen Arbeiterbewegung* (Stuttgart, 1963).

128 For the Paris section of the League of the Just in the early 1840s see Arnold Ruge, *Zwei Jahre in Paris* (1946).

129 F. Engels to Karl Marx, end of December 1846 in *Gesamtausgabe*, Part III, Vol. 1, p. 60.

130 "Things are going splendidly in London. The two branches in West London and East London are growing every day and they have already enrolled some 500 members." (Address of the central executive

committee of the League of the Just, London, February 1847, in G. Winkler (ed.), *Dokumente zur Geschichte des Bundes der Kommunisten*, 1957, p. 89.) In 1853 the police directors Wermuth and Stieber (*op. cit.*, Vol. 1, p. 54) observed that by 1847 "the League must have grown enormously in London, not only in numbers but in influence. Unfortunately at that time the police had no knowledge of the activities of the League."

131 F. Engels, "Zur Geschichte des Bundes der Kommunisten", 1885 (*op. cit.*), p. 11.

132 F. Engels, *op. cit.*, p. 19.

133 J. C. Eccarius wrote an article on the tailoring trade in London: see "Die Schneiderei in London . . ." in the *Neue Rheinische Zeitung. Politisch-ökonomische Revue.* Heft 5 and 6, 1850, pp. 293–303.

134 K. Marx to F. Engels, August 25, 1851 in *Gesamtausgabe*, Part III, Vol. 1, p. 245. For Schabelitz see Tibor Dénés, "Lehr-und Wanderjahre eines jungen Schweizers . . ." in the *Schweizerische Zeitschrift für Geschichte*, Vol. 16, 1966, No. 1, pp. 34–79. Dénés considers that Schabelitz was never a communist "even though he served Marx for some years and was even a member of the Communist League in Paris for a time" (*op. cit.*, p. 67). The first number of the *Deutsche-Londoner Zeitung* appeared on April 4, 1845. Schabelitz was the editor from October 1846 to May 1848.

135 Max Nettlau, "Londoner deutsche kommunistische Diskussion, 1845. Nach dem Protokollbuch des Communistischen Arbeiter Bildungsverein" in the *Archiv für die Geschichte des Sozialismus und der Arbeiterbewegung*, Vol. 10, 1922, pp. 362–91; Ernst Engelberg, "Einiges über die historisch-politischen Charakter des Bundes der Gerechten" in *Wissenschaftliche Zeitschrift der Universität Leipzig*, 1951–2, Heft 5; "Discussions à Londres sur le Communisme Icarien" in the *Bulletin of the International Institute of Social History* (Amsterdam), Vol. 7, 1952, pp. 94–6; and Carl Grünberg, "Hugo Hildebrand über den kommunistischen Arbeiterbildungsverein in London" in *Archiv für die Geschichte des Sozialismus und der Arbeiterbewegung*, Vol. 11, 1925, pp. 458–9.

136 F. Engels, "Zur Geschichte des Bundes der Kommunisten" (*op. cit.*), p. 15.

137 G. Winkler (ed.), *Documente zur Geschichte des Bundes der Kommunisten* (1957), pp. 64–6. The letter (accompanied by a donation to the Silesian weavers) was signed by Schapper, Moll (and others) "on behalf of and in the name of the German Workers Education Society in London."

138 For the *Address to the Working Classes of Great Britain and the United States on the Oregon Question* (1846) see A. R. Schoyen, *The Chartist Challenge* (1958), pp. 138–9.

139 The author of the leaflet was a former grammar school master named Sievers. It appeared as a brochure and was also published in the *Northern Star*, September 26, 1846, and the *Deutsche-Londoner Zeitung*, September 18, 1846. For Engels's criticism of the leaflet see his letter to Karl Marx, September 18, 1846 in *Gesamtausgabe*, Part III, Vol. 1, p. 40. Engels declared that the author had "learned from the English how to write utter nonsense which completely ignores the facts and how to misunderstand a historical process."

140 In Committee Letter No. 3 to the Brussels Correspondence Committee dated October 23, 1846 (*Gesamtausgabe*, Part III, Vol. 1, p. 52)

Engels reported that Kriege had sent a letter to the *Halle* (headquarters) of the League of the Just in Paris. On that date therefore the headquarters of the League was still in Paris. But the address of the League of the Just of November 1846 came from London and stated that the leaders of the London branch of the League "had been authorised to undertake the duties of leadership within the League". The transfer of authority from Paris to London must have taken place after October 23 and before the end of November 1846.

141 F. Engels to K. Marx, end of December 1846 in *Gesamtausgabe*, Part III, Vol. 1, pp. 59–60.

142 The first address of the central executive committee of the League of the Just (November 1846) was printed in the *Demokratisches Taschenbuch für 1848* (Leipzig, 1847), pp. 282–90 and in G. Winkler (ed.), *Dokumente zur Geschichte des Bundes der Kommunisten* (1957), pp. 78–84.

143 Franz Mehring's introduction to the edition of 1914 of Karl Marx, *Enthüllungen über den Kommunisten-Prozess zu Köln*, 1852 (1952), pp. 151–2.

144 F. Engels's introduction of 1885 to K. Marx, *Enthüllungen über den Kommunisten-Prozess zu Köln*, 1852 (edition of 1952), pp. 19–20.

145 The following sentence in the address of February 1847 shows that it was written after the completion of Moll's mission: "We have provisionally reorganized our branches in France and in Belgium." The address of February 1847 is printed in the *Demokratisches Taschenbuch für 1848* (Leipzig, 1847), pp. 290–9 and in G. Winkler (ed.), *Dokumente zur Geschichte des Bundes der Kommunisten* (1957), pp. 85–91.

146 W. Wolff (?), "Der preussische Landtag und das Proletariat in Preussen, wie überhaupt in Deutschland" in the *Kommunistische Zeitschrift*, September, 1847: reprinted in G. Winkler (ed.), *Dokumente zur Geschichte des Bundes der Kommunisten* (1957), pp. 92–105. The article has now been attributed to Engels.

147 For the constitution of the Communist League of 1847 see Wermuth and Stieber, *op. cit.*, Vol. 1, Appendix 10 and G. Winkler (ed.), *Dokumente zur Geschichte des Bundes der Kommunisten* (1957), pp. 106–11.

148 Stephan Born, *Erinnerungen eines Achtundviezigers* (1898), p. 54 *et seq.* and Max Quarck, *Die erste deutsche Arbeiterbewegung* (1924), p. 47.

149 For the debates in the German Workers Education Society on Cabet's emigration plan see Arthur Lehning, "Discussions à Londres sur le Communisme Icarien" in the *Bulletin of the International Institute of Social History* (Amsterdam), Vol. 7, 1952, pp. 94–6 and F. Lessner in *Reminiscences of Marx and Engels* (Foreign Language Publishing House, Moscow), p. 152.

150 The draft manifesto of the central executive committee of the Communist League (1847) was in the form of a catechism. Only paragraphs 15, 18, 19 and 20 (discussed by the German Workers Education Society on October 19 and 26 and November 2 and 23, 1847) have survived. Carl Grünberg attempted to "reconstruct" the catechism from the views expressed in the addresses of the League of the Just of November 1846 and February 1847. Such a "reconstruction" makes the dubious assumption that the views of Karl Schapper and his colleagues had not changed between February 1847 and the summer

of 1847. See Carl Grünberg, "Die Londoner Kommunistische Zeitschrift und andere Urkunden aus den Jahren 1847–8", in *Archiv für die Geschichte des Sozialismus und der Arbeiterbewegung*, Vol. 4, 1921, pp. 249–341.

151 The leading article, entitled "Proletarians" was reprinted by C. Grünberg, *op. cit.*, and summarised by H. Förder, *op. cit.*, pp. 270–2.

152 F. Engels to K. Marx, October 25–26, 1847 in *Gesamtausgabe*, Part III, Vol. 1, pp. 79–84.

153 For the "Principles of Communism" – printed by Iring Fetscher in *Karl Marx–Friedrich Engels*, Vol. 3: *Geschichte und Politik* (I) (Fischer Bücherei, 1966) – see H. Bollnow, "Wer schrieb das Kommunistische Manifest?" in *Göttinger Universitätszeitung*, 1948, No. 6, and H. Bollnow, "Engels' Auffassung von Revolution und Entwicklung in seinen 'Grundsätzen des Kommunismus' (1847)" in *Marxismusstudien*, 1954, pp. 77–144.

154 F. Engels to K. Marx, November 23–24, 1847 in *Gesamtausgabe*, Part III, Vol. 1, pp. 87–9.

155 Gustav Mayer, *Friedrich Engels*, Vol. 1 (1934), p. 285.

156 Hermann Bollnow, "Engels' Auffassung von Revolution und Entwicklung in seinen 'Grundsätzen des Kommunismus' (1847)" in *Marxismusstudien*, Vol. 3, 1954, pp. 77–144.

157 F. Engels, "Grundsätze des Kommunistmus" (1847) in *Gesamtausgabe*, Part I, Vol. 6, pp. 503–22.

158 It has been observed that for Engels "the concept of revolution by peaceful means was an impossibility; only a violent transformation of the existing conditions could improve the position of the proletarians. It would have to be a political, as well as a social revolution" (F. Nova, *Friedrich Engels: His Contributions to Political Theory* (1967), p. 32).

159 A few weeks later in an article in the *Northern Star*, January 22, 1848 Engels declared that "after all the modern bourgeois, with civilisation, industry, order and, at least relative enlightenment following him, is preferable to the feudal lord or to the marauding robber, with the barbarian state of society to which they belong."

160 For this meeting see *La Réforme*, December 5, 1847 (F. Engels), the *Deutsche-Londoner Zeitung*, Number 140 (J. K. Schabelitz), and the *Deutsche-Brüsseler Zeitung*, December 9, 1847 (Marx and Engels)

161 R. Payne, *Marx* (1968), p. 161.

162 T. Dénes, "Lehr – und Wanderjahre eines jungen Schweizers 1845–1848" in the *Schweizerische Zeitschrift für Geschichte*, Vol. 16, 1966, No. 1, p. 72 (note 78).

163 F. Lessner in *Reminiscences of Marx and Engels* (Foreign Languages Publishing House, Moscow), p. 153.

164 F. Lessner, *ibid.*, p. 174.

165 F. Lessner (*ibid.*, p. 153) also stated that the conference lasted for ten days.

166 F. Engels, "Zur Geschichte des Bundes der Kommunisten", Introduction to the edition of 1885 of Karl Marx, *Enthüllungen über den Kommunistenprozess zu Köln*, 1852 (edition of 1952), p. 21.

167 T. Dénes in the *Schweizerische Zeitschrift für Geschichte*, Vol. 16, 1966, No. 1, p. 72.

168 F. Lessner in *Reminiscences of Marx and Engels* (Foreign Languages Publishing House, Moscow), p. 174.

169 Some of these lectures were printed in the *Neue Rheinische Zeitung* between April 5 and April 11, 1849.

170 R. Payne, *Marx* (1968), p. 162.

171 The printer was D. E. Burghard of Bishopgate. See F. Lessner in *Reminiscences of Marx and Engels* (Foreign Languages Publishing House, Moscow), p. 153.

172 The manifesto appeared in the *Deutsche-Londoner Zeitung* between March 3 and July 28, 1848: see T. Dénes, *op. cit.*, p. 64. The Communist Manifesto was also printed in Wermuth and Stieber, *Die Communisten-Verschwörungen des neunzehnten Jahrhunderbs* (two volumes, 1853–4: new edition, 1969), Vol. 1, pp. 209–34.

173 See B. Andréas, *Le manifeste Communiste* (Milan, 1963) and A. J. P. Taylor (ed.), *The Communist Manifesto* (Penguin Books, 1967).

174 F. Engels to Karl Marx, April 25, 1848 in *Gesamtausgabe*, Part III, Vol. 1, p. 100.

175 Thus the communist manifesto was translated into English by Helen Macfarlane (in the *Red Republican*, 1850), Samuel Moore (1888) and Eden and Cedar Paul (1930), and into Russian by Bakunin (1869) and by Plekhanov (1882).

176 A. J. P. Taylor: Introduction to *The Communist Manifesto* (Penguin Books, 1967), p. 36.

177 A. J. P. Taylor (ed.), *op. cit.*, p. 34.

178 A. J. P. Taylor, *The Communist Manifesto* (Penguin Books, 1967), pp. 62–3.

179 For the speeches of Marx and Engels at the meeting of the Brussels Democratic Association on February 22, 1848 see *Célébration à Bruxelles du deuxième anniversaire de la Révolution Polonaise du 22 février 1846* (Brussels, 1848), reprinted in *Marx–Engels Werke*, Vol. 4, p. 519 and p. 522.

180 Max Quarck, *Die erste deutsche Arbeiterbewegung* (Leipzig, 1924), p. 49.

181 See Engels's introduction to a new edition of Wilhelm Wolff, *Die schlesische Milliarde* (1886), pp. 6–7, reprinted in F. Engels, *Biographische Skizzen* (1967), pp. 85–6. In a letter to Marx written on Wednesday and Thursday, March 8–9, 1848 Engels stated that Wilhelm Wolff had left Brussels by train "last Sunday" (i.e. March 5). The police had refused to allow Wolff to go home to collect his belongings (*Gesamtausgabe*, Part III, Vol. 1, p. 94).

182 R. Payne, *Marx* (1968), p. 176.

183 The decisions taken at the meeting in Brussels of the central executive committee of the Communist League in Brussels were printed in Wermuth and Stieber, *Die Communisten-Verschwörungen des neunzehnten Jahrhunderts* (1853: new edition of 1969), Vol. 1, pp. 65–6. The resolutions were signed by Marx, Engels, F. Fischer, Gigot and H. Steingens.

184 *Reminiscences of Marx and Engels* (Foreign Languages Publishing House, Moscow), p. 223. The sum involved was 5,000 francs.

185 Tedesco was free by March 18: see F. Engels to K. Marx, March 18, 1848 in *Gesamtausgabe*, Part III, Vol. 1, p. 97.

186 F. Engels to K. Marx, March 8–9, 1848 in *Gesamtausgabe*, Part III, Vol. 1, p. 94.

187 Georg Weerth in the *Neue Rheinische Zeitung*, June 8, 1848, reprinted in Georg Weerth, *Sämtliche Werke*, Vol. 4 (1957), pp. 39–44. See also an article of September 3, 1848 in *Sämtliche Werke*, Vol. 4, pp. 91–7.

188 F. Engels to K. Marx, March 8–9, 1848 in *Gesamtausgabe*, Part III, Vol. 1, pp. 93–5. A week later Marx told Engels that Gigot "should

be acting with greater energy just now" (K. Marx to F. Engels, March 16, 1848 in *Gesamtausgabe*, Part III, Vol. 1, p. 97).

189 K. Marx to F. Engels, March 12, 1848 in *Gesamtausgabe*, Part III, Vol. 1, p. 96.

190 F. Engels to K. Marx, March 18, 1848 in *Gesamtausgabe*, Part III, Vol. 1, pp. 97–9.

191 Georg Weerth to his mother, March 27, 1848 in Georg Weerth, *Sämtliche Werke*, Vol. 5 (1957), p. 284.

192 The only difference between the new central executive committee of the Communist League (named in Marx's letter to Engels of March 12, 1848 in *Gesamtausgabe*, Part III, Vol. 1, p. 96) and the "committee of the Communist Party in Germany" which issued the seventeen point programme (Wermuth and Stieber, *op. cit.*, pp. 68–9) was that Wallau was a member of the central executive committee of the Communist League but not a member of the "Committee of the Communist Party in Germany".

193 Wermuth and Stieber, *op. cit.*, Vol. 1, pp. 68–9.

194 Karl Marx to F. Engels, March 16, 1848 in *Gesamtausgabe*, Part III, Vol. 1, p. 97.

195 Quoted by Franz Mehring, *Karl Marx* (edition of 1967), p. 162.

196 F. Engels's introduction of 1885 to Karl Marx, *Enthüllungen über den Kommunistenprozess zu Köln*, 1852 (Berlin, 1952), pp. 23–4.

197 Max Quarck, *Die erste deutsche Arbeiterbewegung* (1924), p. 73.

198 F. Engels's introduction of 1885 to a new edition of Karl Marx, *Enthüllungen über den Kommunistenprozess zu Köln,* 1852 (edition of 1952), p. 24.

199 For the reports of Wilhelm Wolff (April 18, 1848), Ernst Dronke (May 5, 1848) and Stephan Born (May 11, 1848) see Franz Mehring's introduction of 1914 to the fourth edition of K. Marx, *Enthüllungen über den Kommunistenprozess zu Köln,* 1852 (edition of 1952), pp. 157–61.

200 Wilhelm Wolff, *Gesammelte Schriften* (Berlin, 1909), p. 12 *et seq.*

201 For C. J. A. Hätzel see Wermuth and Stieber, *op. cit.*, Vol. 1, pp. 44–52 and Vol. 2, p. 54.

202 Wermuth and Stieber, *op. cit.*, Vol. 1, p. 50.

203 A "reserve deputy" was one who had the right to take his seat only if the senior deputy was absent.

204 A "Provisional Central Club", with Born as chairman, had been established at a meeting of about 150 workers held in Berlin at the *café d'artistes* on March 29, 1848.

205 Max Quarck argues that Born did not give up his faith in Marxism as quickly as he stated in his memoirs. Quarck observes that throughout the years 1848 and 1849 Born continued to be strongly influenced by his previous association with Marx and Engels in Brussels and Paris. See Max Quarck, *Die erste deutsche Arbeiterbewegung* (Leipzig, 1924), p. 55.

206 F. Engels to K. Marx, March 18: "Before his flight Dronke was admitted to the League by Willich and his friends. I examined him again here (in Brussels) and explained our views to him. Dronke accepted our principles and so I confirmed his admission to the League. In the circumstances there was little else that I could do even if I had had doubts about him. Moreover Dronke is quite a modest fellow – very young – and seems to me to be open to conviction. I think that if we keep an eye on him and help him to study,

he will become a reliable member of the League." (*Gesamtausgabe*, Part III, Vol. 1, p. 98).

207 Georg Weerth to Karl Marx, March 25–27, 1848 in Georg Weerth, *Sämtliche Werke*, Vol. 4 (1957), p. 282.

208 Georg Weerth to Karl Marx, March 25–37, 1848 in Georg Weerth, *Sämtliche Werke*, Vol. 5 (1957), p. 282.

209 F. Engels, "Marx und die *Neue Rheinische Zeitung* 1848–9" in the *Sozialdemokrat* (Zürich), March 13, 1884, reprinted in K. Marx and F. Engels, *Die Revolution von 1848. Auswahl aus der 'Neuen Rheinischen Zeitung'* (1955), p. 32. See also G. Becker, *Karl Marx und Friedrich Engels in Köln 1848–49* (1963) and Auguste Cornu, *Karl Marx et la révolution de 1848* (1948).

210 Georg Weerth to Karl Marx, March 25–27, 1848 in Georg Weerth, *Sämtliche Werke*, Vol. 5 (1957), p. 282. See also Georg Weerth to his mother, March 27, 1848 (*ibid.*, p. 284).

211 F. Engels, "Marx und die *Neue Rheinische Zeitung* 1848–49" in the *Sozialdemokrat* (Zürich), March 13, 1884, reprinted in Karl Marx and F. Engels, *Die Revolution von 1848* . . . (1955), p. 32.

212 K. Marx to F. Engels, April 24, 1848 in *Gesamtausgabe*, Part III, Vol. 1, p. 99.

213 F. Engels to K. Marx, April 25, 1848 in *Gesamtausgabe*, Part III, Vol. 1, p. 101.

214 F. Engels to K. Marx, May 9, 1848 in *Gesamtausgabe*, Part III, Vol. 1, p. 101.

215 F. Engels, "Marx und die *Neue Rheinische Zeitung* 1848–9" in the *Sozialdemokrat* (Zürich), March 13, 1884, reprinted in Karl Marx and F. Engels, *Die Revolution von 1848* . . . (1955), p. 32.

216 Kurt Hager's introduction to Karl Marx and F. Engels, *Die Revolution von 1848* . . . (1955), p. 7.

217 F. Engels, "Marx und die *Neue Rheinische Zeitung* 1848–9" in the *Sozialdemokrat* (Zürich), March 13, 1884, reprinted in Karl Marx and F. Engels, *Die Revolution von 1848* . . . (1955), pp. 32–3.

218 F. Lessner in *Reminiscences of Marx and Engels* (Foreign Languages Publishing House, Moscow), p. 168.

219 Karl Marx's articles on "Wages and Capital" appeared in the *Neue Rheinische Zeitung* between April 5 and April 11, 1849. The paper informed its readers on April 20 that – owing to Marx's absence from Cologne – this series of articles had been suspended. No more articles by Marx on this subject appeared in the *Neue Rheinische Zeitung*. In July 1849 Marx wrote to Weydemeyer that he would like to finish his essays on "Wages and Capital" – "of which only the first part appeared in the *Neue Rheinische Zeitung*." He hoped that Leske might be able to publish his "Wages and Capital" as a pamphlet. On August 28, 1849, however, Weydemeyer informed Marx that he had been unable to find a publisher for the proposed pamphlet.

220 At the end of November 1848 Marx asked Engels to write an article on the Hungarian campaign and on January 7–8, 1849 Engels replied and enclosed an article (*Gesamtausgabe*, Part III, Vol. 1, pp. 104–5.

221 T. Dénes, "Lehr – und Wanderjahre eines jungen Schweizers 1845–8" in *Schweizerische Zeitschrift für Geschichte*, Vol. 16, No. 1, pp. 77.

222 F. Engels, "Marx und die *Neue Rheinische Zeitung* 1848–9" in the *Sozialdemokrat* (Zürich), March 13, 1884, printed in Karl Marx and F. Engels, *Die Revolution von 1848* . . . (1955), p. 38. For the contributions of Marx and Engels to the *Neue Rheinische Zeitung* see

Marx–Engels Werke, Vols 6 and 7 and a selection of articles in Karl Marx and F. Engels, *Die Revolution von 1848 . . .* (1955). Georg Weerth's articles in the *Neue Rheinische Zeitung* and his novel *Leben und Taten des berühmten Ritters Schnapphahnski* have been printed in Georg Weerth, *Sämtliche Werke,* Vol. 4 (1957), pp. 39–489. Wilhelm Wolff's articles on *Die schlesische Milliarde* were reprinted in 1886 as a pamphlet (with an introduction by F. Engels) by the Verlag der Volksbuchhandlung in Hottingen-Zürich.

223 For articles on the Frankfurt National Assembly see the *Neue Rheinische Zeitung,* June 1 and 7, 1848 and November 23, 1848 in Karl Marx and F. Engels, *Die Revolution von 1848 . . .* (1955), pp. 42–51 and pp. 237–8. For articles on the Prussian National Assembly in Berlin see the *Neue Rheinische Zeitung,* June 4 to 17, 1848 in Karl Marx and F. Engels, *Die Revolution von 1848 . . .* (1955), pp. 52–75.

224 F. Engels, "Marx und die *Neue Rheinische Zeitung* 1848–9" in the *Sozialdemokrat* (Zürich), March 13, 1884 and Karl Marx and F. Engels, *Die Revolution von 1848 . . .* (1955), p. 34.

225 See the article entitled "No more Taxes" in the *Neue Rheinische Zeitung,* November 17, 1848 (supplement) in Karl Marx and F. Engels, *Die Revolution von 1848 . . .* (1955), pp. 236–7.

226 "Der rheinische Städtetag" (*Neue Rheinische Zeitung,* May 4, 1849) and "Belagerungsgelüste" (*Neue Rheinische Zeitung,* May 6, 1849).

227 "Address to the Workers of Cologne" in the *Neue Rheinische Zeitung,* May 19, 1849.

228 *Neue Rheinische Zeitung,* December 31, 1848 and Karl Marx and F. Engels, *Die Revolution von 1848 . . .* (1955), p. 274. A similar point of view was expressed in the democratic *Neue Deutsche Zeitung* on January 6, 1849: "The revolution of 1848 was the last revolution to be made by the proletariat for the benefit of the middle classes. The revolution of 1849 will be the first revolution to be made by the proletariat in the interest of the workers" (quoted in Max Quarck, *Die erste deutsche Arbeiterbewegung 1848–9* (1924), pp. 313).

229 F. Engels, "Marx und die *Neue Rheinische Zeitung* 1848–9" in the *Sozialdemokrat* (Zürich), March 13, 1884, printed in Karl Marx and F. Engels, *Die Revolution von 1848 . . .* (1955), p. 33.

230 *Ibid.*, p. 36.

231 *Neue Rheinische Zeitung,* August 9 to September 7, 1848 in Karl Marx and F. Engels, *Die Revolution von 1848 . . .* (1955), pp. 112–67.

232 *Neue Rheinische Zeitung,* July 3, 1848 in Karl Marx and F. Engels, *Die Revolution von 1848 . . .* (1955), p. 103.

233 "Der magyarische Kampf" (*Neue Rheinische Zeitung,* January 13, 1849) in *Marx–Engels Werke,* Vol. 6, p. 165.

234 "Der demokratische Panslavismus" (*Neue Rheinische Zeitung,* February 15, 1849) in *Marx–Engels Werke,* Vol. 6, p. 275.

235 See articles in the *Neue Rheinische Zeitung,* June 29 and July 1, 1848: Karl Marx and F. Engels, *Die Revolution von 1848 . . .* (1955), pp. 84–97.

236 *Neue Rheinische Zeitung,* May 19, 1849 in Georg Weerth, *Sämtliche Werke,* Vol. 4 (1957), pp. 277–80.

237 See G. Becker, *Karl Marx und Friedrich Engels in Köln 1848–49* (1963).

238 *Neue Rheinische Zeitung,* April 15, 1849.

239 Many years later F. Lessner stated that when he attended the congress

of the German Social Democrat Party in Cologne in 1893 he met some peasants from Worringen. "They still remembered me from 1848 and 1849" (*Reminiscences of Marx and Engels*, Foreign Languages Publishing House, Moscow), p. 157.

240 The last number of the *Neue Rheinische Zeitung* to be printed before the suspension was Number 112 dated September 26, 1848. The printing of Number 113 had already begun on the afternoon of September 26 when publication ceased. On September 30, 1848 the regular subscribers were informed that publication would be resumed on October 5 but in fact Number 114 was dated Thursday, October 12, 1848.

241 The date "September 11" given by Marx (in a letter to Engels, October 26, 1848 in *Gesamtausgabe*, Part III, Vol. 1, p. 102) was a mistake.

242 Extracts from letters written by Engels's mother to her son are taken from Klaus Goebel and Helmut Hirsch, "Engels-Forschungsmaterialen im Bergischen Land" in *Archiv für Sozialgeschichte*, Vol. 10, 1969, pp. 109–34.

243 Karl Marx to F. Engels, November 10, 1848 in *Gesamtausgabe*, Part III, Vol. 1, p. 103.

244 F. Engels, "Von Paris nach Bern" in F. Engels, *Auf Reisen* (1966), pp. 121–59.

245 Karl Marx to F. Engels, October 26, 1848 in *Gesamtausgabe*, Part III, Vol. 1, p. 102.

246 Karl Marx to F. Engels, November 10, 1848 in *Gesamtausgabe*, Part III, Vol. 1, pp. 102–3.

247 Karl Marx to F. Engels, November 29, 1848 in *Gesamtausgabe*, Part III, Vol. 1, pp. 103–4.

248 Georg Weerth to F. Engels, December 10, 1848 (postscript to letter from Stephan Naut to F. Engels) in Georg Weerth, *Sämtliche Werke*, Vol. 5 (1957), p. 291.

249 F. Engels to Karl Marx, December 28, 1848 in *Gesamtausgabe*, Part III, Vol. 1, p. 104.

250 F. Engels to Karl Marx, January 7–8, 1849 in *Gesamtausgabe*, Part III, Vol. 1, pp. 102–6.

251 "Der magyarische Kampf" (*Neue Rheinische Zeitung*, January 13, 1849) in *Marx–Engels Werke*, Vol. 6, pp. 165–76.

252 F. Engels to Karl Marx, July 6, 1852 in *Gesamtausgabe*, Part III, Vol. 1, p. 361. See also G. Zirke, *Der General* (1957), p. 8, where the date of Engels's letter to Marx is given incorrectly as June 6, 1852.

253 *Deutsche Monatshefte für Politik, Wissenschaft, Kunst und Leben* (Stuttgart), Vol. 10 (ii), p. 125; see also G. Zirke, *Der General* (1957), p. 8. Wilhelm Liebknecht later recalled that when he first met Engels in Switzerland in 1849 – after the campaign in Baden – he "learned that the articles that the *Neue Rheinische Zeitung* had published on the revolutionary war in Hungary, and were attributed to a high-ranking officer in the Hungarian army because they always proved to be correct, were written by Engels. And yet, as he himself told me, laughing, he had no other material than all the other newspapers had. This came almost exclusively from the Austrian government, which lied in the most brazen way. It did the same with Hungary as the Spanish government now (1895) with Cuba – it always won. But Engels here made use of his *clairvoyance*. . . . No matter with what scorn of death the Austrian government issued its Münchausen proclamations it had to mention certain facts – the names of the places

where the clashes took place; where the troops were at the beginning and at the end of the battle; the time of the clashes; the troop movements, etc. And out of these tiny bits and pieces Engels with his clear bright eyes put together . . . the real picture of the events in the fighting area. With a good map of the theatre of operations one could conclude with mathematical accuracy from the dates and places that the victorious Austrians were being pushed farther and farther back while the defeated Hungarians continued to go farther and farther forward. The calculation was so correct, too, that the day after the Austrian army had inflicted a decisive defeat on the Hungarians – on paper – it was thrown out of Hungary in complete disarray." (Wilhelm Liebknecht in *Reminiscences of Marx and Engels*, Foreign Languages Publishing House, Moscow, pp. 138–9).

254 *Neue Rheinische Zeitung*, January 13, 1849 in *Marx–Engels Werke*, Vol. 6, pp. 165–76.

255 The speeches made by Marx and Engels in their defence on February 7, 1849 were printed in the *Neue Rheinische Zeitung*, February 14, 1849 (*Marx–Engels Werke*, Vol. 6, pp. 223–39) and as a pamphlet entitled *Zwei politische Prozesse* . . . (Cologne, 1849).

256 Karl Marx to F. Engels, April 23, 1849 in *Gesamtausgabe*, Part III, Vol. 1, pp. 106–7.

257 *Neue Rheinische Zeitung*, May 4, 1849; see also G. Mayer, *Friedrich Engels*, Vol. 1 (1934), p. 332 and H. Hirsch, *Engels* (1968), pp. 57–8.

258 For the rising in Elberfeld in May 1849 see the account (presumably by Engels himself) in the *Neue Rheinische Zeitung*, May 17, 1849 – English translation by W. O. Henderson in *Engels: Selected Writings* (Penguin Books, 1967), pp. 125–7. See also C. Hecker, *Der Aufstand zu Elberfeld im Mai 1849 und mein Verhältniss zu demselben* (Elberfeld, 1849).

259 F. Engels, "Die deutsche Reichsverfassungs-Campagne" in the *Neue Rheinische Zeitung. Politisch-ökonomische Revue*, Heft 1, January 1850 (reprint of 1955), pp. 49–50.

260 Ernst von Eynern, "Friedrich von Eynern. Ein Bergisches Lebensbild" in the *Zeitschrift des Bergischen Vereins*, Vol. 55.

261 *Elberfelder Zeitung*, June 3, 1849 and H. Hirsch, *Engels* (1968), p. 61.

262 *Kölnische Zeitung*, June 9, 1849 and H. Hirsch, *Engels* (1968), p. 62. The warrant was issued on June 6, 1849.

263 F. Engels, "Marx und die *Neue Rheinische Zeitung*" in the *Sozialdemokrat* (Zürich), March 13, 1884: see Karl Marx and F. Engels, *Die Revolution von 1848* . . . (1955), pp. 37–8.

264 F. Engels, "Petty Traders" in the *New York Daily Tribune*, October 2, 1852 (K. Marx (should be F. Engels), *Revolution and Counter-Revolution or Germany in 1848*, edited by Eleanor Marx Aveling, edition of 1952, p. 126).

265 F. Engels, "Die Deutsche Reichsverfassungs-Campagne" in the *Neue Rheinische Zeitung. Politisch-ökonomische Revue*, Heft 1. There is an English translation of this passage in Wilhelm Liebknecht, "Reminiscences of Engels" in *Reminiscences of Marx and Engels* (Foreign Languages Publishing House, Moscow), pp. 140–1.

266 The phrase appeared in an article by Engels in the *New York Daily Tribune*, September 18, 1852: see introduction to W. O. Henderson (ed.), *Engels: Selected Writings* (Penguin Books, 1967), p. 16.

267 F. Engels, "Petty Traders" in the *New York Daily Tribune*, October

2, 1852 (K. Marx – should be F. Engels – *Revolution and Counter-Revolution or Germany in 1848*, edited by Eleanor Marx Aveling, edition of 1952, p. 127).

268 K. Obermann, *Zur Geschichte des Bundes der Kommunisten 1849 bis 1852* (1955), p. 13.

269 F. Engels in *Der Bote für Stadt und Land*, June 3, 1849, reprinted in *Marx–Engels Werke*, Vol. 6, pp. 524–6.

270 Karl Marx to F. Engels, June 7, 1849 in *Gesamtausgabe*, Part III, Vol. 1, p. 109.

271 F. Engels to Jenny Marx, July 25, 1849 in *Gesamtausgabe*, Part III, Vol. 1, p. 109.

272 F. Engels to Jenny Marx, July 25, 1849 in *Gesamtausgabe*, Part III, Vol. 1, p. 109.

273 Klaus Schreiner, *Die badisch-pfälzische Revolutionsarmee 1849* (1956), pp. 39–40.

274 Klaus Schreiner, *Die badisch-pfälzische Revolutionsarmee 1849* (1956), p. 71.

275 F. Engels, "Die deutsche Reichsverfassungs-Campagne" in the *Neue Rheinische Zeitung. Politisch-ökonomische Revue*, Heft 2, February 1850 (reprint of 1955), pp. 164–5. There is an English translation of this passage in *Reminiscences of Marx and Engels* (Foreign Languages Publishing House, Moscow), pp. 143–4.

276 F. Engels to Jenny Marx, July 25, 1849 in *Gesamtausgabe*, Part III, Vol. 1, p. 109 and W. O. Henderson (ed.), *Engels: Selected Writings* (Penguin Books, 1967), pp. 128–9.

277 Karl Marx to F. Engels, August 11, 1849 in *Gesamtausgabe*, Part III, Vol. 1, pp. 110–11.

278 Gustav Mayer, *Friedrich Engels*, Vol. 1 (1934), p. 352.

279 Karl Marx to F. Engels, August 23, 1849 in *Gesamtausgabe*, Part III, Vol. 1, p. 113.

280 Wilhelm Liebknecht described his first meeting with Engels in Switzerland in an article in the *Illustrierte Neue Welt: Kalender für das Jahr 1897*, reprinted (in English translation) in *Reminiscences of Marx and Engels* (Foreign Languages Publishing House, Moscow), pp. 137–48.

281 Gustav Mayer, *Friedrich Engels*, Vol. 1 (1934), p. 356.

282 Georg Weerth to his mother, November 28, 1849 in Georg Weerth, *Sämtliche Werke*, Vol. 5 (1957), p. 338.

283 F. Engels, "Zur Geschichte des Bundes der Kommunisten": introduction to a new edition (1885) of Karl Marx, *Enthüllungen über den Kommunistenprozess zu Köln* (1852–3); F. Engels, "Karl Marx" in *Die Zukunft*, August 11, 1869; Wermuth and Stieber, *Die Communisten-Verschwörungen des neunzehnten Jahrhunderts* (two volumes, 1853–4: reprinted in one volume in 1969); K. Obermann, *Zur Geschichte des Bundes der Kommunisten, 1849–52* (1955); R. Herrnstadt, *Die erste Verschwörung gegen das Internationale Proletariat. Zur Geschichte des Kölner Kommunistenprozesses 1852* (1958); W. Schneider, "Der Bund der Kommunisten im Sommer 1850" in the *International Review of Social History*, Vol. 13, 1968, pp. 29–57.

284 Marx's passport shows that he left Boulogne on August 26, 1849.

285 Karl Marx to J. Weydemeyer, December 19, 1849 in Karl Marx and F. Engels, *Letters to Americans, 1848–95* (1963), p. 18.

286 Karl Marx to J. Weydemeyer, July 27, 1850 in Karl Marx and

J. Weydemeyer, July 27, 1850 in Karl Marx and F. Engels, *Letters to Americans, 1848–95* (1963), p. 19.

287 Jenny Marx, "Short Sketch of an eventful Life" in *Reminiscences of Marx and Engels* (Foreign Languages Publishing House, Moscow), p. 226.

288 4 Anderson Road, Chelsea.

289 Jenny Marx, "Short Sketch of an eventful Life" in *Reminiscences of Marx and Engels*, p. 226.

290 Jenny Marx stated that Marx and his family stayed at the German Hotel for only a week. "One morning our worthy host refused to serve us our breakfast and we were forced to look for other lodgings" (*Reminiscences of Marx and Engels*, p. 226). According to the pamphlet *London Landmarks*, Marx and his family lived in the German Hotel "in April and May 1850" (p. 3). See also R. Payne, *Marx* (1968), p. 233.

291 64 Dean Street, Soho (May 8–December 2, 1850) and then 28 Dean Street (until 1856).

292 Jenny Marx to J. Weydemeyer, May 20, 1850 in *Reminiscences of Marx and Engels*, p. 237.

293 Jenny Marx, "Short Sketch of an eventful Life" in *Reminiscences of Marx and Engels*, p. 227.

294 F. Engels to J. Weydemeyer, April 25, 1850 (postscript) in Karl Marx and F. Engels, *Letters to Americans, 1848–95* (1963), p. 19.

295 Baron Bunsen, the Prussian ambassador in London, reported in February 1851 that, according to information supplied to him by the Home Secretary, the "democratic clubs" in London had about 300 German, 200 Magyar and 40 Polish members. This suggests that there were about 1,000 foreign refugees in London at this time who belonged to political associations. See R. Herrnstadt, *Die erste Verschwörung gegen das Internationale Proletariat* (1958), pp. 225–6.

296 See Yvonne ffrench, *News from the Past, 1805–87*, pp. 375–82. For Chartist approval of the attack on Haynau see *The Red Republican*, September 7 and 14, 1850 and R. G. Gammage, *History of the Chartist Movement, 1837–54* (1854: new edition, 1969), p. 355. Gammage wrote: "What increased the excitement at this time was the visit of the Austrian General Haynau to London, who was assailed by Barclay and Perkins's draymen, and driven into a dustbin, for his merciless cruelties inflicted on the brave Hungarians. Votes of thanks were passed to the draymen at every meeting, for the personal chastisement inflicted on this monster of despotism, who had presumed to pollute the shores of England by his presence".

297 R. Payne, *Marx* (1968), p. 241. The statutes were originally written in French.

298 A Prussian agent described the revolutionary activities of the German exiles in London in a report dated May 2, 1850. Otto von Manteuffel gave a copy to Lord Westmoreland, the British ambassador in Berlin, on May 24. Lord Westmoreland forwarded it to Lord Palmerston. See R. Payne, *Marx* (1968), pp. 234–8.

299 "Prussian Spies in London" in *The Spectator*, *Sun*, and *Northern Star*, June 15, 1850. The letter also appeared in some German newspapers such as the *Westdeutsche Zeitung*, June 20, 1850.

300 Engels gave a more detailed account of the revolution in Germany in 1848–9 in a series of articles in the *New York Daily Tribune* in

1851–2: see Karl Marx (should be F. Engels), *Revolution and Counter-Revolution* (edited by Eleanor Marx, 1896).

301 Wermuth and Stieber, *Die Communisten-Verschwörungen des neunzehnten Jahrhunderts* (two volumes, 1853–4: new edition in one volume, 1969), Vol. 1, Appendix 13, pp. 251–9; appendix to Karl Marx. *Enthüllungen über den Kommunistenprozess zu Köln* (new edition with introduction by F. Engels, Zürich, 1885: reprinted 1952), pp. 124–36; and Iring Fetscher (ed.), *Karl Marx–Friedrich Engels Studienausgabe*, Vol. 3: *Geschichte und Politik* (No. 1, 1966), pp. 90–9.

302 F. Engels, "Zur Geschichte des Bundes der Kommunisten": introduction to Karl Marx, *Enthüllungen über den Kommunistenprozess zu Köln* (edition of 1885: reprinted 1952), p. 27.

303 W. Schneider, "Der Bund der Kommunisten im Sommer 1850" in *International Review of Social History*, Vol. 13, 1968, pp. 29–57.

304 Three of the most important branches of the Communist League in Germany in 1850 were
(i) Cologne, led by Heinrich Bürgers,
(ii) Frankfurt am Main, led by J. Weydemeyer,
(iii) Mainz, led by Friedrich Lessner.

305 The address of the central committee of the Communist League of June 1850 was printed in Wermuth and Stieber, *Die Communisten-Verschwörungen des neunzehnten Jahrhunderts* (two volumes, 1853–4: reprinted in one volume, 1969), Vol. 1, Appendix 14, pp. 260–5.

306 Georg Weerth to Karl Marx, June 2, 1850 in Georg Weerth, *Sämtliche Werke*, Vol. 5 (1957), p. 539.

307 Karl Marx and F. Engels, "Revue. Mai bis Oktober" in the *Neue Rheinische Zeitung. Politisch-ökonomische Revue*, Heft 5–6, May to October 1850, pp. 317–8. See the reprint of the review (introduction by Karl Bittel: Berlin, 1955).

308 F. Engels, "Zur Geschichte des Bundes der Kommunisten": introduction of 1885 to a new edition of Karl Marx, *Enthüllungen über den Kommunistenprozess zu Köln*, 1852–3 (edition of 1952), p. 27.

309 In February 1851 Marx declared that he was "in complete retirement" (Karl Marx to F. Engels, February 11, 1851 in *Gesamtausgabe*, Part III, Vol. 1, p. 146).

310 R. Payne, *Marx* (1968), p. 229.

311 F. Engels to J. Weydemeyer, April 12, 1853 in Karl Marx and F. Engels, *Letters to Americans, 1848–95* (1963), p. 57.

312 R. Payne, *Marx* (1968), p. 243.

313 R. Payne, *Marx* (1968), p. 246.

314 *Neue Rheinisch Zeitung. Politisch-ökonomische Revue* (edited by Karl Marx: reprinted in 1955 with an introduction by Karl Bittel).

315 Jenny Marx, "Short Sketch of an eventful Life" in *Reminiscences of Marx and Engels* (Foreign Languages Publishing House, Moscow), p. 226.

316 Elise Engels to F. Engels, December 2, 1849: "But now your father says, and I must agree with him, that if you follow a path which – to put it mildly – we cannot approve, you must not expect us to support you" (Klaus Goebel and Helmut Hirsch, "Engels – Forschungsmaterialen im Bergischen Land" in *Archiv für Sozialgeschichte*, Vol. 9, 1969, p. 444). See also Elise Engels to F. Engels, April 11, 1850 (*ibid.*, pp. 444–5).

4

THE MANCHESTER YEARS 1850–1870

I. The Years of Storm and Stress, 1850–60

When Marx referred to Engels's years of "storm and stress"[1] he aptly described the period between Engels's return to Manchester in 1850 and the death of his father in 1860. Engels had a robust constitution but there was a history of epilepsy in his family and he stuttered when excited. The strain of life in Manchester, combined with overwork, led to a breakdown in Engels's health between 1857 and 1860. He was ill for six months in the second half of 1857. And in 1860, when his father died, his brother Emil had to come to Manchester to settle Engels's future in the firm as Engels himself was not well enough to attend to the matter.

Engels's life in Manchester was fraught with difficulties. He disliked Manchester and the "philistines" who made up its business community. As soon as he arrived he wrote to Julian Harney that he was disgusted with the place and Harney replied that Manchester was "a damned dirty den of muckworms". "I would rather be hanged in London than die a natural death in Manchester."[2] Engels knew that Marx missed him[3] and he longed to return to London. He detested office work and the drudgery of earning a living in the cotton trade. He was under a continual strain because he was living a double life. He was a businessman by day and a revolutionary writer in the evenings and at week ends. He hoped that his office colleagues and the gentlemen whom he met at the Albert Club or the Cheshire Hunt would not find out about his revolutionary past, his association with Marx, and his hopes for the downfall of capitalism. Engels disliked having to maintain two establishments – his bachelor lodgings where he entertained his middle-class friends and the home which he made for himself and Mary Burns.

To add to these problems there was the fact that Marx was nearly always short of money. The need to send remittances to Marx frequently left Engels without sufficient funds himself. And the attitude of his father, who strongly disapproved of Engels's friendship with Marx, did not help matters. Engels was, however, buoyed up by the firm conviction that there would soon be a revolution. When this happened he planned to leave Manchester at once. But he was doomed to disappointment. Whenever there was a trade recession – as in 1857 – he rejoiced at the imminent fall of the bourgeois society which he detested. Throughout the twenty years that he worked for Ermen and Engels he waited in vain for a revolution that never took place.

Engels's position in the firm of Ermen and Engels was not a happy one. He settled in Manchester because he thought that this was the only way to earn enough money to satisfy his own needs and those of Marx. The brothers Peter and Godfrey Ermen regarded Engels's arrival with considerable misgivings since his presence in the office in South Gate threatened their freedom to run the Manchester business as they pleased. The firm of Ermen & Engels had been founded in 1838.[4] It manufactured sewing thread which was a highly specialised branch of the cotton industry. Its trade mark was three red towers – a device taken from the arms granted to a certain Ludwig van Ermen in the sixteenth century. The firm prospered to such an extent that Friedrich Engels senior had more than doubled his capital in twelve years.[5] It was now run by four partners – the three Ermen brothers (Peter, Anthony and Godfrey) and Friedrich Engels senior. Peter and Godfrey Ermen ran the English branch of the firm – which operated the Victoria Mill in Weaste Lane, Eccles – while Friedrich Engels senior (assisted by Anthony Ermen) ran the German branch at Engelskirchen (20 miles east of Cologne).

While both families were represented in Germany, the Ermen family alone ran the Manchester firm. Moreover Peter and Godfrey Ermen did not devote all their time to the firm of Ermen and Engels. As Ermen Brothers they ran a small spinning mill and bleachworks which were independent of the firm of Ermen and Engels though they both used the same offices in Manchester[6] and Ermen and Engels purchased some of the products made by Ermen Brothers. Peter and Godfrey Ermen realised that though Friedrich Engels was only a clerk in the office he was the eldest son of their partner and was bound to keep his father informed of their activities. The elder Engels suspected that Peter and Godfrey Ermen might be using some of his capital to finance the transactions of Ermen Brothers. They might also be charging Ermen and Engels unduly high prices for goods supplied from their own works. Moreover Peter and Godfrey Ermen also feared that arrival of Friedrich Engels in Manchester might interfere with their plans to find places for the next generation of Ermens in the firm. Young Henry Ermen, for example, joined the firm in the same year as Friedrich Engels.

In December 1850, soon after coming to Manchester, Engels wrote to his brother-in-law Emil Blank that he had been spending his dinner hour on four days a week – when the office was empty – examining the books of Ermen Brothers. It may be doubted if he had any right to do this. He drew up balance sheets for the years 1847–50[7] from which his father could see "how these gentlemen have been using his capital". And he carefully compared the prices charged by Ermen Brothers for goods supplied to Ermen and Engels with the average prices ruling in Manchester at the time of each transaction. Engels told Emil Blank that Peter and Godfrey Ermen were at loggerheads but he did not explain why they had quarrelled. His father had told him that he would not continue the partnership with Peter Ermen any longer than was necessary. He was, however, prepared to maintain his association with Godfrey Ermen.[8] A few days later Engels wrote to Marx that Peter Ermen was "running around like a fox whose tail has been caught in a trap" and was trying to get rid of him. The dispute between the two brothers coupled with Peter Ermen's declared hostility, made it possible for Engels to secure Godfrey Ermen as an ally and to obtain from him confidential information about the firm.[9] Although Engels tried to play off one Ermen brother against the other he disliked both of them. He referred to Peter Ermen as "a little bullfrog", while Godfrey Ermen was "a pig", "a dog", and "shit pants". In the office he found himself in an isolated position since the other clerks – like Charles Roesgen – curried favour with the partners on the spot rather than with the son of the absentee partner.

Jenny Marx's advice to Engels at this time was: "Get yourself firmly entrenched between the two hostile brothers." "Their enmity gives you the opportunity to make yourself indispensable to your worthy papa. In my mind's eye I can already see you as Friedrich Engels, junior, a partner of Friedrich Engels senior."[10] Engels took her advice. Early in February 1851 he told Marx that his father wanted him to stay in Manchester until the future of the firm had been settled satisfactorily.[11] The period of uncertainty might last until 1854 when the existing partnership was due for renewal. Engels added that his father was coming to Manchester in the summer. "I will try to make myself so indispensable here that I will be able to dictate my own terms for staying on."[12] A few weeks later Engels wrote to Marx that his "business letters have enchanted my old man". "My intrigue with my old man has been completely successful – at any rate so far – and I can now definitely settle down here and have my books forwarded from Brussels." He added that he had thought of an ingenious plan which would enable him to watch over his father's interests in Manchester while securing more time for his literary activities. In return for an annual allowance he would act as his father's representative with Ermen and Engels, without holding any appointment with the firm necessitating the keeping of regular office hours.[13] Such an arrangement would certainly have suited Engels but it did not suit his father. Friedrich Engels senior believed that young men in business should attend punctually to their duties in the office. Engels made the best of a bad job and assured his friend Weydemeyer that he now had "a very independent job with many advantages".[14] In fact Engels did not have an "independent" position at this time and his office job had more drawbacks than advantages.

In the summer of 1851 the elder Engels visited Manchester. He hoped to secure the retirement of Peter Ermen, the amalgamation of the two firms (Ermen and Engels and Ermen Brothers), and the appointment of his son to take charge of the Manchester office. Although Engels declined to accept responsibility for running the office his father agreed that his allowance should be fixed at £200 a year. Engels assured Marx that he had made no concessions to his father and that he was free to continue to write in his spare time. And he considered himself free to leave the firm immediately "in the event of a revolution". Although father and son discussed the future of Ermen and Engels amicably enough, their relations quickly deteriorated if politics were discussed.[15]

In September 1851 Friedrich Engels senior asked his son to reduce his expenses from £200 to £150 a year. Engels was furious at this "new trick" and told Marx that he would throw up his business career rather than submit to his father's proposal. Engels admitted that his father "would not earn anything like so much in Manchester this year as he did last year", but this was "due entirely to the bad management of his partners over whom I have no control".[16] In February 1852 Engels wrote that the balance sheet for the previous year would show a "positive loss" for his father and that Godfrey Ermen's reorganisation of the firm was involving him in long hours at the office. "I must attend to business or else everything will go wrong here and my old man will stop my supplies."[17]

In March 1852 the trading loss of Ermen & Engels was confirmed and Engels thought that the partnership would be dissolved and that he would be able to settle in Liverpool and buy cotton for his father.[18] In May Engels wrote to Marx: "My old man will be here next week and then this whole business shit will have to be settled one way or another and my position will be regularised.

Either the partnership will be renewed – which is unlikely – or I will try to persuade my father to withdraw from the firm by the end of the year or possibly even as early as the end of June."[19] In fact – although the partnership with Peter Ermen was to be dissolved at the end of 1853 – the partnership with Godfrey Ermen was renewed. On his return to Germany Friedrich Engels senior wrote to his son that the firms of Ermen Brothers and Ermen & Engels would be amalgamated and that Peter Ermen would leave 10,000 thalers in the firm for six years.[20] The new partnership between Godfrey Ermen and Friedrich Engels senior was signed on June 21, 1852.

A nine year contract, running from June 30, 1855 to June 30, 1864, gave Engels a welcome increase in salary. He received £100 per annum and – what was more important – a five per cent share in the profits of Ermen & Engels. This rose to seven and a half per cent in 1856. Engels's share of the profits was £168 in 1854, £163 in 1855, £408 in 1856, £834 in 1857, £840 in 1858 and £978 in 1859.[21] Although his income had risen, Engels was in financial difficulties in March 1853 when he admitted to Marx that "a reform of my personal expenses is urgently necessary".[22] In June 1853 Engels told Marx that the relations between his father and Godfrey Ermen were far from satisfactory but that his own relations with Charles Roesgen were improving.[23]

In the following year Engels admitted that he had recently been devoting too much of his time to journalism – military articles on the Crimean campaign – with the result that he was neglecting his duties at the office. He had not replied to letters from his father which he had received six months previously.[24] He thought that he had found a way out of his difficulties. He approached the *Daily News* newspaper with the object of becoming its military correspondent. "If all goes well," he wrote to Marx, "I will give up my business career when my father comes here in the autumn and I will then come to London."[25] Marx was delighted. "I hope, Sir," he replied, "you will leave Manchester, Sir, for ever, Sir."[26] But the plan fell through and Engels had to stay in Manchester for many years. In September he was elected a member of the Manchester cotton exchange and Marx congratulated him on becoming "altogether respectable".[27]

In the early 1850s – while the future of the firm was still in doubt – Engels believed that his stay in Manchester would be brief and that he would soon be able to lay down his pen in the office and take up his sword as a leader of the workers in a new revolution. In July 1851 he told Marx that "if a market crash coincides with a very large cotton harvest there will be a fine how do you do here".[28] In February 1852 Engels thought that the revolutionary movement in England had revived and that there was bound to be a commercial crisis by September or October.[29] A year later Engels asserted that in England "the present prosperity, in my opinion, cannot last beyond the autumn" and that on the Continent it would be impossible "for the present situation to outlast the spring of 1854".[30] Once more he was mistaken.

In 1857, however, his hopes rose again when news reached him of the disastrous bank failures in New York. He hastened to Manchester from the Channel Islands where he was recuperating from an illness. As the commercial depression moved across the Atlantic to Europe, Engels once more felt certain that the capitalist system was at last on the verge of collapse. But capitalism survived and there were no revolutions in England or on the Continent.[31] Only a year later Engels had to recognise that in Manchester "business is very good indeed".[32] Many years afterwards Engels admitted that in the 1850s and 1860s the British economy, far from being on the verge of collapse, had been passing through a phase of "unparalleled expansion".[33] Engels's gloomy, but mistaken, prophecies in the 1850s were shared by Marx who confidently anticipated a world wide economic collapse in 1851, 1852, 1853 and 1855.[34]

After the renewal of the partnership Ermen and Engels enjoyed a period of prosperity. A short survey of the firm's history, which appeared in a trade journal in 1897, stated that Ermen and Engels was a flourishing concern in the middle of the nineteenth century. The growth of the business owed something to Godfrey Ermen's "patent for polishing cotton thread". "This gentleman, in conjunction first with Mr Engels senior, and afterwards with Mr Engels's son, conducted the business with great energy and ability. . . ."[35] According to another account of the firm Godfrey Ermen patented several "improved methods of cotton processing". "He retained the right to earn royalties on them wherever he pleased, becoming thereby a moderately wealthy man, apart from his interest in the firm."[36] His thread was sold under the name of "Diamond Thread". (The registration of this trade mark now stands in the name of English Sewing Cotton Co. and still applies.) Godfrey Ermen was worth £400,000 when he died in 1899. As a businessman he was described as vigorous, tough, and shrewd. The absence of references in the Marx–Engels correspondence to Engels's career in business between 1853 and 1856 suggests that the firm was moving in calmer waters than before. And Engels's relations with his father were improving. In 1856 Friedrich Engels senior showed his appreciation of the efficiency with which Engels was watching over his interests in Manchester by sending him a Christmas present of money with which to buy a hunter.[37] Engels appreciated the gift as he was a keen rider to hounds with the Cheshire Hunt.[38] In March 1857, however, Engels complained that he was overwhelmed with work at the office. "In his letters my old man asks a hundred questions about the business which have to be answered."[39]

Although for twenty years his income depended upon the prosperity of Ermen and Engels – and of the Lancashire cotton industry – Engels was always delighted when the firm ran into difficulties or when the industry was depressed. So passionately did he detest the middle classes in general and the Manchester business community in particular that he derived the greatest pleasure from any misfortune that befell them. In the summer of 1851, for example, Engels wrote gleefully that there was likely to be a crash in the cotton market very soon. "Peter Ermen is already shitting his pants when he thinks of it – and that little bullfrog is a good barometer of the state of trade."[40] In the autumn of 1857, when there was an economic crisis, Engels – who was just recovering from a serious illness – declared that "the cotton exchange is the one place where my present low spirits give way to cheerfulness and good humour. Of course this annoys the asses there – as do my gloomy forecasts for the future."[41]

Engels worked in Manchester in an office which he detested not to oblige his father but to secure a regular income in order to help Marx financially. In his view it was imperative for the communist cause that Marx should devote himself entirely to the study of economics. Nothing should be allowed to stand in the way of the completion of Marx's forthcoming masterpiece on the history and structure of the capitalist system. Engels was confident that this book would conclusively prove the validity of the doctrines advocated by the communists. If Marx were to spend all his time in his study or in the reading room of the British Museum he could not be expected to earn his own living. All that Marx earned by his own efforts were fees for newspaper articles and modest royalties from his books but the income derived from these sources was quite insufficient for his needs.

Only the financial support of Engels and other friends saved Marx and his family from the workhouse. Since his student days Marx had failed to manage his financial affairs properly. He was utterly feckless and habitually lived beyond his means. Although he never tired of denouncing the middle classes – and eagerly looked forward to their downfall – he tried to maintain a bourgeois standard of living for himself and his family. When he had money to spend he enjoyed good food and cigars. As soon as he could do so he moved from Soho to a middle class suburb in London. He took his family for holidays to the seaside. He sent his daughters to private schools and secured for them private tuition in the "accomplishments" considered suitable for young ladies in Victorian England. Marx believed that he was entitled to enjoy a higher standard of living than many of the workers whose cause he championed.

Marx was often in arrears with his rent and rates. He ran up debts with tradespeople in a reckless manner. His newsagent had to wait for over a year before his bill was settled. Jenny Marx admitted that "no matter how much we cut down expenses, we could never make ends meet and our debts mounted from day to day and year to year".[42] No wonder that Marx's wife and his housekeeper were familiar figures at the local pawnshop. No wonder that even the children learned how to deceive the shopkeepers. Once little Edgar (Musch) answered the door when the baker called with three loaves. The baker asked the small boy if Mr Marx was at home. "No, he a'nt upstairs," declared Edgar – hastily seizing the loaves and slamming the door.[43] Marx frequently borrowed money without having the faintest idea as to how he could repay the loans. He simply incurred new debts to pay off old debts. Only a court order, a visit from the bailiffs, or a threat to cut off his water or gas would force Marx to meet his financial obligations. He and his wife pestered relations, friends and political associates for gifts or loans. Like Mr Micawber Karl and Jenny Marx waited for something to turn up. And occasionally something did turn up. Then the Marx family would indulge in a spending spree without a thought for the future. Jenny Marx mentioned in her memoirs that in 1856 she obtained small legacies from the estates of her uncle and mother. Debts were paid, Jenny bought a new outfit to go on a visit to Trier, and the family moved from Soho to Hampstead.[44] Engels of course sent some money to pay for the removal.[45]

There were times when Marx and his family were in desperate straits. One winter they were without coal and on another occasion there was no food in the house except bread and potatoes. Sometimes Marx could not call a doctor as he had no money to pay the fee. In his letters to Engels he complained that he could not afford to post a manuscript or buy a newspaper. Writing to Weydemeyer in May 1850 Jenny Marx described how the family had been evicted from their home in Chelsea. Marx was behind with the rent and was in debt to local tradesmen.

> "Finally a friend helped us; we paid our rent and I hastily sold all my beds to pay the chemist, the baker, the butcher and the milkman who – alarmed at the sight of the sequestration – suddenly besieged

me with their bills. The beds which we had sold were taken out and put on a cart. What was happening? It was well after sunset. We were contravening English law. The landlord rushed up to us with two constables, maintaining that there might be some of his belongings among the things and that we wanted to make away abroad. In less than five minutes there were two or three hundred persons loitering around our door – the whole Chelsea mob. The beds were brought in again – they could not be delivered to the buyer until after sunrise next day. When we had sold all our possessions we were in a position to pay what we owed to the last farthing."[46]

The family moved from Chelsea to a couple of rooms in Soho and here Marx's son Guido (Föxchen) died in November 1850. Shortly afterwards Marx asked Engels for money to pay the rent. He explained that his landlady – who was "very poor" – had not received any rent for a fortnight "and she is most importunate in her demands for payment".[47]

In the following year Marx had other worries besides lack of funds. His housekeeper Helene Demuth gave birth to a son on June 23, 1851 and Marx was the father. Jenny Marx was presumably referring to her husband's lapse when she wrote in her memoirs that "in the early summer 1851 an event occurred which I do not wish to relate here in detail, although it greatly contributed to increase our worries, both personal and others".[48] Since he was determined to maintain his position as a respectable family man Marx always denied that he was the father of Helene Demuth's illegitimate child. As usual when he was in a difficulty owing to his own folly he turned to Engels for help. He proposed to let it be known that Engels was the child's father. To add versimilitude to this story the boy was given Engels's christian name. Engels appears to have allowed Marx to do this. When Marx died Engels destroyed all the letters in their correspondence referring to Helene Demuth's child.

It was not until 1962 that Marx's shameful secret became known. Werner Blumenberg found a letter which Louise Freyberger (Engels's housekeeper at the time of his death) had written to August Bebel on September 2, 1898. She recalled that shortly before his death Engels was visited by Marx's daughter Eleanor. At this interview he categorically denied that he was the father of Helene Demuth's child and repeated (what he had already told Samuel Moore and Louise Freyberger) that Marx was the father.[49]

In the circumstances it is hardly surprising that Jenny Marx kept her faithless husband awake at night with her tears. "It makes me furious," he told Engels, "but there is not much that I can do about it."[50] In August 1851 Marx told Weydemeyer that his situation was "indeed distressing". "It will be the end of my wife if it goes on like this for long. The never-ending worries, the pettiest everyday struggles are wearing her out."[51] And in February 1852 he declared: "I have been so plagued by money worries that I haven't even been able to continue my studies at the library, much less write articles."[52]

At this time an agent of the Prussian police gained access to the Marx household. He described the squalor in which the family lived in two rooms in Soho. "In the whole apartment there is not one clean and solid piece of furniture. Everything is broken, tattered and torn, with a half-inch of dust over everything and the greatest disorder everywhere. In the middle of the salon there is a large old-fashioned table covered with an oil cloth, and on it there lie manuscripts, books and newspapers, as well as the children's toys, the rags and tatters of his wife's sewing basket, several cups with broken rims, knives, forks, lamps, an inkpot, tumblers, Dutch clay pipes, tobacco ash – in a word everything topsy turvy, and all on the same table. A seller of second hand goods would be ashamed to give away such a remarkable collection of odds and ends."[53] In 1851 another child (Franzisca) was born. Marx wrote to Engels: "There is literally not a farthing in the house but there is no shortage of bills from petty tradesmen – the butcher, the baker and so forth."[54] And a year later when Franzisca died[55] only a timely gift of £2 from a French émigré made it possible for Marx to buy a coffin so that the child could be decently buried.[56] A third child – Edgar (Musch) – died at an early age in April 1855.[57]

In January 1857 – soon after moving from Soho – Marx was still in financial difficulties. He wrote to Engels: "Today I am actually worse off than I was five years ago when I was wallowing in the very quintessence of filth."[58] Engels declared that this news had come "like a clap of thunder out of a clear sky". If only Marx had mentioned his difficulties a little sooner Engels would have sent him the money which he had just received from his father to buy a horse.[59] In March 1857 Engels was himself short of money and was being dunned by his creditors in the office.[60] In November Marx wrote that he was – as usual – in "financial distress".[61]

In 1858 the situation deteriorated. In January Marx appealed to Engels for help as it was a cold winter and he could not afford to buy any coal. He declared that he would rather be dead and buried than continue to exist in such abysmal poverty.[62] In the summer of the same year he told Engels that he had not had a penny in the house for a month. "I have had to borrow £4 from Schapper to cover essential daily expenses for which cash must be paid. And half of this went in fees in an abortive attempt to raise a loan." At this time Marx's debts amounted to more than £100. "The root of the trouble is that my modest income can never be used to pay for what I need next month. The money is absorbed by regular expenses such as rent, school fees, and payment of interest to the pawnbroker. What remains liquidates just enough debts to avoid being evicted and turned out into the street."[63] Engels gave what help he could but in the following December Marx described his situation as "more dreary and desolate . . . than ever". His wife had to go to the pawnbroker once more to raise money to pay the most pressing bills.[64]

Almost every letter written by Marx to Engels between 1850 and 1870 included a request for money or an acknowledgement of a remittance. It has been calculated from the Marx–Engels correspondence that Marx received about £4,000 from Engels.[65] This does not include sums mentioned in letters that no longer exist or money handed to Marx and not sent through the post. It does not include fees received by Marx for articles written by Engels or the bottles of wine which Engels sent to his friend from time to time. It does not include the money given by Engels to Marx's daughters both during and after the lifetime of their father.

In his first years in Manchester Engels was able to send Marx only small sums – sometimes only postage stamps – as his own income was small.[66] The correspondence records payments of £33 in 1851, £41 in 1852 and £57 in 1853. Then the remittances dropped to only £12 in 1854 and £10 in 1856. But as Engels's income increased so did his remittances to Marx. In 1857 the payments rose to £70. Engels's remittances amounted to £61 in 1858, £52 in 1859 and £159 in 1860.[67] These figures refer only to sums mentioned in the Marx–Engels correspondence. The actual payments were undoubtedly greater than those recorded in the letters which have survived.

From time to time Engels guaranteed loans raised by Marx – for example £30 from Freiligrath[68] and £250 from Dronke.[69] In July 1858 he offered to help Marx to borrow £30 provided that "the guarantee never leaves the lender's portfolio – otherwise I shall be ruined".[70] Engels insisted upon this condition because his contract with Ermen and Engels forbade him to act as a guarantor of a loan. Engels's efforts to rescue Marx from one financial scrape after another sometimes involved him in transactions of a dubious character. In 1851 he asked Marx to secure from Roland Daniels a letter addressed to Engels acknowledging the receipt of £15 which he had not received. In the letter Daniels was to allege that the money had been spent in settling Engels's debts in Cologne. Presumably this letter was to be used to deceive Engels's father. Friedrich Engels senior was to believe that his son had discharged debts in Germany amounting to £15 whereas, in fact, the money would presumably have found its way into Marx's pocket.[71] On May 23, when no letter from Daniels had been received, Engels wrote to Marx that without the letter he would be "in the devil of a fix".[72] Daniels was arrested soon afterwards and it is not known whether he ever wrote the letter that Engels wished to have.[73]

Engels also helped Marx financially in another way. In 1851 Marx was asked by Charles Dana, editor of the *New York Daily Tribune* – whom he had recently met in Cologne – to act as European correspondent for the paper. Since the German press was closed to him Marx welcomed the opportunity of contributing to one of the leading American newspapers. As there was no censorship in the United States he could express his views freely. And he hoped that the £2 which Dana offered for each article would enable him to surmount his financial difficulties. But at this time Marx was not sufficiently proficient in English to write the articles in that language. Delays would be caused if he wrote them in German and had them translated. A simple solution to the difficulty suggested itself to Marx. Engels would write the articles and he would pocket the fee. On August 8, 1851 Marx wrote to Engels: "Freiligrath and I have been invited to become correspondents of the *New York (Daily) Tribune* and we shall be paid for our contributions. This newspaper has the largest circulation in North America. If you can possibly do so I should be glad if you would let me have an article on German affairs – written in English. The article should reach me by Friday morning, August 15. That would be a fine beginning."[74]

The secret of the authorship of the articles was well kept. In 1896 when Eleanor Marx wrote an introduction to a collection of Engels's newspaper articles on the German revolution of 1848 she assumed that her father had written them. In the same year Karl Kautsky edited a German translation of the articles and he too attributed them to Marx. By the summer of 1853 Marx's English had improved sufficiently for him to write some of the articles himself. But he continued to ask Engels to send him contributions for the *New York Daily Tribune*, particularly on military topics such as the campaign in the Crimea.[75] Engels also contributed articles (on Marx's behalf) to *Putnam's Review*[76] and to the *New American Cyclopaedia*.[77]

Engels, the businessman, was kept very busy at the office, while Engels, the journalist, worked long hours in his study in the evenings and at week-ends. On the one hand his father was continually asking for information about the business, while on the other hand,

Marx was insatiable in his demands for more articles to send to Dana. Engels's health was undermined by overwork and by the strain involved in leading a double life and in trying to keep secret his association with Mary Burns and his activities as a journalist. In April 1857 Engels had trouble with his eyes and Marx sent him some drops.[78] A month later he was suffering from glandular fever.[79] By June he had recovered sufficiently to travel to London to see Marx but on returning to Manchester he was soon off work again. On July 14 Marx wrote that he was pleased to learn that there had been some improvement in Engels's condition. He strongly advised his friend not to return to the office but to go to the seaside for a rest. If he failed to take this advice there was a real danger of a relapse followed by an attack of consumption. Marx added: "Surely you do not seek the glory of sacrificing yourself on the altar of Ermen and Engels! Let Mr Ermen shift for himself."[80]

At the end of July 1857 Engels went to Waterloo near New Brighton. He wrote to Marx that he was suffering from glandular fever, that he was in severe pain, and that he could not sleep. He was "crooked, lame and weak".[81] From Waterloo Engels went first to Ryde (Isle of Wight) and then to Jersey. News of the economic crisis in New York led Engels to believe that the long awaited collapse of the capitalist system was at hand.[82] He hurried back to London in November only to suffer a relapse and to be "condemned to four days of hot compresses".[83] Back in Manchester he reported that his doctor (Martin Heckscher) was agreeably surprised at his rapid progress towards recovery. He arranged to work at the office for only part of the day.[84] Early in December Engels assured Marx that he was now in good health.[85] On the last day of 1857 he wrote that he had greatly enjoyed seven hours in the saddle with the Cheshire Hunt. He was confident that exercise on the hunting field would soon restore his health to normal.[86]

In February 1858 Engels was ill again. This time he was suffering from inflammation of the skin and from piles. He found it inconvenient to sit down except on a horse.[87] Marx attributed this relapse to years of overwork in the period of "storm and stress" in Manchester.[88] But Engels's indisposition did not prevent him from riding and he boasted that he had cleared a five foot fence – his highest jump so far.[89] Marx congratulated his friend on his "equestrial performances" but pleaded with him not to take unnecessary risks.[90] Engels replied that if he were to break his neck it would not be by falling off a horse.[91] But Engels did fall off his horse[92] and – as is clear from a letter to Victor Adler in 1892 – he subsequently suffered from the effects of his injury.[93]

Engels appears to have enjoyed reasonably good health for most of 1858 and 1859. In December 1859, however, he was ill once more. In the following April Marx twice enquired anxiously about Engels's health.[94] In May 1860 the state of Engels's health was so unsatisfactory that his brother Emil had to come to Manchester to discuss Engels's future with Godfrey Ermen now that Friedrich Engels senior had died.[95] Many years later Engels wrote that he would never forget the help that Emil gave him in 1860. He recalled that at that time he had been so ill as to be "incapable of taking a single necessary decision".[96]

It has been seen that during his first ten years in Manchester Engels placed not merely his purse but also his pen at Marx's disposal. He put his own literary plans on one side to meet Marx's almost insatiable demands for articles which would be sent to American editors as Marx's work and for which Marx would be paid. In 1858 and 1859 two events occurred which at last encouraged Engels to resume the *rôle* of an independent commentator on political affairs. They were the so-called "New Era" in Prussia in 1858 and the war between Austria and France in northern Italy in 1859. Prince Wilhelm became Regent of Prussia in October 1858 owing to the mental illness of his brother Frederick William IV. Within a month he had dismissed not only Otto von Manteuffel, the Minister President, but all his colleagues as well except for von der Heydt and Louis Simons. There were those in Germany and in Austria who imagined that the disappearance of the reactionary ministry would inaugurate a "New Era" of liberal reform and that Prussia might renew her challenge to Austria for the leadership of the German states. Their hopes – and fears – proved to be groundless. The Regent had all the characteristics of a Prussian officer and he had no intention of allowing any wind of change to blow through his dominions. But the appointment of a new ministry did lead to a revival of political discussion in Prussia for the first time for many years. As Bismarck remarked to his sister: "It certainly looks as if the world of politics is going to be a little less boring in the future."[97] And Marx was quick to notice that there was some relaxation in the way in which the censorship was applied in Prussia. "We are no longer in the era of 1850–8", he remarked to Engels in 1860.[98] Engels lost no time in taking advantage of the situation.

Moreover within a few months of assuming office the new Prussian ministry had to face a crisis in foreign affairs – the war of Italian unification in which France was supporting Piedmont against Austria. Prussia had to decide whether to ally herself with Austria or to remain neutral. Here was a vital political issue and

Engels quickly came forward to give the German public the benefit of his views on the problem. In February 1859 Engels suggested to Marx that he should write a pamphlet on the political and military aspects of the war in Italy which he was confident would break out soon. Marx enthusiastically approved. "*Po und Rhein* is a brilliant idea," he wrote, "and you should get to work on it immediately." He suggested that the brochure should appear anonymously in the hope that readers would assume that the author was "a great general". "The democratic dogs and liberal chumps will see that we are the only chaps who are not struck dumb in this miserable era of peace." Marx added that he had approached Lassalle to ask him to find a publisher for the pamphlet in Berlin.[99] A few days later Marx suggested that Engels should take a few days off from the office to complete the pamphlet.[100] On March 4 Engels informed Marx that the pamphlet would be finished in a few days.[101] *Po und Rhein* appeared in April: 1,000 copies were printed. Marx soon revealed in *Das Volk* that Engels was the author of the pamphlet.[102] Early in 1860 Marx congratulated Engels on the appearance of a favourable review of *Po und Rhein* in the *Allgemeine Militärzeitung*, published in Darmstadt. He wrote: "Your pamphlet has established your position in Germany as a military critic."[103] In 1861, when Marx was visiting Lassalle in Berlin, he wrote to Engels that it was believed in the most exalted military circles that *Po und Rhein* had been written by a Prussian general.[104] In 1860 Engels wrote a sequel to *Po und Rhein* entitled *Savoyen, Nizza und der Rhein*.[105]

The campaign in Italy caused some alarm in England where the evidence of France's military strength led some people to believe that Napoleon III was following in his uncle's footsteps and was planning other wars of aggression. There was a panic and in May 1859 the government authorised the formation of local Volunteer Corps to support the regular army in the event of a French invasion. Engels was always interested in the raising of civilian forces and he wrote an article on a review of the Volunteers which took place at Newton le Willows in August 1860. The article appeared in the *Allgemeine Militärzeitung* on September 8 and (in English translation) in the *Volunteer Journal for Lancashire and Cheshire* on September 14. Marx was delighted when the article received favourable notices in the leading London newspapers and declared that "it was sensational".[106] Engels subsequently wrote further articles on the Volunteers and other military topics for the *Volunteer Journal for Lancashire and Cheshire*, some of which were published in Manchester as a sixpenny pamphlet.[107] A review in the

United Services Gazette praised the pamphlet and declared that it had been "modestly and carefully written".[108]

The years 1859–60 were a turning point in Engels's career in Manchester. His membership of the Cheshire Hunt and the Albert Club gave him a certain standing in the community. His involvement in the Schiller celebrations of 1859 showed that he was beginning to take a lead in the affairs of the German community in Manchester. The death of his father in March 1860 at last opened up the prospect of a partnership and a degree of financial independence that he had never known before. At the same time the publication of his two pamphlets on the war in Italy and the articles on the Volunteer movement showed that Engels could still play a *rôle* as a political and military commentator, independent of Marx. There was, however, one event in Engels's life at this time which he was glad to forget in later years. In September 1859 he was involved in a drunken brawl during which he struck an Englishman with his umbrella and injured him in the eye. The Englishman threatened to sue Engels for damages. Engels complained bitterly that if the case came to court he would have no chance of success. In his view English justice was heavily weighted against "a bloody foreigner". He recognised that – even if he settled out of court – this escapade would be an expensive business. The final outcome of the affair is not known.[109]

II. The Cotton Lord, 1860–70

There were significant changes in Engels's way of life in Manchester in the 1860s. His father died in 1860; Mary Burns three years later. His father's death enabled Engels to reach an agreement with Godfrey Ermen which paved the way to a partnership. The death of Mary Burns closed an epoch in Engels's life. "I felt that with her I had buried all that was left of my youth."[110]

On securing his partnership Engels gained an improved status in the firm and on the Cotton Exchange. His income increased and he took a more active part in the social and cultural life of Manchester. He enjoyed the confidence of the German community in Manchester and became chairman of the executive committee of the Schiller Anstalt (Schiller Institute). He served on various committees – the Albert Club[111] and the Society for the Relief of Really Deserving Distressed Foreigners[112] for example – and during the Franco–Prussian war he served on a committee which raised over £1,000 to provide comforts for the German wounded. He subscribed £5 a month to this fund.[113] Engels rode with the Cheshire Hunt[114] and attended the Hallé concerts.

Some of Engels's "philistine" friends may have known of his revolutionary activities in Germany in 1848 and 1849 but his participation in the risings in Elberfeld and Baden could now be dismissed as the youthful escapades of one who was a welcome guest in some of the most respected households in Manchester. And if the authorities of his home town could leave him in peace when he visited his family in 1860 and 1862 the businessmen of Manchester could overlook his indiscretions of long ago.

Yet Engels still lived two separate lives. He continued to maintain one establishment as a businessman and another as a revolutionary writer. He flouted middle class morality by living with Mary Burns who was not his wife. In February 1862 he told Marx that he was "living with Mary nearly all the time".[115] And when Mary died he lived with her sister Lizzie, whom he did not marry until she was on her deathbed. It was not until he retired from business in 1869 that he gave up his lodgings in Dover Street.[116] Moreover his bourgeois friends were still puzzled that one who was a pillar of the Cotton Exchange on week days should not be a pillar of a place of worship on Sundays. Normally Engels succeeded in keeping the world of the bourgeoisie at arm's length outside office hours but he admitted to Jenny Marx that at Christmas time, when he received many invitations from middle class friends, he could not help feeling that he had "a foot in the bourgeoisie camp."[117]

While his business activities reached their climax in the 1860s his work for the cause of world revolution also achieved a measure of success. When the Communist League collapsed, Marx and Engels had no organisation for the propagation of their views. Engels had written to Marx in 1851: "We are at last – and for the first time in many years – so situated that we can show the world that we can do without popular applause and that we are not dependent upon any political party anywhere in the world. We are now completely isolated from any sort of low party intrigues."[118]

In the 1860s, however, the situation changed. The International Working Men's Association now gave Marx and Engels a new platform from which to preach their doctrines. In Germany the workers' movement revived – though under the leadership of Lassalle whose policy and ambitions aroused Marx's deepest suspicions. But there were disciples of Marx – such as Liebknecht – who disseminated his ideas in Germany with a freedom that had not existed in the 1850s. Above all the first volume of Marx's *Das Kapital* appeared in 1867 and Engels felt that the sacrifices which he had made to finance the author had not been in vain.

Engels had not been long in Manchester before Jenny Marx wrote that she hoped that he would become a partner in the firm of Ermen and Engels and would be "a great cotton lord".[119] When the elder Friedrich Engels died it seemed possible that Jenny Marx's prophecy would come true. Engels now had a strong claim to a partnership. On his father's death he hoped to secure a share in the German branch of the firm but his brothers – Hermann, Emil and Rudolf – argued that they alone should control the business at Engelskirchen. They were prepared to agree that £10,000 should be placed in the Manchester firm in Engels's name so that he could secure a partnership there. Engels pointed out – and his brother-in-law Emil Blank agreed with him – that his brothers were in a secure position as partners in a flourishing concern. But he had been left to the tender mercies of Godfrey Ermen. He might have a moral claim to step into his father's shoes as a partner in the Manchester firm but he had no legal claim. Engels eventually accepted the proposal put forward by his brothers because he did not wish his mother to be distressed by an unseemly family quarrel over the inheritance.[120]

Godfrey Ermen did not want to have Engels as a partner. He disliked Engels and he wished to keep control of the firm of Ermen and Engels in his own hands. Moreover when Engels's father died in 1860 Godfrey Ermen again went into business on his own by reviving the firm of Ermen Brothers. This firm (which was independent of Ermen and Engels) now operated the Bridgewater Mill at Pendlebury and Henry Ermen – who had been with Ermen and Engels for ten years – was its manager. And another member of the Ermen family (Francis Julian Ermen) had joined the firm as recently as 1859. Godfrey Ermen was establishing his young nephews in the firms under his control and he did not want Engels to be in a position to thwart his plans.

Engels, however, had two cards up his sleeve. He knew that Godfrey Ermen needed capital. Not only had Godfrey Ermen founded the Bridgewater Mill (Ermen Brothers) but he had secured Bencliffe Mill at Lane End, Eccles for the firm of Ermen and Engels.[121] If Engels were to leave the firm he would naturally take his capital with him. Again if Godfrey Ermen refused to have Engels as a partner – or even to make a firm promise of a partnership in the future – then Engels could threaten to establish a cotton business of his own and enter into competition with Godfrey Ermen.

On April 8, 1860 Engels wrote to Marx that, on returning to Manchester from Barmen – his first visit in 11 years – he had been able to secure a firm basis on which to negotiate with Godfrey Ermen by gaining the support of Charles Roesgen.[122] A few days later he told his brother Emil that Godfrey Ermen had offered to pay their mother the capital which their father had invested in the

Manchester firm. And he would continue to employ Engels for another four years under the terms of their existing contract – a contract which Jenny Marx described as "disadvantageous".[123] When Engels rejected this proposal Godfrey Ermen agreed to offer Engels a partnership in 1864. If Godfrey Ermen refused, Engels threatened to set up his own business. Engels now wrote to Emil that "Charles (Roesgen) is more devoted to our interests than ever and actually believes that we can make Godfrey do anything that we want – perhaps even force him to retire."[124] Roesgen underestimated Godfrey Ermen!

At this time Engels fell ill and Emil Engels came to Manchester to complete the negotiations. Engels hoped "to make the contract as onerous as possible for Godfrey Ermen so that, when the critical moment comes, he will be glad to be rid of me".[125] Godfrey Ermen now promised to admit Engels to a partnership in 1864, provided that (by that time) Engels had invested £10,000 in the firm. This would represent about one fifth of the capital of Ermen and Engels. But it was not until September 25, 1862 that Godfrey Ermen and Engels signed a contract containing "provisions for an eventual partnership between them". The agreement covered the period from April 7, 1860 to June 30, 1864 (when the nine year contract of 1855 expired) and provided that Engels should receive 10 per cent of the profits of the firm. He was also paid 5 per cent interest on his capital. These arrangements gave Engels a substantial increase in his income.[126]

There was no improvement in the early 1860s in the relations between Godfrey Ermen and Engels. Godfrey Ermen hoped that Engels would do something which could be regarded as a breach of contract and then he could force Engels to leave the firm. Engels was determined not to give Godfrey Ermen the satisfaction of catching him out in any breach of his contract. In December 1860 he wrote to Marx: "As far as Godfrey Ermen is concerned it is imperative that I should appear to live within my income. I have not done so during the last financial year. Godfrey Ermen must on no account be able to use this against me in the forthcoming negotiations."[127] In January 1863 Engels warned his friend that he could not raise a loan for Marx from a moneylender. If Godfrey Ermen heard of such a transaction he would be able to dismiss Engels for breach of contract.[128]

In the early 1860s, while Engels was waiting for his partnership, the Lancashire cotton industry suffered its worst slump up to that time. The industry secured about three quarters of its raw material from the United States. During the American civil war the southern states were blockaded by the North and could not export their raw cotton. The effects of the blockade upon the English cotton industry were delayed because recent bumper cotton crops had encouraged Lancashire merchants and manufacturers to make heavy purchases of raw cotton. For a time the Lancashire industry survived by using existing stocks. But eventually raw cotton became scarce and expensive. The average price of Middling Orleans (Uplands) at Liverpool rose from 6¼d per lb in 1860 to 27½d per lb in 1864. Efforts to secure cotton from regions other than America – from India or Egypt for example – had only a limited success. About 50 mills had ceased production by November 1861 while 119 were on short time. A year later over 400,000 operatives were unemployed or on short time. As late as the last week in May 1865 nearly 125,000 operatives were still out of work. Engels believed that hunger would drive the Lancashire workers to revolt and that capitalism and bourgeois society would collapse. But this did not happen. There was very little violence in Lancashire. A Factory Inspector praised the "silent resignation" and the "patient self-respect" of the cotton operatives while the Poor Law Board reported that "the working classes in the cotton manufacturing districts have conducted themselves generally with admirable patience under their privations".[129] Karl Marx denounced the Lancashire workers for "behaving like sheep" during the crisis. "Such a thing has never been heard of in the world."[130] He was naturally delighted when riots broke out in Stalybridge.[131]

There are a few references to the Cotton Famine in the Marx–Engels correspondence. In March 1862 Engels told Marx that trade was bad and that his income would almost certainly decline. "We have large stocks of goods in hand and we cannot sell anything. Our hands are tied until the Americans settle their affairs. We may lose all the profits that we might expect to make by the end of the year."[132] In the following September Engels complained that he was seriously overworked in the office owing to the cotton crisis. Prices had gone up fivefold and customers had to be kept informed of successive rises. Engels was not consistent in his assessment of the way in which the crisis was affecting different branches of the industry. In one breath he asserted that only commission houses were pocketing large profits – there was nothing left over for the owners of cotton mills – while in another he declared that anyone in the industry who showed a little courage could make money out of the great "cotton swindle". Alas, "the worthy Godfrey Ermen is a shit pants" and Ermen and Engels did not have the nerve to take advantage of the situation.[133] In November 1862 Engels wrote that there was grave distress among the cotton operatives. Dr Gumpert had told him that many undernourished patients were being admitted to hospital.[134] Early in 1863 Engels reported that the cotton market was very depressed. "Prices are no longer rising just now and we cannot sell anything."[135] In November 1864 Engels had some caustic comments to make on the public works which had been started to provide work for the unemployed cotton operatives. He claimed that – out of a total expenditure of £230,000 – only £12,000 had been spent on wages. "The Act for the relief of the distressed factory operatives has been turned into an Act for the relief of the undistressed middle classes. . . ."[136] In the same month Engels admitted somewhat gloomily that trade was at last improving. "It is a pity that nowadays a commercial crisis never seems to come really to the boil!"[137] But in 1865 Engels wrote to Marx that trade was poor again. Bankruptcies however were rare because creditors were willing to accept part of the debts owing to them from cotton firms in full settlement of their claims. "Observe the glory of commercial morality. Goods ordered today have fallen in price by 3d, 4d, or 5d a lb by the time that they are delivered. Firms indulge in all sorts of chicanery and dishonesty to wriggle out of contracts involving financial loss. And so I am kept busy at the office with numerous disputes and recriminations."[138]

In 1864, when the Cotton Famine was nearly over, Engels called upon Godfrey Ermen to implement their agreement of 1862 and admit him to a partnership. He had now invested his inheritance of £10,000 in the business.[139] Godfrey Ermen could not prove any breach of the agreement of 1862 on Engels's part. But before accepting the inevitable, Godfrey Ermen brought his brother Anthony into the business as a partner and as manager of Bencliffe Mill. Anthony Ermen, who had formerly worked in the German branch of the firm, invested only £500 in the English firm. Godfrey Ermen brought Anthony into the Manchester business so that when Engels became a partner he would be confronted by a united front of two Ermen brothers. With a brother running the Bencliffe Mill at Eccles (Ermen and Engels) and a nephew managing his own Bridgewater Mill at Pendlebury, Godfrey Ermen could feel that the Ermen family was firmly entrenched in the two businesses.

On June 30, 1864 Articles of Agreement for the establishment of a partnership were signed by Godfrey Ermen, Anthony Ermen and Friedrich Engels. But this was not the end of the matter. A deed of partnership had still to be drawn up. In July 1864 Engels wrote to Marx that he was engaged in lengthy negotiations with Godfrey Ermen and the lawyers on this deed. Godfrey Ermen, stubborn to the last, refused to recognise Engels as his partner until the deed had been signed and sealed.[140] Engels was furious that Godfrey Ermen should delay recognition of his new status in the firm until the last possible moment. It was not until September 1864 that Engels was at last able to let Marx know that "the partnership affair is settled at last, the deed is signed, and I hope to have five years of peace as far as this affair is concerned".[141] It is not without significance that in the very letter in which he told Marx of his partnership Engels should have reflected that "as a man gets older, the desire to retire grows; if that is impossible, then his health suffers".[142] Engels celebrated his partnership by moving to a larger house and by taking a holiday in Schleswig-Holstein.

The agreement between Godfrey Ermen, Anthony Ermen and Friedrich Engels made it very clear who was the senior partner and who were the junior partners. Godfrey Ermen held four fifths of the capital and was not under any obligation to devote all his time to the affairs of Ermen and Engels. But Engels did have to devote all his time to the business and was made responsible for running the office. He was required to live within ten miles of Manchester Royal Exchange. He had no claim to the profits of Godfrey Ermen's Bridgewater Mill or on the fees earned by Godfrey Ermen from his inventions. The great advantage that Engels derived from the agreement was a substantial improvement in his financial position. He now had an annual income of £500 – five per cent interest on the £10,000 which he had invested in the firm – and his share of the profits was increased from ten to twenty per cent. Engels was entitled to draw £1,000 per annum for living expenses, in anticipation of his share of the profits. This may not have turned him into a wealthy "cotton lord" but it did mean that he enjoyed a good income and was in a position to assist Karl Marx financially to an even greater extent than in previous years.

As partners Godfrey Ermen and Friedrich Engels ran a flourishing business. Their large four-storey Bencliffe Mill at Eccles employed about 800 operatives who were "profitably and regularly employed".[143] But the partnership was not a happy one. Seldom can so ill assorted a pair have tried to run a business together. They had disliked each other when Engels – a penniless refugee from Germany – had worked in the office as a junior clerk. They disliked each other just as much when Engels had forced himself on Godfrey Ermen as a partner. Engels had been a partner for only a year when he complained that "our office is like a pig stye" because Godfrey Ermen had appointed three inexperienced clerks and had insisted that, in accordance with the terms of the contract, Engels must "teach them how to do their work".[144] And a little later he told Marx that he could not guarantee a loan for him because "I am forbidden by my contract to act as a surety, and – in view of my present relations with Monsieur Godfrey – he would seize at any chance to put me wrong before a court of arbitration."[145] Engels was getting his own back on Godfrey Ermen when he advised his brother Hermann "not normally to buy your sewings from us". "If you do, Godfrey Ermen will always try to palm off his yarn from Pendlebury."[146] Engels knew that Godfrey Ermen would pass orders on to his own Bridgewater Mill (Pendlebury) rather than to the Ermen and Engels Bencliffe Mill (Eccles).

In 1867 Engels wrote:

> "In two years my contract with that swine Godfrey runs out and as things are I doubt very much whether either of us will wish to renew it. Indeed it is not improbable that we will part company even sooner. If that happens I will give up my career in commerce completely because if I were to set up a business of my own I would have to work very hard for five or six years without achieving anything worth mentioning and then I would have to slave away for another five or six years to garner the harvest of the first five years. And that would ruin my health completely. I long desperately for freedom from business which is a dog's life. I am becoming utterly demoralised by the time wasted in commercial activities. So long as I am in business I am not fit for anything. The situation has become much worse since I have shouldered the heavier responsibilities of being the partner in full charge of the office. Were it not for the increased income I would gladly return to my old job as a clerk. In any case my business career will draw to a close in a few years and then my income will be very much reduced. I am very concerned as to what I am to do about you when that happens. But on retirement from business I expect to arrange something for you – unless of course there is a revolution which would put an end to all our financial plans."[147]

But no revolution occurred to free Engels from his office desk. In June 1867 he told Marx that he was having "all sorts of rows" with Godfrey Ermen;[148] in October he reported that the disputes in the office were enough to send him off his head;[149] and in November he wrote to his brother Hermann that from time to time he was quarrelling both with Godfrey Ermen and with Anthony Ermen.[150] In the following year Engels and Godfrey Ermen opened discussions on the dissolution of their partnership.[151] In November 1868 Engels suggested that he might be willing to continue the partnership for three years if he could become a sleeping partner with no office duties. He would in this case leave his capital in the firm.[152] Godfrey Ermen countered this proposal with an offer to buy Engels out – so gaining complete control of the firm – provided that Engels would promise not to set up a rival firm during the next five years. No sum of money was mentioned, however, and Engels doubted whether – in the existing state of trade – Godfrey Ermen would make an acceptable offer.

Engels told Marx that he aimed at securing enough capital to be able to make Marx an allowance of £350 per annum for the next five or six years.[153] In December 1868 Engels wrote that his discussions with Godfrey Ermen were continuing. "I cannot trust the dog across the road and I must negotiate with the greatest care." Although no contract for the dissolution of the partnership had yet been drawn up Engels explained to Marx that luckily he had a letter from Godfrey Ermen – and a memorandum which had been given to the solicitor – which outlined an agreed basis for a contract. Engels added that Godfrey Ermen was urging him to draw his money out of the firm before the partnership was dissolved. Engels refused to do this in case it should weaken his position in the concluding stages of the negotiations. In January 1869 Engels received a draft of the proposed agreement.[154] He complained that Godfrey Ermen was employing delaying tactics to spin out the negotiations.[155]

In May 1869 Engels withdrew £7,500 of his capital from the firm[156] and on June 30 – when the partnership agreement lapsed – he retired, although the contract for the dissolution of the partnership had not yet been signed. All that had been arranged was that Engels should receive £1,750 as his share of the goodwill. The contract dissolving the partnership – which was not signed until August 10[157] – provided for a payment of nearly £5,000 (inclusive of the goodwill). If one adds this £5,000 to the £7,500 withdrawn from the firm by Engels in May it appears that Engels received about £12,500 from Godfrey Ermen. This sum represents little more than the capital invested by Engels in the business and it looks as if Godfrey Ermen drove a hard bargain as far as the goodwill was concerned. On December 9, 1869 Engels wrote to Marx: "Everything is settled with Godfrey. He paid me the last of my money yesterday and from now onwards we shall presumably turn our backsides on each other if we meet again."[158] So ended a business association of over twenty years.

On the day of his retirement Engels wrote to Marx: "Hurrah! I have finished with sweet commerce today and I am a free man. I settled all the main points yesterday with the worthy Godfrey and he had to give way completely."[159] To his mother he wrote: "Since yesterday I am a new man – and ten years younger. Instead of going to the gloomy city I took a walk for a few hours in the country. I am sitting at my desk in a comfortably furnished room where I can open the window without having smuts deposited by the smoke. There are flowers in my window and some in front of the house. Here I can work much better than in my dingy room in the office where I had a view of the courtyard of a public house."[160] He told Marx's daughter Jenny: "I am just now in the honeymoon of my newly-recovered liberty, and you will not require to be told that I enjoy it amazingly."[161] Eleanor Marx was visiting Engels at this time and she later recalled: "I shall never forget the triumph with which he exclaimed: 'For the last time' as he put on his boots to go to the office for the last time. A few hours later we were standing at the gate waiting for him. We saw him coming over the little field opposite the house where he lived. He was swinging his stick and singing, his face beaming. Then we set the table for a celebration and drank champagne and were happy."[162] And Marx sent his "dear Fred" his "sincere congratulations on your escape from Egyptian captivity". "In honour of the occasion I drank a glass more than is necessary to quench one's thirst – but late at night and not first thing in the morning like a Prussian policeman."[163]

Engels was unable to secure a very favourable financial settlement when his partnership with Godfrey Ermen was dissolved. Godfrey Ermen took advantage of the fact that Engels was determined not to renew the partnership agreement. He also knew that Engels wished to retire from business and had no intention of establishing a firm of his own. So he drove a hard bargain. All that Engels secured was the return of the capital that his family had invested in the firm and a mere £1,750 as his share of the goodwill. Engels's contempt for his former partner can be seen from a letter which he wrote to Godfrey Ermen five years after their partnership had been dissolved. In 1874 Godfrey Ermen asked Engels if he would allow the firm to continue to be called "Ermen and Engels". Engels made Godfrey Ermen wait for three months before replying and then he rejected Ermen's request. He declared that so long as the firm was known as "Ermen and Engels" he might, in certain circumstances, be liable for debts incurred by the firm although he had ceased to be a partner.[164] So the name of the firm was changed to Ermen and Roby.

As Engels's income increased so did his payments to Marx. In 1866 he sent Marx £240 and in 1867 he made him an annual allowance of £350.[165] But Marx's expenses were increasing since his family was growing up and he persisted in trying to maintain a middle-class standard of living for himself, his wife and his three daughters. He told his friend Dr Kugelmann that he had "to keep up appearances"[166] and that he needed between £400 and £500 a year to live in London.[167] His two elder daughters left school in the summer of 1860 but they continued to have private tuition in

French, Italian, music and drawing. Marx's earnings from journalism and from royalties seldom exceeded £100 and he made no serious attempt to secure full-time employment. In 1862 his Dutch cousin August Philips attempted to obtain a clerkship for Marx in the office of a railway company.[168] Marx told Engels in September that he hoped to take up the appointment soon[169] but Marx failed to secure the post since his handwriting was so difficult to read.[170]

Marx was continually in debt and had to pay from 20 to 30 per cent interest on the small sums that he borrowed.[171] In 1861 he went to Germany and Holland to try to raise some money and he secured an interest-free loan from his uncle Lion Philips – to be repaid out of his inheritance when his mother died.[172] The Marx family promptly indulged in a spending spree so that by the end of 1861 Marx was in debt again. This time he owed £100.[173]

The year 1862 was one of serious financial difficulties for Marx and the situation was aggravated by the fact that an industrial exhibition was being held in London. Marx could not afford to let his daughters join in the festivities in which their schoolfriends participated. Nor could he entertain Lassalle – who visited him in the summer – as he would have wished.

In March 1862 Marx received a "pig dirty letter" from his landlord demanding £20 rent which was 12 months overdue.[174] In June he wrote to Engels: "My wife tells me every day that she wishes that she were in her grave with her children and I do not blame her. The humiliation, the distress, and the anxiety brought about by the situation in which we find ourselves are positively indescribable."[175]

Marx complained bitterly of the indignities that he suffered at the hands of his creditors. There was the "piano man" from whom he was buying a piano on hire purchase so that his daughters could have singing lessons. The piano man was "an exceedingly uncouth fellow" – "a brutal dog" – who actually expected the instalments to be paid punctually.[176] And the grocer was a "pig dog" who refused to give Marx any more credit and insisted that future transactions must be on a cash basis![177]

There was a serious crisis in Marx's financial affairs at the end of 1862. In December of that year Jenny Marx went to Paris to try to secure money from "an old friend who had become rich and remained generous". But her friend died a few days after her arrival.[178] In January 1863, on a day when there was no food or coal in the house, the brokers' men arrived. On the same day Marx received a letter from Engels informing him of Mary Burns's death. Marx was so depressed by his own worries that when he next wrote to Engels he dismissed Mary's death in a couple of sentences and went on to discuss his own financial problems. He declared that unless he could borrow a substantial sum from a moneylender or an insurance company he could not keep the family together. Engels complained bitterly of Marx's callous behaviour and Marx was quick to appreciate that this time he had gone too far. He promptly apologised and Engels replied that he was glad not to have lost his best friend at the same time as he had lost Mary Burns. Marx now wrote that unless he could raise some money quickly he would have to go bankrupt. His two elder daughters would have to earn their living as governesses while he and his wife and youngest daughter would go to the City Model Lodging House. Once more Engels came to the rescue. He borrowed £100 himself and sent the money to Marx with a clear warning that he could send no more – except very small sums – for the next six months.[179]

In July 1863 Marx borrowed £250 from Dronke, a former member of the Communist League who now enjoyed an income of £1,000 a year.[180] Engels guaranteed the loan.[181] In 1864 two legacies improved Marx's financial position. On December 2, 1863 Marx informed Engels that his mother had died. Although he had "one foot in the grave" – a large carbuncle having been cut out only a few weeks previously – Marx declared that he was "more necessary than the old woman" and asked Engels for enough money to travel to Trier and Zalt Bommel to collect his legacy.[182] Engels sent him £10 and shortly afterwards he sent another £10 to Jenny Marx to pay a butcher's bill.[183] Marx spent Christmas 1863 at Zalt Bommel with his uncle Lion Philips, "a marvellous old boy", who was the executor of his mother's will.[184] Marx's inheritance amounted to £575, some of which he had already received. In May 1864 Wilhelm Wolff died[185] and left Marx £825.[186]

So in a single year Marx had two windfalls amounting together to about three times as much as he needed to maintain his family for a year. In June 1864 Marx boasted to his uncle Lion Philips that he had made over £400 by dabbling in stocks and shares.[187] But when he wrote to Engels a few days later he merely claimed that he "could have made a killing on the Stock Exchange" if he had had some money.[188] It is doubtful if Marx was telling the truth when he wrote to his uncle about his successful speculation.[189]

When Marx secured the money due to him from his mother's estate he forgot about model lodging houses. The legacy, wrote Jenny Marx, "enabled us to free ourselves from obligations, debts, pawnbroker etc.". She found "a very attractive and healthy house which we fitted out very comfortably and relatively smartly".[190]

By Easter 1864 Marx and his family had moved from Kentish Town to No. 1 Modena Villas.[191] Soon afterwards Wilhelm Wolff died and Marx received a second legacy which afforded his family "a year free from worry".[192] It also paid for a holiday at the seaside, a ball for Marx's daughter and "some smaller parties".[193]

The legacies were quickly spent and within a year Marx was again in debt. In July 1865 he told Engels that for eight weeks he had relied upon visits to the pawnbroker to secure money for household expenses. He had spent £500 in repaying debts and in furnishing his new home. He admitted that he had been living beyond his means. He appealed for help and Engels promptly sent him £50.[194] In August 1865 Engels sent Marx £20 to satisfy the butcher, the "very troublesome" landlord and the "tax-gatherers".[195] Another £15 was sent in November when Marx wrote that his wife was "desolate" at the importunities of the landlord and various tradespeople.[196] Marx persuaded his landlord to wait until the middle of February for two thirds of the current quarter's rent. He declared that unless his financial position improved he would have to leave England for a country such as Switzerland where he could live more cheaply.[197] At the end of 1865 he complained: "I have lost much time in running around all over the place to fix things up right and left. But I can satisfy one creditor only by falling into the clutches of another."[198]

Marx's financial position deteriorated in 1866. In January he complained that he was short of money – and he had "minus zero" to keep his family.[199] In August Engels declared that he could not make Marx a larger allowance than £200 per annum, though he held out the hope that "if everything goes well I may be able to rustle up another £50".[200] In October Marx appealed to Dr Kugelmann for help.

> "My economic position has become so bad as a result of my long illness and the many expenses which it entailed, that I am faced with a financial crisis in the *immediate* future, a thing which, apart from the direct effects on me and my family, would also be disastrous for me politically, particularly here in London, where one must 'keep up appearances'. What I wanted to ask you was: Do you know anybody, or a few persons (in no circumstances must the matter become *public*), who could lend me about 1,000 thalers at 5 or 6 per cent interest for at least two years? I am now paying 20 to 30 per cent interest for the small sums which I borrow, but even so I cannot put off my creditors for much longer and I am therefore faced with the break-up of our household."[201]

When Dr Kugelmann suggested that if Engels were fully informed of the facts he might be able to give Marx greater financial help

Marx replied sharply: "You mistake my relations with Engels. He is my most intimate friend. I have *no secrets* from him. Had it not been for him I should long ago have been compelled to take up 'business'. Therefore in no circumstances do I want any third person to intervene with him on my account. He also obviously can only act within certain limits."[202]

Marx's failure to pay his rent was one of his most serious difficulties. On October 2, 1866 Engels sent Marx £45 for the landlord. It was characteristic of Marx's inability to handle his financial affairs that he did not know how much he owed. He thought that he owed £46 so that he still had to find £1. He borrowed this from his obliging baker Mr Whithers. But when the account came to be settled Marx discovered that it amounted to £48 15s 0d. So he called upon the baker a second time and borrowed £2 15s 0d![203]

The year 1867 opened with new financial worries. The ownership of the house which Marx rented changed hands and the new landlord asked for the prompt payment of the last quarter's rent. And as usual Marx was in debt to the butcher, the grocer, and the tax collector. Engels sent him £20 in February.[204] In the following month Marx decided that he must take the manuscript of the first volume of *Das Kapital* to his publisher in Hamburg in person. He asked Engels for enough money to redeem his clothes from the pawnbroker and to pay his fare. Engels sent Marx £30 and Jenny Marx £10.[205] In May 1867 Marx wrote to Engels from Hanover – where he was the guest of Dr Kugelmann – that he urgently needed a few hundred pounds. He dreaded returning to London where new debts were piling up. On the other hand he declared: "I confidently hope and believe that by next year I shall have enough money to undertake a radical reform of my finances so that I shall at last be able once more to stand entirely upon my own feet."[206]

Nothing came of his good resolution. Instead of economising when he returned to London Marx gave a dance for his daughters, explaining that the young ladies would lose caste with their friends if the dance were not held. He asked Engels for some hock and claret. Engels sent the wine and £10 as well.[207] Three weeks later Marx wrote to Engels that he had just spent £45 to send his daughters to Bordeaux for a holiday. In August he wrote that he would have to pay £11 taxes immediately and also £1 15s 0d interest to the pawnbroker and £4 to two "shit-grocers".[208] In October Marx declared that he must have peace "for some weeks" from his creditors and he decided to raise a loan in London. Engels reminded Marx that, in view of his contract with Godfrey Ermen, it was impossible for him to act as a guarantor of the loan.[209] But he wrote to the Atlas Insurance Company that "from confidential information I am convinced that Mr Marx will be in a position to repay the loan when due".[210] He sent Marx £30 on November 28 for "immediate necessities".[211] In December 1867 Marx drew £150 from the insurance company but £45 of this had to be used immediately to repay a loan from Borkheim.[212]

In 1868 Marx described himself as "a poor devil who is as hard up as a church mouse".[213] He told Dr Kugelmann in March: "My circumstances are very harassing, as I have been unable to do any additional work which would bring in money, and yet certain appearances must be maintained for the children's sake."[214] At this time Marx became alarmed lest his poverty should adversely affect the marriage prospects of his daughter Laura who was engaged to Paul Lafargue. Marx was anxious to prevent Lafargue – and his family in Bordeaux – from learning of his financial difficulties. And there was the problem of providing Laura with a dowry and an adequate trousseau. Marx told Engels that he could not "send her into the world like a beggar".[215] He appealed in vain to his relations in Holland for a loan and he postponed the wedding as long as possible. But a time came when no further excuses for delay could be made and the marriage took place in April.

Engels sent Marx £150 between March and July 1868 but on July 23 Marx declared that he still needed £20 for Laura's linen and that his only hope of raising some money was to borrow once more from an insurance company.[216] In August Marx was again in urgent need of money to satisfy the landlord, the tax collector and other creditors.[217] Engels sent Marx £25 on August 21[218] and £20 on August 28 – "your landlord will have to console himself with that for the time being".[219] In the following month Engels sent £167 to repay the loan from an insurance company which had been raised the year before.[220] Marx still complained that Laura's trousseau was not complete[221] and in October Engels sent Marx £100. He was able to do this because Borkheim had agreed to wait until the following February for the settlement of an account (amounting to £72) for wines supplied to Engels, Dr Gumpert and Charles Roesgen.[222] In a letter dated October 4 Marx acknowledged the receipt of the £100 but stated that he still had debts amounting to £100.[223] Shortly afterwards Marx asked for more money, this time to pay a quarter's rent and the water rate.[224]

On November 25, 1868, Engels wrote to Marx that he would shortly be retiring from business. In his discussions with his partner Godfrey Ermen he hoped to secure a capital sum which would produce an income sufficient for both Marx and himself. Engels had already warned Marx that when he retired there would be a drop in his income.[225] Now he asked Marx two questions. First, what did Marx owe? Secondly, could Marx live on £350 a year in future? Engels hoped to be able to allow Marx £350 per annum during the first five or six years after retirement. After that he hoped – perhaps optimistically – that Marx's income from royalties would increase. In later years Engels thought that he would be able to allow Marx only £150 per annum. Engels warned Marx – not for the first time – that when his debts had been paid he must learn to live within his income.[226] Marx replied that he was "quite knocked down" by Engels's generosity. He stated that he owed well over £200 – and not £100 as he had estimated only a few weeks before – but he assured Engels that an allowance of £350 per annum would be "quite adequate". He admitted that in recent years he had spent more than this owing to the need to pay high school fees and to entertain Lafargue whose visit had "greatly increased our expenses". "If all my debts were paid I would be able to insist upon a strict administration of our domestic finances." Marx added that his financial situation was so serious that his daughter Jenny had – without asking his permission – taken a post as a daily governess. Marx clearly felt that it would be difficult to keep up appearances in the future if one of his daughters went out to work.[227]

In 1869 Engels retired from business. The capital which he withdrew from the firm of Ermen and Engels enabled him to send Marx – in addition to a quarterly allowance of £87 10s 0d[228] – the sum of £100. Engels wrote to Marx in August 1869 that he hoped that the £100 "will cause your debts to vanish for ever".[229] The money was very welcome. A few months previously Marx had again complained of financial stringency. He had paid for his wife and two daughters to go on a holiday to Paris to see the Lafargues and he was being dunned by a gentleman from New York for a debt of £15 incurred thirteen years previously.[230] In 1870 Engels settled in London. The two friends now wrote to each other much less frequently than before and there are comparatively few references to Marx's finances in the correspondence after 1870.[231]

The responsibility of running the office of Ermen and Engels made it impossible for Engels to do as much writing as he wished. No major work from his pen appeared in the 1860s. In 1866 Marx tried to persuade Engels to have his book on *The Condition of the Working Class in England* reprinted with an appendix covering the period 1844–66. He was sure that the task could be accomplished in three months.[232] In the following year Marx told Dr Kugelmann that he believed that he had persuaded Engels to do this.[233] But Engels never brought his account of the condition of the English workers up to date and it was not until 1892 that a second edition of his book appeared in Germany. Engels, however, wrote many articles in the 1860s for newspapers and periodicals. The most important were on military topics such as those on the English volunteer movement,[234] the Seven Weeks War,[235] and the Franco–Prussian war.[236] Among his writings on international politics three articles on the Polish question deserve mention.[237] Engels also succeeded in placing some anonymous reviews of Karl Marx's *Das Kapital* in various German newspapers. He wrote one pamphlet at this time in which he offered some advice to the German Workers Party on its policy concerning the constitutional conflict in Prussia.[238] After his retirement Engels could devote more time to his studies and to his writing. In the spring of 1870 he told Marx that he had been working in Chetham's Library. "During the last few days I have again spent a good deal of time sitting at the four-sided desk in the alcove where we sat together twenty-four years ago. I am very fond of the place. The stained glass window ensures that the weather is always fine there."[239]

Despite his office duties and his work as a journalist Engels found time to do some public work in Manchester. He became chairman of the committee of the Schiller Anstalt,[240] a club which grew out of the celebrations held in 1859 to mark the 100th anniversary of Schiller's birth. Carl Siebel, a distant relative of Engels, helped to organise the festivities in the Free Trade Hall. Engels thought that the organising committee was "a crowd of jackasses"[241] and told Jenny Marx that the local "philistines" were very annoyed because he and Wilhelm Wolff "refuse to have anything to do with the Schiller celebrations".[242] But Engels relented to the extent of attending both a rehearsal of *Wallensteins Lager* and the celebrations on November 11. He declared that the failure of the first part of the programme – "a complete washout" – was retrieved by the success of the second part. And Engels enjoyed himself at a party held after the entertainment was over.[243]

The organisers had hoped to make a profit with which to start a German club but ended up with a deficit of £150.[244] Nevertheless the Schiller Anstalt was established in 1860 at Carlton Buildings in Cooper Street (the former Mechanics Institute) with Dr Louis Borchardt as chairman of the committee and Charles Hallé as one of the vice-chairmen.[245] Despite their earlier opposition to the formation of the club Engels and his friends Wilhelm Wolff and Schorlemmer joined the Schiller Anstalt and Wolff left the club £100 in his will.[246]

Engels stated that Dr Gumpert persuaded him to join the Schiller Anstalt.[247] He was certainly a member in May 1861 when he sharply rebuked the librarian of the club for sending him a peremptory reminder that a book which he had borrowed should be returned. Engels wrote to the committee that if the club's correspondence was conducted in this way its members would never feel homesick. The receipt of such a communication – reminiscent of a letter from a German police commissioner – would make them feel that they were still in the Fatherland – that "beloved police state".[248] A year later Engels complained that the Schiller Anstalt was being overrun by Jews and had become a "Jerusalem club".[249]

Despite his earlier antipathy towards the club Engels agreed to serve on its committee in July 1864 and he was elected chairman shortly afterwards.[250] He told Marx that he had accepted the office to annoy Dr Borchardt, the previous chairman.[251] Engels was an efficient and energetic chairman under whose guidance the Schiller Anstalt made rapid progress. By 1866 it had 300 members. It had a library of 4,000 volumes and a reading room with 55 newspapers and periodicals. It had a regular programme of lectures while provision was also made for various activities such as musical recitals, choral singing and gymnastics.[252] The club became the focus of the social and cultural life of the German community in Manchester. When Ludwig Mond came to England as a young man he "found a warm welcome" at the Schiller Anstalt and made friends with Carl Pieper with whom he was later associated in business.[253]

In 1866 the lease of Carlton Buildings expired and the Schiller Anstalt faced the problem of finding a new club house. The committee decided to build rather than to lease fresh premises and in March 1866 Engels told Marx that the building appeal of the Schiller Anstalt was keeping him very busy every evening.[254] On March 19 the committee appealed to members of the German community to subscribe to a fund for this purpose. The members of the club had already raised nearly £1,200 in a few days. Engels had subscribed £20.[255] It was estimated that between £5,000 and £5,500 would be needed to carry out the committee's scheme.[256]

On June 28, 1867 the committee circularised subscribers to the building fund. The appeal had produced only £2,875 so far. Depressed trade probably accounted for the failure of the appeal to reach its target. The committee had not been able to find either a suitable plot of land to purchase or suitable premises to rent in the centre of the city. But an extension had been secured (until June 1868) of the lease of Carlton Buildings, though the rent went up from £225 to £450 per annum. In the circumstances – and in view of the rising cost of land in the city centre – the committee recommended that the club should move to somewhere near All Saints where land was cheaper than in the business quarter of Manchester.[257]

The finding of a suitable plot of land and erection of a new building (Rylands House) involved Engels in much hard work. In March 1868 he wrote that "the accursed affair of the infernal Manchester Schiller Anstalt" had reached a crisis and that everything rested upon his shoulders. He was confident that he could "bring the matter to a successful conclusion, despite Borchardt and various other German cliques."[258] On March 29 he wrote:

> "The infernal Schiller Anstalt affair has kept me on tenterhooks all the week. Yesterday I was able to settle the business. Some blunders by my chief adjutant threw everything into the melting pot again. Had I failed I would indeed have been the laughing stock of Manchester for to be 'done' in business and to get oneself 'sold' is naturally the worst that can happen to anyone here. Now I have achieved a triumph I can retire honourably from the whole business. There are plenty of people who will now push themselves forward to take an active part in the affairs of the Schiller Anstalt."[259]

Despite his triumph Engels complained on June 24 that he was still having trouble "on account of the building of the Schiller Anstalt".[260]

Engels resigned from the committee in September 1868.[261] He told Marx that, in his absence, "the fellows on the committee of the Schiller Anstalt – instigated by the Bradford Schiller Verein – invited that swine Vogt to lecture here. Of course I resigned at once. The swine arrives tomorrow".[262] Karl Vogt had been a member of the Frankfurt National Assembly who had since been in the pay of Napoleon III. Marx had denounced Vogt in 1860 in a virulent pamphlet.[263] Although Engels resigned from the committee he remained a member of the Schiller Anstalt.[264] The committee appealed to him to resume his membership of the committee and he did so in 1870[265] when money was being raised for the relief of the German wounded in the Franco–Prussian war.[266] When Engels left Manchester in 1870 he had the satisfaction of knowing that he had played an important part in securing the removal of the Schiller Anstalt to better premises at Rylands House in Chorlton on Medlock.

A month before Engels resigned from the committee of the Schiller Anstalt an article on the club appeared in a local journal. The writer declared that "the present prosperity of the Schiller Anstalt" had been achieved only after a struggle between "the advocates of culture and the advocates of conviviality". The high-minded founders of the Schiller Anstalt had wished "to impart a literary and artistic character to the institution" but many of the members wanted to have a purely social club. The writer of the article declared that although "the convivial party triumphed" experience had shown that "beer and culture have taken quite kindly to one another".[267]

Engels was also a member of the Albert Club and served on its committee throughout the 1860s.[268] This club had been established in 1842 in Clifford Street by a group of young Germans who were working in Manchester. In 1859 the Albert Club moved to larger premises at the junction of Oxford Road and Dover Street. The club house was described in 1869 as "a handsome and commodious building". "It stands some yards back from Oxford Street, and has a piece of garden ground, or shrubbery, in front, with a semi-circular carriage drive, and two large gates for the ingress and egress of vehicles. Externally, it has more the appearance of a suburban residence of a private gentleman than of a club-house." On the ground floor there was a library, a newsroom, and a dining-room while upstairs there was a billiard room, a smoking room, a card room, a committee room and a private dining-room. A visitor declared that the smoking room was "the best room of its kind in Manchester – certainly it is much superior to any club smoke room now extant in this city." The club had 96 members in 1866 and 120 three years later. About half the members were English and half were foreigners. The German members included Engels, Godfrey Ermen, Dr Borchardt, and Dr Gumpert while Samuel Moore was one of the English members. The annual subscription was five guineas.[269] Engels retained his membership of the Albert Club after he moved to London.[270]

When Engels left Manchester he could look back with some satisfaction on the twenty years that he had spent there. He had kept his post with Ermen and Engels despite Godfrey Ermen's efforts to get rid of him. In the end he had secured his partnership. His earnings, which had grown as time went on, were sufficient to enable him to supply Marx with funds that he so urgently needed. And on retirement, though Godfrey Ermen drove a hard bargain, he secured a financial settlement which made it possible for him – at the age of 50 – to live in comfort in London as a retired gentleman. He was able to make Marx a regular allowance. Now at last he was free from the office duties that had proved so irksome and he had no further contact with the "philistines" in the Manchester cotton trade whom he detested. Now he could spend all his time in furthering the cause of Marxian socialism. Engels had never liked Manchester and he left for a pleasant house in Regent Park Road with no regrets. From time to time he had news of the German colony in Manchester from his friends Schorlemmer and Gumpert while Charles Roesgen kept him in touch with the fortunes of Ermen and Engels. Not long after Engels settled in London Roesgen gave him an account of the fire that caused serious damage to the Bencliffe Mill at Eccles.[271] Engels had achieved the main purpose of his stay in Manchester. He had seen the appearance of the first volume of Karl Marx's *Das Kapital*, the work which he believed would prove once and for all the validity of the socialist philosophy.

Much of the Manchester that Engels knew so well disappeared in the hundred years that elapsed after his departure. The office in which he worked has been demolished and slum clearance operations around the University on both sides of Oxford Road has swept away many of the streets that he frequented. Ermen and Engels (later Ermen and Roby) became part of the English Sewing Cotton Company and the Manchester Cotton Exchange – once the most important in Europe – has closed its doors for ever. The Albert Club and the Schiller Anstalt have vanished. Only the words "Albert Club" on a pillar box in Oxford Road still remind us that the club once existed on the other side of the street. Happily visitors to Manchester can still see in Chetham's Library the desk in a pleasant alcove at which Marx and Engels once studied economics together.

NOTES

1 Karl Marx to F. Engels, February 10, 1858 in *Gesamtausgabe*, Part III, Vol. 2, p. 285.

2 Julian Harney to F. Engels, December 16, 1850 in F. G. and R. M. Black (ed.), *The Harney Papers* (1969), p. 258.

3 On February 11, 1851 Karl Marx wrote that he was living "in complete retirement". "You will appreciate how much I miss you and how I wish that I could discuss my problems with you" (*Gesamtausgabe*, Part III, Vol. 1, p. 146).

4 For the firm of Ermen & Engels see articles in the *Eccles Advertiser*, February 11, 1871, the *Warehousemen and Drapers' Trade Journal*, 1894 ("The Manufacture of Sewing Cotton"), and *The Drapers' Record*, September 18, 1897 ("New Cotton Combinations. The English Sewing Cotton Ltd"); H. E. Blyth, *Through the Eye of a Needle . . .* (1947), p. 11; A. C. G. Ermen, R.N., "Cotton and Communism" (1964: typescript) and "The Three Red Towers" (1965: typescript in Eccles Public Library); J. B. Smethurst, "Ermen & Engels" in *Marx Memorial Library Quarterly Bulletin*, January–March 1967, pp. 5–11) and "Ermen & Engels in Eccles" (typescript).

5 F. Engels to Karl Marx, July 6, 1851 in *Gesamtausgabe*, Part III, Vol. 1, pp. 212–13.

6 6 South Gate, St Mary's, Manchester.

7 See document M7 in the Marx–Engels archives (Amsterdam).

8 F. Engels to Emil Blank, December 3, 1850 in *Marx–Engels Werke*, Vol. 27, pp. 451–2.

9 F. Engels to Karl Marx, December 7, 1850 in *Gesamtausgabe*, Part III, Vol. 1, p. 123.

10 Karl Marx to F. Engels, December 2, 1850 (postscript by Jenny Marx) in *Gesamtausgabe*, Part III, Vol. 1, p. 120.

11 On February 5, 1850 Friedrich Engels senior wrote to F. Engels: "I am indeed delighted that you would be willing to stay in Manchester. You are in the right place there. You are better placed than anyone else to represent me there" (Marx–Engels archives, Amsterdam, L. 1588).

12 F. Engels to Karl Marx, February 5, 1851 in *Gesamtausgabe*, Part III, Vol. 1, p. 143.

13 F. Engels to Karl Marx, February 26, 1851 in *Gesamtausgabe*, Part III, Vol. 1, p. 159.

14 F. Engels to K. Weydemeyer, January 23, 1852 in K. Marx and F. Engels, *Letters to Americans, 1848–95* (1963), p. 33.

15 F. Engels to Karl Marx, July 6, 1851 in *Gesamtausgabe*, Part III, Vol. 1, pp. 212–13.

16 F. Engels to Karl Marx, September 8, 1851 in *Gesamtausgabe*, Part III, Vol. 1, p. 258.

17 F. Engels to Karl Marx, February 17, 1852 in *Gesamtausgabe*, Part III, Vol. 1, pp. 319–20.

18 F. Engels to Karl Marx, March 2 and 18, 1852 in *Gesamtausgabe*, Part III, Vol. 1, p. 328 and p. 332.

19 F. Engels to Karl Marx, May 4, 1852 in *Gesamtausgabe*, Part III, Vol. 1, pp. 347–8.

20 Friedrich Engels senior to F. Engels, June 30, 1852 and December 20, 1853 in the Marx–Engels archives (Amsterdam), L. 1609.

21 Gustav Mayer, *Friedrich Engels* (two volumes, 1934), Vol. 2, pp. 12, 29, 61, 107 and 172–5.

22 F. Engels to Karl Marx, March 4, 1853 in *Gesamtausgabe*, Part III, Vol. 1, p. 451.

23 F. Engels to Karl Marx, June 6, 1853 in *Gesamtausgabe*, Part III, Vol. 1, pp. 479–80.

24 F. Engels to Karl Marx, April 21, 1854 in *Gesamtausgabe*, Part III, Vol. 2, pp. 20–1.

25 F. Engels to Karl Marx, April 3, 1854 in *Gesamtausgabe*, Part II, Vol. 2, p. 15.

26 Karl Marx to F. Engels, April 14, 1854 in *Gesamtausgabe*, Part III, Vol. 2, p. 16.

27 Karl Marx to F. Engels, September 2, 1854 in *Gesamtausgabe*, Part III, Vol. 2, p. 50.

28 F. Engels to Karl Marx, July 30, 1851 in *Gesamtausgabe*, Part III, Vol. 1, p. 224.

29 F. Engels to J. Weydemeyer, February 27, 1852 in K. Marx and F. Engels, *Letters to Americans 1848–95* (1963), pp. 40–2.

30 F. Engels to J. Weydemeyer, April 12, 1853 in K. Marx and F. Engels, *Letters to Americans 1848–95* (1963), pp. 53–9.

31 F. Engels to Karl Marx, November 6 and 15, 1857 in *Gesamtausgabe*, Part III, Vol. 2, p. 238 and p. 242.

32 F. Engels to Karl Marx, October 16, 1858 in *Gesamtausgabe*, Part III, Vol. 2, p. 339.

33 *Neue Zeit*, July 1888.
34 Werner Blumenberg, *Marx* (1962), p. 121.
35 *Drapers' Record*, September 18, 1897.
36 Captain A. C. G. Ermen, R.N., *The Three Towers* (typescript in Eccles Public Library), John Smethurst, "Ermen and Engels" in the *Marx Memorial Library Quarterly Bulletin*, No. 41, January–March 1967, pp. 5–11 and "Ermen and Engels in Eccles" (typescript). Bennet Woodcroft, *Alphabetical Index of Patentees of Inventions* (1854: new edition 1969) recorded the granting of a patent to Godfrey Ermen on June 17, 1851 for "a method or apparatus for finishing yarns or threads".
37 F. Engels to Karl Marx, January 22, 1857 in *Gesamtausgabe*, Part III, Vol. 2, p. 166.
38 There is a reference to the cost of keeping the hunter "Jack" in a letter from Charles Roesgen to Friedrich Engels on October 27, 1857 (Marx–Engels archives, Amsterdam, L. 5434). See also the documents on the "Cheshire Hunt Covert Fund" in the March–Engels archives, Amsterdam, 1918).
39 F. Engels to K. Marx, March 11, 1857 in *Gesamtausgabe*, Part III, Vol. 2, p. 171.
40 F. Engels to Karl Marx, July 30, 1851 in *Gesamtausgabe*, Part III, Vol. 1, p. 224.
41 F. Engels to Karl Marx, November 15, 1857 in *Gesamtausgabe*, Part III, Vol. 2, p. 241.
42 Jenny Marx, "Short Sketch of an eventful Life" in *Reminiscences of Marx and Engels* (Foreign Languages Publishing House, Moscow), p. 230.
43 Jenny Marx to F. Engels, April 27, 1853 in *Gesamtausgabe*, Part III, Vol. 1, p. 468.
44 Jenny Marx, "Short Sketch of an eventful Life", in *Reminiscences of Marx and Engels* (Foreign Languages Publishing House, Moscow), p. 229.
45 Karl Marx to F. Engels, September 22, 1856 in *Gesamtausgabe*, Part III, Vol. 2, p. 145.
46 Jenny Marx to J. Weydemeyer, May 20, 1850 in *Reminiscences of Marx and Engels* (Foreign Languages Publishing House, Moscow), pp. 237–8.
47 Karl Marx to F. Engels, January 6, 1851 in *Gesamtausgabe*, Part III, Vol. 1, p. 125.
48 *Reminiscences of Marx and Engels* (Foreign Languages Publishing House, Moscow), p. 227.
49 Werner Blumenberg, *Marx* (Rowohlt, 1962), pp. 115–18.
50 Karl Marx to F. Engels, July 31, 1851 in *Gesamtausgabe*, Part III, Vol. 1, p. 226.
51 Karl Marx to J. Weydemeyer, August 2, 1851 in K. Marx and F. Engels, *Letters to Americans 1848–95* (1963), p. 24.
52 Karl Marx to J. Weydemeyer, February 20, 1852, *ibid.*, p. 37.
53 *Archiv für Geschichte des Sozialismus*, Vol. 10 (1922), pp. 56–8 and Robert Payne, *Marx* (1968), pp. 251–2.
54 Karl Marx to F. Engels, March 31 and April 2, 1851 in *Gesamtausgabe*, Part III, Vol. 1, pp. 179–80.
55 Karl Marx to F. Engels, April 14, 1852 in *Gesamtausgabe*, Part III, Vol. 1, p. 337.

56 *Reminiscences of Marx and Engels* (Foreign Languages Publishing House, Moscow), p. 228.
57 Karl Marx to F. Engels, April 6, 1855 in *Gesamtausgabe*, Part III, Vol. 2, p. 87.
58 Karl Marx to F. Engels, January 20, 1857 in *Gesamtausgabe*, Part III, Vol. 2, p. 163.
59 F. Engels to Karl Marx, January 22, 1857 in *Gesamtausgabe*, Part III, Vol. 2, pp. 165–6.
60 F. Engels to Karl Marx, March 20, 1857 in *Gesamtausgabe*, Part III, Vol. 2, p. 175.
61 Karl Marx to F. Engels, November 13, 1857 in *Gesamtausgabe*, Part III, Vol. 2, p. 239.
62 Karl Marx to F. Engels, January 28, 1858 in *Gesamtausgabe*, Part III, Vol. 2, p. 279.
63 Karl Marx to F. Engels, July 15, 1858 in *Gesamtausgabe*, Part III, Vol. 2, pp. 327–30.
64 F. Engels to Karl Marx, December 11, 1858 in *Gesamtausgabe*, Part III, Vol. 2, pp. 350–1.
65 The calculation has been made by the Marx–Engels Institute in Moscow.
66 For example £1 on January 8, 1851; £1 on February 5, 1851; £5 on May 8, 1851 and postage stamps on April 25, 1851 in *Gesamtausgabe*, Part III, Vol. 1, pp. 128, 140, 195 and 341.
67 D. Rjazanov's introduction to *Gesamtausgabe*, Part III, Vol. 2, pp. xvii–xx.
68 F. Engels to Karl Marx, February 6, 1861 in *Gesamtausgabe*, Part III, Vol. 2, pp. 11–12.
69 F. Engels to Karl Marx, April 8, 1863 in *Gesamtausgabe*, Part III, Vol. 3, p. 135.
70 F. Engels to Karl Marx, July 16, 1858 in *Gesamtausgabe*, Part III, Vol. 2, pp. 330–2. For details of the transaction see Karl Marx to F. Engels, July 20, 1858 (*ibid.*, p. 332), July 25, 1858 (*ibid.*, pp. 332–3), August 8, 1858 (*ibid.*, p. 333).
71 F. Engels to Karl Marx, May 1, 1851 in *Gesamtausgabe*, Part III, Vol. 1, p. 189. On May 3 Marx replied that he would write to Daniels as requested (*ibid.*, p. 191).
72 F. Engels to Karl Marx, May 23, 1851 in *Gesamtausgabe*, Part III, Vol. 1, p. 208.
73 Karl Marx to F. Engels, June 16, 1851 in *Gesamtausgabe*, Part III, Vol. 1, p. 210.
74 Karl Marx to F. Engels, August 8, 1851 in *Gesamtausgabe*, Part III, Vol. 1, p. 229.
75 See K. Marx, *The Eastern Question . . . 1853–56* (edited by Eleanor Aveling and Edward Aveling, 1897).
76 K. Marx to F. Engels, June 15, 1855 in *Gesamtausgabe*, Part III, Vol. 2, pp. 89–90.
77 F. Engels to K. Marx, April 22, 1857 and May 28, 1857 in *Gesamtausgabe*, Part III, Vol. 2, pp. 185–6 and pp. 1967 and C. A. Dana to Karl Marx, June 11, 1857 in *Gesamtausgabe*, Part III, Vol. 2, pp. 197–8. See also *Gesamtausgabe*, Part III, Vol. 2, pp. 200–1, 217–18, 221–4, 231, 237, 267, 270, 276, 282–3, 290, 300–1, 336, 418, 419, 421.
78 Jenny Marx to F. Engels, April 12, 1857 and F. Engels to Karl Marx, April 22, 1857 in *Gesamtausgabe*, Part III, Vol. 2, p. 184 and p. 187.

79 F. Engels to Karl Marx, May 28, 1857 and Karl Marx to F. Engels, June 15, 1857 in *Gesamtausgabe*, Part III, Vol. 2, p. 196 and p. 197.
80 Karl Marx to F. Engels, July 14, 1857 in *Gesamtausgabe*, Part III, Vol. 2, p. 202.
81 F. Engels to Karl Marx, July 30, 1857 in *Gesamtausgabe*, Part III, Vol. 2, pp. 204–5.
82 F. Engels to K. Marx, November 15, 1857 in *Gesamtausgabe*, Part III, Vol. 2, p. 242.
83 F. Engels to K. Marx, November 6, 1857 in *Gesamtausgabe*, Part III, Vol. 2, p. 238.
84 F. Engels to K. Marx, November 15, 1857 in *Gesamtausgabe*, Part III, Vol. 2, p. 239.
85 F. Engels to Karl Marx, December 9, 1857 (Gesundheitgut) in *Gesamtausgabe*, Part III, Vol. 2, p. 254.
86 F. Engels to Karl Marx, December 31, 1857 ("Das bringt meine Gesundheit schon auf den Strumpf") in *Gesamtausgabe*, Part III, Vol. 2, p. 266.
87 F. Engels to Karl Marx, February 8, 1858 in *Gesamtausgabe*, Part III, Vol. 2, pp. 284–5.
88 Karl Marx to F. Engels, February 10, 1858 in *Gesamtausgabe*, Part III, Vol. 2, p. 285.
89 F. Engels to Karl Marx, February 11, 1858 in *Gesamtausgabe*, Part III, Vol. 2, p. 287.
90 Karl Marx to F. Engels, February 14, 1858 in *Gesamtausgabe*, Part III, Vol. 2, p. 288.
91 F. Engels to Karl Marx, February 18, 1858 in *Gesamtausgabe*, Part III, Vol. 2, p. 289.
92 Karl Marx to F. Engels, December 10, 1859 in *Gesamtausgabe*, Part III, Vol. 2, p. 444.
93 F. Engels to V. Adler, September 25, 1892 in *Victor Adlers Aufsätze, Reden und Briefe*, Heft 1: *Victor Adler und Friedrich Engels* (1922), p. 53.
94 Karl Marx to F. Engels, April 17 and 24, 1860 in *Gesamtausgabe*, Part III, Vol. 2, pp. 481–2.
95 F. Engels to Karl Marx, May 7, 1860 in *Gesamtausgabe*, Part III, Vol. 2, p. 484. Friedrich Engels senior died on March 20, 1860.
96 F. Engels to Charlotte Engels, December 1, 1884 in *Marx–Engels Werke*, Vol. 36, pp. 247–8 and H. Hirsch (ed.), *Friedrich Engels: Profile* (1970), p. 99.
97 Bismarck to his sister, November 12, 1858 in Horst Kohl (ed.), *Bismarckbriefe 1836–1872* (1897), p. 168.
98 Karl Marx to F. Engels, September 25, 1860 in *Gesamtausgabe*, Part III, Vol. 2, p. 509.
99 Karl Marx to F. Engels, February 25, 1859 in *Gesamtausgabe*, Part III, Vol. 2, p. 365. See also a second letter written on the same day (*ibid.*, pp. 366–9).
100 Karl Marx to F. Engels, March 3, 1859 in *Gesamtausgabe*, Part III, Vol. 2, p. 370.
101 F. Engels to Karl Marx, March 4, 1859 in *Gesamtausgabe*, Part III, Vol. 2, p. 371.
102 Karl Marx to F. Engels, June 7, 1859 in *Gesamtausgabe*, Part III, Vol. 2, p. 398.
103 Karl Marx to F. Engels, January 11, 1860 in *Gesamtausgabe*, Part III, Vol. 2, p. 453.

104 Karl Marx to F. Engels, May 7, 1861 in *Gesamtausgabe*, Part III, Vol. 3, p. 17.
105 F. Engels to Karl Marx, January 31, 1860 and February 4, 1860 in *Gesamtausgabe*, Part III, Vol. 2, p. 458 and p. 465.
106 Karl Marx to F. Engels, October 2, 1860 in *Gesamtausgabe*, Part III, Vol. 2, p. 514.
107 F. Engels, *Essays addressed to Volunteers* (1861).
108 *United Services Gazette*, March 23, 1861.
109 F. Engels to Karl Marx, September 22, 1859 (where the victim of Engels's assault was described as a *Schweinhund*) and October 3, 1859 in *Gesamtausgabe*, Part III, Vol. 2, p. 417 and p. 421.
110 F. Engels to Karl Marx, January 26, 1863 in *Gesamtausgabe*, Part III, Vol. 3, p. 121.
111 The premises of the Albert Club were in Chorlton on Medlock, first at 26 Clifford Street and then at 315 Oxford Road. For Engels's election to the committee of the Albert Club see letters from the secretary dated December 29, 1859 and December 31, 1862 in the Marx–Engels archives, L. 42 (4) (5), Amsterdam. Members of the club in 1866 included Dr Gumpert, Dr Borchardt and Samuel Moore. See F. P. Schiller, "Friedrich Engels und die Schiller Anstalt in Manchester" in *Marx–Engels Archiv*, ed. D. Rjazanov, Vol. 2, 1927, p. 488 (footnote) and J. A. Petch, "Dover House (315 Oxford Road). A Link with Friedrich Engels" in the *Transactions of the Lancashire and Cheshire Antiquarian Society*, Vol. 72, 1962, pp. 167–9.
112 The secretary of this society in 1868 was W. Berlach whose offices were at 35 Princess Street, Manchester. See F. P. Schiller, "Friedrich Engels und die Schiller Anstalt in Manchester" in *Marx–Engels Archiv*, ed. D. Rjazanov, Vol. II, 1927, p. 490 and H. Whellan & Co., *Directory of Manchester and Salford* (1853).
113 See Marx–Engels archives, M. 22 (Amsterdam).
114 See receipts (£10) for Engels's annual subscription to the Cheshire Hunt Covert Fund in the Marx–Engels archives, M. 18 (Amsterdam).
115 F. Engels to Karl Marx, February 28, 1862 in *Gesamtausgabe*, Part III, Vol. 3, p. 55.
116 F. Engels to Karl Marx, April 4, 1869 in *Gesamtausgabe*, Part III, Vol. 4, p. 176.
117 F. Engels to Jenny Marx, January 3, 1868 in *Gesamtausgabe*, Part III, Vol. 4, p. 1.
118 F. Engels to Karl Marx, February 13, 1851 in *Gesamtausgabe*, Part III, Vol. 1, p. 148.
119 Karl Marx to F. Engels (postscript by Jenny Marx), December 2, 1850 in *Gesamtausgabe*, Part III, Vol. 1, p. 120.
120 F. Engels to Elise Engels, February 13, 1861 in *Gesamtausgabe* in *Marx–Engels Werke*, Vol. 30, pp. 582–3. He wrote: "Nothing in the world would induce me to contribute – even in the most trifling manner – to darkening the closing years of your life by taking part in a family dispute concerning the inheritance". See also F. Engels to Elise Engels, February 27, 1861 (*ibid.*, pp. 585–6). In this letter Engels wrote that "affairs with Godfrey Ermen are as good as settled".
121 Bencliffe Mill was acquired by Ermen and Engels at some time between 1852 and 1858.
122 F. Engels to K. Marx, April 8, 1860 in *Gesamtausgabe*, Part III, Vol. 2, p. 477.

123 Jenny Marx in *Mohr und General* (1965), p. 226.
124 F. Engels to Emil Engels, April 11, 1860 in *Marx–Engels Werke*, Vol. 30, p. 528.
125 F. Engels to Karl Marx, May 7, 1860 in *Gesamtausgabe*, Part III, Vol. 2, p. 484.
126 The contract between Godfrey Ermen and Friedrich Engels of September 25, 1862 is preserved in the Lancashire Record Office at Preston. A draft of the contract (in German), lacking three paragraphs, is preserved in the Marx–Engels archives, H. 11 in Amsterdam. See also F. Engels to Karl Marx, May 10, 1860 in *Gesamtausgabe*, Part III, Vol. 2, p. 485.
127 F. Engels to Karl Marx, December 3, 1860 in *Gesamtausgabe*, Part III, Vol. 2, p. 524.
128 F. Engels to Karl Marx, January 26, 1863 in *Gesamtausgabe*, Part III, Vol. 3, p. 121.
129 W. O. Henderson, *The Cotton Famine, 1861–65* (Manchester University Press, second edition 1969), pp. 107–8.
130 Karl Marx to F. Engels, November 17, 1862 in *Gesamtausgabe*, Part III, Vol. 3, p. 111.
131 Karl Marx to F. Engels, March 24, 1863 in *Gesamtausgabe*, Part III, Vol. 3, p. 134.
132 F. Engels to Karl Marx, March 5, 1862 in *Gesamtausgabe*, Part III, Vol. 3, pp. 57–8.
133 F. Engels to Karl Marx, early September 1862 and September 9, 1862 in *Gesamtausgabe*, Part III, Vol. 3, pp. 99–110.
134 F. Engels to Karl Marx, November 5, 1862 in *Gesamtausgabe*, Part III, Vol. 3, p. 107.
135 F. Engels to Karl Marx, January 26, 1863 in *Gesamtausgabe*, Part III, Vol. 3, pp. 121–2.
136 F. Engels to Karl Marx, November 9, 1862 in *Gesamtausgabe*, Part III, Vol. 3, p. 201.
137 F. Engels to Karl Marx, November 2, 1864 in *Gesamtausgabe*, Part III, Vol. 3, p. 194.
138 F. Engels to Karl Marx, April 12, 1865 in *Gesamtausgabe*, Part III, Vol. 3, p. 260.
139 Engels wrote to his brother Hermann on May 24, 1864 that "Godfrey Ermen would be able to repudiate our contract if the £10,000 which I have promised to invest were short by a single penny" (*Marx–Engels Werke*, Vol. 30, p. 663).
140 F. Engels to Karl Marx, July 5, 1864 in *Gesamtausgabe*, Part III, Vol. 3, p. 183.
141 F. Engels to Karl Marx, September 2, 1864 in *Gesamtausgabe*, Part III, Vol. 3, p. 186. The "Articles of Agreement" between Godfrey Ermen and Friedrich Engels (June 30, 1864) are in the Lancashire Record Office at Preston.
142 F. Engels to Karl Marx, September 2, 1864 in *Gesamtausgabe*, Part III, Vol. 3, p. 186.
143 *Eccles Advertiser*, February 11, 1871.
144 F. Engels to K. Marx, October 4, 1865 in *Gesamtausgabe*, Part III, Vol. 3, pp. 292–3.
145 F. Engels to Karl Marx, October 11, 1867 in *Gesamtausgabe*, Part III, Vol. 3, p. 431.
146 F. Engels to Hermann Engels, April 6, 1866 in *Marx–Engels Werke*, Vol. 30, p. 511.

147 F. Engels to Karl Marx, April 27, 1867 in *Gesamtausgabe*, Part III, Vol. 3, p. 386.
148 F. Engels to Karl Marx, June 16, 1867 in *Gesamtausgabe*, Part III, Vol. 3, p. 393.
149 F. Engels to Karl Marx, October 11, 1867 in *Gesamtausgabe*, Part III, Vol. 3, p. 432.
150 F. Engels to Hermann Engels, November 27, 1867 in *Marx–Engels Werke*, Vol. 30, p. 571.
151 F. Engels to Karl Marx, September 18, 1868 in *Gesamtausgabe*, Part III, Vol. 4, p. 94.
152 F. Engels to Karl Marx, November 23, 1868 in *Gesamtausgabe*, Part III, Vol. 4, p. 129.
153 F. Engels to Karl Marx, November 29, 1868 in *Gesamtausgabe*, Part III, Vol. 4, p. 130–1.
154 F. Engels to Karl Marx, January 25, 1869 in *Gesamtausgabe*, Part III, Vol. 4, p. 150.
155 F. Engels to Karl Marx, January 29, 1869 in *Gesamtausgabe*, Part III, Vol. 4, p. 153.
156 Gustav Mayer, *Friedrich Engels*, Vol. 2, p. 172.
157 The agreements of June 24 and August 10, 1869 concerning the winding up of the Ermen–Engels partnership of 1864 are in the Lancashire Record Office at Preston. For the last stages of the negotiations between Godfrey Ermen and Engels see F. Engels to Karl Marx, July 25, July 30, August 12, December 9 and December 16, *Gesamtausgabe*, Part III, Vol. 4, pp. 210, 215, 221, 256 and 261.
158 F. Engels to Karl Marx, December 9, 1869 in *Gesamtausgabe*, Part III, Vol. 4, p. 256.
159 F. Engels to Karl Marx, July 1, 1869 in *Gesamtausgabe*, Part III, Vol. 4, p. 198.
160 Gustav Mayer, *Friedrich Engels*, Vol. 2, p. 173.
161 Friedrich Engels to Jenny Marx (Marx's daughter), July 9, 1869 in E. Bottigelli, "Sieben unveröffentliche Dokumente von Friedrich Engels" (*Friedrich Engels 1820–1970*: Forschungsinstitut der Friedrich Ebert Stiftung, Vol. 85, 1971, p. 320).
162 Eleanor Marx's essay on Engels in the *Sozialdemokratische Monatsschrift*, November 30, 1890; English translation in *Reminiscences of Marx and Engels* (Foreign Languages Publishing House, Moscow), pp. 185–6.
163 Karl Marx to F. Engels, July 3, 1869 in *Gesamtausgabe*, Part III, Vol. 4, p. 199.
164 F. Engels to Godfrey Ermen, June 1, 1874 in M. Jenkins, *Friedrich Engels in Manchester* (1951). The letter is preserved in the Lancashire Record Office at Preston.
165 F. Engels to Karl Marx, March 28, 1869 in *Gesamtausgabe*, Part III, Vol. 4, p. 173.
166 Karl Marx to L. Kugelmann, October 13, 1866 in Karl Marx, *Letters to Dr Kugelmann*, p. 42. Later he wrote to Kugelmann that "certain appearances must be maintained for the children's sake". (*Ibid.*, p. 64).
167 Karl Marx to L. Kugelmann, March 17, 1868 in Karl Marx, *Letters to Dr Kugelmann*, p. 65.
168 Arnold Künzli, Karl Marx, *Eine Psychographie* (1966), p. 254.
169 Karl Marx to F. Engels, September 10, 1862 in *Gesamtausgabe*, Part III, Vol. 3, p. 102.

170 Karl Marx to L. Kugelmann, December 28, 1862 in Karl Marx, *Letters to Dr Kugelmann*, p. 24.
171 Karl Marx to L. Kugelmann, October 13, 1866 in Karl Marx, *Letters to Dr Kugelmann*, p. 42.
172 Jenny Marx in *Mohr und General* (1965), p. 228.
173 Karl Marx to F. Engels, December 9, 1861 in *Gesamtausgabe*, Part III, Vol. 3, p. 48.
174 Karl Marx to F. Engels, March 3, 1862 and April 28, 1862 in *Gesamtausgabe*, Part III, Vol. 3, p. 56 and p. 62.
175 Karl Marx to F. Engels, June 18, 1862 in *Gesamtausgabe*, Part III, Vol. 3, p. 77.
176 Karl Marx to F. Engels, June 30, 1862 and August 7, 1862 in *Gesamtausgabe*, Part III, Vol. 3, p. 82 and p. 91.
177 Karl Marx to F. Engels, November 14, 1862 in *Gesamtausgabe*, Part III, Vol. 3, p. 108.
178 Jenny Marx in *Mohr und General* (1965), p. 229.
179 F. Engels to Karl Marx, January 7, 1863 (death of Mary Burns), Karl Marx to F. Engels, January 8, 1863 (Marx's reply), F. Engels to Karl Marx, January 13, 1863 (Engels's rebuke to Marx), K. Marx to F. Engels, January 24, 1863 (Marx's apology), F. Engels to Karl Marx, 1863 (reconciliation), Karl Marx to F. Engels, January 28, 1863 (further apologies from Marx) in *Gesamtausgabe*, Part III, Vol. 3, pp. 117–22.
180 Jenny Marx to Joseph Weydemeyer, March 11, 1861 in *Mohr und General* (1965), p. 261.
181 F. Engels to Karl Marx, June 24, 1863; Karl Marx to F. Engels, July 6, 1863 in *Gesamtausgabe*, Part III, Vol. 3, pp. 147–8.
182 Karl Marx to F. Engels, December 2, 1863 in *Gesamtausgabe*, Part III, Vol. 3, pp. 157–8.
183 F. Engels to Karl Marx, December 3, 1863; Karl Marx to F. Engels, December 4 and 22, 1863; F. Engels to Karl Marx, January 3, 1864 in *Gesamtausgabe*, Part III, Vol. 3, pp. 158–63.
184 Karl Marx to F. Engels, December 22, 1863 in *Gesamtausgabe*, Part III, Vol. 3, p. 160.
185 F. Engels to Karl Marx, May 2, 1864; Karl Marx to F. Engels, May 23, 1864 in *Gesamtausgabe*, Part III, Vol. 3, p. 171.
186 F. Engels to Karl Marx, March 11, 1865 in *Gesamtausgabe*, Part III, Vol. 3, p. 252 (Marx received £824 14s 9d).
187 W. Blumenberg, *Marx* (1962), p. 114; A. Künzli, *Karl Marx . . .* (1966), p. 255.
188 Karl Marx to F. Engels, July 4, 1864 in *Gesamtausgabe*, Part III, Vol. 3, p. 182.
189 There is no evidence to support the assertion by R. Payne in *Marx* (1968) that Marx was "becoming a passably rich man as the result of these dubious speculations" (p. 353).
190 Jenny Marx in *Reminiscences of Marx and Engels* (Foreign Languages Publishing House, Moscow), p. 233.
191 Renamed Maitland Park Road in 1868.
192 Jenny Marx in *Reminiscences of Marx and Engels* (Foreign Languages Publishing House, Moscow), p. 233.
193 Jenny Marx, "Kurze Umrisse eines bewegten Lebens" in *Mohr und General* (1965), p. 232.
194 Karl Marx to F. Engels, July 31 and August 5, 1865 in *Gesamtausgabe*, Part III, Vol. 3, p. 278 and p. 281.

195 Karl Marx to F. Engels, August 19 and 22, 1865; F. Engels to Karl Marx, August 21, 1865 in *Gesamtausgabe*, Part III, Vol. 3, pp. 288–91.

196 Karl Marx to F. Engels, November 8 and 15, 1865; F. Engels to Karl Marx, November 13, 1865 in *Gesamtausgabe*, Part III, Vol. 3, pp. 293–4.

197 Karl Marx to F. Engels, November 20, 1865 in *Gesamtausgabe*, Part III, Vol. 3, p. 296.

198 Karl Marx to F. Engels, December 26, 1865 in *Gesamtausgabe*, Part III, Vol. 3, p. 299.

199 Karl Marx to F. Engels, February 14, 1866 in *Gesamtausgabe*, Part III, Vol. 3, p. 309.

200 F. Engels to Karl Marx, August 10, 1866 in *Gesamtausgabe*, Part III, Vol. 3, p. 356.

201 Karl Marx to L. Kugelmann, October 13, 1866 in Karl Marx, *Letters to Dr Kugelmann*, p. 42.

202 Karl Marx to L. Kugelmann, October 25, 1866 in Karl Marx, *Letters to Dr Kugelmann*, p. 44.

203 Karl Marx to F. Engels, September 26, October 1 and 3, 1866; F. Engels to Karl Marx, October 2, 1866 in *Gesamtausgabe*, Part III, Vol. 3, pp. 358–61.

204 Karl Marx to F. Engels, January 10, February 21 and February 25, 1867 in *Gesamtausgabe*, Part III, Vol. 3, pp. 373–6.

205 Karl Marx to F. Engels, March 27 and April 24, 1867; F. Engels to Karl Marx, April 4 and 27, 1867 in *Gesamtausgabe*, Part III, Vol. 3, pp. 378–85.

206 Karl Marx to F. Engels, May 7, 1867 in *Gesamtausgabe*, Part III, Vol. 3, pp. 388–9.

207 Karl Marx to F. Engels, June 22 and 27, 1867; F. Engels to Karl Marx, June 24 and 26, 1867 in *Gesamtausgabe*, Part III, Vol. 3, pp. 395–403.

208 Karl Marx to F. Engels, August 14, 1867 in *Gesamtausgabe*, Part III, Vol. 3, pp. 406–7. In this letter Marx acknowledged that Engels had sent him "very large sums of money" in 1867.

209 Karl Marx to F. Engels, October 4, 1867; F. Engels to Karl Marx, October 11, 1867 in *Gesamtausgabe*, Part III, Vol. 3, pp. 429–31.

210 Karl Marx to F. Engels, November 28, 167; F. Engels to Karl Marx, December 4, 1867 in *Gesamtausgabe*, Part III, Vol. 3, p. 452 and p. 458. The medical examination in connection with the loan appears to have been somewhat perfunctory: see Karl Marx to F. Engels, December 7, 1867 in *Gesamtausgabe*, Part III, Vol. 3, p. 459.

211 F. Engels to Karl Marx, November 28, 1867; Karl Marx to F. Engels, November 29, 1867 in *Gesamtausgabe*, Part III, Vol. 3, pp. 453–4.

212 Karl Marx to F. Engels, December 14, 1867 in *Gesamtausgabe*, Part III, Vol. 3, p. 463.

213 Karl Marx to F. Engels, January 8, 1868 in *Gesamtausgabe*, Part III, Vol. 4, p. 8.

214 Karl Marx to L. Kugelmann, March 6, 1868 in Karl Marx, *Letters to Dr Kugelmann*, p. 64.

215 Karl Marx to F. Engels, February 15, 1868 in *Gesamtausgabe*, Part III, Vol. 4, p. 22.

216 Karl Marx to F. Engels, July 23, 1868 in *Gesamtausgabe*, Part III, Vol. 4, p. 76.

217 Karl Marx to F. Engels, August 13, 1868 in *Gesamtausgabe*, Part III, Vol. 4, p. 83.

218 Karl Marx to F. Engels, August 21, 1868 in *Gesamtausgabe*, Part III, Vol. 4, p. 85.
219 F. Engels to Karl Marx, August 28, 1868 in *Gesamtausgabe*, Part III, Vol. 4, p. 87.
220 Karl Marx to F. Engels, September 9, 1868 in *Gesamtausgabe*, Part III, Vol. 4, p. 89.
221 Karl Marx to F. Engels, September 16 and 19, 1868 in *Gesamtausgabe*, Part III, Vol. 4, p. 93 and p. 95.
222 F. Engels to Karl Marx, October 2, 1868 in *Gesamtausgabe*, Part III, Vol. 4, p. 105.
223 Karl Marx to F. Engels, October 4, 1868 in *Gesamtausgabe*, Part III, Vol. 4, p. 107.
224 Karl Marx to F. Engels, October 15 and 24, 1868 in *Gesamtausgabe*, Part III, Vol. 4, p. 113 and p. 118.
225 F. Engels to Karl Marx, April 27, 1867 in *Gesamtausgabe*, Part III, Vol. 3, p. 386.
226 F. Engels to Karl Marx, November 25, 1868 in *Gesamtausgabe*, Part III, Vol. 4, pp. 130–1.
227 Karl Marx to F. Engels, November 30, 1868 in *Gesamtausgabe*, Part III, Vol. 4, p. 131.
228 F. Engels to Karl Marx, February 25 and March 28, 1869 in *Gesamtausgabe*, Part III, Vol. 4, p. 157 and p. 173.
229 F. Engels to Karl Marx, August 3, 1869 in *Gesamtausgabe*, Part III, Vol. 4, p. 217.
230 Karl Marx to F. Engels, May 21, 1869 in *Gesamtausgabe*, Part III, Vol. 4, p. 193.
231 F. Engels to Karl Marx, May 11, 1870; Jenny Marx to F. Engels, September 13, 1870 in *Gesamtausgabe*, Part III, Vol. 4, p. 324 and p. 384.
232 Karl Marx to F. Engels, February 10, 1866 in *Gesamtausgabe*, Part III, Vol. 3, pp. 305–6.
233 On July 13, 1867 Marx wrote to Dr Kugelmann that he hoped "to induce Engels to write and publish the second volume from 1845 down to the present day. I have finally succeeded to the extent of obtaining a promise that he will set about it" (Karl Marx, *Letters to Dr Kugelmann*, p. 48).
234 Published in the *Volunteer Journal for Lancashire and Cheshire* in 1860–1.
235 Published in the *Manchester Guardian*, June 20 to July 6, 1866.
236 Published in the *Pall Mall Gazette*, 1870–1.
237 Published in *The Commonwealth* in 1867.
238 F. Engels, *Die preussische Militärfrage und die deutsche Arbeiterpartei* (1865).
239 F. Engels to Karl Marx, May 15, 1870 in *Gesamtausgabe*, Part III, Vol. 4, p. 328.
240 F. P. Schiller, "Friedrich Engels und die Schiller-Anstalt in Manchester" in the *Marx–Engels Archiv* (edited by D. Rjazanov), Vol. 2, 1927, pp. 483–93; W. Blumenberg, "Friedrich Engels und die Schiller-Anstalt in Manchester" in the *Bulletin of the International Institute of Social History* (Amsterdam), Vol. 5, 1950; and an anonymous article in *The Sphinx* (Manchester), August 29, 1868, p. 48.
241 F. Engels to Karl Marx, November 4, 1859 in *Gesamtausgabe*, Part III, Vol. 2, p. 430.

242 F. Engels to Jenny Marx, November 5, 1859 in *Gesamtausgabe*, Part III, Vol. 2, pp. 432–3.

243 F. Engels to Karl Marx, November 17, 1859 in *Gesamtausgabe*, Part III, Vol. 2, p. 435. A copy of the programme of the Schiller Festival in Manchester (November 11, 1859) is preserved in the public library at Wuppertal. The prologue was written by Alfred Meissner, the festive stanzas by E. Slomans, and the epilogue by Carl Siebel.

244 F. Engels to Karl Marx, November 17, 1859 in *Gesamtausgabe*, Part III, Vol. 2, p. 434.

245 The premises were leased to eight years at a rent of £225 per annum. A copy of the statutes of the Schiller Anstalt (1860) is preserved in the Manchester Central Reference Library.

246 F. Engels to Karl Marx, March 6 and 11, 1865 in *Gesamtausgabe*, Part III, Vol. 3, p. 249 and p. 252.

247 F. Engels to Karl Marx, March 19, 1868 in *Gesamtausgabe*, Part III, Vol. 4, p. 31.

248 V. Stoessel (librarian of the Schiller Anstalt) to F. Engels, May 2, 1861 in F. P. Schiller, "Friedrich Engels und die Schiller-Anstalt in Manchester" (in *Marx–Engels Archiv*, edited by D. Rjazanov, Vol. 2, 1927) and F. Engels to the committee of the Schiller Anstalt, May 23, 1861 in *Marx–Engels Werke*, Vol. 30, pp. 596–8.

249 F. Engels to Carl Siebel, June 4, 1862 in *Marx–Engels Werke*, Vol. 30, pp. 624–5. This letter was first published in the *Deutsche Zeitung*, October 16, 1920.

250 A. Burkhard (acting secretary of the Schiller Anstalt) to F. Engels, July 8, 1864 in the Marx–Engels archives, L. 858 (Amsterdam).

251 F. Engels to Karl Marx, November 7, 1864 in *Gesamtausgabe*, Part III, Vol. 3, p. 200.

252 Circular of the Schiller Anstalt (Manchester, March 19, 1866) signed by F. Engels (chairman), J. G. Wehner (treasurer) and A. Burkhard (secretary).

253 J. M. Cohen, *The Life of Ludwig Mond* (1956), p. 73.

254 F. Engels to Karl Marx, March 5, 1866 in *Gesamtausgabe*, Part III, Vol. 3, p. 312.

255 Schiller Anstalt correspondence in Marx–Engels archives, M. 17 (Amsterdam).

256 Circular of the Schiller Anstalt (Manchester, March 19, 1866).

257 Circular of the Schiller Anstalt to subscribers to the Building Fund (Manchester, June 28, 1867). The circular was signed by F. Engels (chairman), J. G. Wehner (treasurer), and A. Davisson (secretary).

258 F. Engels to Karl Marx, March 19, 1868 in *Gesamtausgabe*, Part III, Vol. 4, p. 31.

259 F. Engels to Karl Marx, March 29, 1868 in *Gesamtausgabe*, Part III, Vol. 4, p. 35.

260 F. Engels to Karl Marx, June 24, 1868 in *Gesamtausgabe*, Part III, Vol. 4, p. 64.

261 For Engels's letter of resignation (September 16, 1868) see W. Blumenberg, "Friedrich Engels und die Schiller-Anstalt in Manchester" (in the *Bulletin of the International Institute of Social History, Amsterdam*, Vol. 5, 1950).

262 F. Engels to Karl Marx, September 16 and 30, 1868 in *Gesamtausgabe*, Part III, Vol. 4, p. 91 and p. 104.

263 Karl Marx, *Herr Vogt* (1860); reprinted in *Marx–Engels Werke*, Vol. 14, p. 381.

264 F. Engels to Karl Marx, August 12, 1869 and August 10, 1870 in *Gesamtausgabe*, Part III, Vol. 4, p. 221 and p. 363.

265 On April 28, 1870 A. Davisson wrote to F. Engels: "I have the honour to inform you that at the election held today you were elected a member of the committee for the business year 1870–1" (F. P. Schiller, "Friedrich Engels und die Schiller-Anstalt in Manchester", *Marx–Engels Archiv*, ed. D. Rjazanov, Vol. 2, 1927).

266 Engels subscribed £5 a month to this fund: see J. G. Wehner to F. Engels, August 3, 1870 (receipt for £5) in the Marx–Engels archives, M. 22 (Amsterdam).

267 Anonymous article on "The Schiller Anstalt" in *The Sphinx* (Manchester), August 29, 1868, p. 48.

268 See letters from the secretary of the Albert Club to F. Engels, December 29, 1859 and December 31, 1862 in the Marx–Engels archives, L. 42 (4) (Amsterdam). See also J. A. Petch, "Dover House (315 Oxford Road). A Link with Friedrich Engels" in the *Transactions of the Lancashire and Cheshire Antiquarian Society*, Vol. 72, 1962, pp. 167–9 and an anonymous article in *The Sphinx* (Manchester), May 1, 1869, p. 43. There is a brief reference to the Albert Club in F. P. Schiller, "Friedrich Engels und die Schiller-Anstalt in Manchester" in the *Marx–Engels Archiv* (edited by D. Rjazanov), Vol. 2, 1927, p. 488 (footnote).

269 Anonymous article on "The Clubs of Manchester. The Albert" in *The Sphinx* (Manchester), May 1, 1869, p. 43.

270 See, for example, P. Ziegler to F. Engels, January 23, 1873 (acknowledging the receipt of Engels's annual subscription) and February 19, 1874 in the Marx–Engels archives, L. 6477 (Amsterdam).

271 Charles Roesgen to F. Engels, February 12, 1871. For Roesgen's letters to Engels see the Marx–Engels archives, L. 5423 to 5447 (Amsterdam). The fire is described in an article in the *Eccles Advertiser*, February 11, 1871.

5

FRIENDS IN EXILE

I. Wilhelm Wolff[1]

Karl Marx dedicated the first volume of *Das Kapital* "to the memory of my very dear friend Wilhelm Wolff, bold and faithful champion of the proletarian cause". Jenny Marx recalled her first meeting with "our dear Wilhelm Wolff" in Brussels in 1846 and declared that this was the beginning of "a close bond of friendship which ended only with the death of our dear Lupus in May 1864".[2] Engels wrote that when Wolff died "Marx and I mourned our most trusted companion while the revolutionary cause in Germany lost a valued fighter who could never be replaced."[3]

In a sketch of Wolff's career Engels mentioned that "for several years Wolff was my only friend in Manchester who shared my political views". "It is not surprising that we met nearly every day and that I had many opportunities of admiring his judgment on current affairs – which was almost instinctively correct." Engels and Wolff discussed the good old days when they fought for their ideals shoulder to shoulder with Marx in Brussels, London and Cologne. Their working days were now spent in the society of middle class "philistines" but in their leisure hours they could dream of a bright new world in which there would be no place for Manchester cotton lords. Before he sank into obscurity in Manchester Wilhelm Wolff had been a revolutionary journalist and communist agitator. As a champion of the oppressed peasants and handloom weavers of his native Silesia, as a leading member of the Communist League, and as an editor of the *Neue Rheinische Zeitung* he had earned the hatred of the Prussian authorities.

Wilhelm Wolff was born in the Silesian village of Tarnau (Kreis Schweidnitz)[4] on June 21, 1809. His father was a smallholder and a carpenter and – since feudal obligations survived in Silesia at this time – he had to work on the manor farm in the summer and to help with the threshing of his landlord's corn in the winter. A small wage was paid for these services. Since members of a peasant's family generally had to work on their lord's estate Wolff as a child performed feudal services for the Countess of Fürstenberg. His personal experience of life in Tarnau enabled him in later years to write about the grievances of the Silesian peasants with unrivalled authority. It was far from easy in those days for the son of a peasant in Silesia to break away from the social class in which he was born. But his teachers recognised his academic abilities and his parents gave him what help they could so that he was able to attend the grammar school at Schweidnitz and later the University of Breslau where he read classics. He earned money by coaching to enable him to continue his studies.

In December 1831, when he had been at the University for two years, Wilhelm Wolff joined the students' association. The revolution in France of 1830 had generated a revival of liberal agitation in Germany which culminated in a great open air demonstration at Hambach in 1832 (to demand more freedom for the press) and an abortive attempt to seize the guard house at Frankfurt in 1833. There was a revival of students associations which had been forbidden by the Carlsbad Decrees. At the beginning of the winter term of 1832 Wilhelm Wolff was elected to the post of first secretary of the Breslau students association and he played an active part in recruiting new members. Moritz Elsner, one of his friends, later recalled that Wolff, though not a duelling man or a drinking man, was popular among the students and had a considerable influence over them. He was the leading spirit in a small left-wing group – always a minority of the student body as a whole – which was engaged in political discussions. It was due largely to Wolff's efforts that the radical ideas current in the Universities of south west Germany were brought to Breslau. Wolff's friends now established themselves as a separate group within the students' association. They discussed such problems as the future of Poland, the need for a Prussian constitution, and the social question. In May 1833 – immediately after the attack on the Frankfurt guard house – the Prussian authorities took stern measures to suppress student unrest and in some universities arrests were made. This led to the dissolution of the radical group in Breslau. Wolff left the University early in 1834 and took a post in Striegau as a private tutor to earn money to continue his studies.

A senior legal official named Koch was sent to Breslau to investigate the political activities of the students. He soon realised that Wolff had been a leading figure in the students association. Wolff was brought to Breslau in July 1834 for questioning and he was subsequently arrested. It was not until March 1835 that he was charged not only with being a member of a students' association but also with *lèse-majesté*. His defence was that the students' association had been engaged only in academic and social – and not in political

– activities and that nothing that he had said or written amounted to *lèse-majesté*. Wolff was found guilty and sentenced to six years imprisonment for being a member of a students' association and to two years for *lèse-majesté*. The first sentence was reduced to one year but the second sentence had to be served in full. Including the time spent in goal before his trial Wolff was in prison for four years. The sentence was served in the fortress of Silberberg where many other political prisoners – including the poet Fritz Reuter – were incarcerated.

Wolff was released at the end of July 1838. His health had suffered owing to the rigours of his imprisonment. It was now very difficult for him to make a living since his sentence barred him from public employment or from completing his University studies. He could not even teach as a private tutor without securing a licence from the authorities. Wolff was fortunately able to obtain a post as a tutor in the household of the Polish patriot Count Titus Dzialynski whose estates lay at Kurnik in the province of Posen. Dzialynski had taken an active part in the Polish rising of 1830–1 and his estates had been confiscated. Some years elapsed before he was allowed to resume possession of his estates. He was glad to employ Wolff who had suffered so much at the hands of the Prussian authorities. Dzialynski was a scholar, engaged upon the compilation of a collection of old Lithuanian laws (1330–1529) and it is possible that Wolff assisted his patron in editing these documents. Since Wolff lived in Posen for two years he had ample opportunities of seeing how the local peasants, farm labourers and craftsmen lived. Their lot was no better than those of the workers in Silesia.

In the summer of 1840 Wolff returned to Silesia. If he hoped that Frederick William IV's accession would be followed by a relaxation of the supervision which the police exercised over him he was to be disappointed. He secured a post in Ratibor in the household of a merchant and as he had no teaching licence he was nominally a house-guest and not a tutor. Wolff wrote some articles for the *Schlesische Provinzialblätter* at this time. As he was closely watched by the authorities his contributions were anonymous and consequently it has been difficult for historians to identify them. He returned to politics by taking part in a controversy concerning the hymns sung in Protestant churches in Silesia. Some of the traditional hymns, written in an age when the Pietists exercised great influence, were now regarded by progressive churchmen as highly unsuitable for modern services. The issue, of little importance in itself, focused attention upon the conflict within the Church between the conservative supporters of traditional Pietism and the supporters of a liberal wind of change in Church affairs. Wolff attacked the extreme Pietists for the same reason that Engels criticised Dr Krummacher of Elberfeld–Barmen.

Wilhelm Wolff's contribution to the controversy was to hold the Pietists up to ridicule by printing a verse which he claimed to have found in an old hymnbook:

> Ich bin ein echtes Rabenaas
> ein wahres Sündenknüppel
> der seine Sünden in sich frass
> so wie der Rost die Zwibbel
> Herr Jesu, nimm mich Hund beim Ohr
> wirf mir den Gnadenknochen vor
> und schmeiss mich Sündenlümmel
> in deinen Gnadenhimmel.

Engels declared that the verse "spread like wildfire throughout the country to the amusement of the godless and the fury of the godly".[5]

At the end of 1842 Wilhelm Wolff left Ratibor for Striegau and by the middle of 1843 he was back in Breslau. Here he again made contact with left wing students – he met Ferdinand Lassalle who was an undergraduate at this time[6] – but on the whole he devoted himself to journalism rather than to political activities. Breslau had changed since Wolff's student days. The building of railways was turning Breslau from a sleepy provincial capital into a bustling commercial centre of a region that was passing through the early stages of an industrial revolution. The Silesian workers were facing the problems of long hours, low wages, harsh factory discipline and poor housing. Factories were driving village craftsmen out of business. Silesia, however, had its own special problems. The old established linen industry had failed to revive after the Napoleonic wars and was still declining owing to its inability to meet foreign competition. The relations between the owners of mines and factories and their workers was complicated by the fact that – at any rate in Upper Silesia – most of the employers were Germans while most of the workers were Poles. National differences aggravated disputes between management and men. Feudal services and dues survived in the country districts of Silesia. The growth of industrial towns would in any case have made it difficult for village craftsmen – weavers and millers for example – to survive in the surrounding country districts. But many smallholders and peasants were still liable to render services and to make ancient feudal payments to the lord of the manor and this greatly aggravated the situation. Moreover the feudal lords in Silesia still controlled the local law courts which dealt with minor offences and also the police in the villages. Peasants who indulged in poaching or stealing wood received no mercy at the hands of their landlords. The grievances of peasants and craftsmen were therefore as serious as those of the miners and the factory workers.

It was no easy matter for a political journalist with pronounced radical views to survive in Breslau in the early 1840s especially if he had already served a sentence for *lèse-majesté*. Wolff had to contend with a censor who would refuse to permit any criticism of the government to be published and the editor of the papers to which he contributed could see from the fate of the *Rheinische Zeitung* what happened to those who defied the censor. Wolff survived for a couple of years by devoting himself to descriptive writing. He gave vivid accounts of housing conditions in Breslau and the rising of the weavers in 1844 and he let the facts speak for themselves. The threat of censorship forced him to be circumspect in making comments that might be regarded as attacks upon established institutions. Sometimes he was able to write more freely when he contributed to newspapers outside Prussia – even outside Germany – where press censorship was less vigorously enforced.

Wolff's articles on the housing of the workers in Breslau and on the miserable condition of the Silesian weavers made him known far beyond the borders of his native province. In November 1843 he gave a vivid description of the appalling conditions prevailing in a Breslau municipal reception centre for the temporary accommodation of homeless persons. The wretched inmates lived in squalid dilapidated overcrowded rooms which had once been used as a prison. They lacked adequate food and fuel. The article created a sensation and its author became known as "Kasematten Wolff" since the premises which he had described were called "Kasematten".[7] Treitschke has observed that Wolff's description of the sufferings of the homeless in Breslau gave the Germans a salutary shock. They realised that there was just as serious a housing problem in German towns as in English or French manufacturing regions.[8] Only a few weeks after it had published the "Kasematten" article the *Breslau Zeitung* declared that "our attention has suddenly been called to the problem of the condition of the proletariat. We lived quietly and peacefully, amusing ourselves at theatres, concerts and dances but now poverty has reared its ugly head." "And all at once our consciences have been pricked and we are visiting the lodgings of the poor and we are subscribing to funds to alleviate distress."[9] Moreover Wolff's description of the lodgings of the homeless in Breslau gave an impetus to further revelations not only of the housing condition of the urban workers[10] but also of the grievances of the peasants and the weavers in the country districts of Silesia.

In June 1844 there were two days of disturbances among the handloom weavers in the Silesian villages of Peterswaldau and Langenbielau. The premises of the firms of Zwanziger and Dierig were destroyed. The rising was quickly put down by troops and some 80 arrests were made. The affair might well have been forgotten as a minor incident in a distant province. But it proved to be the signal for industrial unrest in Breslau, Magdeburg, Berlin and elsewhere. Germans began to realise that they too would have to face the social problems which had led to the rising of the workers in Lyons in the 1830s and in Lancashire in 1842. Wilhelm Wolff played an important part in bringing home to the German people the full significance of the disturbances in Silesia. He visited various mountain villages in the textile regions to examine the causes of the affair on the spot. His article on "The Distress and the Rising of the Silesian Weavers" appeared in Püttmann's *Deutsches Bürgerbuch für 1845*.

In this essay Wolff described the wretched situation of the peasant weavers of his native province. He wrote:

> "I have often met these poor hungry frozen wretches trudging many miles in the most horrible weather to bring a finished piece of cloth to the merchant. At home his wife and children awaited his return. A single bowl of potato soup had been their only meal in a day and a half. The weaver was taken aback at the price which he had been offered for weaving the cloth. But the merchant was quite adamant and even the clerks and apprentices in the office adopted a shamefully hardhearted attitude towards the poor weaver. He took what was offered and went home in despair. Frequently he was paid in gold at the rate of three silver Thalers and six groschen for one gold ducat but when he changed his ducats into silver money he obtained only two Thalers and 28 groschen or even less. Other merchants had introduced the English truck system. The weavers were paid in kind and not in cash. Since most of the weavers were in debt to their employer they had to accept goods at the price fixed by the merchant. So the merchants had the weavers in a cleft stick. If a weaver protested against this treatment the merchant simply blamed the poor state of trade."

Wolff gave an account of the events in Peterswaldau and Langenbielau which was very different from the official version put out by the Prussian authorities. And he showed that the disturbances were due not merely to local circumstances but to deep-rooted injustices inherent in a rural society dominated by feudal overlords and capitalist merchants. The events in Silesia had not been brought about simply by low wages or a shortage of food. They heralded the appearance on the German scene of the proletariat as a political force.[11]

Wolff's articles on the housing of the poor and the weavers' rising brought him into the limelight and by the second half of 1844 he was contributing to *Vorwärts*, the organ of left wing German exiles in Paris with which Marx was closely associated. In this paper and in the *Schlesische Chronik* he attacked the Prussian junkers and Prussian militarism with his accustomed vigour. It was obviously only a question of time before the authorities would take action to silence so dangerous a critic of the régime. Criminal proceedings were initiated against Wolff in the autumn of 1845 and he was sentenced to three months' imprisonment early in the following year. He fled to Breslau to avoid arrest and made his way to London where he was soon in touch with members of the German Workers' Education Society and the League of the Just. In April 1846 he settled in Brussels.

Engels later recalled his first meeting with Wolff. He wrote:

> "If I remember rightly it was towards the end of April 1846 – when Marx and I were living in a suburb of Brussels and were collaborating in writing a book (*The German Ideology*) – that we were told that a gentleman from Germany wished to see us. We found ourselves in the presence of a small but sturdily built man. He impressed us as a kindly man of quiet determination. His figure was that of an East German peasant, and he wore the sort of clothes that one would expect to see in a little market town in East Germany. This was Wilhelm Wolff. He had infringed the press laws and had escaped from the Prussian authorities who would have put him in prison. When we first saw him we did not realise what an exceptional character lay behind so modest an exterior. But within a few days Marx and I had formed a close friendship with this new colleague in exile and we realised that we were dealing with no ordinary mortal. He soon revealed his intellectual powers – sharpened by studying classics – his fund of humour, his firm grasp of difficult theoretical problems, his burning hatred of all the oppressors of the proletariat, and his quiet but energetic character. Marx, Wolff and I worked together in friendly collaboration for several years. We stood shoulder to shoulder in times of strife; we were united in victory and defeat; we were together in good times and in bad. And only then did we really appreciate the full extent of Wolff's immense strength of character, his complete reliability – of which there could be no shadow of doubt whatever – and the powerful sense of duty and responsibility towards friend and foe, and towards himself."[12]

In Brussels Wilhelm Wolff found employment in Sebastian Seiler's press bureau which supplied German newspapers with foreign news. Wolff contributed to left-wing journals such as the *Deutsche-Brüsseler Zeitung*[13] and the *Westphälisches Dampfboot*.[14] He was associated with the Brussels Correspondence Committee through which Marx and Engels kept in touch with communist groups throughout western Europe. Wolff visited London with Engels in the summer of 1847 to attend the first congress of the Communist League. Wolff represented the Brussels and Engels the Paris workers. At the end of August 1847 a German Workers Association was established in Brussels and Wilhelm Wolff became its secretary. He was one of the Association's most popular lecturers on current affairs at its weekly meetings. Wolff was also a member of an international Democratic Association which was set up in Brussels in November 1847.[15]

Revolution broke out in Brussels in February 1848 but within a few days government troops were in control of the city. Wilhelm Wolff was arrested and harshly treated by the police before being expelled from Belgium.[16] He joined several socialist colleagues in Paris where he sat on the executive committee of the Communist League and signed the document which set forth the League's immediate objectives in Germany.[17]

When the revolution spread to Germany in March 1848 Wilhelm Wolff returned to Silesia by way of Mainz, Cologne and Berlin. In a report to the League of April 18, 1848 he declared that he had seen few signs of activity on the part of the League's supporters. In Cologne the League was moribund. In Berlin all that Wolff could do was to persuade Hätzel to try to revive interest in communism.[18] In Breslau the local communist organisation was defunct.[19] Wilhelm Wolff endeavoured to rally the communist supporters in Breslau and he toured the neighbouring country districts to campaign on behalf of radical candidates seeking election to the Frankfurt National Assembly. He was himself a candidate in Breslau but he was only elected as a "substitute member". This meant that he could take his seat only if the representative for Breslau was absent from the National Assembly.[20] Engels subsequently declared that Wolff's mission to Breslau had been "highly successful".[21]

When Marx and Engels established the *Neue Rheinische Zeitung* in Cologne Wilhelm Wolff joined them and became an editor of the paper. He was now aged 39 and he was one of the most senior members of the editorial board. He was a conscientious editor and if any colleagues were absent they were sure that "Lupus would see that the paper went punctually to press". At this time Wolff gave weekly lectures on current affairs to the local Democratic Society. Friedrich Lessner later recalled that when he joined this society he "got to know Wilhelm Wolff who often gave talks on current political events. It was a real pleasure to hear that man speak. His vigorous, humorous way of giving a political survey was admired by everybody: he could group even the better known and less exciting events so skilfully and deal with a matter seriously or satirically according to its nature."[22] On September 14, 1848 Wolff and Engels addressed a public meeting in the Frankenplatz to protest against the declaration of a state of siege and the suspension of the *Neue Rheinische Zeitung*.[23]

When legal proceedings were initiated against the editors of the *Neue Rheinische Zeitung* Wilhelm Wolff went to the Palatinate but soon returned to Cologne and resumed his duties on the paper. He secured lodgings near his office and seldom appeared on the streets for fear of being arrested. The most important articles which he wrote were those on *Die Schlesische Milliarde* (March 22–April 25, 1849). Once more he attacked the great landowners of Silesia who still refused to surrender their feudal privileges.[24]

The *Neue Rheinische Zeitung* was suppressed on May 19, 1849 and since the editors were threatened with legal proceedings they all left Cologne. Wilhelm Wolff went to Frankfurt where, in the absence of the representative from Breslau, he addressed the Assembly as a "substitute member". He charged the Assembly – and the Reichsverweser – with cowardice in the face of mounting reaction. His words fell upon deaf ears. Wolff joined the rump of the assembly which moved to Stuttgart. But Württemberg troops dispersed the assembly and Germany's first elected parliament came to an end.

Wolff went into exile again – first to Zürich and then (in June 1851) to London where he joined Marx and Engels.[25] He had difficulty in earning a living. Weerth tried to secure a post for him as an agent for a German firm but without success[26] and Engels asked Dr John Watts if he could find Wolff some employment in Manchester.[27] Wolff was offered the post of editor of the *New-Yorker Staatszeitung*[28] but he decided to stay in England. In March 1853 Marx wrote that "Lupus (Wolff) grows older from day to day and becomes more crotchety",[29] and later in the same year Wolff described his situation as one of "dreadful distress".[30] Eventually Dr Borchardt, a German doctor living in Manchester who had known Wolff in Breslau, offered to find pupils for him if he came to Manchester as a teacher of languages. Borchardt sent Wolff £10 for his travelling expenses.[31] Wolff's departure from London in September 1853 was marred by a childish squabble with Marx over a book which Marx had borrowed from him and failed to return. Marx wrote to Engels that Wolff was a senile old fool soaked in gin[32] and it was some months before Engels was able to effect a reconciliation between Marx and Wilhelm Wolff.[33]

From 1854 until his death ten years later Wilhelm Wolff lived in Manchester. He did not return to journalism and he did not resume his political activities. The fiery revolutionary who had defied the Prussian authorities in Breslau and Cologne became an obscure tutor living in Chorlton on Medlock and presiding over harmless social gatherings at the Chatsworth Inn frequented by German clerks working in Manchester offices.[34] In a letter to Marx in 1854 Engels mentioned that Wolff sometimes drank more than was good for him. On one occasion he emerged from a public house late at night and became involved in a brawl in which he lost his money and his watch. In February 1858, however, Engels wrote that Wolff was "trying to retire from drinking".[35]

By 1859 Wilhelm Wolff – according to Marx – was "fairly well off". He stayed with Marx in 1861 and his host declared that "in spite of his gout the old fellow looks quite young".[36] At this time Jenny Marx described Wilhelm Wolff as "the same old fellow we used to know". "He is highly respected in Manchester, and the chief opponent of this confirmed bachelor is now his landlady who sometimes keeps him short of tea, sugar or coal."[37] In that year Marx and Lassalle discussed the possibility of founding a new left-wing journal in Germany and Marx suggested that Wilhelm Wolff should be one of the editors. But nothing came of this project.

Only visits from Engels and letters from Weerth and other old friends reminded Wolff of the stirring days of the revolution of 1848. But he had not been forgotten on the Continent and when he went to France on holiday in August 1857 he was kept under constant surveillance by the police. There was an echo from the past in 1863 when Wolff came across a copy of Fritz Reuter's *Ut mine Festungstid*.[38] Through the publisher, Wolff got in touch with the poet. Reuter at once sent his cordial greetings to his former companion in Silberberg prison.[39]

Wilhelm Wolff fell ill early in 1864. Marx came to Manchester to see his old friend for the last time. Wolff died on May 9.[40] Marx and Engels attended the funeral. Freiligrath was unable to do so.[41] In a letter to his wife Marx mentioned that he had paid a tribute to his old friend at the graveside. "I do not think that anyone in Manchester was held in such universal esteem as our poor little fellow."[42] Wolff's estate amounted to £1,370. After bequests of £100 each had been made to Engels, Borchardt and the Manchester Schiller Anstalt, the residue of £818 16s 11d was left to Karl Marx.[43]

II. Georg Weerth[44]

Shortly after settling in Manchester in 1851 Engels wrote to his friend Weydemeyer that "so long as Weerth is in Bradford, we have established a regular switchback service between the two cities, since the journey by rail takes only two and a half hours".[45] For a brief period in 1851–2, before Wilhelm Wolff settled in Manchester, Weerth was the only friend of Engels who lived fairly near at hand. He was in Bradford for much of the time between the middle of August 1851 and October 1852 and he lodged with Engels in Manchester for a week or two before leaving for the West Indies in November 1852. Engels and Weerth had known each other since the 1840s when Engels had worked as a clerk in Manchester and Weerth had held a similar post in Bradford. Together they had studied the condition of the English workers. Weerth had been a close friend and a strong supporter of Marx and Engels in the days of the Brussels Correspondence Committee, the Communist League, and the *Neue Rheinische Zeitung*. Engels held him in high regard as "the first and most important poet of the German proletariat".[46]

Georg Weerth was born in 1822 at Detmold. He was the third son of Pastor Ferdinand Weerth, the General Superintendent of the Lutheran Church in the Principality of Lippe. The Weerth and Freiligrath families were close neighbours and Georg Weerth's earliest contact with radical ideas may have been through Ferdinand Freiligrath, the revolutionary poet. It was a curious coincidence that the sleepy little town of Detmold should have provided the *Neue Rheinische Zeitung* with its two literary editors.

After attending the local grammar school Weerth embarked upon a business career at the age of fourteen. His first post was in Elberfeld with the textile firm of J. H. Brink and Co. Four years later, in 1840, he moved to Cologne where he served for a year in the offices of Count Meinertshagen. Early in 1841 he went to Bonn to serve as a clerk in the firm of Friedrich aus'm Weerth who was his father's cousin. He was able to attend some lectures at the University of Bonn as a visiting student.[47] In some humorous sketches of office life, written in 1845–8, Friedrich aus'm Weerth appeared as "Herr Preiss" who was depicted as a thoroughly unscrupulous and hypocritical merchant whose life was devoted to making money. All Georg Weerth's disgust with the world of commerce in which he felt himself trapped were expressed in his attacks upon the unsavoury character of Herr Preiss. In a letter to Marx the author declared that "old Weerth" would wring his neck if he found out that he was the merchant depicted as Herr Preiss.[48] In the summer of 1843 Georg Weerth gave up his post in Bonn owing to "a foolish indiscretion"[49] and he was fortunate, later in the year,[50] to secure an appointment as a clerk at £120 a year with the firm of Philip Passavant and Co. of Bradford.[51] He worked in Bradford from December 1843 to April 1846.[52]

Weerth took an instant dislike to Bradford and to its more prosperous inhabitants. He described Bradford as "the most disgusting manufacturing town in England"[53] – "dirty, foggy, smoky and cold".[54] "Every other English industrial centre is a paradise when compared with this filthy hole." "There can be no doubt whatever that here in Bradford one is living in the very home of Lucifer himself."[55] Bradford might have a larger population than Cologne but it had "no theatre, no social life, no decent hotel, no reading room, and no civilised human beings – only Yorkshiremen in torn frock coats, shabby hats and gloomy faces".[56] The English were a "cold hypocritical race" of "barbaric money grubbers".[57] "From the prime minister to the humblest shopkeeper the English behave in a shameful manner behind the mask of religion."[58] Weerth was envious of the rich. He denounced George Cheetham whose "enormous wealth has been amassed by ruining many thousands of his workers".[59] When the head of the firm for which he worked – an old gentleman from whom he had received many kindnesses – retired to Greenhill Hall at Bingley he wrote: "These old merchants live a good life. Let's hope that we can soon kick them all out of their fine mansions. I cannot bear to think of anybody enjoying an unfair share of the good things of life."[60]

Before long Georg Weerth told his mother that he was "completely absorbed in politics and socialism".[61] His conversion to socialism was due to Engels's influence, to envy of the rich, to sympathy for the factory workers, and to his study of economics.[62] His acceptance of Marxist doctrines can be seen from his observation that "the political history of a country is directly associated with its economic development. All too often political events stem directly from economic changes. What may appear at first sight to be a sudden unexpected event is nearly always the result of a slow process of development over a long period of years".[63] Just as Engels studied the way in which the Manchester cotton operatives worked and lived so Weerth examined the condition of the Bradford workers. His accounts of the working class and the poor law in *Sketches of British Social and Political Life* show how carefully Weerth studied the social question in England.[64] His friend Dr John Little McMichan – a Scottish surgeon practising in the working class district of Bradford – showed him round local slums, hospitals, prisons and workhouses. On one occasion Weerth was present when applicants for poor relief were being interviewed.[65] What he saw in Bradford led Weerth to "cherish and respect" the English workers because they were "intelligent and energetic men". He detested "the monied classes" who treated the workers "like beasts of burden – like merchandise – like machines". The workers had become the "outcasts of modern society".[66]

A common interest in the condition of the English workers brought Weerth and Engels together. The first reference to Engels in Weerth's correspondence is a letter of May 22, 1844 in which Weerth mentioned that he was going to Manchester at Whitsun when he hoped to meet "a German philosopher buried in that dark city".[67] After his visit Weerth wrote: "I spent the day with my friend Engels exploring the great city of Manchester."[68] Engels later recalled how he and Weerth had enjoyed "many a happy Sunday together".[69] Weerth, like Engels, took a lively interest in the political movements of the time. He admired the oratory of Feargus O'Connor and he supported the Chartist cause which he regarded as the spearhead of revolution in England. He was less impressed by speakers at meetings organised by the Anti-Corn Law League and by supporters of new railway companies.[70] He shared Engels's political philosophy and regarded private property as the root of all evil.[71] Like Engels he believed that England was ripe for revolution and that the next slump would herald the fall of capitalism and the triumph of the proletariat. In December 1844 he declared that two bad harvests and a commercial crisis would spark off a revolution. "And it will be no revolution against royal power or parliamentary follies, or religion. It will be a revolution against property." "The next trade slump will throw thousands of workers onto the streets. It will spark off a revolt that will lead to attacks upon property. The last time that there was a revolt in Lancashire and Yorkshire the workers simply grumbled and went on strike. Next time they will attack the homes of the rich and seize for themselves the necessities of life. Next time they will go on strike for so long that a complete social revolution will be inevitable."[72] In January 1845 Weerth wrote that England was ready for "an explosion which will blow up the greater part of society as it exists today".[73] A few months later he wrote to his brother Wilhelm: "I hope that a slump will come soon. When it comes the English constitution will go to the devil. A democratic constitution will take its place and this will inevitably lead to the triumph of socialism."[74]

In the summer of 1845 Georg Weerth's health deteriorated, partly because of overwork and partly because of Bradford's polluted atmosphere and "the fearful raw north east wind".[75] The elder Passavant suggested that he should have a holiday in Southport but Weerth thought that Paris would be a better place in which to recuperate. He decided to visit Brussels on the way and then a sprained ankle prevented him from going any further. In Brussels he stayed in the same house as Karl Marx[76] and met the members of a small group of Marx's disciples who were engaged in revolutionary propaganda. He described himself as a follower of the "ragged trousered Communists".[77] Weerth, however, had no intention of becoming a full time agitator or of eking out a living as a journalist. He appreciated the comforts of life too much to leave the world of business behind him. His ambition was to escape from the drudgery of an office stool by becoming a commission agent on the Continent. Such a post would enable him to travel and to find time for some political activity. He returned to Bradford for the winter of 1845–6. In April 1846 Weerth left the firm of P. Passavant and became an agent in France, Holland and Belgium[78] for Emanuel and Son, a textile firm with offices in Bradford, Hamburg and Moscow.[79]

In April 1846 Weerth left Bradford for Brussels which was his headquarters for the next two years. Although he made frequent business trips in Belgium, Holland and France[80] he was in Brussels often enough to keep in close touch with Marx and Engels and their political associates. He told his brother Wilhelm: "I have decided once and for all that I am going to devote myself to my business and to making money and that all other activities must take second place."[81] His political activities included writing for the left-wing *Deutsche Brüsseler Zeitung* and serving on the committee of the *Association Démocratique* of Brussels.[82] In September 1847 an international congress, sponsored by the *Association Belge pour la Liberté Commerciale* was held in the Hôtel de Ville of Brussels and was attended by over 300 economists, manufacturers, and parliamentarians from Britain and the Continent.[83] When Weerth heard that the congress proposed to discuss the question: "Will the carrying out of universal Free Trade benefit the working classes?", he put his name down as a speaker. On September 18 Dr Bowring, one of the English delegates, was unable to speak because of a sore throat and the chairman unexpectedly called Weerth to the rostrum. Weerth declared that since no representatives of the working class were present at the conference he would speak on their behalf. He spoke of the wretched condition of the workers in industrialised societies and he claimed that Free Trade would not bring about the slightest improvement in their lot. He warned the manufacturers: "If you do not take care you will have to fear an irruption of your own workmen, and they will be more terrible to you than all the Cossacks in the world."[84]

In spite of his sore throat Dr Bowring immediately replied to Weerth. He denied that Weerth had any right to represent the English workers and he argued that the abolition of the Corn Laws in Britain had been followed by a substantial increase in food imports – indicating an improvement in the workers' standard of living. Marx had prepared a speech for the congress but did not have an opportunity of delivering it.[85] Weerth's speech was widely reported in the press[86] and the obscure commercial traveller suddenly obtained a certain recognition as a political figure.[87] Julian Harney declared: "'All men are brethren' is becoming something more than a string of words, when a German, at a conference of delegates from several nations, is seen to rise in defence of the much-wronged people of England."[88]

At the end of November 1847 Weerth told his mother that he was very busy. "By accident I have now become a well known figure and my services are always in demand. But I generally decline all engagements so as to maintain my independence."[89] Various left wing organisations solicited his support and he had visions of playing an important role at the forthcoming meeting of the Communist League in London. Engels became alarmed and appealed to Marx to stop Weerth from going to England. He declared that Weerth "has always been too lazy until his success at the Free Trade Congress launched him into politics. And what's more, he actually wants to go as an 'independent delegate'."[90] Engels considered that Weerth had little aptitude for revolutionary politics and that he could best serve the communist cause by exercising his undoubted literary talents.

On February 25, 1848, when he was in Rotterdam, Weerth heard the news of the establishment of the Second Republic in France.[91] He hurried to Paris to see for himself the triumph of the revolution which he hoped would bring the socialists to power all over Europe. He rejoiced that "one of the finest nations in the world has regained its independence in three days". "It has swept away with bag and baggage the meanest rogue to wear a crown together with the clique that supported him."[92] Weerth joined a committee which organised a demonstration of German residents in Paris in support of the Republic. The Germans marched to the Town Hall and the poet Herwegh presented the republican authorities with an address of congratulation. Weerth told his mother that this had been one of the most wonderful days in his life.[93] But Weerth's most memorable experience in Paris was his visit to the Tuileries. His friend Henri Imbert,[94] whom he had known in Brussels, was now in charge of an old people's home in the palace. Weerth acquired some letters of historical interest as souvenirs of his visit.[95]

On his return to Brussels Weerth found that trade was so slack that he had plenty of time for politics.[96] Engels declared that he had become "a furious republican on the rampage".[97] When the revolution spread to Germany Weerth returned to the Rhineland where he had discussions with Heinrich Bürgers and Karl Ludwig d'Ester[98] and then with Marx and Engels concerning the establishment of a radical newspaper.[99] When the first number of the *Neue Rheinische Zeitung* appeared in Cologne on June 1, 1848 Weerth edited its literary supplement. Engels declared that no other German newspaper had so humorous and so biting a literary supplement.[100] Weerth indulged in bitter attacks upon the German princes, nobles and middle classes.[101] He quoted extracts from right-wing journals with satirical comments. He poked fun at the tiny German principalities – like his native Lippe-Detmold – which had survived from an earlier age but were out of place in the modern world.

Weerth fiercely attacked the Prussian junkers in a series of essays that were turned into a novel and published by Hoffman and Campe of Hamburg under the title *The Life and Deeds of the Famous Knight Schnapphahnski* (1849). Here Weerth described a number of highly unedifying episodes in the life of a Prussian junker. When Weerth had written about Herr Preiss he had described a businessman whose character – for all its faults – was not without some redeeming features. But there were no redeeming features in the character of the Knight Schnapphahnski who was depicted as a coward, a thief, a seducer, and a man of no principles who was guilty of one infamous action after another. Schnapphahnski's adventures were based upon events in the life of Prince Felix Lichnowski who was murdered by a savage mob on the outskirts of Frankfurt in September 1848. Weerth claimed that in his novel he had recounted events which had actually occurred.[102] Although Weerth's novel was a political satire of unusual merit it was soon forgotten. Subsequently Friedrich Engels and Franz Mehring tried to rescue it from oblivion. It was not until 1957 that a new edition was published in Weerth's collected works.

At the end of September 1848 the *Neue Rheinische Zeitung* had to suspend publication for a few weeks and Weerth retired to Bingen. Soon after the paper again appeared – in October – Freiligrath joined the staff as one of its editors. This made it possible for Weerth to leave Cologne early in 1849 and to resume his business career as a commission agent in the textile trade, though he continued to send contributions to the *Neue Rheinische Zeitung*.[103]

He realised that the revolution now had little chance of success in Germany and he decided that it was time that he started to earn his living again. Weerth was in Hamburg on January 1849 and in England in February. In Yorkshire he made a tour of the woollen and linen districts. In London he met Julian Harney and attended a debate in the House of Commons.[104] When he was in Cologne again (in April) he visited the Countess of Hatzfeld in Düsseldorf and went with her to see Lassalle in prison. He declared that Lassalle was the most brilliant man – other than Marx – whom he had ever met.[105] On May 12 he was summoned to appear before a Cologne court to answer a charge of having slandered the landed aristocracy in Prussia in his novel on Schnapphahnski. He ignored the summons and left the country. On July 4, 1849 he was found guilty and sentenced to three months' imprisonment.[106]

Meanwhile Weerth was travelling in Belgium and France. In June 1849 he was in Paris and saw the suppression of the riots which, in his view, clinched "the victory of the counter-revolutionary party".[107] From Paris he went to Liége where the police locked him up for a night and then expelled him across the Dutch frontier. In July he was in Hamburg on business and early in August he was again in Paris where he visited Marx. At Calais he met Lola Montez by chance and had the privilege of hearing "from her own charming lips the story of many of her adventures".[108] During the autumn of 1849 he was in England. He spent a fortnight in Liverpool before deciding to settle in London for the time being. He rented an office at 42 Cornhill. Jenny Marx in her memoirs mentioned that at this time she arrived in London from France. Weerth "met me when I arrived, sick and exhausted, with my three poor persecuted children. He found accommodation for me in a boarding house in Leicester Square belonging to a master tailor."[109] In November Weerth met Engels who had just arrived in London by sea from Genoa after taking part in the Baden rising.[110]

In January 1850 Weerth's appeal against his conviction for slandering the Prussian aristocracy was rejected.[111] He had the choice of ignoring the court – at the cost of liability to arrest if ever he crossed the Prussian frontier – or of serving his sentence in Cologne. Weerth decided that exile from Germany would make it impossible for him to conduct his textile agency[112], and – against Marx's advice[113] – he surrendered to the Cologne authorities and served his sentence.

Weerth was in prison from February 25 to May 26, 1849. He was well treated since he could order food from outside, buy books and newspapers, and receive visitors. When he was free again he made it clear to Marx that his career as a revolutionary agitator was over.

He proposed to hide in "the quietest mousehole" that he could find. "I no longer believe in the possibility of revolution in Germany," he wrote on June 2, 1849. "For me there is a Fatherland only because I enjoy its cheap Moselle wine and because I can crack feeble jokes about it."[114] He visited England and Scotland in August.[115] He boasted to his mother that "in business affairs I deal only with the men at the top". Nathan Rothschild gave him letters of introduction in connection with a forthcoming business trip to Spain and Portugal.[116] By August he was in Oporto. Weerth travelled extensively in these countries and was not back in Germany until February 1851. From Hamburg he wrote to Marx: "What is the riddle of my restlessness? Why cannot I sit peacefully on my backside for more than ten minutes? The answer is the revolution which has robbed me of all peace of mind."[117] And he told Engels: "Time is money and one needs hard cash for the future. You may be bored but you are right to stick to Manchester. Boredom brings in the money. Wealth does not come from having a good time. Only money can help us today and tomorrow."[118] In April 1850 Weerth told Marx that his literary work had ended when the *Neue Rheinische Zeitung* ceased publication. "It makes sense for *you* to write on economics. But it is simply a waste of time for me to try to entertain fools by cracking feeble jokes."[119]

In July 1851 Weerth was Marx's guest in London and in August he was in Bradford where he stayed – except for business trips to the Continent – for rather more than twelve months. As Engels had now settled in Manchester the two friends were able to meet from time to time.[120] But Weerth was soon complaining about the horrible weather and the horrible inhabitants of Bradford and he longed to return to Spain.[121] Although the Communist League had been revived Weerth was not invited to join it again.[122] Perhaps Marx thought that Weerth was not a sufficiently dedicated Communist since – even when an editor of the *Neue Rheinische Zeitung* – he had given his business interests priority over his political activities. And now Weerth showed no sign of complying with requests from Marx and Engels that he should contribute to a socialist journal edited by Joseph Weydemeyer in the United States.[123] Marx may have considered that Weerth could best be used as a courier and that he would be more effective in that capacity as a businessman who was no longer a party member. In 1852 Weerth rendered his last service to the revolutionary cause by sending Marx business envelopes which were intended to deceive the police and the postal authorities in Prussia.[124] Marx used the envelopes to send material to his friends in Germany who were

Jenny Marx (née Westphalen), 1814–1881

Helene Demuth, 1823–1890

Family Group (about 1861)
back: Karl Marx and Friedrich Engels
front: Marx's daughters – Jenny, Eleanor, and Laura

assisting in the defence of the Communist leaders on trial in Cologne.

It was at about this time that Weerth severed his connection with Emanuel and Son,[125] and joined the firm of Steinthal & Co. of Bradford, Manchester and Hamburg.[126] He was in Hamburg in the summer of 1852 and returned to London in September of that year. Marx, with whom he stayed for a few days, grumbled to Engels: "You know that I am very fond of Weerth but it is painful to have such a fine gentleman as a guest when I am floundering in all this filth."[127] In October Weerth was in Bradford and in Manchester where he stayed with Engels.[128] He was back in London at the end of November on his way to Southampton to catch a boat for St Thomas in the West Indies.

Weerth's last visits to Marx before leaving England did not pass off smoothly. Marx found it difficult to forgive a former editor of the *Neue Rheinische Zeitung* for washing his hands of revolutionary activities and devoting himself entirely to business and to overseas travel. Marx wrote to Engels on December 3, 1852:

> "I was very busy and in no amiable frame of mind when Weerth called on Sunday. He asked me in a haughty and superior manner what I really proposed to write about the Cologne trial. I replied by asking him what he thought he was going to do in the West Indies and in fifteen minutes he was off. On Tuesday evening he was back again, remarking that he had not intended to come but that Freiligrath had persuaded him to do so. He said that I had been very busy and bad-tempered on Sunday. I permitted myself the observation that for nine-tenths of the time that I had known Herr Weerth he had generally been short tempered and full of complaints and that was something of which I could not be accused. After I had given him a dressing down he recovered his spirits and returned to his old self again. But I feel that Weerth has become damnably bourgeois and takes his business career far too seriously. . . ."[129]

Weerth was away from Europe from the end of 1852 to the middle of 1855. His travels, not without hazards, took him to Porto Rico,[130] Venezuela,[131] Mexico,[132] California,[133] and the Argentine.[134] He was in London again in June 1855 and soon went to Germany to visit his firm in Hamburg and his mother in Detmold. His correspondence in 1855 includes several love letters to Betty Tendering to whom he proposed marriage. In a letter of October 2, 1855 he declared that he was tired of Europe and intended to live in the West Indies. He assured Betty that he would give up travelling and settle in Havana where he could earn as large a salary as that of a Prussian general or minister of state.[135] But Betty Tendering declined his offer of marriage. In the autumn of 1855 Weerth was in England and met Marx and Engels. Marx wrote to Lassalle at this time: "Weerth does not write essays any more but he speaks them instead and his companions can enjoy his lively actions, his mimicry and his infectious laughter." On November 17, 1855 Weerth left Europe for the West Indies. He died of fever in Havana on July 30, 1856 at the age of 34.[136] Weerth's early promise had not been fulfilled and it was long after his death before his contribution to German literature came to be appreciated.

III. Carl Schorlemmer[137]

In the 1860s Engels spent some of his Saturday evenings at the Thatched House Tavern in Manchester[138] in the company of some young German scientists who were working in the chemical industry which was developing in Lancashire and Cheshire. Some of them eventually became heads of important chemical firms. Heinrich Caro[139] worked as a research chemist for Roberts, Dale & Co. (Manchester), returned to Germany in 1866, and later became managing director of the *Badische Anilin- und Sodafabrik* (Ludwigshafen). Ludwig Mond[140] joined John Brunner in 1871 to establish an undertaking at Winnington in Cheshire which made soda by the Solvay ammonia process. Philipp Pauli[141] worked for the United Alkali Co. (Evans & MacBryde) at St Helens and for the Sulphate of Copper Company. On returning to Germany he ran his own chemical works first at Ziegenhausen (by Heidelberg) and then at Rheinau (by Mannheim). In the early 1880s he erected a chemical works for Meister, Lucius & Brüning and eventually became the managing director of this great undertaking.

At the convivial meetings at the Thatched House Tavern[142] the chair was generally taken by Carl Schorlemmer, a lecturer in chemistry at Owens College, Manchester. Engels and Schorlemmer became close friends. In March 1865 Engels told Marx that a chemist, whom he had met at the Schiller Anstalt, had explained Tyndall's "sunbeam experiment" to him.[143] The chemist was probably Schorlemmer and this may well have been one of their first meetings. In June 1867 in a letter to Engels, Marx sent his "best compliments" to Schorlemmer.[144] In May of the following year Engels wrote to Marx that Schorlemmer was "one of the best chaps I have met for a long time".[145] It was fortunate for Engels that he should have met an "ideal teacher and adviser"[146] just when he was embarking upon the study of science. Schorlemmer was an ideal teacher since he was not only a good research chemist but he was also one of the few scientists of his day who took a really broad view of his subject and tried to integrate the study of chemistry with that of all other branches of science. His book on *The Rise and Development of Organic Chemistry* has been described as "the marxist contribution to summarising the theoretical and practical progress of chemistry in the nineteenth century".[147]

Carl Schorlemmer was 14 years younger than Engels, having been born in Darmstadt in 1834. His father, a master carpenter, wanted him to become a craftsman but his mother encouraged him to carry on with his education after he left the elementary school. He studied for three years at the Darmstadt technical college and then worked in pharmacies at Gross-Umstedt and Heidelberg. At the University of Heidelberg he attended lectures given by the distinguished chemist R. W. Bunsen. Schorlemmer decided to adopt chemistry rather than pharmacy as a profession and he studied at the University of Giessen under Heinrich Will and Hermann Kopp during the summer semester of 1859.[148] It was from Kopp that Schorlemmer learned to appreciate the historical aspects of his subject. Many years later he dedicated his book on *The Rise and Development of Organic Chemistry* to his former teacher. Schorlemmer did not stay at Giessen to work for his doctorate but migrated to England where he lived for the rest of his life.[149]

Engels states that when Schorlemmer came to Manchester he was employed by the chemist Angus Smith. This appointment must have been of short duration since in the autumn term of 1859 Schorlemmer became private assistant to Professor H. E. Roscoe at Owens College which was then situated in Quay Street. Schorlemmer secured the appointment on the recommendation of his friend Wilhelm Dittmar[150] who had just been promoted to the position of demonstrator in the chemistry department.

Schorlemmer, then aged 24, was only two years younger than his professor. Two years previously Roscoe had succeeded Edward Frankland as head of the chemistry department at a time when the college "was at the lowest ebb of its fortunes".[151] There were only 15 students in the department in 1857. It was largely owing to the efforts of Roscoe and Schorlemmer that the chemistry department eventually became one of the most important in the country. When Schorlemmer died the number of students in the chemistry department had risen to 120.[152]

Roscoe found that he had secured the services of a colleague whose "power of work was simply prodigious".[153] Schorlemmer proved himself to be a dedicated scientist who devoted himself to pure research. Throughout his life he was contemptuous of men like Karl Vogt whose only skill lay in popularising the discoveries of others.[154] On taking up his post in Manchester Schorlemmer's first task was to investigate the composition of solutions of halogen acids under different pressures.[155] Then in 1861 – when Schorlemmer had succeeded Dittmar as demonstrator in the chemical laboratory[156] – Roscoe received from John Barrow (manufacturer of hydro-carbon oils at the Dalton Chemical Works at Gorton) some samples of light oils obtained from cannel-coal tar. Schorlemmer analysed these samples and wrote an article on "the hydrides of alcohol radicals existing in the products of the destructive distillation of cannel-coal". This was the first of many papers which Schorlemmer wrote on the normal paraffins. His experiments showed that all the paraffin hydro-carbons – whether derived from coal tar, from natural petroleum, or by synthesis – formed a single series. If his theory were correct then certain hitherto unknown substances must exist and he proceeded to prepare them – pentane, heptane, diispropyl – in the laboratory.

The paper which Schorlemmer delivered before the Chemical Society in April 1872 on "the chemistry of the hydro-carbons" summarised ten years' work on the subject. Engels recalled that when he first knew Schorlemmer he "often had facial injuries when he came to see me. One cannot take liberties with the paraffins. These substances – almost unknown in those days – continually exploded when Schorlemmer was carrying out his experiments and he bore many honorable scars as a result of his researches. But for the fact that he wore spectacles he might have lost his sight."[157]

In the late 1860s Carl Schorlemmer made a name for himself in scientific circles. The results of his researches appeared in the *Proceedings of the Royal Society* between 1865 and 1871. A leading German chemical journal mentioned his work in 1866.[158] On May 10, 1868 Engels wrote to Marx that he could soon expect a visit from Schorlemmer who had been asked to lecture to the Royal Society. The invitation, declared Engels, was

> "a great triumph for him, because Frankland – the leading chemist in London[159] – has criticised all Schorlemmer's research. It will be the making of Schorlemmer if he gets a few more invitations of this kind. I am delighted for Schorlemmer, who puts up with a very poor academic post in Manchester simply because he has the use of a laboratory where he can get on with his research."[160]

Schorlemmer became a member of the German Academy of Naturalists (Leopoldina) (1857), the German Chemical Society of Berlin (1868),[161] and the Manchester Literary and Philosophical Society (1870),[162] and he achieved the distinction of being elected a Fellow of the Royal Society in 1871.[163] He was elected to a lectureship at Owens College in 1873 and to a chair in organic chemistry – the first in England – in the following year. When applying for the chair he submitted a testimonial from the eminent Russian scientist A. M. Butlerov, who was the author of a pioneer work on organic chemistry (1864) and an authority on the derivatives of petroleum.[164] The Principal of Owens College observed that Carl Schorlemmer's promotion was

> "the well-earned reward of many years' devotion – with conspicuous success and with a single-minded enthusiasm not too common in our age – to science pursued for its own sake and to the laborious work of academic life."

When Roscoe resigned his chair in 1885, Carl Schorlemmer was involved in a dispute with the authorities of Owens College. In a letter of November 1, 1886 to the chairman of the committee of the College Council, Roscoe discussed Schorlemmer's position with regard to the appointment of a new Professor of Chemistry. He wrote:

> "Should the Committee come to the conclusion that their new Professor is to be specially an Inorganic Chemist I desire to point out, in justice to the present Professor of Organic Chemistry, that a reorganisation of his duties, and of his remuneration, should be brought about. Professor Schorlemmer occupies a position in his branch of science second to none, the work he has done for the department during 25 years has been most important, as shown by the Honours gained by his students in the Universities both of London and Victoria, and by the fact that his books are the text-books in all the German schools and universities. Under myself – for reasons which I need not specify – Professor Schorlemmer has been contented to work. But he feels (and rightly feels) that to be placed in a similar position under a stranger is more than he can agree to. Hence, if the Committee desire to procure a continuance of Professor Schorlemmer's services in concert with a new specially Inorganic Chemist, his position will have to be altered. My own idea is that the advanced students in Organic Chemistry might be placed under his special charge, and that he should have control of and authority over them in the laboratory as he has hitherto had in the lecture room, and that a proper proportion of the laboratory fees of such students should be paid over to him."

At one stage of the dispute the University authorities terminated Carl Schorlemmer's appointment as a professor – though not as a University teacher – but fortunately changed their minds. The Chemistry Professorship Committee recommended "that the Council should consider whether it is possible to make provision for Professor Schorlemmer, as the Committee understands to be his wish, of laboratory accommodation for private research".[165]

In August 1887 Schorlemmer acted as vice-president of the

chemical section of the British Association when it met in Manchester. In the following year he was awarded an honorary degree by the University of Glasgow where his old friend Dittmar was teaching at the Andersonian College. At the ceremony Professor Simpson described Schorlemmer as "one of the greatest living writers and authorities on organic chemistry".[166]

Schorlemmer's publications were of two kinds. In his earlier writings he described his experiments and advanced his theories in contributions to scientific journals. His later writings dealt with various aspects of chemistry – both organic and inorganic – in a more general fashion. He published 60 papers in the *Journal of the Chemical Society*, 21 contributions to *Liebigs Annalen*, while some of his articles appeared in the proceedings of the Royal Society and Manchester Literary and Philosophical Society. In 1868 he translated into German (and revised) a beginners' textbook on chemistry by Roscoe.[167] His three major works were *A Manual on the Chemistry of the Carbon Compounds* (1874),[168] *The Rise and Development of Organic Chemistry* (1879),[169] and (in collaboration with Roscoe) a *Systematic Treatise on Chemistry* (1878–89).[170] Schorlemmer had a much larger share in the writing of this book than Roscoe. Hartog described this book as "the most extensive and at the same time readable textbook on the subject". Schorlemmer also began to write a history of chemistry but this was never completed.[171] Unlike many of his contemporaries, Schorlemmer dealt not only with the theoretical side of his subject but also with the practical application of chemistry to the world of industry. And his historical works (published and unpublished) were far more than descriptions of the development of chemistry over the ages. Schorlemmer regarded the study of the history of chemistry as an essential first step to an understanding of the nature of the subject.

Engels observed that Schorlemmer was a communist before he met Marx and Engels. "All we had to do was to give him a grounding in economics to support the firm conclusions which he had reached by himself long before this."[172] Schorlemmer was admitted to the intimate circle of Marx's disciples and was known by various nicknames such as Jollymeier and Chlormeier. In 1867 he assisted in correcting the proofs of the first volume of *Das Kapital*. He joined the First International and the German Social Democrat Party. Roscoe stated that he knew little of Schorlemmer's political views "for these he did not obtrude upon his friends, though he had decided ones".[173] Privately Schorlemmer did all in his power to further the socialist cause and to help its supporters. In 1881 he tried to help a young Russian scientist – in exile because of his political views – to find work in England.[174] In public, however, he kept his politics to himself. In 1870 he emerged from the seclusion of his laboratory to go to France with J. G. Wehner to deliver supplies of schnaps, wine, blankets and other comforts to German soldiers wounded in the Sedan campaign.[175] The funds were raised in Manchester by a committee of the German Association for the Relief of the Wounded.[176] Engels was the secretary of the Manchester committee. On September 10 Marx informed Engels that Schorlemmer had visited him on his way to the Continent.[177] On September 17 Schorlemmer wrote to Engels from Bouillon (in Belgium) that he had reached Sedan and had distributed some of the comforts to the wounded in a Prussian and a Bavarian field hospital in Remilly.[178] He praised Wehner for being "a splendid commander" of the little expedition who made everybody work hard. He signed the letter: "Your Jollymeyer who feels very jolly." In the 1880s Carl Schorlemmer frequently visited the Continent to attend scientific conferences[179] and to keep Marx and Engels in touch with their political associates abroad.

Marx and Engels were fortunate to have a communist as their adviser on scientific matters. Engels wrote that Schorlemmer

> "was probably the only leading scientist of his day who was not ashamed to acknowledge his debt to Hegel. At a time when most people despised Hegel, Schorlemmer venerated him. And Schorlemmer was right. Anyone who hopes to achieve anything in the field of the theory of science – anyone who tries to discover a synthesis of different branches of scientific knowledge – must beware of looking upon natural phenomena as static or permanent. Many scientists do this. But natural phenomena should be regarded as factors in a state of flux or transition. Even today the theory of science can still best be studied with the aid of Hegel's philosophy."[180]

Marx and Engels considered that the principles of dialectical materialism should be applied to science as well as to history and economics[181] and their scientific studies were greatly helped by expert advice from Carl Schorlemmer.[182] Engels's letter of May 30, 1873 on "some dialectical ideas about the natural sciences" was seen and approved by Schorlemmer who made such comments as "Very good, I agree", "Quite right" and "That's the point".[183] Schorlemmer gave copies of his books to Marx and Engels. In 1867 Marx wrote that he was "extremely pleased with Schorlemmer's textbook".[184] When Engels moved from Manchester to London in 1870 he corresponded regularly with Schorlemmer on scientific and political matters. Engels's *Anti-Dühring* and his unfinished *Dialectics of Nature* were influenced by Schorlemmer's ideas.

By the 1870s Schorlemmer had secured widespread recognition

as one of the leading chemists of the day. His professional salary and his royalties ensured him an income adequate for his modest bachelor needs. But, as Roscoe observed, Schorlemmer "lived and died a poor man, though had he chosen he might have amassed a large fortune".[185] When he died his personal estate was just under £2,000.[186] Schorlemmer's researches were now concerned with the derivatives of the hydro-carbons hexane and heptane, with aurine colouring matter and (in collaboration with R. S. Dale) with suberic acid from cork. His interests had widened and he devoted much of his time to a systematic analysis of the facts and theories of chemistry. In his books and lectures he tried to assess the significance of chemistry as one aspect of the entire range of scientific knowledge.

Schorlemmer remained in close touch with his friends in London and in Germany. In his vacations he often visited Marx and Engels and he travelled on the Continent to meet fellow scientists and socialist friends. He once had a disagreeable experience in Germany because of his political views. He was on his way from Switzerland to Darmstadt when the police found a box containing copies of a banned socialist journal which were being smuggled into Germany from Switzerland. "The police," wrote Engels, "naturally assumed that the socialist professor was the culprit. From the police point of view a chemist is an academically trained smuggler. So they searched the homes of his mother and his brother. But the professor was in Höchst. A telegram was immediately sent to Höchst and the professor's belongings were examined. But this time the police discovered something that they had not expected to find – a British passport. When the Anti-Socialist Law was passed, Schorlemmer had become a naturalised British subject.[187] The sight of a British passport sufficed to bring the police search to a halt. The police had no wish to become involved in a dispute with the British government. The affair caused a great sensation in Darmstadt and was worth at least 500 votes to the Social Democrats at the next election."[188]

After Marx's death Engels looked forward more than ever to Schorlemmer's visits. The two friends could no longer go for 18 mile walks, as they had done twenty years earlier, but they could enjoy less strenuous holidays together. In the 1880s, however, Schorlemmer's health declined. He suffered from earache, catarrh and a nervous disability. In the summer of 1888 a doctor told Ludwig Schorlemmer that his brother Carl had no chance of living to a ripe old age.[189] Later in that year he was able to accompany Engels, Aveling and Eleanor Marx on a trip to the United States and Canada. In 1890 Schorlemmer and Engels went to Norway for a holiday. On his return Schorlemmer was ill for some time, suffering from earache and deafness.[190] But the root of the trouble appears to have been lung cancer. In May 1892 Engels learned from Dr Gumpert and Roscoe that Schorlemmer was sinking.[191] When Schorlemmer made his will on May 19 his arm was paralysed so that he could not sign his name but had to make a mark. Engels went to Manchester early in June to see his friend for the last time. Schorlemmer died on June 27 at the age of 58 and was buried in the Southern Cemetery in Manchester.

Engels told Schorlemmer's brother Ludwig that he was sorry that Schorlemmer had had a Christian burial. A Unitarian minister had taken the service. Engels wrote that he could have insisted that the funeral should be a secular one. But in that case he would have had to deliver a funeral oration praising Schorlemmer as a socialist rather than as a chemist. And that would have meant that "the whole English bourgeois press would have attacked me for using Carl's funeral as an excuse for making a useless political demonstration in front of mourners who would be indifferent or even hostile to the socialist cause but who could not make their views known at a funeral". So Engels simply laid a wreath upon Schorlemmer's grave on behalf of the German Social Democrat Party.[192]

When Schorlemmer died his colleague Arthur Schuster wrote that Schorlemmer

> "was not only an investigator in a special branch of chemistry; he was a scholar with an extensive command of many branches of science. His large acquaintance with the complicated history and his perhaps unique knowledge of the bewildering literature of his subject marked him out as the one man who could write a systematic treatise on organic chemistry."[193]

At the same time Roscoe described Schorlemmer as a man

> "of retiring, most modest and unassuming disposition.[194] To only a few of his intimates, German and English, were his true colours visible. As a laboratory teacher he was excelled by few, merely as a lecturer by many. But although, like some other eminent lecturers, his diction may have been faulty, the staple article was there, and I never met a real student amongst all those who passed through his hands who did not express his admiration for the man, and his sense of obligation which he felt for the masterly instruction Schorlemmer always gave."[195]

That Schorlemmer was "not a brilliant lecturer"[196] is confirmed by one of his students who wrote that "his lectures were read without emphasis or pause from notes held close to his nose".[197] But

Smithells stated that although Schorlemmer "had neither the graces of the orator nor the arts of the populariser, his lectures were admirable in construction and suggestiveness".

When Schorlemmer died Engels was anxious that his manuscripts should be published. Engels wrote to Laura Lafargue on July 7, 1892:

> "The manuscripts he left may cause some trouble. The most interesting one is in the history of chemistry – 1. The Ancients, 2. Alchemy, 3. latro-chemistry, up to the seventeenth century; a fragment, and the third part not completed, but still full of new views and discoveries. Then a lot of work on organic chemistry. But as he has *two* works in the press at the same time (1. his own organic chemistry, 2. his and Roscoe's big book) it will be pretty hard to distinguish which belongs to which. One of his executors is a chemist (Siebold) but hardly knows enough about the theory of science to distinguish. And Roscoe is red hot after the manuscript as he knows too well that *he* cannot finish the book. I have told the executors in my opinion they might let Roscoe have what belongs to the Roscoe–Schorlemmer book on binding himself to let the heirs participate in the profits of the pending volume (German and English) in the same way as Schorlemmer himself would have done. As Roscoe was elected yesterday for Manchester, he will no doubt pounce upon the executors at once, so I wrote them yesterday giving a full account of what I considered ought to be done in the matter."[198]

Only a week before his own death Engels wrote to Dr Louis Siebold concerning the publication of Schorlemmer's manuscripts.[199]

Engels had always held Schorlemmer in the highest esteem. In 1883 he wrote that "next to Marx there can be no doubt that Schorlemmer is the most famous figure in the European socialist movement".[200] He complained to Philipp Pauli – an old friend from the days of the Thatched House Tavern – that English and German "University donkeys" had failed to recognise Schorlemmer's true greatness.[201] There is little substance in Engels's accusation. The fact that Schorlemmer had been elected a Fellow of the Royal Society and other learned bodies suggests that the academic world recognised the high qualities of Schorlemmer's scholarship.

Soon after his death, Schorlemmer's friends in Manchester set up a committee to raise funds to build a laboratory in his memory. Philipp Pauli wrote to Engels that he would support the project and Engels replied: "I am in complete agreement with you that each of us should send Perkins a subscription towards the erection of a laboratory to be named after Schorlemmer."[202] On May 3, 1895 the Schorlemmer chemical laboratory at Owens College was opened by Ludwig Mond[203] who had himself subscribed £500.[204]

The laboratory provided accommodation for 36 students. Half the cost had been defrayed by public subscription.

On the following day a leading article in the *Manchester Guardian* paid a warm tribute to Carl Schorlemmer. "Schorlemmer himself was recognised by all those who spoke yesterday and indeed by all who knew him, as a lover of chemistry for its purely intellectual – and to him its greatest – rewards. He studied it in its more abstract and its historical aspects; he coveted neither the honour nor the material advantages which lay within his grasp; and all his life he remained known but to a few, and relatively poor. Nevertheless his work forms the cornerstone of the comprehensive theories which within recent years have given chemists so marvellous a mastery over the transformations of matter, and which have directly led to those triumphs in chemical industry which now employ many thousands of workers."[205]

In 1964 the 130th anniversary of Schorlemmer's birth was marked in the German Democratic Republic by the publication of a collection of essays on his life and work.[206] At the same time the College of Chemistry at Leuna (by Merseburg) was renamed the Technical College for Chemistry Carl Schorlemmer.[207]

IV. Eduard Gumpert[208]

There are several references in the Marx–Engels correspondence to Eduard Gumpert, a German doctor who practised in Manchester for many years. He was not only Engels's doctor but also his friend. There is no evidence to suggest that he was a socialist but the fact that Engels thought it worth while to ask Dr Gumpert if he would buy five shares in the *Beehive*[209] suggests that Dr Gumpert may have held left-wing political views.

Dr Gumpert, a native of Hesse, was born in 1834. He qualified as a doctor at the University of Würzburg in 1855 and settled in Manchester as a general practitioner shortly afterwards. In 1856 Dr A. G. Merei and Dr James Whitehead had set up a second children's hospital in Manchester, the first having been established by Dr Borchardt two years earlier. When Dr Merei died in 1858 Dr Gumpert joined Dr Whitehead as an honorary consulting physician at the Clinical Hospital for the Diseases of Children which was situated in Stevenson Square. This hospital moved to larger premises at Park Place, Cheetham Hill Road in 1867. Dr Gumpert served the hospital for 35 years.[210] He was a leading figure in the German colony in Manchester and was a member of the Schiller Anstalt.

The first reference to Dr Gumpert in the Marx–Engels correspondence was in May 1858 when Marx asked Engels how Dr

Gumpert was progressing as a horseman.[211] Jenny Marx told Engels that Dr Gumpert was the only doctor in whom Marx had confidence.[212] Marx and Engels persuaded some of their friends – Schorlemmer and Samuel Moore for example – to seek his advice. Although Marx had a doctor in London he often asked Engels for advice from Dr Gumpert on the treatment of his boils, carbuncles and liver disorders. Dr Gumpert doubted whether he should treat a patient of another doctor. Nevertheless from time to time he prescribed arsenic to alleviate the carbuncles. Dr Gumpert found it difficult to appreciate the niceties of English medical etiquette. There was, for example, the occasion on which Dr Gumpert paid a visit of condolence to a friend who was not a patient. The body of a child who had died of scarlet fever was in the house. Dr Borchardt, the family physician, was present and Dr Gumpert suggested that it was inadvisable to allow other children in the same room as the dead child. Dr Borchardt took offence at what he regarded as Dr Gumpert's unjustified interference. The dispute between the two doctors came before the local medical council which decided that "Dr Gumpert had committed a breach of medical etiquette, though he was morally right".[213]

Whenever he was in Manchester Marx consulted Dr Gumpert and on his advice took the waters at Harrogate and Carlsbad.[214] During Wilhelm Wolff's last illness Engels was dissatisfied with Dr. Borchardt's treatment of the patient and insisted upon calling in Dr Gumpert for a second opinion.[215] In 1891 when Samuel Moore returned to England from a tour of duty in Nigeria he immediately went to Dr Gumpert for a checkup.[216] In the following year Dr Gumpert attended Carl Schorlemmer in his last illness.[217]

Dr Gumpert died on April 20, 1893 at the age of fifty-nine[218] and Engels travelled from London to Manchester to attend the funeral.[219] The only criticism of Dr Gumpert to be found in the Marx–Engels correspondence is Engels's complaint that Dr Gumpert persuaded him to join the Schiller Anstalt and to take office as president. He blamed Dr Gumpert for getting him involved in some unpleasantness in the Schiller Anstalt in connection with the search for new premises.[220]

V. Carl Siebel[221]

For a short time in 1859–60 Engels saw a good deal of Carl Siebel of Barmen whom he described as a "distant relative". Siebel was born in 1836, the son of a wealthy merchant and – although he had literary aspirations – he was destined for a business career. He completed his training in England between 1856 and 1860 and was in Manchester at the end of that period. He was in Manchester for only a little more than a year but when he returned to Barmen he kept in touch with Engels.

The first reference to Siebel in the Marx–Engels correspondence is on January 27 1859 when Engels mentioned that Siebel – then 23 years of age – had called upon him. Freiligrath had already told Engels that Siebel, whom he had met in London, was "a decent chap" who had an income of £1,000 a year.[222] Siebel had written some poetry and his story of Jesus of Nazareth (1856) had highly displeased the Pietists of Elberfeld and Barmen. Siebel's ambition was to make a name for himself as a romantic poet.[223]

Writing to his mother on April 20, 1859 Engels declared that she had no cause to worry about young Siebel's conduct in Manchester. He assured her that Siebel nearly always stayed at home in the evening. "I doubt whether there are 20 young men of his age in Manchester who lead such respectable lives." Engels discussed Siebel's poetry and observed that although his writing was still quite immature, Siebel was by no means without talent. He had advised Siebel to stop writing poetry for a time and to make a thorough study of the works of the classical poets "of all peoples".

Engels told his mother that although "Siebel's father may perhaps imagine that I am stuffing his son's head with all sorts of nonsense I assure you that I have used all my influence to prevent him from spending too much time writing poetry". He was confident that when he was a little older and a little wiser Siebel would become "a really good fellow capable of producing literary work of a high standard".[224] Shortly after receiving this letter Engels's mother was visited by Carl Siebel. He wrote to Engels that his mother had been delighted to have news of her son in Manchester.[225] In a letter to Jenny Marx of December 22, 1859 Engels wrote about Siebel in less favourable terms than in the letter to his mother. He now declared that Siebel was "an abominable poet" though he had the saving grace of knowing that he was "a humbug".[226] In letters to Marx he called Siebel "a waster"[227] and "an utter charlatan – and what is more he knows it".[228] Marx, too, had a poor opinion of Siebel's literary efforts but all the same he asked Engels to persuade Siebel to write some verses for the short-lived *Das Volk*, a paper which was published in London under the auspices of the German Workers Educational Association.[229]

Carl Siebel looked up to Friedrich Engels who was a good deal older and more experienced than himself. He knew about Engels's activities in 1848–9 as an editor of the *Neue Rheinische Zeitung* and as a revolutionary leader in Elberfeld and Baden. He admired

Engels as a writer and as a man of action and he was soon converted to his political ideas. When he got to know Marx he recognised that he was in the presence of a born leader of men. Although Siebel played no active part in politics he was prepared to give Marx and Engels any help that he could behind the scenes. The arrival of a new faithful disciple suited Marx and Engels even if they regarded him as a humbug and a charlatan.

In February 1860 Engels told Marx that Siebel had many contacts and could be useful in making Engels's pamphlet on *Savoyen, Nizza und der Rhein* widely known in Germany.[230] This was to be Siebel's modest *rôle* in the Marxian movement in the 1860s. Through his contacts with publishers, booksellers and editors he did all that he could to publicise the books and pamphlets of Marx and Engels. When the first volume of *Das Kapital* appeared Siebel worked hard to place favourable reviews of it in German newspapers and periodicals.

The 100th anniversary of Schiller's birth fell on November 10, 1859 and the German colony in Manchester celebrated the event by holding a festival in the Free Trade Hall on the following day. Carl Siebel took the initiative in organising the celebrations. He recited Alfred Meissner's prologue, wrote the epilogue and produced scenes from Schiller's *Wallensteins Lager*.[231] He managed to interest Engels in the celebrations although at first Engels was reluctant to become involved. Engels told Marx that he was holding himself aloof and declared that the members of the organising committee were "asses without exception".[232] Wilhelm Wolff also declined to support the project. But eventually Engels gave Siebel some assistance with the production of *Wallensteins Lager* and he attended two rehearsals. He was present at the festival and enjoyed himself afterwards at a party – which lasted until four in the morning – attended by the players and singers. Engels told Marx that the organisers had hoped to make a profit so that they could found a Schiller Anstalt (Schiller Institute) in Manchester. They lost £150.[233] But the Schiller Anstalt was founded. On February 4, 1860 Carl Siebel lectured to the Schiller Anstalt on modern German poetry.[234] Despite his earlier opposition Engels joined the Schiller Anstalt. In 1862 he complained to Siebel that the club was dominated by Jews whose extravagant schemes would lead to the bankruptcy of the institute.[235] Yet two years later Engels accepted the position of President of the Schiller Anstalt.

In the summer of 1860, when on a visit to Barmen, Siebel met and became engaged to Reinhilde von Hurter. Engels did not consider it to be a suitable match. He referred to the lady as "a young female philistine" and to Siebel as "a greenhorn".[236] They were married in the autumn.[237] At this time he distributed copies of Marx's *Karl Vogt* to the editors of various German newspapers and journals.[238] In April and May of the following year Marx was in Elberfeld for a few days. He wrote to Engels that he had met Siebel. "I dined at his house one evening." "He has a charming young wife who sings well and adores her Carl." "I liked her – up to a point. Siebel himself has not changed." Siebel entertained Marx at the radical California Club in Barmen where his health was drunk by the members.[239]

Anyone who enjoyed the honour of Marx's acquaintance was sooner or later asked for a loan and Carl Siebel was no exception.[240] But Siebel, though anxious to help, claimed that he was not in a position to do so. On December 23, 1861 he wrote to Engels: "Can you send Marx 60 to 90 thalers? I will return the money to you at the end of January. I like Marx and I regret that I cannot assist him just now – hence my request to you."[241]

In 1864 Marx enlisted Siebel's help to foster the growth of the First International in Germany. He asked Siebel to persuade Carl Klings, a leader of the workers in Solingen, to recommend to a forthcoming conference at Düsseldorf of Lassalle's German Workers Union, that this association should become affiliated to the First International.[242] In the following year Engels had bad news of Siebel. Emil Blank told him that Siebel was "always drunk and his wife was thinking of divorcing him".[243] Nevertheless Engels kept in touch with Siebel and asked him to send to the *Düsseldorfer Zeitung* a notice concerning his pamphlet on the Prussian military question and the German workers' party.[244] In August 1865 Marx declared that Siebel's most recent patriotic verses were worse than anything that he had written in the past.[245]

Two years later Siebel was seriously ill and went to Madeira to recuperate. Engels hoped that when "amicus Siebel" returned he would help to make *Das Kapital* widely known in Germany.[246] In May 1867 Siebel wrote to Marx suggesting that either Marx or Engels should stand as a socialist candidate in Barmen at the first elections to the new Reichstag of the North German Federation.[247] But Marx and Engels had no intention of leaving England at this time. In September 1867 Engels told Marx that Siebel had fallen ill again and would not be of much help to them in the future,[248] but in October Siebel wrote to Engels from Honnef – a spa on the Rhine – offering to try to place anonymous reviews (written by Engels) of the first volume of *Das Kapital* in various German papers.[249] In the following month Engels went to Liverpool to see Siebel when he was embarking for Madeira.[250]

Despite chronic ill-health Siebel was still determined to do all in his power to assist Marx through his contacts with German editors. Siebel succeeded in placing reviews of Marx's book in four German papers, including the *Düsseldorfer Zeitung*.[251] In May 1868 Engels learned from his mother that Siebel had died in Barmen at the age of 32 soon after returning home from Madeira.[252] When Marx heard the news he declared that Siebel was "a good fellow" whose death was "a grievous loss".[253]

VI. English Friends

Engels had many English acquaintances but few English friends. As a businessman, a journalist, a military correspondent, and a rider to hounds he had ample opportunities of making social contacts in Manchester. But there could be no true friendship between Engels and his middle class acquaintances whom he called "philistines" and he told Bebel later that when he lived in Manchester he had always refused to become involved in the "social treadmill" of the bourgeoisie.[254] One might have expected Engels to have made friends with Chartists or radicals. For a time Engels hoped to convert the Chartist leaders to Marx's doctrines. In January 1851 he told Marx that he hoped to establish "a little club" of Chartists in Manchester to discuss the Communist Manifesto which had recently been translated into English.[255] But his efforts were unsuccessful. Since none of the Chartist groups was prepared to swallow the Marxist creed they never enjoyed Engels's full confidence. Marx and Engels welcomed faithful disciples but they could never work for long with those whose political ideas were different from their own.

On his first visit to England Engels had met some of the Chartist leaders such as Harney and Leach. Engels admired Harney[256] as an uncompromising revolutionary, a supporter of the international working class movement, and the editor of the *Northern Star* which he regarded as "the only newspaper which contains reports of all aspects of the workers' movement".[257] Engels became a contributor to the *Northern Star*. Marx and Engels probably met Harney when they visited England in 1845. As early as 1846 Harney joined the League of the Just which eventually became the Communist League.[258] In 1847 Marx and Engels spoke at a banquet in London commemorating the Polish rising of 1830.[259] A resolution calling for the establishment of an international association of democrats was proposed by Harney and carried by the assembled company. Harney visited France after the outbreak of the revolution in February 1848 when Marx had reconstituted the central committee of the Communist League

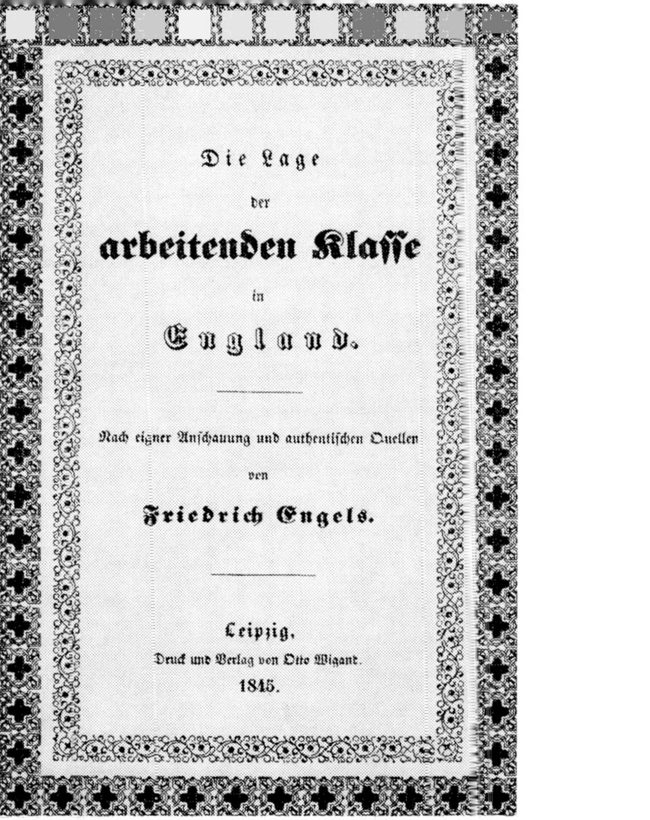

Die Lage
der
arbeitenden Klasse
in
England.

Nach eigner Anschauung und authentischen Quellen
von
Friedrich Engels.

Leipzig.
Druck und Verlag von Otto Wigand.
1845.

Frontispiece of the first edition of Friedrich Engels, *The Condition of the Working Class in England (1845)*

Lodgings of Friedrich Engels in Manchester, 1858–1864
6 Thorncliffe Grove (off Oxford Road)

Desk in Chetham's Library, Manchester, at which Marx and Engels worked together in 1846

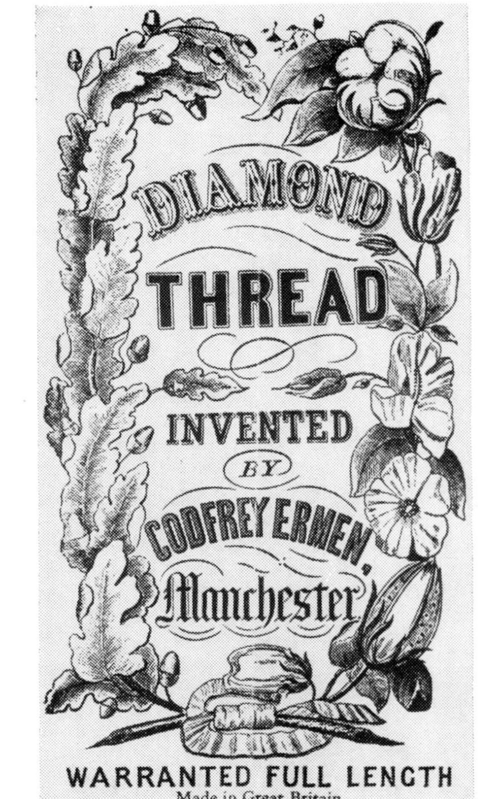

Advertisement of Godfrey Ermen's "Diamond Thread"

in Paris.[260] In April 1848 Engels was so confident of the success of the Chartists that he offered to bet his brother in law Emil Blank any sum that Harney would step into Lord Palmerston's shoes within a couple of months.[261]

In 1850 in London – after the failure of the revolution – Harney signed the statutes of the Universal Society of Revolutionary Communists which were drawn up by Marx and Engels. In his *Democratic Review* he published an article by Engels on the Ten Hour Question[262] and in his *Red Republican* he published Helen Macfarlane's translation of the Communist Manifesto which was described as "the most revolutionary document ever given to the world". When Engels moved to Manchester in 1850 Harney sympathised with his misfortune and declared that he would rather be hanged in London than die a natural death in that "damned dirty den of muckworms".[263]

In 1851 the Chartists were moving towards a socialist programme and the aims approved at their convention of March in that year have been described as "a statement of socialist policy which was not bettered until the twentieth century".[264] Yet at this very time Marx and Engels – described by Harney as "friends of long standing"[265] – ceased to collaborate with him. This was because when the exiles from the Continent quarrelled among themselves Harney declined to support the Marxist faction to the exclusion of other revolutionary groups. When Harney and Ernest Jones were rivals for the leadership of the remnants of the Chartist party in the early 1850s Marx and Engels supported Jones. Marx, writing to Engels in July 1851, was happy to report that Harney's *Friend of the People* was losing ground while the sale of Jones's *Notes of the People* was increasing.[266] Engels and Harney did not entirely lose touch with one another. They met in Jersey in 1857 when Engels was recuperating from an illness and Harney was editing the Jersey *Independent*. Engels wrote contemptuously that Harney was "an exceedingly stupid creature who feels quite at home here as a member of the petty bourgeoisie".[267] Over twenty years later – on a visit to the United States – Engels met Mrs Harney and wrote to Sorge in August 1888: "She says Harney will come to London in October where I shall then see him."[268] In the summer of 1891 Engels and Harney met in the Isle of Wight. On Engels's death Harney paid a warm tribute to one who had been his "friend and occasional correspondent for more than half a century".[269]

In his book on *The Condition of the Working Class in England* Engels quoted from a pamphlet written by James Leach entitled *Stubborn Facts from the Factories*. The pamphlet had appeared anonymously and Engels was the first to identify the author. Leach had been a weaver and was now a bookseller and printer in a small way. He had been the president of the provisional executive of the National Charter Association in Manchester in 1840 and had served as vice-chairman of the Chartist National Convention in London in 1842. After the disturbances in the north of England in that year Leach had been one of a number of Chartists who had been arrested on charges of seditious conspiracy. At his trial in March 1843 he defended his right to expose the evils of the factory system and to champion the Chartist cause. He was convicted on one count but the sentence was quashed on a technicality. Back in Manchester Leach resumed his activities as a political agitator, addressed meetings in support of the Charter and the Ten Hours Bill. He opposed the Anti-Corn Law League and tried to disrupt its meetings. He was arrested again in 1848. Gammage declared that Leach was a relaxed speaker in public. "For fact and argument there were but few of the speakers of that period who excelled him."[270] Engels regarded Leach as "an upright, trustworthy and capable fellow".[271] He referred to Leach as his "good friend".[272] But the friendship was not renewed when Engels returned to Manchester. There are only two references to Leach in Engels's letters to Marx. The first letter described a debate between Ernest Jones and James Leach in January 1851 at which Engels was present. The second mentioned Leach's attendance in the same month at a Chartist conference in Manchester.[273]

Ernest Jones,[274] another Chartist with whom Engels was associated, was born in Berlin and brought up on his father's estate in Holstein. His father was Major Charles Jones, veteran of the Peninsular and Waterloo and equerry to the Duke of Cumberland who came to the throne of Hanover as Ernest I. Ernest Jones came to England at the age of 19 and qualified as a barrister. He joined the Chartists and soon became one of the leaders of the left wing of the movement which was prepared to attain its ends by physical force rather than by peaceful means. He was one of the most effective Chartist orators. Engels's friend Georg Weerth wrote: "Jones, a master of the two most powerful modern languages, combined in his speeches a profound German scholarship with unlimited English drive. His speeches at the great meetings of the Fraternal Democrats were probably received with greater enthusiasm than those of any other speaker."[275] The violence of one of Jones's speeches earned him a term of imprisonment in 1848.

Engels does not appear to have made contact with Jones during his first stay in England in 1842–4. They probably met when Engels visited England in 1845 and 1847. Since he had been educated in Germany and spoke German Jones could understand

Engels's philosophical arguments in favour of communism. But he was never converted to Marx's doctrines. Ernest Jones was in touch with the international working class movement before 1848. He was, for example, a member of the German Workers Educational Association in London. The German tailor Friedrich Lessner recalled Jones's visits to the Association and described him as a "courageous and self-sacrificing agitator" and a "resolute and fearless leader".[276] Marx and Jones met at the end of 1847 when they spoke at a banquet held to commemorate the anniversary of the Polish revolution of 1830.[277]

The first reference to Jones in the Marx–Engels correspondence is in March 1848 when Marx informed Engels that Jones was in Paris and in touch with the newly elected central committee of the communist party. It has been seen that in 1851 when Jones and Harney were rivals for the support of the rump of the Chartist party Marx and Engels supported Jones and contributed to his *Notes to the People* and *The Peoples Paper*. On March 18, 1852 Engels wrote to Marx that Ernest Jones now had a real chance of reviving the Chartist movement.

> "From all I see, the Chartists are so completely disorganised and scattered and at the same time so short of useful people, that they must either fall completely to pieces and degenerate into cliques . . . or they must be reconstituted on an entirely new basis by a fellow who knows his business. Jones is quite on the right lines for this, and we may well say that he would not have got onto the right road without our teaching, for he would never have discovered how the only basis on which the Chartist party can be reconstituted – namely, the instinctive hatred of the workers for industrial bourgeoisie – can be not only preserved but enlarged, developed and based on enlightened propaganda, whilst on the other hand one must still be progressive in opposing reactionary desires and prejudice amongst the workers."[278]

A year later Marx reported that *The People's Paper* was financially sound and that Ernest Jones was planning to address a number of meetings in the provinces.

In 1857, however, Marx and Engels were disappointed at the tactics adopted by Ernest Jones. They criticised him for failing to take advantage of the discontent caused by the slump of that year to rouse the masses in the factory districts. Marx complained that instead of doing this Jones was trying to co-operate with the middle class radicals.[279] In October 1858 Engels declared that "the Jones affair is truly disgusting".[280] The English workers were becoming more bourgeois in character and Jones was losing his old fire. Early in 1859 Marx wrote to Weydemeyer: "I have broken with Ernest

Jones. Despite my repeated warnings and despite the fact that I accurately predicted what would happen – namely, that he would ruin himself and disorganise the Chartist party – he nevertheless took the course of trying to reach an agreement with the radical bourgeoisie. Now he is a ruined man, and the harm he has caused to the British proletariat is enormous."[281]

When the last of the Chartist newspapers collapsed Jones settled in Manchester (1861) and practised at the bar. On the establishment of the International Working Men's Association Marx urged Engels to persuade Jones to set up a branch of the Association in Manchester – but added the warning: "Have an eye on Jones! He is a fellow too clever by half."[282] But Jones seems to have shown little interest in the new association. Marx complained in 1865: "Ernest Jones is here. He was very agreeable socially speaking. But, between ourselves, he keeps in touch with our Association only because it will help him from an electoral point of view."[283] Engels replied that he could never find Jones at home. "We must let Jones go his own way."[284] Marx thought that it would be useful to "co-operate with Jones for a time" – in view of a forthcoming meeting in Manchester of delegates from the International Working Men's Association and the Reform League.[285]

Jones's policy of co-operating with the radicals – and even with the Liberals – continued to be a disappointment to Marx and Engels. In September 1868 Engels told Marx that he had actually heard Jones call Gladstone "a great leader of the working classes". "Once more he has been too clever by half."[286] Two months later Engels described Ernest Jones as a faithful servant of Gladstone and Bright.[287] He had only contempt for Jones's efforts to enter Parliament with the support of the Liberal vote. In the following year Marx asked Engels if he would contribute to the expenses of a demonstration to be held in Trafalgar Square to support Ernest Jones. But early in 1869 Jones died suddenly at the age of 50. On January 29 Engels wrote to Marx: "Tomorrow, with an enormous procession, Jones is to be buried in the same churchyard where Lupus lies. The fellow is really a loss. His bourgeois phrases were only hypocrisy after all, and here in Manchester there is no one who can take his place with the workers. They will disintegrate again completely and fall right into the net of the bourgeoisie. Moreover he was the only educated Englishman among the politicians who was, at bottom, entirely on our side."[288]

Another Englishman with whom Engels was on friendly terms was Edward Jones of Manchester. Frank Hall wrote that as a young man Edward Jones "was exceptionally well informed, and so marked was his gift of speech that one of the Manchester papers described him as 'a young Demosthenes'. He became a protégé of a Mr Engels, a Manchester merchant, who almost adopted him as a son and sent him to the Mechanics Institute for further training in order to qualify him for public life." Edward Jones played an important part in the activities of the Manchester branch of the International Working Men's Association which met in the Union Chambers near the Town Hall.[289] When Eugène Dupont moved from Manchester Edward Jones became the leading figure in the branch and kept Engels informed of its activities. In 1872 he acted as secretary to the Nottingham congress of the English Federal Council of the First International.

Engels's closest English friend was Samuel Moore. Born in 1838 at Bamford in Derbyshire, Moore studied at Trinity College, Cambridge and graduated in 1862. He then ran a cotton spinning mill at Ancoats[290] and, when the undertaking failed, he embarked – at the age of 40 – upon the study of law at Lincoln's Inn where he qualified as a barrister. Samuel Moore and Engels met in Manchester in 1863.[291] Moore shared the political views of Marx and Engels and when he was given the nickname "King Coal" he could feel that he had been admitted to the inner circle of Marx's closest disciples. Moore joined the International Working Men's Association, the receipt of his subscription of £5 being noted in the minutes of the General Council in September 1866.[292] Moore, however, did not play an active part in politics. His significance in the early socialist movement lay in the fact that he translated most of the first volume of *Das Kapital* into English.

The earliest references to Moore in the Marx–Engels correspondence are in 1865 when Moore purchased a few shares in the *Beehive* journal and joined Engels on a fortnight's holiday in Germany and Switzerland.[293] In June 1867 Engels wrote to Marx that he had found an English translator for *Das Kapital*. Samuel Moore would translate the book. "He knows enough German to read Heine fluently and he will soon master your style. . . . It goes without saying that the translation will be done under my personal supervision. . . . He is an industrious and reliable fellow and he has as much theoretical knowledge as one can expect from an Englishman."[294] In the autumn of 1867 Moore went to Eisenach to study German for six weeks in preparation for his work as translator of *Das Kapital*.[295] In November Engels wrote to Marx that the translation was now in hand.[296]

For many years Moore made little progress with the translation. In January 1869 Engels wrote that Moore was studying Marx's earlier book *Kritik der politischen Ökonomie*.[297] In the 1870s, when Engels had moved to London, there is no mention of the translation in Engels's correspondence. Only after Marx died in 1882 was the question raised again. In 1883 Engels told Laura Lafargue that he hoped to find a publisher for Moore's English version of *Das Kapital*. He praised Samuel Moore's specimen translation as being "very good and lively".[298] In the following year Engels wrote that he proposed to let Moore have most of Marx's parliamentary papers "for use with the translation".[299] Most of the translation was done in 1883–4. In April 1884 Engels wrote to Laura Lafargue that it had been suggested that Aveling might assist with the translation. Engels doubted whether Aveling's knowledge of German was adequate for this purpose.[300] Moore completed the translation in 1886 with some help from Aveling, and it was published in the following year.[301] In 1887 Samuel Moore made a new translation of the Communist Manifesto.[302]

Samuel Moore was appointed Chief Justice of the territories of the Royal Niger Company in 1889 and held this post until 1899. Engels wrote that Moore would get six months leave every other year as well as "good pay, and the expectation of returning in eight years or so an independent man".[303] In 1890 Engels told Kautsky that Moore was subject to attacks from malaria every six or eight weeks but the attacks were quite mild and there were no after effects. Early in 1891, however, Engels wrote that "Sam Moore is seriously ill".[304] Moore recovered and when he returned to England on his first leave Engels wrote to Laura Lafargue that he "likes the climate and the easy life amazingly".[305] In England he had another attack of malaria.[306] On December 1, 1891 Engels wrote that Moore had returned to Lagos "and would be back in the arms of his black wife in about a week or ten days".[307] Moore was in England again at the end of 1892. Engels mentioned that Moore had visited him in London in November of that year.[308] Engels consulted Samuel Moore when he drew up his will.[309] Moore was in London at the time of Engels's last illness. On one occasion when Engels was in Eastbourne Moore went to Victoria Station to catch Dr Freyberger – Engels's doctor – as he left the train so as to get the latest news of the patient's condition. When Engels died Moore attended the funeral and paid a brief tribute to his old friend. Moore retired in 1899 and died at his home at Castleton Hall, Derbyshire on July 20, 1911.[310]

VII. The "Philistines"

Although in later years Engels declared that "it is possible to enjoy a personal friendship with somebody with whom one differs in politics"[311] it may be doubted whether he had any close friends among the middle classes in Manchester with whom he came in contact through his business and social activities. Some of these "philistines" – as he called them – were in the cotton trade while some were members of the flourishing German colony in Manchester. It was a real hardship for Engels to be forced to associate day after day with English businessmen. In 1845 he had savagely attacked the English bourgeoisie. He declared:

> "I have never seen so demoralised a social class as the English middle classes. They are so degraded by selfishness and moral depravity as to be quite incapable of salvation. And here I refer to the bourgeoisie proper (in the narrower sense of the term) – and in particular to the 'Liberal' section of the English middle classes which supports the repeal of the Corn Laws. The middle classes have a truly extraordinary conception of society. They really believe that all human beings (themselves excluded) and indeed all living things and inanimate objects have a real existence only if they make money or help to make it. Their sole happiness is derived from gaining a quick profit. They feel pain only if they suffer a financial loss. Every single human quality with which they are endowed is grossly debased by selfish greed and love of gain. Admittedly the English middle classes make good husbands and family men. They have also all sorts of so-called 'private virtues'. In the ordinary daily affairs of life they seem to be as respectable and as decent as the members of any other middle class. One finds them better than Germans to deal with in business. The English do not condescend to that petty haggling which characterises the German trader with his pathetically limited horizon. But what is the use of all that? When all comes to all what really matters to the Englishman is his own interest and above all his desire to make money."[312]

Yet Engels did not find the society of members of the middle class quite so disagreeable as one might suppose. He told Marx: "It is sad but true that here in Manchester the ordinary bourgeois fellow is the one who is easiest to get on with since he drinks and tells smutty stories . . . and one can laugh at him."[313] There are not many references to his "philistine" friends in Engels's letters to Marx. One would like to know more about the solicitor Isaac Hall (who described himself as "an old friend")[314] and the manufacturer Alfred Knowles – "fatty Knowles", who went bankrupt in 1868 and paid his creditors 7s 6d in the pound.[315] Engels joined the Albert Club, the Schiller Anstalt, and the Cheshire Hunt[316] but he seldom mentioned the names of fellow members of these organisations. He did tell Marx that his "philistine" friends knew of his association with Mary Burns[317] and sent their condolences when she died.[318]

In later life Engels sometimes recalled his years in Manchester.

One of his stories concerned the attitude of the "philistines" to smoking. When being entertained by a manufacturer he was invited to retire to the kitchen for a smoke since no gentleman would smoke a cigar in the presence of ladies. To illustrate the strength of sabbatarianism, Engels recalled lunching with a middle class family on a Sunday and being asked which service he had attended. He replied that he always took a walk in the country on a Sunday morning. His host observed that Engels held rather "peculiar religious views" – "somewhat socinian, I think". Belfort Bax, reporting the story, commented that " 'somewhat socinian' was about the extreme limit of heterodoxy conceivable to a respectable middle class mind".[319]

Two of the "philistines" mentioned in the Marx–Engels correspondence were Louis Borchardt and John Watts. Borchardt[320] was born in Landsberg an der Warthe (Brandenburg) in 1813 and qualified as a doctor in Berlin in 1838. He practised in Breslau and organised medical relief measures during the typhus epidemic in Silesia in 1845. He was a democratic agitator during the revolution of 1848 and was imprisoned when the reaction triumphed. On his release he migrated to England and settled in Bradford where he met H. M. Steinthal of Messrs. Steinthal & Co. When Steinthal moved to Manchester, Dr Borchardt followed him in 1852 and built up "an excellent practice among the wealthy classes".[321] His interest in revolutionary politics declined. He joined the Liberals and became president of the Withington branch of the South East Lancashire Liberal Association.

In 1853 Dr Borchardt was appointed honorary physician to the General Dispensary for Children (opened in 1829) at 25 Back King Street, Pool Fold. In 1854 this dispensary moved to North Parade, St Mary's and a little hospital of six beds was added to it. The dispensary and hospital were charitable institutions supported by public subscription. In his first report on the hospital Dr Borchardt observed that many working class children died owing to inadequate home nursing when they fell ill and he urged the provision of additional hospital accommodation – including a fever ward – for sick children.[322] In 1860 the children's hospital was moved to a larger house (30 beds) in Bridge Street. In the following year there were 236 admissions. Between 1873 and 1878 the hospital – now the Royal Manchester Children's Hospital – was transferred to large new premises at Pendlebury. When Dr Borchardt retired in 1878 a ward in the new hospital was named after him, and a marble bust of the doctor was placed at the entrance to the ward. Dr Borchardt has been described as "an efficient administrator", but "he was not very popular because of his autocratic attitude and intolerance of contradiction".[323] On one occasion he was criticised for dismissing a colleague without giving any reason for doing so.

Dr Borchardt met Marx and Engels through Wilhelm Wolff. Dr Borchardt and Wolff came from Silesia and had probably met in Breslau in the 1840s. The first reference to Dr Borchardt in the Marx–Engels correspondence is in a letter from Marx in 1852. Marx hoped that Dr Borchardt would persuade Steinthal to recommend Wolff to some of his business friends in London.[324] In September 1852 Dr Borchardt sent Wolff £10 so that he could come to Manchester[325] and subsequently Dr Borchardt helped Wolff to find private pupils. Wilhelm Wolff later showed his appreciation by leaving Dr Borchardt £100 in his will.[326]

Engels had a poor opinion of Dr Borchardt but maintained contact with him for Wilhelm Wolff's sake. He regarded Dr Borchardt as "a mendacious character"[327] and "a louse"[328] while Marx dismissed him as "a philistine liberal".[329] Engels was contemptuous of Dr Borchardt's professional skill. In 1858 he complained that Dr Borchardt was not giving Wilhelm Wolff proper treatment[330] and in 1864 – during Wolff's last illness – he insisted that Dr Gumpert should be called in to give a second opinion.[331] Dr Borchardt did not forgive Dr Gumpert for his intervention and the two doctors quarrelled again a few years later when Dr Gumpert suggested that Dr Borchardt should not allow children into a bedroom in which a child that had died of scarlet fever was lying. Both Engels and Dr Borchardt were members of the Schiller Anstalt. Engels was persuaded to become President of this institution because he hoped to annoy Dr Borchardt by doing so.[332] In their correspondence Marx and Engels frequently made derogatory remarks about Dr Borchardt. In 1868, for example, Engels regaled Marx with a scandalous piece of gossip concerning Dr Borchardt's alleged improper relations with a lady who was his patient. Engels declared that Dr Borchardt's position in Manchester had received a "severe shock". "Many people dare to speak about him in a disrespectful way." "And he has lost some of his elegance and cheerfulness."[333] Nevertheless Marx and Engels did not break off relations with Dr Borchardt. In 1859 they tried – apparently unsuccessfully – to persuade him to subscribe to the socialist periodical *Das Volk*.[334] In 1873, when Marx was on a visit to Manchester, Dr Borchardt called upon him. Dr Borchardt died in 1883.

John Watts,[335] a crippled tailor, played a leading *rôle* in the public life of Manchester in the middle of the nineteenth century. He was self-taught and he eventually secured a position as assistant secretary and librarian at the Mechanics Institute in Coventry. In

1841 he became a full-time lecturer for the National Society of Rational Religionists at the Hall of Science in Manchester. In his well attended lectures on Sundays Watts denounced revealed religion and capitalism and advocated atheism and the type of socialism preached by Robert Owen. Later his views changed. He supported radical rather than socialist reforms and he made his peace with the clergy. He became a strong supporter of such causes as the co-operative movement, free public libraries, state schools and technical education. He was a prolific pamphleteer and in 1866 he wrote a book on *Facts of the Cotton Famine.* On his first visit to Manchester Engels attended some of Watts's lectures and gave a vivid description of one of them in an article which he contributed to a Swiss radical journal in 1843. Here he described Watts as "an important fellow", whose writings showed "considerable talent".[336] In *The German Ideology* Marx and Engels mentioned Watts's pamphlet on *Facts and Fictions of Political Economists* with approval.[337] But in 1846 Engels complained that Watts was aiming "at becoming respectable in the eyes of the middle classes, despite his far from respectable atheism and socialism".[338] In 1850, when he was back in Manchester, Engels took an even less favourable view of Watts who had become "a faithful disciple of M. Proudhon" and "a completely radical humdrum bourgeois".[339] Watts was actually "on the best of terms with the Bishop of Manchester".[340] Engels, however, decided to "keep on good terms" with Watts who, after all, was "just as endurable as the other philistines here".[341] In 1851 he asked Watts to help Wilhelm Wolff to find a suitable post in Manchester.[342] In 1854 he secured from Watts a letter of introduction to the editor of the *Daily News* since he hoped to become the military correspondent of that paper.[343] But in 1858 when Marx asked Engels to approach Watts for a loan from the People's Provident Assurance Company (of which he was the managing director) Engels replied that he had "fallen out with the fellow".[344] The quarrel appears to have been patched up since in 1863 Engels did call upon Watts in a vain effort to borrow money – on Marx's behalf – from the People's Provident Assurance Company.[345] In 1866 Marx asked Engels to see Watts to secure from him a copy of a pamphlet entitled *On Machinery* which Watts had written.[346] In the first volume of *Das Kapital* Marx attacked a recent pamphlet by Watts[347] as "a positive cesspool of ancient and rotten apologetic commonplaces". He added that "at one time this same Watts traded in Owenism, and in 1842 published a pamphlet entitled *Facts and Fictions of Political Economists.* Among other things he said: 'Property is robbery.' But that was a long time ago".[348]

NOTES

1 Soon after Wilhelm Wolff's death Engels wrote to Marx (on June 9, 1864) that they should write a short biography of Wolff but it was not until 1876 that Engels wrote a brief account of Wolff's life in a series of articles in *Die Neue Welt* (July 1 to November 25, 1876). In 1886 these articles formed the basis of Engels's introduction to a reprint of Wolff's eight articles on *Die Schlesische Milliarde* which had originally appeared in the *Neue Rheinische Zeitung*. This brief biography has been reprinted in two editions of Wolff's works – one edited by Franz Mehring (1909) and one by E. Reiche (1954). It appears also in *Karl Marx–Friedrich Engels: Werke*, Vol. 19, pp. 53–88 and in F. Engels, *Biographische Skizzen* (1967), pp. 77–104. See also Willy Klamitter's essay on Wilhelm Wolff in *Schlesische Lebensbilder*, Vol. 1 (1922), pp. 266–70; Helmut Bleiber, "Wilhelm Wolff's Auftreten in Breslau in Frühjahr 1848" in *Zeitschrift für Geschichtswissenschaft*, 1958, Heft 6, pp. 1310 *et seq.*; and Walter Schmidt, *Wilhelm Wolff, sein Weg zum Kommunisten 1809–1846* (1963).

2 *Mohr und General: Erinnerungen an Marx und Engels* (1965), p. 207 and Jenny Marx, "Short Sketch of an eventful Life" in *Reminiscences of Marx and Engels* (Foreign Languages Publishing House, Moscow), p. 223.

3 F. Engels, *Biographische Skizzen* (1967), p. 103.

4 Wilhelm Wolff was born in Tarnau, Kreis Schweidnitz and not – as Engels stated (*Biographische Skizzen*, 1967, p. 78) – in Tarnau near Frankenstein.

5 For the "Rabenaas" hymn see F. Engels, *Biographische Skizzen* (1967), p. 83, Walter Schmidt, *Wilhelm Wolff. Sein Weg zum Kommunisten 1809–46* (1963), p. 127 and D. Hoffmann "Die Rabenaastrophe" in *Correspondenzblatt für Geschichte der evangelischen Kirche Schlesiens*, Vol. 6, Lignitz, 1898, (Heft 1, p. 71).

6 H. Oncken, *Lassalle* (Third edition, 1920), p. 34.

7 Wilhelm Wolff, "Die Kasematten" in the *Breslau Zeitung*, November 18, 1843, reprinted in *Der Aufruhr der Weber in Schesien (Juni 1844) und andere Schriften* (edited by Karl Bittel) (Berlin, 1952).

8 Heinrich Treitschke, *Deutsche Geschichte im neunzehnten Jahrhundert*, Vol. 5 (edition of 1927), p. 510.

9 *Breslau Zeitung*, December 5, 1843 and W. Schmidt, *Wilhelm Wolff. Sein Weg zum Kommunisten 1809–46* (1963), p. 177.

10 In 1844 the poor law doctor Alexander Schneer described some of the workers' houses in Breslau as "pigsties rather than habitations fit for human beings" (*Über die Zustände der arbeitenden Klassen in Breslau* (1844), p. 25 and W. Schmidt, *op. cit.*, p. 168).

11 F. W. Wolff, "Das Elend und der Aufruhr in Schlesien" (written at the end of June 1844) in Püttmann's *Deutsches Bürgerbuch* (Darmstadt, 1845). Reprinted in Eduard Bernstein, *Documente des Sozialismus*, Vol. 1 (1902), pp. 296–313, Wilhelm Wolff, *Der Aufruhr der Weber in Schlesien* (Juni 1844) *und andere Schriften* (edited by Karl Bittel, 1952), and Carl Jantke and Dietrich Hilger, *Die Eigentumlosen* (1965), pp. 157–78. Wolff's views on the weavers rising in Silesia were similar to those held by Marx, Engels and the members of the German Workers' Educational Society in London. See Karl Marx, "Kritische Randglossen zu dem Artikel, Der König von Preussen und

die Sozialreform. Von einem Preussen" (1844) in *Gesamtausgabe*, Part I, Vol. 3 (1932) and a letter from the German Workers' Educational Society in London to the editor of the Hamburg *Telegraph* in G. Winkler (ed.), *Dokumente zur Geschichte des Bundes der Kommunisten* (1957), pp. 64–6. The letter stated: "We accuse society which treats us like pariahs, lays insupportable burdens upon us, gives us no rights and allows us to rot in hunger and distress."

12 F. Engels, *Biographische Skizzen* (1967), p. 103.

13 At one time a number of Wilhelm Wolff's contributions to the *Deutsche Brüsseler Zeitung* were erroneously attributed to Engels.

14 Wilhelm Wolff may have been the author of an article on the Prussian Landtag and the proletariat which appeared in the *Kommunistische Zeitschrift* (the London organ of the newly established Communist League) in September 1847. The article has also been attributed to Engels.

15 F. Engels, introduction of 1885 to Karl Marx, *Enthüllungen über den Kommunistenprozess zu Köln*, 1852 (edition of 1952), p. 20 and F. Mehring, Karl Marx (edition of 1967), pp. 150–1.

16 Marx wrote that the police "tore off his spectacles, spat in his face, kicked him and cursed him" (R. Payne, *Marx*, 1968, p. 176).

17 The members of the executive committee were Marx, Engels, Wilhelm Wolff (formerly of Brussels) and Bauer, Moll and Schapper (formerly of London).

18 Wilhelm Wolff's gloomy account of the situation in Berlin was confirmed shortly afterwards by Stephan Born who wrote to Marx on May 11, 1848 that the local branch of the Communist League had been dissolved.

19 For Wilhelm Wolff's report of April 18, 1848 see Franz Mehring's introduction of 1914 to the fourth edition of Karl Marx, *Enthüllungen über den Kommunistenprozess zu Köln*, 1852 (reprinted as an appendix to the edition of 1952, pp. 157–8).

20 For Wilhelm Wolff's activities in Silesia in 1848 see H. Bleiber, "Wilhelm Wolff's Aufenthalt in Breslau im Frühjahr 1848" in the *Zeitschrift für Geschichtswissenschaft*, 1958, Heft 6, p. 1310 *et seq.*

21 F. Engels's introduction of 1885 to Karl Marx, *Enthüllungen über den Kommunistenprozess zu Köln*, 1852 (edition of 1952, p. 25).

22 Friedrich Lessner in *Reminiscences of Marx and Engels* (Foreign Languages Publishing House, Moscow), p. 156.

23 Friedrich Lessner, *op. cit.*, p. 156 and R. Payne, *Marx* (1968), p. 186.

24 These articles were reprinted in 1886: see Wilhelm Wolff, *Die Schlesische Milliarde* (introduction by Friedrich Engels) (Hottingen-Zürich, 1886) and Wilhelm Wolff, *Gesammelte Schriften* (edited by Franz Mehring, 1909).

25 See Georg Weerth to Ferdinand Lassalle, May 3, 1851 for Weerth's efforts to secure papers for Wilhelm Wolff that would enable him to travel to England (Georg Weerth, *Sämtliche Werke*, Vol. 5, p. 507).

26 Georg Weerth to Engels, November 24, 1851: "My plan for Lupus has fallen through" (Georg Weerth, *Sämtliche Werke*, Vol. 5, p. 432).

27 Engels to Marx, August 21, 1851 in *Gesamtausgabe*, Part III, Vol. 1, p. 243.

28 Marx to Weydemeyer, August 2, 1851 in K. Marx and F. Engels, *Letters to Americans, 1848–1895* (New World Books, 1963), p. 23.

29 Marx to Engels, March 10, 1853 in *Gesamtausgabe*, Part III, Vol. 1, p. 457.

30 F. Engels, *Biographische Skizzen*, (1967), p. 102.
31 Engels to Marx, September 19, 1853 in *Gesamtausgabe*, Part III, Vol. 1, p. 504.
32 Wolff was only aged 44 but Marx and Engels referred to him as "the old man".
33 Marx to Engels, September 7, 1853 in *Gesamtausgabe*, Part III, Vol. 1, pp. 499–501 and A. Künzli, *Karl Marx, Eine Psychographie* (1966), p. 365. In another letter Marx complained of Wilhelm Wolff's "infamous insolence" (October 8, 1853 in *Gesamtausgabe*, Part III, Vol. 1, p. 508). For the reconciliation see Marx to Engels, January 25, 1854 in *Gesamtausgabe*, Part III, Vol. 2, p. 4 and A. Künzli, *op. cit.*, p. 366.
34 Friedrich Engels to Jenny Marx, April 16, 1857: "The old gentleman is now very popular with a group of German clerks who gather at the Chatsworth Inn from time to time. Wolff takes the chair every Sunday evening in a most dignified manner. The German clerks and the English philistines who frequent the inn would be lost without him" (*Gesamtausgabe*, Part III, Vol. 2, pp. 184–5). The Chatsworth Inn (proprietor J. Royle) was situated in Boundary Lane, Chorlton on Medlock (W. Whellan, *Directory of Manchester and Salford*, 1853, p. 472).
35 Friedrich Engels to Karl Marx, March 23, April 3, 1854 and February 11, 1858 in *Gesamtausgabe*, Part III, Vol. 2, pp. 12, 15 and 286.
36 Karl Marx to Joseph Weydemeyer, February 1, 1859 in Karl Marx and Friedrich Engels, *Letters to Americans, 1848–95* (New World Books, 1963), p. 60; Karl Marx to F. Engels, July 1, 1868, Part III, Vol. 3, p. 29.
37 Jenny Marx to Louise Weydemeyer, May 11, 1861 in *Mohr und General: Erinnerungen an Marx und Engels* (1965), p. 261. Marx considered that Horace Mayhew's definition of an old bachelor applied to Wilhelm Wolff. He quoted from an article by Horace Mayhew in the *London Illustrated News*: "Symptoms of being a confirmed old Bachelor: When a man cannot go anywhere without his umbrella, that's a symptom. When a man thinks everyone is cheating him, that's a symptom. When a man does all the shopping himself etc." (Karl Marx to Friedrich Engels, August 25, 1857 in *Gesamtausgabe*, Part III, Vol. 2, p. 162).
38 Friedrich Engels to Karl Marx, August 25, 1857 in *Gesamtausgabe*, Part III, Vol. 2, pp. 210–11.
39 For Wilhelm Wolff's letter to Fritz Reuter of December 30, 1863 see the *Zeitschrift für Geschichtswissenschaft*, 1957, Heft 6, p. 1244. An extract from Reuter's reply of January 12, 1864 was given by Engels in his *Biographische Skizzen* (1967), p. 80. Reuter declared that he was still waiting for revolution to break out in Germany. The constitutional conflict in Prussia was at its height and Reuter wrote: "If only the Prussians would at least refuse to pay their taxes. That is the only way to get rid of Bismarck and company and kill off the old king with sheer vexation."
40 Wilhelm Wolff was buried in the (now disused) cemetery in Ardwick.
41 Ferdinand Freiligrath to Karl Marx, May 10 and 11, 1864 in F. Mehring, "Freiligrath und Marx in ihrem Briefwechsel" in *Ergänzungshefte zur Neuen Zeit*, Vol. 12, April 12, 1912.
42 Karl Marx to Jenny Marx, May 13, 1864 in *Marx–Engels Werke*, Vol. 30, pp. 659–60.
43 For Wilhelm Wolff's will see the documents in the Wolff papers at

the International Institute of Social History (Amsterdam). See also F. Engels to Karl Marx, March 6, 1865 in *Gesamtausgabe*, Part III, Vol. 3, p. 251 and Jenny Marx, "Short Sketch of an Eventful Life" in *Reminiscences of Marx and Engels* (Foreign Languages Publishing House, Moscow), p. 233.

44 For Georg Weerth see his collected works – Georg Weerth, *Sämtliche Werke* (ed. Bruno Kaiser, five volumes, 1956–7) and F. Engels, "Georg Weerth, der erste und bedeutendste Dichter des deutschen Proletariats" in *Der Sozialdemokrat*, June 7, 1883 reprinted in F. Engels, *Biographische Skizzen* (1967), pp. 107–14; Karl Weerth, *Georg Weerth. Der Dichter des Proletariats* (1930); Horst Bunke, *Georg Weerth 1822–1856. Ein Überblick über sein Leben und Wirken* (1956); Marianne Lange, "Das Vermächtnis Georg Weerths – eine grosse Tradition unserer sozialistischen Literatur" in *Einheit. Zeitschrift für Theorie und Praxis des wissenschaftlichen Sozialismus*, Vol. 12, 1957, Heft 10, pp. 1288–98; Marianne Lange, *Georg Weerth. Der erste und bedeutendste Dichter des deutschen Proletariats* (1957); Florian Vassen, *Georg Weerth. Ein politischer Dichter des Vormärz und der Revolution von 1848–49* (1971).

45 F. Engels to J. Weydemeyer, January 23, 1852 in Karl Marx and F. Engels, *Letters to Americans, 1848–1895* (New World Books, 1963), p. 33.

46 F. Engels, *Biographische Skizzen* (1967), p. 108.

47 Georg Weerth to his brother Wilhelm, March 26, 1842 in Georg Weerth, *Sämtliche Werke*, Vol. 5, p. 54.

48 George Weerth to Karl Marx, December 18, 1845 in Georg Weerth, *Sämtliche Werke*, Vol. 5, p. 188.

49 George Weerth to Friedrich aus'm Weerth, January 22, 1845: "Having been guilty of a foolish indiscretion in the summer of 1843 I have not dared to write to you since . . ." (Georg Weerth, *Sämtliche Werke*, Vol. 5, p. 146). For details of the indiscretion see Georg Weerth to his mother, September 8, 1843 (*ibid.*, Vol. 5, pp. 83–9). Weerth had improperly shown someone a private letter from the local burgomaster to his employer.

50 For a short time after leaving the firm Georg Weerth worked for August aus'm Weerth (son of Friedrich aus'm Weerth) and lived in his house. He drew no salary but August aus'm Weerth undertook to pay off Georg Weerth's debts. But when he left Bonn some of Georg Weerth's debts were still unpaid and some tradesmen's accounts were sent to his mother. See Georg Weerth to his mother, September 8, 1843, July 18, 1847 and September 14, 1847 in *Sämtliche Werke*, Vol. 5, pp. 83–9, pp. 254–9, and pp. 263–5.

51 Philip Passavant & Co. (worsted yarn merchants of Bradford) was a subsidiary of S. Passavant (Manchester) – Philip being the eldest son of S. Passavant. The offices of the Bradford firm were in Chapel Lane (1842), Tyrrel Street (1845) and Cheapside (1847). In 1845 S. Passavant gave up his business in Manchester and retired to Greenhill Hall, Bingley. See Georg Weerth to his mother, May 29, 1845 in *Sämtliche Werke*, Vol. 5, p. 160. In 1845 Georg Weerth was earning £149 a year. If he had received £150 he would have had to pay £5 in income tax (*ibid.*, Vol. 5, p. 152).

52 Georg Weerth's first letter from Bradford to his mother was dated December 21, 1843 (*Sämtliche Werke*, Vol. 5, p. 108). On April 18, 1846 Georg Weerth wrote to his mother that he had left Bradford on

April 11 (*ibid.*, p. 202). Weerth was in Brussels in July and August 1845.

53 Georg Weerth to his brother Ferdinand, January 10, 1844 in Georg Weerth, *Sämtliche Werke*, Vol. 5, 1957, p. 111.

54 Georg Weerth to his mother, January 9, 1846 in Georg Weerth, *Sämtliche Werke*, Vol. 5, p. 194.

55 Georg Weerth, *Sämtliche Werke*, Vol. 3, *Skizzen aus dem sozialen und politischen Leben der Briten*, p. 165.

56 George Weerth to his brother Ferdinand, January 10, 1844 in Georg Weerth, *Sämtliche Werke*, Vol. 5, p. 111.

57 Georg Weerth to his mother, January 12, 1845 in Georg Weerth, *Sämtliche Werke*, Vol. 5, p. 144.

58 Georg Weerth to Friedrich aus'm Weerth, January 22, 1845 in Georg Weerth, *Sämtliche Werke*, Vol. 5, p. 147.

59 Georg Weerth to his mother, January 12, 1845 in Georg Weerth, *Sämtliche Werke*, Vol. 5, p. 144. The firm was George Cheetham and Sons, 43 Spring Gardens, Manchester – described in the local directory as "spinners and manufacturers by power". The family resided in Stalybridge.

60 Georg Weerth to his mother, May 29, 1845 in Georg Weerth, *Sämtliche Werke*, Vol. 5, p. 161. Weerth wrote in his novel on Schnapphanski: "May the devil take the idle rich and the West Indian planters. One day the workers will destroy the idle rich and the slaves will destroy their masters" (Georg Weerth, *Sämtliche Werke*, Vol. 4, p. 313).

61 Georg Weerth to his mother, May 29, 1845 in Georg Weerth, *Sämtliche Werke*, Vol. 5, p. 160.

62 Georg Weerth to his brother Wilhelm, April 12, 1845 in Georg Weerth, *Sämtliche Werke*, Vol. 5, p. 157. He wrote: "The principal subject that I am studying at present is economics. I have nearly finished Adam Smith and I will then get down to some other rogues – Malthus, Ricardo and MacCulloch. These rubbishy works are full of lies."

63 Georg Weerth, *Sämtliche Werke*, Vol. 3, p. 7.

64 Georg Weerth, *Sämtliche Werke*, Vol. 3.

65 Georg Weerth to his mother, November 22, 1844 and May 29, 1845 in Georg Weerth, *Sämtliche Werke*, Vol. 5, p. 138 and p. 160. In 1847 Dr John Little McMichan lived at 23 Thornton Buildings, Bridge Street, Bradford. In an article in the *Rheinische Jahrbücher*, Vol. 1, 1845 Weerth wrote: "Mac is a Scot who, after studying in Glasgow and Edinburgh, became a ship's doctor on a Greenland whaler. 'I got a great cold there,' he told me, 'and I was glad to come ashore at Liverpool after 2½ years at sea. I settled in York which is a truly ancient aristocratic hole. Some really pretty girls run around there and I actually fell in love with one of them. What folly! I had no money and everything went wrong. I moved to Bradford as a pale castaway and for some time now I have been knocking about among the factory workers.' " (Georg Weerth, *Sämtliche Werke*, Vol. 3, p. 493).

66 F. Engels, "The Free Trade Congress in Brussels" in the *Northern Star*, No. 520, October 9, 1847 (quoting Weerth's speech).

67 Georg Weerth to his mother, May 22, 1844 in Georg Weerth, *Sämtliche Werke*, Vol. 5, p. 125.

68 Georg Weerth to his mother, July 6, 1844 in Georg Weerth, *Sämtliche Werke*, Vol. 5, p. 128.

69 F. Engels, *Biographische Skizzen* (1967), p. 109.
70 Georg Weerth to his mother, February 18, 1845 (*Sämtliche Werke*, Vol. 5, p. 153), for a description of "a railway meeting" and Georg Weerth to Karl Marx, December 25, 1845 (*ibid.*, Vol. 5, pp. 191–4) for a description of a "monster meeting" at Wakefield organised by the Anti-Corn Law League.
71 Georg Weerth to his brother Wilhelm, April 12, 1845 in Georg Weerth, *Sämtliche Werke*, Vol. 5, p. 156. He wrote: "Private property is the major cause of public misery."
72 Georg Weerth to his brother Wilhelm, December 24, 1844 in Georg Weerth, *Sämtliche Werke*, Vol. 5, p. 140.
73 Georg Weerth to Friedrich aus'm Weerth, January 22, 1845 in Georg Weerth, *Sämtliche Werke*, Vol. 5, p. 149.
74 Georg Weerth to his brother Wilhelm, April 12, 1845 in Georg Weerth, *Sämtliche Werke*, Vol. 5, p. 156. Georg Weerth wrote to his mother on January 9, 1846: "It is highly probable that we shall soon have a splendid revolution here and I rejoice in the prospect with all my heart."
75 Georg Weerth to his mother, July 17, 1845 in Georg Weerth, *Sämtliche Werke*, Vol. 5, p. 168.
76 19 au bois Sauvage, Ste Gudule. See Georg Weerth, *Sämtliche Werke*, Vol. 5, pp. 165–6. During part of Weerth's stay in Brussels Marx and Engels were away on a visit to Manchester.
77 Georg Weerth to his mother, July 19, 1845 in Georg Weerth, *Sämtliche Werke*, Vol. 5, pp. 170–3.
78 Georg Weerth to his mother, March 23, 1846 in Georg Weerth, *Sämtliche Werke*, Vol. 5, p. 200.
79 The Hamburg house was run by Wolff and Steinthal, the Bradford house by Rickmann and Schütt.
80 When Weerth visited Paris in March 1847 he met Friedrich Engels. Weerth to his mother, April 18, 1847: "I was in Paris on March 20 and had breakfast with my friend Engels in the rue Rivoli." (*Sämtliche Werke*, Vol. 5, p. 252).
81 Georg Weerth to his brother Wilhelm, November 18, 1846 in *Sämtliche Werke*, Vol. 5, p. 239.
82 Georg Weerth to his mother, November 28, 1847 in Georg Weerth, *Sämtliche Werke*, Vol. 5, p. 277. Lucien Jottrand was president of this association and Marx was vice-president.
83 See *Congrès des Economistes réunis à Bruxelles par les soins de l'association belge pour le liberté commerciale. Session de 1847. Seánces, 16, 17 et 18 Sept* (Brussels, 1847) – and "Economistes, Congrès de" in Coquelin and Guillaumin, *Dictionnaire de l'Economie Politique* (two volumes, 1854), Vol. 1, pp. 671–2.
84 F. Engels, "The Free Trade Congress in Brussels" (published anonymously) in the *Northern Star*, No. 520, October 9, 1847; Georg Weerth in *Sämtliche Werke*, Vol. 2, pp. 128–33; and Georg Weerth to his brother Wilhelm, September 26, 1847 in *Sämtliche Werke*, Vol. 5, pp. 265–75.
85 F. Engels, "Speech of Dr Marx on Protection, Free Trade and the Working Classes" in the *Northern Echo*, October 9, 1847.
86 According to Engels (in a letter to Marx, September 28, 1847) Weerth's speech appeared in *l'Atelier* as a supplement (*Gesamtausgabe*, Part III, Vol. 1, 1929, p. 75). *The Times* dismissed Weerth's speech as "Chartist commonplace" (*Northern Star*, October 9, 1847).

87 Georg Weerth to his brother Wilhelm, September 26, 1847 in Georg Weerth, *Sämtliche Werke*, Vol. 5, p. 274.

88 *Northern Star*, October 30, 1847 and A. R. Schoyen, *The Chartist Challenge* . . . (1958), p. 154.

89 Georg Weerth to his mother, November 28, 1847 in Georg Weerth, *Sämtliche Werke*, Vol. 5, p. 277.

90 F. Engels (in Paris) to Karl Marx (in Brussels), November 23–4, 1847 in *Gesamtausgabe*, Part III, Vol. 1 (1929), p. 89.

91 Weerth to his mother, February 25, 1849 in George Weerth, *Sämtliche Werke*, Vol. 5, p. 300.

92 Georg Weerth to his mother, March 11, 1848 in Georg Weerth, *Sämtliche Werke*, Vol. 5, p. 281.

93 *Ibid*., p. 281.

94 Imbert had been a former editor of the Marseilles workers' newspaper *Le Peuple Souverain* (1833–4) and a vice-president of the Brussels *Association Dėmocratique* (1847).

95 Georg Weerth, "Ein Besuch in den Tuilerien" in the *Kölnische Zeitung*, April 1 and 2, 1848 and in *Sämtliche Werke*, Vol. 4, pp. 17–26. See also Georg Weerth to his mother, March 27, 1848. For Julian Harney's visit to the Tuilleries at this time see A. R. Schoyen, *The Chartist Challenge* . . . (1958), p. 159.

96 Georg Weerth to his mother, March 27, 1848: "There is no business to be done as nobody thinks of buying or selling" (Georg Weerth, *Sämtliche Werke*, Vol. 5, p. 286.

97 Engels (in Brussels) to Marx (in Paris), March 18, 1848 in *Gesamtausgabe*, Part III, Vol. 1, p. 99.

98 Georg Weerth (Cologne) to Karl Marx (Paris), March 28, 1848: "Communism is a word that inspires terror here. People would stone anyone who openly admitted that he was a communist. Bürgers and d'Ester are talking about a new newspaper but I think that it is very doubtful whether the necessary capital can be raised. It would be a good idea if you would come here instead of studying in Paris." (Georg Weerth, (*Sämtliche Werke*, Vol. 5, p. 282). These discussions were also mentioned by Weerth in a letter of March 27, 1848 to his mother (*ibid*., Vol. 5, p. 284).

99 Editor's note to Georg Weerth, *Sämtliche Werke*, Vol. 5, pp. 286–7.

100 F. Engels, "Georg Weerth" in *Biographische Skizzen* (1967), p. 109.

101 Georg Weerth's articles, which appeared in the *Neue Rheinische Zeitung* between June 1848 and May 1849 have been reprinted in his *Sämtliche Werke*, Vol. 4 (1957), pp. 39–284.

102 Varnhagen von Ense noted in his diary on August 24, 1849 that actual incidents in Lichnowski's career had been reproduced by Weerth in his novel. In 1858 Weerth's friend Eduard Vehnse wrote that the author had told him "that his novel on Schnapphahnski was based upon authentic sources". Engels writing in 1883 stated: "The facts are all true" (Georg Weerth, *Sämtliche Werke*, Vol. 4, p. 10 and p. 529).

103 For example Weerth wrote articles on political affairs in England which appeared in the *Neue Rheinische Zeitung* on March 7, 1849 (*Sämtliche Werke*, Vol. 4, pp. 173–81) and May 19, 1849 – the last number of the newspaper (*Sämtliche Werke*, Vol. 4, pp. 277–80). See also Georg Weerth to his mother, May 18, 1849 in *Sämtliche Werke*, Vol. 5, pp. 304–5.

104 Georg Weerth to his mother, February 23–25, 1849 in *Sämtliche Werke*, Vol. 5, pp. 296–301.

105 Georg Weerth to his mother, April 11, 1849 in *Sämtliche Werke*, Vol. 5, pp. 302–4.

106 Introduction to Georg Weerth, *Sämtliche Werke*, Vol. 4, pp. 11–12.

107 Georg Weerth to his brother Wilhelm, June 16, 1849 in Georg Weerth, *Sämtliche Werke*, Vol. 5, pp. 309–18.

108 Georg Weerth to his mother, August 12, 1849 in *Sämtliche Werke*, Vol. 5, pp. 309–318.

109 Jenny Marx, "Short Sketch of an Eventful Life" in *Reminiscences of Marx and Engels* (Foreign Languages Publishing House, Moscow), p. 225.

110 Georg Weerth to his mother, September 16 and November 28, 1849 in Georg Weerth, *Sämtliche Werke*, Vol. 5, pp. 329–32 and pp. 336–9 and George Weerth to his brother Ferdinand, December 15, 1849 (describing his travels from June 13, 1849 to the end of 1849) in Georg Weerth, *Sämtliche Werke*, Vol. 5, pp. 339–42.

111 Georg Weerth's letters to the president of the Cologne court (*Landesgericht*) July 20, 1849; September 29, 1849; and October 11, 1849 are printed in Georg Weerth, *Sämtliche Werke*, Vol. 5, pp. 320, 332 and 334.

112 Georg Weerth to his brother Wilhelm, April 16, 1850 in Georg Weerth, *Sämtliche Werke*, Vol. 5, p. 351.

113 Georg Weerth to Karl Marx, May 2, 1850 in *Sämtliche Werke*, Vol. 5, p. 355.

114 Georg Weerth to Karl Marx, June 2, 1850 in Georg Weerth *Sämtliche Werke*, Vol. 5, p. 359.

115 Georg Weerth to his mother, August 2, 1850 in Georg Weerth, *Sämtliche Werke*, Vol. 5, pp. 360–2.

116 Georg Weerth to his mother, September 1–3, 1850 in Georg Weerth, *Sämtliche Werke*, Vol. 5. p. 364.

117 Georg Weerth to Karl Marx, March 3, 1851 in Georg Weerth, *Sämtliche Werke*, Vol. 5, p. 391.

118 Georg Weerth to Friedrich Engels, March 3, 1851 in Georg Weerth, *Sämtliche Werke*, Vol. 5, p. 393.

119 Georg Weerth to Karl Marx, April 28, 1851, in Georg Weerth, *Sämtliche Werke*, Vol. 5, p. 403. Marx wrote to Engels on May 3, 1851: "I have just had a letter from Weerth. He is very discontented. He is bored by long noses and smoked meats. . . . You know friend Weerth. He gets bored most readily when he is enjoying middle class comforts." (*Gesamtausgabe*, Part III, Vol. 1, p. 190).

120 There are several references to meetings between Engels and Weerth at this time in the Marx-Engels correspondence and in Weerth's collected works. For example Engels mentioned Weerth's visits to Manchester in letters to Marx of August 27, 1851 (*Gesamtausgabe*, Part III, Vol. 1, p. 251), October 27, 1851 (*ibid.*, p. 283), December 16, 1851 (*ibid.*, p. 300), October 14, 1852 (*ibid.*, p. 408), October 18, 1852 (*ibid.*, p. 413), November 27, 1852 (*ibid.*, p. 437). See also letters from Weerth to Engels on October 20 and 23, 1851, and of January 1852 and October 6 and 9, 1852 (in Georg Weerth, *Sämtliche Werke*, Vol. 5).

121 G. Weerth to F. Engels, November 24, 1851 in Georg Weerth, *Sämtliche Werke*, Vol. 5, p. 432: F. Engels to K. Marx, October 27, 1851 in *Gesamtausgabe*, Part III, Vol. 1, p. 284; K. Marx to F. Engels, February 4, 1852 in *Gesamtausgabe*, Part III, Vol. 1, p. 316.

122 G. Weerth to K. Marx, October 26, 1852 in Georg Weerth, *Sämtliche Werke*, Vol. 5, pp. 454–5. At the Cologne trial of leaders of the Communist League the prosecutor alleged that Weerth was a member of the central committee of the League. A similar statement appeared in the *Neue Preussische Zeitung*. In fact Weerth was not a member of the League in 1852.

123 Jenny Marx to F. Engels, January 8, 1852; F. Engels to K. Marx, January 22, 1852 in *Gesamtausgabe*, Part III, Vol. 1, p. 304 and p. 309.

124 Jenny Marx to Adolph Cluss, October 28, 1852 in Georg Weerth, *Sämtliche Werke*, Vol. 5, p. 456.

125 Georg Weerth to F. Engels, November 26, 1851, January 16, 1852 and August 24 1855 in Georg Weerth, *Sämtliche Werke*, Vol. 5, pp. 433, 437 and 481. Steinthal had formerly been jointly in charge of the Hamburg branch of Emanuel and Son. He is mentioned in the Marx-Engels correspondence: *Gesamtausgabe*, Part III, Vol. 1, pp. 282, 416, 477 and 479.

126 Georg Weerth to Karl Marx, October 11, 1852 in Georg Weerth, *Sämtliche Werke*, Vol. 5, p. 454. Steinthal & Co were described as commission merchants of 2 Lower Mosley Street in W. Whellan, *Directory of Manchester and Salford* (1853), p. 301.

127 Karl Marx to F. Engels, September 28, 1852 in *Gesamtausgabe*, Part III, Vol. 1, p. 402.

128 F. Engels to K. Marx, October 18, 1852 in *Gesamtausgabe*, Part III, Vol. 1, p. 413.

129 K. Marx to F. Engels, December 3, 1852 in *Gesamtausgabe*, Part III, Vol. 1, p. 440.

130 Georg Weerth to his mother, February 2 and June 14, 1853 in Georg Weerth, *Sämtliche Werke*, Vol. 5, pp. 456–9.

131 Georg Weerth to Heinrich Heine, July 17, 1853 from Angostura (Cindad Bolivar) in Georg Weerth, *Sämtliche Werke*, Vol. 5, pp. 460–4.

132 Georg Weerth to his mother from Tepic, December 14–17, 1853 in Georg Weerth, *Sämtliche Werke*, Vol. 5, pp. 464–8.

133 Georg Weerth to his mother from San Francisco, February 1854 in Georg Weerth, *Sämtliche Werke*, Vol. 5, pp. 468–72.

134 George Weerth to Heinrich Heine from Buenos Ayres, April 1, 1855 in Georg Weerth, *Sämtliche Werke*, Vol. 5, pp. 472–9.

135 Quoted in Georg Weerth, *Sämtliche Werke*, Vol. 5, p. 486.

136 Wilhelm Wolff to Karl Marx, August 28, 1856 (conveying news of Weerth's death) in George Weerth, *Sämtliche Werke*, Vol. 5, p. 500. Marx wrote: "The news of Weerth's death came as a great shock to me. It is hard to realise what has happened" (K. Marx to F. Engels, September 1856 in *Gesamtausgabe*, Part III, Vol. 2, p. 146).

137 For Carl Schorlemmer see articles by A. Spiegel in the *Berichte der Deutschen Chemischen Gesellschaft*, Vol. 25, 1892, p. 1106; by F. Engels in *Vorwärts*, July 3, 1892; by H. E. Roscoe in the *Proceedings of the Royal Society*, Vol. 7, p. vii and in *Nature*, August 25, 1892; by H. B. Dixon in the *Memoirs of the Manchester Literary and Philosophical Society*, Vol. 7, 1892, p. 191; by Professor Schuster in the *Manchester Guardian*, June 28, 1892; by P. J. Hartog in the *Dictionary of National Biography*, Vol. 50, p. 439; by Hans von Liebig in the *Hessische Biographien*, Vol. 1, 1912, p. 439; by S. Unger in the *Wissenschaftliche Zeitschrift der Universität Rostock*, Vol. 2 (3), 1953; and by H. Grohn in the *Technische Hochschule für*

Chemie Carl Schorlemmer. Festschrift 1954–64 (Merseburg, 1964). See also H. Zimmermann (ed), *Carl Schorlemmer* (1964: collection of essays); Karl Heinig, *Carl Schorlemmer, der erste marxistische Chemiker* (Humboldt University, Berlin, 1968: typescript thesis; copy in the University of Manchester Library and J. K. Roberts, *The life and work of Carl Schorlemmer* (M.Sc. thesis, Manchester University, 1972).

138 The Thatched House Tavern was in Newmarket Place, Market Street, Manchester: see W. Whellan, *Directory of Manchester and Salford*, 1853, p. 424.

139 For Heinrich Caro see *Berichte der Deutschen Chemischen Gesellschaft*, Vol. 45, 1912, pp. 1987–2024: E. Darmstaedter in G. Bugge (ed.), *Buch der grossen Chemiker*, Vol. 2, 1930, pp. 298–309; and *Neue Deutsche Biographie*, Vol. 3, p. 152. Heinrich Caro (1834–1910) came to England in 1859 and was employed by the firm of Roberts, Dale & Co. (Manchester). He returned to Germany in 1866.

140 For Ludwig Mond see J. M. Cohen, *The Life of Ludwig Mond* (1956) and W. H. Chaloner, *People and Industries* (1963), p. 86–97.

141 For Philipp Pauli see H. Reisenegger, "Zu Dr. Paulis achtzigstem Geburtstag" in the *Chemiker-Zeitung*, February 23, 1916 and information supplied by D. F. Soun, archivist of the Farbewerk Hoechst A. G. The following correspondence is preserved in the International Institute of Social History (Amsterdam) – seven letters from Engels to Philipp Pauli, two letters from Engels to Ida Pauli, eleven letters from Ida Pauli to Engels, and one letter from Marx to Ida Pauli.

142 There are references to the Thatched House Tavern in two letters from A. Davisson to F. Engels (February 2 and December 12, 1867 in the Marx-Engels archives (Amsterdam), L.1079 and L.1082.

143 F. Engels to Karl Marx, March 6, 1865 in *Gesamtausgabe*, Part III, Vol. 3, p. 250.

144 Karl Marx to F. Engels, June 3, 1867 in *Gesamtausgabe*, Part III, Vol. 3, p. 393.

145 F. Engels to Karl Marx, May 10, 1868 in *Gesamtausgabe*, Part III, Vol. 4, p. 54.

146 Gustav Mayer, *Friedrich Engels*, Vol. 2 (1934), p. 311.

147 Karl Heinig, *Carl Schorlemmer, der erste marxistische Chemiker* (Humboldt University, Berlin, 1968: typescript thesis), p. 96.

148 Schorlemmer matriculated at the University of Giessen on May 11, 1859.

149 Engels was mistaken in stating (in *Vorwärts*, July 3, 1892) that Schorlemmer settled in England in 1858, the correct date is 1859.

150 Wilhelm Dittmar (1833–92) worked under Sir Lyon Playfair at Edinburgh University in the 1860s and subsequently became Professor of Chemistry at the Andersonian College at Glasgow. See article on W. Dittmar by A. Crum Brown in *Nature*, March 24, 1892, p. 493.

151 E. Fiddes, *Chapters in the History of Owens College and of Manchester University* (1937), p. 47.

152 For the early history of the chemistry department of Manchester University see H. E. Roscoe, *Record of Work done in the Chemical Department of the Owens College 1857–1887* (1887), Colin Campbell, "The Chemistry Department" in *The Journal of the University of Manchester*, Vol. 1, No. 3, 1939, and G. N. Burkhardt, "The School of Chemistry in the University of Manchester" in the *Journal of the Royal Institute of Chemistry*, September 1954, p. 450. For H. E.

Roscoe see *The Life and Experiences of Sir H. E. Roscoe written by himself* (1906), T. E. Thorpe, *The Rt. Hon. Sir Henry Enfield Roscoe: a biographical Sketch* (1916), and the *Dictionary of National Biography*, Supplement 1912–21.

153 *Manchester Guardian*, May 4, 1895.

154 F. Engels to Karl Marx, January 10, 1868 in *Gesamtausgabe*, Part III, Vol. 4, p. 9.

155 H. B. Dixon, "Memoir of . . . Carl Schorlemmer" in the *Memoirs of the Manchester Literary and Philosophical Society*, Vol. 7, 1892, p. 191.

156 The Calendar of Owens College for 1862 – 3 stated that the Professor of Chemistry was "assisted in the instruction of students by Mr. C. Schorlemmer, F.C.S." The salary of an assistant in the chemical laboratory was £80 a year. This was raised to £100 in 1872.

157 F. Engels in *Vorwärts*, July 3, 1892. In a letter to Marx, March 7, 1869 (*Gesamtausgabe*, Part III, Vol. 4, p. 167) Engels stated that Schorlemmer had been injured when a bottle of phosphorus had exploded. Roscoe stated that acid burns left Schorlemmer with a permanent scar on one of his hands (*Nature*, August 25, 1892).

158 *Jahresbericht für Chemie*, Vol. 10, 1866, p. 535 and p. 537.

159 Sir Edward Frankland (1825–99), formerly professor of Chemistry at Owens College, was Professor of Chemistry at the Royal Institution (1863–8) and at the Royal College of Chemistry (1865). See *Dictionary of National Biography*, Supplement II, p. 237.

160 F. Engels to K. Marx, May 10, 1868 in *Gesamtausgabe*, Part III, Vol. 4, p. 54. Carl Schorlemmer's papers on "Researches in the Hydro-carbons of the Series Cn H2n+2" appeared in the *Proceedings of the Royal Society* in 1865, 1868, 1870 and 1871. In 1870 Schorlemmer was living at 192 Brunswick Street close to the site to which Owens College was to move from the centre of the city in 1873. When he became naturalised in 1879 Schorlemmer's address was 114 Rumford Street, Chorlton on Medlock. At the time of his death in 1892 Schorlemmer was living in Hyde Grove, Chorlton on Medlock.

161 Carl Schorlemmer was elected a corresponding member of the German Chemical Society of Berlin at its meeting on November 11, 1868. He was described as "C. Schorlemmer Dr.phil.Manchester" but he did not have a doctorate at this time.

162 Schorlemmer's membership certificate was signed by J. P. Joule, Schunck, Binney, Gaskell and H. E. Roscoe.

163 In 1864 Schorlemmer received a grant of £30 from the Royal Society to assist him in his research.

164 Carl Schorlemmer to Alexander Mikhaiovich Butlerov, March 24, 1874 in Karl Heinig, *Carl Schorlemmer, der erste marxistische Chemiker* (Humboldt University, Berlin: thesis 1968), p. 173. A. M. Butlerov was born in 1828 and died in 1886. The centenary of his birth was marked by the publication of a collection of essays (in Russian) in his honour (British Museum Library, Ac. 1125/119).

165 H. E. Roscoe's letter of November 1, 1886 is in the records of the University of Manchester.

166 *Glasgow Herald*, April 28, 1888.

167 H. E. Roscoe, *Kurzes Lehrbuch der Chemie* (third edition, 1871).

168 H. B. Dixon stated that this was "the first systematic treatise on modern organic chemistry". For a review of the German translation of this book (*Lehrbuch der Kohlenstoffverbindung*) see the *Chemisches Zentralblatt*, 1895, p. 403.

169 There was a German edition (1889) and a French translation by Claparède. A new English edition of 1894 – twice as long as the first edition – was revised by Schorlemmer's pupil Arthur Smithells. Schorlemmer had presented Engels with a copy of the first edition of *The Rise and Development of Organic Chemistry* (1879) while Smithells sent Engels a copy of the edition of 1894. (See *Ex Libris Karl Marx und Friedrich Engels*, 1867, p. 182). The book was dedicated by Schorlemmer to his former teacher Hermann Kopp.

170 German edition: *Ausführliches Lehrbuch der Chemie* (1877 onwards). Engels declared (in a letter to Bernstein) that it was common knowledge that most of this book had been written by Schorlemmer. Roscoe corresponded with his former teacher Robert Bunsen about this book. The correspondence is preserved in the University Library at Heidelberg.

171 The manuscript of Carl Schorlemmer's history of chemistry (which was not completed) is preserved in the library of the University of Manchester. One section covers the age of alchemy and another deals with the age of medical chemistry. The manuscript has been described by Karl Heinig in H. Zimmermann (ed.), *Carl Schorlemmer* (1964), pp. 77–85 and is mentioned by J. R. Partington in his *A History of Chemistry*, Vol. 4 (1964), p. 774.

172 F. Engels, *Biographische Skizzen* (1967), p. 174.

173 H. E. Roscoe in *Nature*, August 25, 1892, p. 395.

174 Carl Schorlemmer to A. M. Butlerov, January 29, 1881 and Butlerov's reply in Karl Heinig, *Carl Schorlemmer, der erste marxistische Chemiker* (Humboldt University, Berlin, 1968: typescript thesis), pp. 175–6. Karl Heinig also reproduces an undated letter from Carl Schorlemmer to Karl Marx referring to the young Russian scientist.

175 F. Engels to Karl Marx, September 7, 1870 in *Gesamtausgabe*, Part III, Vol. 4, p. 380. J. G. Wehner was for many years the treasurer of the Schiller Anstalt in Manchester. In the advertising columns of the *Manchester Guardian*, August 6, 1870 there was an appeal for funds for the German wounded on behalf of the German Ladies Circle (*Frauenverein*) in Manchester.

176 See the *Manchester Guardian*, August 6, 1870 for a report on the work of the London central committee of the German Association for the Relief of the Wounded.

177 Karl Marx to F. Engels, September 10, 1870 in *Gesamtausgabe*, Part III, Vol. 4, p. 328.

178 Carl Schorlemmer (at Bouillon) to F. Engels, September 17, 1970 in Karl Heinig, *Carl Schorlemmer, der erste marxistische Chemiker* (Humboldt University, Berlin, 1968: typescript thesis), p. 180.

179 In 1867, for example, Carl Schorlemmer attended the natural history conference at Frankfurt am Main.

180 F. Engels, *Biographische Skizzen* (1967), p. 147.

181 In the preface to the second edition of *Anti-Dühring* Engels wrote in 1885: "Marx and I were pretty well the only people to rescue conscious dialectics from German idealist philosophy and apply it in the materialist conception of nature and history. But a knowledge of mathematics and natural science is essential to a conception of nature which is dialectical and at the same time materialist."

182 See, for example, F. Engels to K. Marx, June 16 and 24, 1867 and K. Marx to F. Engels, January 3, 1868 in *Gesamtausgabe*, Part III, Vol. 3, pp. 394, 398, and Part III, Vol. 4, p. 2.

183 F. Engels to K. Marx, May 30, 1873 in *Gesamtausgabe*, Part III, Vol. 4, pp. 396–8 and English translation in F. Engels, *Selected Writings* (edited by W. O. Henderson, 1967), pp. 393–9.

184 K. Marx to F. Engels, December 7, 1867 in *Gesamtausgabe*, Part III, Vol. 3, p. 461.

185 *Manchester Guardian*, May 4, 1895.

186 Schorlemmer made a will on May 19, 1892 (witnessed by his solicitor G. W. Fox and his doctor E. Gumpert) leaving his property to his mother.

187 Carl Schorlemmer became a naturalised British citizen on May 17, 1879.

188 F. Engels, *Biographische Skizzen* (1967), pp. 149–50.

189 Ludwig Schorlemmer to F. Engels, May 30, 1892 in Marx–Engels archives (Amsterdam), L.5613.

190 F. Engels to Karl Kautsky, September 18, 1890 in B. Kautsky (ed.), *Friedrich Engels' Briefwechsel mit Karl Kautsky* (1955), p. 262.

191 F. Engels to Laura Lafargue, June 9, 1892 in *F. Engels – Paul and Laura Lafargue Correspondence*, Vol. 3, p. 179; F. Engels to Karl Kautsky, June 11, 1892 in B. Kautsky (ed.), *Friedrich Engels' Briefwechsel mit Karl Kautsky* (1955), pp. 342–3; H. E. Roscoe to F. Engels, May 27, 1892 and Engels's reply, May 28, 1892 in the Marx–Engels archives (Amsterdam), K. 1401.

192 F. Engels to Ludwig Schorlemmer, July 1, 1892 in H. Hirsch (ed.), *Friedrich Engels: Profile* (1970), pp. 364–5 and G. Mayer, *Friedrich Engels*, Vol. 2 (1934), p. 553.

193 *Manchester Guardian*, June 28, 1892. Arthur Schuster (1851–1934) was professor first of applied mathematics (1881–8) and then of physics (1888–1907) at Owens College.

194 Schorlemmer's modesty may be seen from his reply to a letter from a German correspondent asking for particulars of Schorlemmer's career. He wrote on June 23, 1886:

> Since you wish to know something about my extremely uninteresting career, I beg to inform you that I was born in Darmstadt on September 30, 1834. My chemical studies began there at the Polytechnic School. Then, for a time, I followed the profession of a pharmaceutical chemist but I subsequently continued my studies in Giessen and went to Manchester in 1859 as Roscoe's assistant. There I became lecturer in organic chemistry and in 1874 I was appointed Professor of Organic Chemistry, a post which I still hold.

See Karl Heinig, *Carl Schorlemmer, der erste marxistische Chemiker* (Humboldt University, Berlin, 1968: typescript thesis), p. 177. Schorlemmer's letter is preserved in the Deutsches Museum in Munich.

195 H. E. Roscoe in *Nature*, August 25, 1892, p. 394.

196 *Manchester Guardian*, June 28, 1892.

197 See *Obituary Notices of Fellows of the Royal Society*, No. 19, p. 184.

198 F. Engels to Laura Lafargue, July 7, 1892 in *F. Engels – Paul and Laura Lafargue Correspondence*, Vol. 3, p. 182.

199 Quoted by Karl Heinig in Hans Zimmermann (ed.), *Carl Schorlemmer* (1964), p. 84.

200 F. Engels to E. Bernstein, February 27, 1883 in Gustav Mayer, *Friedrich Engels*, Vol. 2 (1934), p. 553.

201 F. Engels to P. Pauli, January 11, 1893, quoted by Karl Heinig in Hans Zimmermann (ed.), *Carl Schorlemmer* (1964).

202 F. Engels to Philipp Pauli, January 11, 1893 in Karl Heinig, *Carl Schorlemmer, der erste marxistische Chemiker* (Humboldt University, Berlin, 1968: typescript thesis), p. 171.
203 *Manchester Guardian*, May 4, 1895.
204 Subscribers to the Schorlemmer memorial fund included H. E. Roscoe, H. Simon, W. H. Perkin (and his son), E. Donner, Heinrich Caro, C. P. Scott, Mrs Rylands, the *Badische Anilin Fabrik*; and Messrs Meister, Lucius & Brüning. By September 25, 1893, £2,015 16s had been raised. Later donations brought the fund up to £2,440. See *Schorlemmer Memorial: First List of Subscribers* in the Marx-Engels archives, S.55 (Amsterdam).
205 *Manchester Guardian*, May 4, 1895.
206 Hans Zimmermann (ed.), *Carl Schorlemmer* (1964).
207 See *Festschrift: Technische Hochschule für Chemie Carl Schorlemmer 1954–1964* (Merseburg, 1964).
208 For a brief obituary notice of Dr E. Gumpert see the *Manchester Guardian*, April 24, 1893.
209 F. Engels to Karl Marx, May 12, 1865 in *Gesamtausgabe*, Part III, Vol. 3, p. 270.
210 E. W. Jones, *The History of the Manchester Northern Hospital for Women and Children* (Manchester, 1933), p. 52. The name of the hospital was changed in 1902 to the "Manchester Northern Hospital for Women and Children".
211 Karl Marx to F. Engels, May 31, 1858 in *Gesamtausgabe*, Part III, Vol. 2, p. 321.
212 Jenny Marx to F. Engels, January 17, 1870 in *Marx-Engels Werke*, Vol. 22, p. 507.
213 F. Engels to Karl Marx, April 26, 1868 in *Gesamtausgabe*, Part III, Vol. 4, p. 44 and F. Engels to V. Adler, October 23, 1892 in *Victor Adlers Aufsätze, Reden und Briefe*, Heft 1: *Victor Adler und Friedrich Engels* (1922), pp. 56–7.
214 Karl Marx (Harrogate) to F. Engels (London), November 30, 1873 in *Gesamtausgabe*, Part III, Vol. 4, p. 408. "I visited Gumpert on Thursday. He is quite bald and he has aged a good deal." See also Karl Marx to Dr Kugelmann, January 19 and May 18, 1874 in Karl Marx, *Letters to Dr Kugelmann*, pp. 134–5.
215 F. Engels to Karl Marx, April 24 and May 1, 1864 in *Gesamtausgabe*, Part III, Vol. 3, pp. 168–9.
216 F. Engels to Laura Lafargue, March 20, 1891 and F. Engels to Paul Lafargue, April 3, 1891 in *F. Engels – Paul and Laura Lafargue Correspondence*, Vol. 3, 1891–5, pp. 39 and 45.
217 F. Engels to Paul Lafargue, May 19, 1892 and F. Engels to Laura Lafargue, June 9 and July 7, 1892 in *F. Engels – Paul and Laura Lafargue Correspondence*, Vol. 3, 1891–5, pp. 175–6, 179 and 181–2. See also F. Engels to August Bebel, June 20, 1892 in F. Engels, *Briefe an Bebel* (1958), p. 227.
218 *Manchester Guardian*, April 22 and 24, 1893.
219 F. Engels to Laura Lafargue, April 25, 1893 in *F. Engels – Paul and Laura Lafargue Correspondence*, Vol. 3, 1891–5, pp. 258–9.
220 F. Engels to Karl Marx, March 18, 1868 in *Gesamtausgabe*, Part III, Vol. 4, p. 31.
221 For Carl Siebel (1836–68) see the *Allgemeine Deutsche Biographie*, Vol. 34, pp. 166–7; J. V. Bredt, *Geschichte der Familie Siebel* (1937); G. Werner, "Romantiker Wuppertals: Barmer Dichter Karl Siebel

starb vor hundert Jahren" in *Westdeutsche Rundschau*, May 31, 1968; Klaus Goebel, "Zum hundertsen Todestag Carl Siebel" in *Romerike Berge*, Vol. 18, 1968–9, p. 45 and H. Hirsch's introduction to *Friedrich Engels: Profile* (1970), pp. 17–20.

222 F. Engels to Karl Marx, January 27, 1859 in *Gesamtausgabe*, Part III, Vol. 2, p. 359.

223 H. Hirsch's introduction to *Friedrich Engels: Profile* (1970), p. 17.

224 F. Engels to Frau Elise Engels, April 20, 1859 in H. Hirsch (ed.), *Friedrich Engels: Profile* (1970), pp. 162–3.

225 Carl Siebel to F. Engels, May 28, 1859, quoted in H. Hirsch's introduction to *Friedrich Engels: Profile* (1970), p. 18.

226 F. Engels to Jenny Marx, December 22, 1859 in *Gesamtausgabe*, Part III, Vol. 2, p. 451.

227 F. Engels to Karl Marx, November 4, 1859 in *Gesamtausgabe*, Part III, Vol. 2, p. 432.

228 F. Engels to Karl Marx, February 7, 1860 in *Gesamtausgabe*, Part III, Vol. 2, p. 467.

229 Karl Marx to F. Engels, August 13, 1859 in *Gesamtausgabe*, Part III, Vol. 2, p. 414.

230 F. Engels to Karl Marx, February 4, 1860 in *Gesamtausgabe*, Part III, Vol. 2, pp. 465–66.

231 See the programme: *Manchester Schiller Festival, Free Trade Hall, November 11, 1859* (Taylor, Garnett, Evans & Co., Printers, "Guardian" Office, Manchester). For the Schiller festival see the *Manchester Guardian*, September 17 and 20, October 22, and November 3, 5, and 9, 1859.

232 F. Engels to Karl Marx, November 4, 1859 in *Gesamtausgabe*, Part III, Vol. 2, pp. 432.

233 F. Engels to Karl Marx, November 17, 1859 in *Gesamtausgabe*, Part III, Vol. 2, pp. 435–6.

234 *Manchester Guardian*, February 6, 1860.

235 F. Engels to Carl Siebel, July 4, 1862 in H. Hirsch (ed.), *Friedrich Engels: Profile* (1970), p. 250.

236 F. Engels to Karl Marx, August 15, 1860 in *Gesamtausgabe*, Part III, Vol. 2, p. 502.

237 F. Engels to Karl Marx, October 5, 1860 in *Gesamtausgabe*, Part III, Vol. 2, pp. 515–16. Engels added: "She will wear the breeches".

238 Karl Marx to F. Engels, September 25, 1860 in *Gesamtausgabe*, Part III, Vol. 2, pp. 510–11.

239 Karl Marx to F. Engels, May 10, 1861 in *Gesamtausgabe*, Part III, Vol. 3, p. 22.

240 Karl Marx to F. Engels, December 27, 1861 in *Gesamtausgabe*, Part III, Vol. 3, p. 52.

241 Carl Siebel to F. Engels, December 23, 1861 in H. Hirsch's introduction to *Friedrich Engels; Profile* 1970), p. 20.

242 Karl Marx to Carl Klings, October 4, 1864 and Karl Marx to Carl Siebel, December 22, 1864 in *Marx-Engels Werke*, Vol. 31, pp. 417–18 and p. 436.

243 F. Engels to Karl Marx, February 5, 1865 in *Gesamtausgabe*, Part III, Vol. 3, p. 227 (postscript).

244 Karl Marx to F. Engels, March 7, 1865 and F. Engels to Carl Siebel, February 27, 1865 in *Marx-Engels Werke*, Vol. 31, p. 94 and p. 456. A review of Engels's pamphlet appeared in the *Barmer Zeitung* (March 9, 1865) and in the *Düsseldorfer Zeitung*.

245 Karl Marx to F. Engels August 5, 1865 in *Gesamtausgabe* Part III, Vol. 3, p. 282.
246 F. Engels to Karl Marx, April 27, 1867 in *Gesamtausgabe* Part III, Vol. 3, p. 385.
247 Carl Siebel to Karl Marx, May 1, 1867 (H. Hirsch ed.) *Friedrich Engels: Profile* (1970), pp. 199.
248 F. Engels to Karl Marx, September 11, 1867 in *Gesamtausgabe*, Part III, Vol. 3, p. 422.
249 F. Engels to Karl Marx, October 22, 1867 in *Gesamtausgabe*, Part III, Vol. 3, p. 438.
250 F. Engels to Karl Marx, November 10, 1867 in *Gesamtausgabe*, Part III, Vol. 3, pp. 447–8.
251 The review in the *Düsseldorfer Zeitung* is reprinted in H. Hirsch (ed.), *Friedrich Engels: Profile* (1970), pp. 172–3. Reviews also appeared in the *Barmer Zeitung* (F. Engels to Jenny Marx, January 3, 1868 in *Marx–Engels Werke*, Vol. 32, p. 531), the *Elberfelder Zeitung* and the *Frankfurter Börsen Zeitung*.
252 F. Engels to Karl Marx, May 15, 1868 in *Gesamtausgabe*, Part III, Vol. 3, Siebel died on May 9, 1868 and was buried in the cemetery in Barmen in the Bartholasstrasse.
253 Karl Marx to F. Engels, May 16, 1868 in *Gesamtausgabe*, Part III, Vol. 3, p. 56.
254 F. Engels to August Bebel, February 2, 1892 in Friedrich Engels, *Briefe an Bebel* (1958), p. 210.
255 F. Engels to Karl Marx, January 8, 1851 in *Gesamtausgabe*, Part III, Vol. 1, p. 129.
256 For Julian Harney see F. G. and R. M. Black (ed.), *The Harney Papers* (1969); A. R. Schoyen, *The Chartist Challenge* (1958), John Saville's introduction to the facsimile reprint of *The Red Republican* and the *Friend of the People* (two volumes, 1966) and Peter Cadogan, "Harney and Engels" in the *International Review of Social History*, Vol. 10, Part 1, 1965. Engels's friend Georg Weerth wrote that "Harney, a brilliant orator, was the first Englishman to offer the hand of friendship to Schapper, Bauer, and Moll, the three Germans who ran the German Workers Education Association in London. Harney established that close co-operation between the English and German workers that led to the foundation of the Society of Fraternal Democrats" (Georg Weerth, *Sämtliche Werke*, Vol. 3, 1957, pp. 373–74).
257 F. Engels, *The Condition of the Working Class in England* (translated by W. O. Henderson and W. H. Chaloner, 1958 and 1971), p. 254 and "Das Fest der Nationen in London" in the *Rheinische Jahrbücher zur zur gesellschaftlichen Reform*, 1846 and *Marx-Engels Werke*, Vol. 2, p. 616. For the *Northern Star* see E. L. H. Glasgow, "The Establishment of the *Northern Star* Newspaper" in *History*, February–June, 1954, pp. 54–67.
258 *Northern Star*, December 4, 1848.
259 H. Förder, *Marx und Engels am Vorabend der Revolution* (1960), p. 158 (note 3).
260 Karl Marx to F. Engels, March 12, 1848 in *Gesamtausgabe*, Part III, Vol. 1, p. 96. Harney, Jones and McGrath presented an address from the Chartists and the Fraternal Democrats to the people of Paris.
261 F. Engels to Emil Blank, April 15, 1848 in *Marx-Engels Werke*, Vol. 27, pp. 476–8.

262 *Democratic Review*, No. 10, March 1850.
263 Julian Harney to F. Engels, December 16, 1850 in F. G. and R. M. Black (ed.), *The Harney Papers* (1969), p. 258.
264 J. Saville in his introduction to the reprint of *The Red Republican* and the *Friend of the People* (1966), p. x. The Chartist programme of March 1851 was printed in the *Friend of the People*, April 12 and 19, 1851 and in the *Northern Star*, June 12, 1851.
265 The *Friend of the People*, March 15, 1851, p. 107.
266 K. Marx to F. Engels, July 31, 1851 (postscript) in *Gesamtausgabe*, Part III, Vol. 1, p. 226. In addition to the *Northern Star* Harney was editor of the *Democratic Review* (1849–50), the *Red Republican* (June–November 1850) and *The Friend of the People* (first series – December 7, 1850 to July 26, 1851: second series – February 7 to April 24, 1852). In 1852 *The Friend of the People* and the *Northern Star* were merged. The new journal was called *The Star of Freedom*. Harney also edited the *Vanguard* from January to March 1853.
267 F. Engels to K. Marx, October 19, 1857 in *Gesamtausgabe*, Part III, Vol. 2, pp. 231–2.
268 F. Engels (Boston) to F. A. Sorge, August 28, 1888 in K. Marx and F. Engels, *Letters to Americans 1848–95* (1963), p. 202.
269 *Newcastle Weekly Chronicle*, August 17, 1895 and *Reminiscences of Marx and Engels* (Foreign Languages Publishing House, Moscow), pp. 192–3. Edward Aveling was exaggerating somewhat when he referred to Harney as "one of the oldest and closest friends of Engels" (*The Labour Prophet*, Numbers 45 and 46, 1895).
270 R. G. Gammage, *History of the Chartist Movement* (second edition, 1894: reprinted 1969), p. 211.
271 F. Engels, *The Condition of the Working Class in England* (translated by W. O. Henderson and W. H. Chaloner, 1958), pp. 151–2.
272 *Ibid.*, p. 342 (article in *Das Westfälische Dampfboot*, 1846, p. 21).
273 F. Engels to K. Marx, January 8 and 29, 1851 in *Gesamtausgabe*, Part III, Vol. 1, p. 128 and p. 135.
274 For Ernest Jones see J. Saville (ed.), *Ernest Jones: Chartist* (1952).
275 Georg Weerth, *Sämtliche Werke*, Vol. 3 (1957), p. 374.
276 *Reminiscences of Marx and Engels* (Foreign Languages Publishing House, Moscow), p. 154.
277 *Northern Star*, December 4, 1847 and J. Saville, *op. cit.*, p. 27.
278 F. Engels to K. Marx, March 18, 1852 in *Gesamtausgabe*, Part III, Vol. 1, p. 331.
279 K. Marx to F. Engels, November 24, 1857 in *Gesamtausgabe*, Part III, Vol. 2, p. 247.
280 F. Engels to K. Marx, October 7, 1858 in *Gesamtausgabe*, Part III, Vol. 2, p. 340.
281 K. Marx to J. Weydemeyer, February 1, 1859 in K. Marx and F. Engels, *Letters to Americans, 1848–95* (1963), pp. 60–61.
282 K. Marx to F. Engels, February 13, 1865 in *Gesamtausgabe*, Part III, Vol. 3, p. 237.
283 K. Marx to F. Engels, May 9, 1865 in *Gesamtausgabe*, Part III, Vol. 3, p. 268.
284 F. Engels to K. Marx, May 12, 1865 in *Gesamtausgabe*, Part III, Vol. 3, p. 270.
285 K. Marx to F. Engels, May 13, 1865 in *Gesamtausgabe*, Part III, Vol. 3, p. 271.

286 F. Engels to K. Marx, September 1, 1868 in *Gesamtausgabe*, Part III, Vol. 4, p. 88.
287 F. Engels to K. Marx, November 10, 1868 in *Gesamtausgabe*, Part III, Vol. 4, p. 126.
288 F. Engels to K. Marx, January 29, 1869 in *Gesamtausgabe*, Part III, Vol. 4, p. 153.
289 Frank Hall, *A Northern Pioneer. The Story of J. R. Lancashire* (1927), p. 116 and pp. 134–5. Hall refers to him as "Edwin Jones" but his Christian name was "Edward". There are references to Edward Jones's political activities in H. Collins and C. Abramsky, *Karl Marx and the British Labour Movement* (1965).
290 The firm of Samuel M. Moore & Son, cotton spinners, 2 Mill Street, Ancoats, is listed in W. Whellan, *Directory of Manchester and Salford* (1853), p. 226.
291 In an address given at Engels's funeral Samuel Moore stated: "I made the acquaintance of Fredrick Engels in the year 1863 in Manchester" (*Reminiscences of Marx and Engels*, Foreign Languages Publishing House, Moscow, p. 359).
292 *Documents of the First International* (Moscow and London), Vol. 2: Council Meeting, September 25, 1866, p. 34.
293 F. Engels to Karl Marx, May 12, July 15 and August 16, 1865 in *Gesamtausgabe*, Part 3, Vol. 3, pp. 270, 277 and 287.
294 F. Engels to Karl Marx, June 24, 1867 in *Gesamtausgabe*, Part III, Vol. 3, pp. 397–8.
295 F. Engels to Karl Marx, September 2 and October 22, 1867 in *Gesamtausgabe*, Part III, Vol. 3, p. 416 and p. 438.
296 F. Engels to Karl Marx, November 28, 1867 in *Gesamtausgabe*, Part III, Vol. 3, p. 453.
297 F. Engels to Karl Marx, January 29, 1869 in *Gesamtausgabe*, Part III, Vol. 4, p. 153.
298 F. Engels to Laura Lafargue, June 2 and September 19, 1883 in *Friedrich Engels – Paul and Laura Lafargue Correspondence*, Vol. 1, p. 137 and p. 146.
299 F. Engels to Laura Lafargue, February 5, 1884 in *Friedrich Engels – Paul and Laura Lafargue Correspondence*, Vol. 1, pp. 169–70.
300 F. Engels to Laura Lafargue, April 18 and May 26, 1884 in *Friedrich Engels – Paul and Laura Lafargue Correspondence*, Vol. 1, pp. 194–6 and 205–7.
301 F. Engels to Laura Lafargue, November 24, 1886 in *Friedrich Engels – Paul and Laura Lafargue Correspondence*, Vol. 1, pp. 395–9.
302 F. Engels to F. A. Sorge, March 10, 1887 in K. Marx and F. Engels, *Letters to Americans* 1848–95 (1963), p. 177. See also F. Engels to Wilhelm Liebknecht, February 23, 1888 in G. Eckert (ed.), *Wilhelm Liebknecht: Briefwechsel mit Karl Marx und Friedrich Engels* (1963), p. 305.
303 F. Engels to Laura Lafargue, June 11, 1889 in *F. Engels – Paul and Laura Lafargue Correspondence*, Vol. 2, p. 276.
304 F. Engels to K. Kautsky, September 18, 1890 and January 7, 1891 in B. Kautsky (ed.), *Friedrich Engels' Briefwechsel mit Karl Kautsky* (1955), p. 262 and p. 268.
305 F. Engels to Laura Lafargue, May 4, 1891 in *F. Engels – Paul and Laura Lafargue Correspondence*, Vol. 3, p. 58.
306 F. Engels to K. Kautsky, June 29, 1891 in B. Kautsky (ed.), *Friedrich Engels' Briefwechsel mit Karl Kautsky* (1955), p. 305.

307 F. Engels to Laura Lafargue, December 1, 1891 in *F. Engels – Paul and Laura Lafargue Correspondence*, Vol. 3, p. 148.
308 F. Engels to Julie Bebel, November 29, 1892 in F. Engels, *Briefe an Bebel* (1958), p. 262.
309 F. Engels to Laura Lafargue and Eleanor Marx, November 14, 1894 in *F. Engels – Paul and Laura Lafargue Correspondence*, Vol. 3, pp. 341–2. Copies of Engels's will (July 29, 1893), a codicil and a letter to his executors are preserved in the Marx-Engels archives, M.53 (Amsterdam).
310 *Manchester Guardian*, July 22, 1911. Samuel Moore's name appears in the Colonial Office List for 1898. At his death Samuel Moore's estate was valued at £2,821 (Probate Registry). In the index to *Reminiscences of Marx and Engels* (Foreign Languages Publishing House, Moscow) it is stated that Samuel Moore died in 1912. This is a mistake. For letters from Samuel Moore to Laura Lafargue and Eleanor Marx see the Marx-Engels archives, G.160, G.330, G.331, and G.161 (Amsterdam).
311 F. Engels to Conrad Schmidt, September 12, 1892 in Helmut Hirsch, *Friedrich Engels: Profile* (1970), p. 109.
312 F. Engels, *The Condition of the Working Class in England* (translated and edited by W. O. Henderson and W. H. Chaloner, 1958 and 1971), pp. 311–12.
313 F. Engels to Karl Marx, August 21, 1851 in *Gesamtausgabe*, Part III, Vol. 1, p. 244.
314 Isaac Hall to F. Engels, May 28, 1869 in the Marx-Engels archives, L.2140–2150 (Amsterdam).
315 For Alfred Knowles see *Gesamtausgabe*, Part II, Vol. 3, pp. 277 and 297 and Vol. 4, pp. 19, 137, 150 and 395. The name of the firm was H. Knowles and Son.
316 F. Engels to Karl Marx, January 22, 1857, December 31, 1857 and February 11, 1858 in *Gesamtausgabe*, Part III, Vol. 2, p. 116, p. 266, and p. 286. See also Karl Marx to his daughter Jenny, January 11, 1865 in *Marx-Engels Werke*, Vol. 31, p. 442.
317 F. Engels to Karl Marx, May 1, 1854 in *Gesamtausgabe*, Part III, Vol. 2, p. 26.
318 F. Engels to Karl Marx, January 13, 1863 in *Gesamtausgabe*, Part III, Vol. 3, p. 118.
319 E. Belfort Bax, *Reminiscences and Reflections* (1918), quoted in *Reminiscences of Marx and Engels* (Foreign Languages Publishing House, Moscow), pp. 305–7.
320 For Dr Louis Borchardt see his obituary in the *Manchester Guardian*, November 16, 1883. F. Boase states in his *Modern English Biography*, Vol. 1 (1892: new edition, 1965) that Borchardt was born in 1813. If this is correct he would have been 70 years of age when he died in 1883. But according to Borchardt's obituary in the *Manchester Guardian* he was 67 at the time of his death. For Louis Borchardt see also Dr A. Holzel, "Paediatrics in Manchester a Hundred Years ago" (History of Medicine Lecture, February 25, 1969: typescript).
321 *Manchester Guardian*, November 16, 1883.
322 A copy of the first report of the General Hospital for Sick Children (Manchester) is in the Medical Library of the University of Manchester.
323 Dr A. Holzel, *Paediatrics in Manchester a Hundred Years Ago* (History of Medicine Lecture, February 25, 1969) (typescript).

324 Karl Marx to F. Engels, June 2, 1853 in *Gesamtausgabe*, Part III, Vol. 1, p. 477.
325 F. Engels to Karl Marx, September 19, 1853 in *Gesamtausgabe*, Part III, Vol. 1, pp. 503–4.
326 F. Engels to K. Marx, March 6 and March 11, 1865 in *Gesamtausgabe*, Part III, Vol. 3, p. 249 and pp. 251–2.
327 F. Engels to K. Marx, June 6, 1853 in *Gesamtausgabe*, Part III, Vol. 1, p. 479.
328 F. Engels to K. Marx, May 1, 1864 in *Gesamtausgabe*, Part III, Vol. 3, p. 170.
329 Karl Marx to F. Engels, September 28, 1861 in *Gesamtausgabe*, Part III, Vol. 3, p. 41.
330 F. Engels to Karl Marx, August 10, 1858 in *Gesamtausgabe*, Part III, Vol. 2, p. 335.
331 F. Engels to Karl Marx, May 1, 1864 in *Gesamtausgabe*, Part III, Vol. 3, p. 169.
332 F. Engels to Karl Marx, November 7, 1864 in *Gesamtausgabe*, Part III, Vol. 3, p. 200.
333 F. Engels to Karl Marx, February 2, 1868 in *Gesamtausgabe*, Part III, Vol. 4, pp. 19–20.
334 F. Engels to Karl Marx, July 18, August 10, August 13, 1859: Karl Marx to F. Engels, August 13 and 26 in *Gesamtausgabe*, Part III, Vol. 2, pp. 403–15.
335 For John Watts (1818–1887) see the *Dictionary of National Biography*, Vol. 60, p. 71; The *Bee Hive*, August 14, 1875; an obituary notice in the *Manchester Guardian*, February 6, 1887.
336 F. Engels, "Briefe aus London" in the *Schweizerische Republikaner*, June 9, 1843. See also F. Engels, "Progress of Social Reform on the Continent" in *The New Moral World*, November 4, 1843.
337 Karl Marx and F. Engels, *The German Ideology* (English edition of 1965), p. 227. Watts was described as a "tailor and doctor of philosophy".
338 F. Engels to the Communist Correspondence Committee in Brussels, September 16, 1846 in *Gesamtausgabe*, Part III, Vol. 1, p. 35.
339 F. Engels to Karl Marx, December 17, 1850 in *Gesamtausgabe*, Part III, Vol. 1, p. 122.
340 F. Engels to Karl Marx, February 5, 1851 in *Gesamtausgabe*, Part III, Vol. 1, pp. 142–3.
341 F. Engels to Karl Marx, August 21, 1851 in *Gesamtausgabe*, Part III, Vol. 1, pp. 243–4.
342 F. Engels to Karl Marx, August 21, 1851 in *Gesamtausgabe*, Part III, Vol. I, pp. 243–4.
343 F. Engels to Karl Marx, April 3, 1854 in *Gesamtausgabe*, Part III, Vol. 2, p. 15.
344 F. Engels to Karl Marx, July 16, 1858 in *Gesamtausgabe*, Part III, Vol. 2, p. 331.
345 F. Engels to Karl Marx, January 13 and 26, 1863 in *Gesamtausgabe*, Part III, Vol. 3, p. 118 and p. 121.
346 Karl Marx to F. Engels, February 10 and 13, and March 2, 1866 in *Gesamtausgabe*, Part III, Vol. 3, p. 306, p. 309, and p. 312.
347 John Watts, *Trade Societies and Strikes. Machinery and Co-operative Societies* (Manchester, 1865).
348 Karl Marx, *Capitalism* (Everyman Edition, 1930), Vol. 2, p. 600 (footnote 1).

DOCUMENTS

I

TO THE WORKING CLASSES OF GREAT BRITAIN, 1845[1]

Working Men,

To you I dedicate a work, in which I have tried to lay before my German countrymen a faithful picture of your condition, of your sufferings and struggles, of your hopes and prospects. I have lived long enough amidst you to know something about your circumstances; I have devoted to their knowledge my most serious attention, I have studied the official and non-official documents as far as I was able to get hold of them. I have not been satisfied with this, I wanted more than a mere *abstract* knowledge of my subject, I wanted to see you in your homes, to observe you in your every-day life, to chat with you on your condition and grievances, to witness your struggles against your oppressors. I have done so: I forsook the company and the dinner parties, the port-wine and champagne of the middle classes, and devoted my leisure hours almost exclusively to the intercourse with plain working men; I am both glad and proud of having done so. Glad, because thus I was induced to spend many a happy hour in obtaining a knowledge of the realities of life – many an hour, which else would have been wasted in fashionable talk and tiresome etiquette; proud, because thus I got an opportunity of doing justice to an oppressed and calumniated class of men who with all their faults and under all the disadvantages of their situation, yet command the respect of every one but an English money-monger; proud, too, because thus I was placed in a position to save the English people from the growing contempt which on the Continent has been the necessary consequence of the brutally selfish policy and general behaviour of your ruling middle class.

Having, at the same time, ample opportunity to watch the middle

[1] This address appeared (in English) as a preface to the original (1845) German edition of F. Engels, *The Condition of the Working Class in England* (translated and edited by W. O. Henderson and W. H. Chaloner, 1958).

classes, your opponents, I soon came to the conclusion that you are right, perfectly right in expecting no support whatever from them. Their interest is diametrically opposed to yours, though they always will try to maintain the contrary and to make you believe in their most hearty sympathy with your fates. Their doings give them the lie. I hope to have collected more than sufficient evidence of the fact that – be their words what they please – the middle class intend in reality nothing else but to enrich themselves by your labour while they can sell its produce, and to abandon you to starvation as soon as they cannot make a profit by this indirect trade in human flesh. What have they done to prove their professed good-will towards you? Have they ever paid any serious attention to your grievances? Have they done more than paying the expenses of half a dozen commissioners of enquiry, whose voluminous reports are damned to everlasting slumber among heaps of waste paper on the shelves of the Home Office? Have they even done as much as to compile from those rotting blue-books a single readable book from which everybody might easily get some information on the condition of "free born Britons"? Not they indeed, those are things they do not like to speak of – they have left it to a foreigner to inform the civilised world of the degraded situation you have to live in.

A foreigner to *them*, not to *you*, I hope. Though my English may not be pure, yet, I hope you will find it *plain* English. No working man in England – nor in France either, by-the-bye – ever treated me as a foreigner. With the greatest pleasure I observed you to be free from that blasting curse, national prejudice and national pride, which after all means nothing but *wholesale selfishness*. I observed you to sympathise with everyone who earnestly applies his powers to human progress – may he be an Englishman or not – to admire everything great and good, whether nursed on your native soil or not. I found you to be more than mere *Englishmen*, members of a single, isolated nation, I found you to be MEN, members of the great and universal family of mankind, who know their interest and that of all the human race to be the same. And as such, as members of this family of "One and Indivisible" Mankind, as Human Beings in the most emphatical meaning of the word, as such I, and many others on the Continent, hail your progress in every direction and wish you speedy success. Go on then, as you have done hitherto. Much remains to be undergone; be firm, be undaunted – your success is certain, and no step you will have to take on your onward march will be lost to our common cause, the cause of Humanity!

Barmen (Rhenish Prussia) Friedrich Engels
March 15, 1845.

II

REVIEW OF FRIEDRICH ENGELS, *THE CONDITION OF THE WORKING CLASS IN ENGLAND,* 1845[1]

No one denies the existence of working class poverty and distress and this is obviously one of the gravest problems to be faced in our present turbulent age. Today every government tries to check the growth and to ameliorate the evil consequences of this distress. If these efforts are to achieve success it is of vital importance that the causes and nature of social distress should be examined, particularly when it occurs in an acute form. England undoubtedly possesses the largest industrial working class and we must examine conditions there in order to appreciate the obstacles to be surmounted if a country is to achieve power and success without suffering the social evils and dangers that have afflicted the British nation. The history of events in England is for us Germans a text-book of practical experience in which we can study the growth of poverty and the degradation of the proletariat. The seeds of these evils – their fundamental causes – already exist in Germany. Fortunately our social structure rests upon a broader basis than that of England and the strong sense of social responsibility of our governments provides a stronger defence against the evil of poverty than exists in England. Nevertheless the danger is there and so the causes of social distress should be thoroughly examined.

One of our contributors recently asserted that because the aristocracy has gained complete control over the state in England it must accept responsibility for the distress that exists among the lower classes. He also argued that – owing to the industrial revolution – the English proletariat, deprived of all landed property, was bound to sink into a condition of poverty. There is a grain of truth in this even though it may be an over-simplification. The growth of the industrial proletariat always appears to be associated with

[1] *Allgemeine Preussische Zeitung,* October 31, November 1 and 7, 1845 reprinted in J. Kuczynski, *Die Geschichte der Lage der Arbeiter unter dem Kapitalismus,* Vol. 8, pp. 170–85 and in C. Jantke and D. Hilger, *Die Eigentumlosen* (1965), pp. 406–25.

the progress – still incomplete – of the modern world. The dissolution of the medieval economy and the general changes that have taken place with regard to the possession of land have meant that both the ownership of property and the exercise of a trade are much less restricted now than they were in former times. Not only in England but also on the Continent former serfs have secured their freedom. At the same time, however, they have lost the protection of a feudal lord that they once enjoyed and they have sunk into the position of a working class which owns no land or other property. Where the feudal system has been most completely abolished and where property and labour have been completely freed from all restrictions – that is where the most grievous social evils exist. This is what has happened in England. The English nobles, firmly established as great landlords, have monopolised both the government of the country and the real power in society. They have made it impossible for property to be shared by other classes in society. If one looks at the influence of the economic changes that have occurred in the present century from this point of view it becomes clear that the aristocracy has a responsibility for the distress of the English proletariat since the industrial revolution has taken place within the framework of an aristocratic constitution.

Friedrich Engels, in the book which we are reviewing, considers the main cause of the origin of the English proletariat to be what we regard as only the means by which this class has developed. By adopting this false approach Engels ignores the sound principles of social theory. Engels states that the modern proletariat arose in the second half of the eighteenth century when the invention of the steam engines and new cotton machines gave the impetus to an industrial revolution – a revolution "which at the same time transformed the entire bourgeois society whose importance in world history is only now beginning to be recognised". Thus Engels believes that the origins of the modern proletariat are to be sought in the inventions of new machines. But this was an event which was only important in the history of technology. It could become of social significance only within a certain definite legal framework. Because he starts from a false principle Engels makes erroneous assumptions and reaches erroneous conclusions when he deals with the more fundamental causes of social evils in an industrial society and with the methods that should be adopted to remove those evils. The author appears to be a young man in a hurry and he has used the state of affairs in England – and the future consequences of this state of affairs – to support the well known morbid principles advocated by socialists today. We believe, on the contrary, that the origins of the distress of the modern workers are to be found in the early beginnings of the development of our present society. We believe that this distress can be removed in a state governed by strong sound monarchical principles. This can be done by exploiting the freedom both of capital and of labour. Consequently we regard Engels's discussion of the origin of the modern proletariat and the methods by which present day social evils should be removed as the least satisfactory part of his book. And in examining Engels's work in more detail we shall not be much concerned with his views on this matter. We shall be dealing with the main part of Engels's book which gives a full account of the gradual growth and the present situation of the English workers. This brief but clear and – above all – comprehensive survey is worthy of praise. We have not seen any other book which gives the reader so clear and so full an account of the subject.

In his historical introduction Engels describes in outline the growth of the modern English factory workers (and their families) and he discusses their present economic and social condition. Formerly the ancestors of most of the factory operatives of today were domestic textile workers who led an uneventful existence in villages which were fairly close to large towns. They combined spinning and weaving with the cultivation of smallholdings. In those days cloth was sold mainly in the home market. As yet there was no cut-throat competition between manufacturers – this being brought about later by the struggle for overseas markets – and there were no drastic reductions in wages. Moreover, as the textile workers lived in isolation in the country districts they did not compete seriously among themselves. These workers were able to rent smallholdings and they enjoyed a standard of life superior to that of the proletariat. The daily routine and the outlook of these early English industrial workers was similar to that of some German workers today. They led a quiet and uneventful existence and they did not experience any drastic changes in their way of life or standard of living.

The stability of this society was first shaken in 1764 when James Hargreaves of Standhill near Blackburn in north Lancashire, invented the jenny which enabled a spinner to operate from 16 to 18 spindles. Before this invention the ratio of spinners to weavers had been three to one and there was normally always a shortage of yarn. But now the weavers were unable to cope with all the available yarn while at the same time there was an increased demand for cloth owing to the fall in its price. So there was a shortage of weavers and their piece-work rates increased substantially. In these circumstances the income of the weavers rose so that they gradually gave up cultivating their smallholdings. In time the peasant-weavers disappeared and became simply weavers who were dependent upon wages and could therefore be classed as members of the proletariat. Hitherto, as far as possible, spinning and weaving had taken place under one roof. Now, however, it required as much strength to operate a jenny as a loom so that men turned to spinning and supported their families by this work. And sometimes women ceased to use their old obsolete spinning wheels and they and their families lived on the earnings of the weaver. The machine which originated the development of the industrial proletariat also stimulated the growth of the agricultural proletariat. There grew up a class of large tenant farmers who cultivated from 50 to 200 Morgen of land abandoned by the peasant-weavers. These farmers worked the land so efficiently that they forced the yeomen to sell their holdings and to swell the ranks of the new wage-earning industrial and agricultural proletariat. Improvements continued to be made in both industry and agriculture. After the jenny came Arkwright's spinning machine (throstle) of 1767, Samuel Crompton's mule of 1785 (combining the jenny with the throstle), and Cartwright's power loom of 1804 which enabled human energy to be replaced by a natural force. Steam engines now drove more and more machines while new processes were invented which involved linking the operations of various machines. Almost everywhere the machine triumphed over the old domestic craftsman.

Engels describes this continuous triumph of machinery over the domestic craftsman in England in various industries – such as cotton, wool, linen, silk, lace, hosiery, bleaching, calico printing, coal, iron and pottery – and also in agriculture. This led to an incredible growth of population and national wealth as well as a complete transformation of the English countryside. We are told that 60 or 80 years ago England was still a country – like all others – with small towns, a few simple branches of manufacture, and a relatively large but widely dispersed agricultural population. Now England has become a country like no other in the world – a country with a capital of two and a half million inhabitants, with huge factory towns, with an industry which supplies the whole world with manufactured products. It is a country which makes practically everything with the most complex machinery. It is densely populated and its people are industrious and intelligent. Two thirds of the English people are engaged in industrial occupations. And the industrial proletariat is a new social class, which might be described as a new nation with customs and needs of its own. It differs completely from any class which has existed in the past. Britain's great industrial and commercial cities have arisen as if by magic. At least three quarters of the people who live in them are workers. Only petty traders and a few surviving craftsmen make up the lower middle class in these cities. The new type of industry became important only when machines replaced tools and factories replaced workshops. While the former middle class workers – the domestic craftsmen – became wage earning factory workers, the former great merchants became the owners of great industrial establishments. The lower middle classes were pushed aside so that society came to be divided simply into capitalists and workers. And this occurred not only in large-scale industry but also in the old domestic crafts and in commerce. Master craftsmen and their journeymen and apprentices were replaced by wealthy capitalists and by workers who could not rise out of the class in which they found themselves. Manufactured products were made in factories and not in domestic workshops. The principle of the division of labour was strictly applied. Small master could no longer compete with large factories and they were eventually engulfed by the new proletariat. At the same time the disappearance of domestic crafts and the destruction of the lower middle class made it impossible for the workers to aim at improving their status or to aim at rising into the middle class. Formerly it had always been possible for a craftsman to establish himself as an independent master and eventually to employ journeymen and apprentices himself. But now the master has been displaced by the factory owners. A large amount of capital is needed to establish a factory. Consequently the workers – who once had the chance of rising to middle class status as master craftsmen – have now become virtually imprisoned in the straightjacket of a social class from which there is no escape. From the day of his birth a member of the proletariat has no future except as an industrial worker. And this has led the workers to become united in a single independent social class. It is an important class which defends its economic interests through its own political movement. Engels has set himself the task of describing the present condition of this class.

By equating the growth of the proletariat with the establishment of the factory system Engels is arguing from false premises without appreciating the true state of affairs and so he inevitably reaches erroneous conclusions. We have already tried to indicate the real origins of the modern proletariat. We ask ourselves: Why should industry plunge the workers into poverty and distress and turn them into a proletariat? Certainly not because industry, as such, brings distress in its wake. If that were true then industry would be an evil whereas in fact it benefits humanity. The unsatisfactory condition of the workers can be explained by the fact that when modern industry began to grow in England the impact of the new type of economy was felt by a society in which it was already inevitable that the workers would fall upon evil days. It is a law of nature that human beings have the right to expect that if they exercise their talents and work hard they should be able to maintain themselves and their families at a decent standard of living. And this is what actually happens in a healthy society. It is true that the new inventions and the new factories provided people with work but the structure of society – and the political constitution which was in force – denied the workers an adequate standard of living. The English worker was "free" in the sense that he was left to his own devices. He owned no property and he enjoyed no aid from the state. His daily wages simply covered his daily needs. But England is a country with a constitution which not only guarantees the most extreme form of personal liberty but also allows the greediest of human passions to flower unchecked. Moreover a small group of wealthy persons has been able to gain control over all effective political power. It is most unfortunate that this autocratic power has not been checked in any way by the higher authority of the monarchy. In a country with such a constitution the worker is in an utterly helpless situation. On gaining his "freedom" by exchanging his smallholding (which had assured him a modest living) for so-called "free" work in the factory the worker lost his former patron (whose interests had always coincided with his own) and now he has no claims and no rights. In the end he has been forced by grim necessity to work for such low wages that he is virtually engaged in forced labour. He has been left to face his troubles by himself and he has become a stranger in his own country. This has been a scandalous denial of the elementary law of nature by which a worker should expect to earn enough for his modest needs by honest toil. Consequently it is quite clear that it would be wrong to condemn industry as such for the present distress of the proletariat. We should condemn the unsound social conditions which existed at the time when the modern proletariat arose as a separate class. Industry should not be regarded as the fundamental cause of the distressed condition of the factory workers. Industry has merely been the means by which distress has been fostered and aggravated.

We have felt it necessary to state clearly our views concerning the fundamental causes of the rise of the proletariat because this enables us to appreciate the results that have followed from the development of this new social class. This is all the more necessary in view of the fact that Engels considers that the present distress of the workers is due entirely to the expansion of modern industries. Not only does he argue that the English middle classes have been responsible for the wretched condition of the proletariat but – because of the enormity of the social evils of the present day – he actually charges them with "social murder". It is obvious from our point of view that no single class can be made responsible for the distress of the workers. The middle classes have simply adopted a logical and inevitable policy with regard to a situation that they themselves have not brought about.

When describing conditions that exist today Engels has adopted a sensible and comprehensive plan. In order to cover the whole ground he has grouped the proletariat into several sub-divisions since different sections of the workers have reached different stages of economic and social development. The textile operatives were the first to feel the impact of the industrial revolution and their way of life has been changed more than that of other workers. The coalminers and the miners of metal ores come next in this respect and they are followed first by the farmworkers and then by the Irish labourers. Since the whole proletariat has been affected by the same economic and social changes Engels has given his readers a general survey of the entire working class before dealing with particular sections of the proletariat. By doing this he has been able to draw attention to certain special features which have characterised particular groups of workers. The first half of his book is devoted to this broad survey while the second half deals with certain sections of the working class.

Engels considers that one factor which has had a significant influence upon the growth and the present condition of the vast mass of the workers has been the rapid concentration of the population in certain new large industrial cities. Every one of these big towns has its slum – or slums – where the workers suffer great hardships in horribly overcrowded conditions. Engels condemns the "barbarous indifference and selfish harshness" of the capitalists who have allowed the workers to sink into a condition of incredible wretchedness. Throughout England – except for some parts of London – the workers live in the worst houses in the worst quarters of the towns. Their houses are generally constructed in long terraces. The houses are built of brick and are two or three storeys high. The streets in the slums are generally unpaved, bumpy, dirty, full of animal and vegetable refuse, and covered with stagnant pools, yet lacking in sewers or gutters. There is an absence of fresh air owing to the lack of any planned housing developments in urban working class districts. Here people live in hopelessly overcrowded conditions. Sickness is rife owing to the foul air. We cannot follow

Engels through all the slums that he has visited. He first saw the London districts of St Giles, Whitechapel and Bethnal Green where several families are nearly always to be found packed in a single room without furniture or bedding. Then he describes Nottingham, Birmingham, Leeds, Bradford and the wealthy Lancashire towns. Finally he gives an account of Manchester. Woodcuts and a town plan illustrate his detailed description of the greatest centre of manufactures in industrial Britain. Engels tells us about the way of life of the workers – their dwellings, clothes and food – and he paints a dramatic and shattering picture of their physical and moral degradation.

We will give some extracts from his account of Manchester to illustrate Engels's description of the manufacturing districts of Britain. These quotations show how the author – wrongly in our opinion – accuses industry itself of being the root cause of social evils. In fact industry is simply the channel through which social evils are brought to light. Engels paints a grim picture of the badly constructed houses, the filth and the foul air of the Old Town of Manchester. He writes:

> "This, then, is the Old Town of Manchester. On re-reading my description of the Old Town I must admit that, far from having exaggerated anything, I have not written vividly enough to impress the reader with the filth and dilapidation of a district which is quite unfit for human habitation. The shameful lay-out of the Old Town has made it impossible for the wretched inhabitants to enjoy cleanliness, fresh air, and good health. And such a district of at least twenty to thirty thousand inhabitants lies in the very centre of the second city in England, the most important factory town in the world! It is here that one can see how little space human beings need to move about in, how little air – and what air! – they need to breathe in order to exist, and how few of the decencies of civilisation are really necessary in order to survive. It is true that this is the *Old Town* and Manchester people stress this when their attention is drawn to the revolting character of this hell upon earth. But that is no defence. Everything in this district that arouses our disgust and just indignation is of relatively recent origin and belongs to the industrial age. The two or three hundred houses which survive from the earliest period of Manchester's history have long ago been deserted by their original inhabitants. It is only industry which has crammed them full of the hordes of workers who now live there. It is only the modern age which has built over every scrap of ground between these old houses to provide accommodation for the masses who have migrated from the country districts and from Ireland. It is only the industrial age which has made it possible for the owners of these shacks, fit only for the accommodation of cattle, to let them at high rents for human habitations. It is only

modern industry which permits these owners to take advantage of the poverty of the workers to undermine the health of thousands to enrich themselves. Only industry has made it possible for workers who have barely emerged from a state of serfdom to be again treated as chattels and not as human beings. The workers have been caged in dwellings which are so wretched that no one else will live in them, and they actually pay good money for the privilege of seeing these dilapidated hovels fall to pieces about their ears. Industry alone has been responsible for all this and yet this same industry could not flourish except by degrading and exploiting the workers. It is true that this quarter of the town was originally built on a poor site, which offered few prospects for satisfactory development. But have either the landowners or the authorities done anything to improve matters when new buildings were erected? Far from adopting any such policy those responsible for recent developments have built houses in every conceivable nook and cranny. Even small passages which were not absolutely necessary have been built over and stopped up. The value of the land rose with the expansion of industry. The more the land rose in value the more furious became the search for new building sites. The health and comfort of the inhabitants were totally ignored, as a result of the determination of landlords to pocket the maximum profit. No hovel is so wretched but it will find a worker to rent it because he is too poor to pay for better accommodation."[2]

Engels concludes his chapter on the working class districts of the industrial towns with the following observations:

"The working classes of the great cities exhibit a variety of standards of living. In favourable circumstances some of them enjoy, at least temporarily, a modest prosperity. Sometimes high wages can be earned, particularly for the hardest kinds of physical labour, and this provides reasonable living accommodation and a respite from the consumption of poor quality food. This standard of living, poor it may seem to the middle classes, is prized by the worker, who has almost certainly known the real meaning of want. In bad times, however, the unlucky worker may sink into the deepest poverty, actually culminating in homelessness and death from starvation. On the average the condition of the worker approximates much more closely to the worst we have described than to the best. The various standards of living cannot be equated with any particular group of workers. It is never possible to single out any particular group of workers as permanently enjoying a satisfactory standard of living. While it is true that particular groups of workers have an advantage over their fellows and are relatively well off, nevertheless the condition of all workers is liable to fluctuate so violently that every single worker is faced with the possibility of

[2] F. Engels, *The Condition of the Working Class in England* (translated and edited by W. O. Henderson and W. H. Chaloner, 1958), pp. 63–4.

> passing through the stages that lead from relative comfort to extreme poverty and even death from starvation. Practically every English worker can recall considerable vicissitudes in his own personal fortunes. . . ."[3]

In a separate chapter Engels suggests that competition is both the immediate cause of this state of affairs and the most powerful factor influencing its development. He argues that in a modern middle class society there is a "war of all against all" – a struggle between different social classes and also a struggle between individuals in the same social group. The workers compete one against the other. Similarly the members of the middle classes also compete one against the other. The weaver operating a power loom competes with the weaver operating a hand loom. The hand loom weavers compete among themselves, the badly paid or unemployed endeavouring to oust their better paid employed rivals. The conflict between the workers themselves is the darkest aspect of the present condition of the proletariat and it is the sharpest weapon which the middle classes can wield against the working class. "This explains the rise of trade unions, which represent an attempt to eliminate such fratricidal conflict between the workers themselves. It explains, too, the fury of the middle classes against trade unions, and their ill-concealed delight at any setback which the unions suffer." If we examine the nature of this competition more closely we shall see that Engels is right when he criticises competition as the immediate cause of the present distress of the workers. This is because such competition – in the form in which it operates in England – has deprived the propertyless and unprotected worker of his status as a human being and has degraded him to the level of an inanimate object, the price of which rises and falls according to the law of supply and demand. It is, however, a mistake to assume that this sort of competition – the competition that completely abolishes freedom of property and freedom of labour – is a necessary condition of industry everywhere in the world. It is true that this has happened in England but it has happened only because of the nature of industrialisation in that country. We repeat our view that in England it is not industry as such but it is the political framework and the social structure of the country which has allowed industrialisation to develop in association with completely unrestricted competition.

By failing to discover the fundamental cause of the conditions that he describes the author has sketched a false background for his account of the English workers. On the other hand Engels gives

[3] *Ibid.*, pp. 86–7.

a very detailed description of the situation as it exists today. He carefully describes the actual consequences of unbridled competition and of the deep moral degradation of the English workers. And he shows how this situation conforms to the doctrines enunciated by the well known economist Adam Smith. There is much that is new and interesting in Engels's discussion of the failure to establish a balance between the competition among the workers themselves and the competition (among the employers) to secure the services of workers. The first (competition among the workers) has always been stronger than the second (competition among the employers for labour) and this has happened despite the continual expansion of industry and the ever increasing demand for labour. Consequently the surplus population of unemployed has sunk into the deepest poverty. Engels believes that this is due to the commercial crises which are an essential feature of modern industry. His arguments on this aspect of the problem suffer, from time to time, by being advanced in a somewhat exaggerated fashion. Engels says that at the present time the production and consumption of goods occurs in an utterly haphazard manner and is undertaken not with the object of satisfying ascertained wants but simply to make a profit. Such a system – with everybody concentrating his attention on making money – inevitably leads to the existence of surpluses on the markets of the world. Thus England supplies many countries with a vast variety of manufactured products. Even though the manufacturer may know what quantities of each product are annually consumed in every country he cannot possibly know what stocks of goods are being held in warehouses and shops abroad. Still less can he be expected to know what quantities of goods his competitors are sending to particular foreign markets. All that he can do is to observe the continual fluctuations in the price of goods and from that he can make an uncertain guess as to the demand for his products abroad and as to the volume of goods held in warehouses abroad. So he sends his goods abroad blindly without really knowing whether they will be sold or not. His exports go out into the blue and what happens then depends more or less upon chance. In the light of even moderately optimistic reports everybody exports what he can and before long the market is glutted. And then sales decline and cash returns fall so that before long the English workers are thrown out of employment.

In the early days of industrialisation these crises were confined to particular branches of trade and to particular markets but as time went on competition exercised a unifying influence so that workers in one branch of manufacture who were unemployed, moved into other branches of industry where the necessary skills could most easily be learned. Similarly goods which were superfluous in one market were ruthlessly thrown onto another market. Gradually these crises, which occurred with considerable regularity, came to merge together and now a universal crisis happens every five years – following upon a brief period of boom and general prosperity. When there is a crisis the home market and all the foreign markets are full of English manufactured products which are only being consumed quite slowly. An industrial depression casts its shadow upon all branches of trade. The small manufacturers and merchants – those who cannot manage without quick cash payments for their goods – go bankrupt. The larger manufacturers and traders stop making goods when the crisis is at its height. They close their factories or they work "short time" – that is to say their factories are open only for half a day instead of a full day. The wages of the factory workers fall because of the lack of profitable business, the reduction in hours of work, and the competition from those workers who are unemployed. The whole proletariat suffers severe distress. Small savings are quickly spent. Welfare organisations are overwhelmed with applications for help. The poor rates are doubled – even trebled – without solving the problem. The number of workers who are actually starving increases and all of sudden a terrifying number of the "surplus population" appear on the scene.

This situation lasts for a time and people survive as best they can – or they fail to survive. And then gradually there is an improvement. The goods which have been stored are consumed. Owing to the depression some time elapses before the gaps can be filled. Eventually rising prices and optimistic reports on the state of the market encourage a resumption of industrial production. The markets are generally far distant from the factories and while the first new supplies are on their way the demand continues to grow. The first goods to arrive are snapped up quickly since traders anticipate still higher prices for their next consignments. Then speculators step in and buy up particular types of goods, expecting to make large profits when they eventually unload them onto the market. This speculation drives prices up still further so that other traders are encouraged to place fresh orders. When news of these events reaches England the manufacturers begin to expand their output. New factories are built and everything is done to take full advantage of favourable trading conditions. Once more the speculators take a hand – with the same results as those which occurred in the foreign markets. Prices rise and goods are stored in the hope that prices will rise still further in the future. The industrial economy is working to full capacity. Then the fly by night speculators who trade with fictitious capital and survive by living on credit, appear on the scene. They are ruined if they cannot sell their goods at once. These speculators fling themselves into the universal rush for quick profits. Their unbridled passion for money increases the feverish pace of trade. There is a mad increase in prices and output and a wild race for profits in which even the coolest and most experienced traders are involved. In the factories the workers are hammering, spinning and weaving as if every man, woman and child in the world needed more goods – as if thousands of millions of new consumers had been discovered on the moon. A time comes when the fly by night speculators in the consuming countries – who need cash urgently – begin to sell goods at less than the prevailing market price. Other traders follow suit. Then prices topple and the speculators throw all their goods onto the market. Now the market is in disorder; credit collapses; one trading house after another stops payment; one bankruptcy follows another. People realise that there are three times as many goods chasing customers as are required. The news reaches England where, in the meantime, production has gone ahead by leaps and bounds. Here too there is a panic. Bankruptcies abroad lead to bankruptcies in England. There is a slump and many trading houses take fright and throw all their goods onto the market. This simply makes matters worse. And now the crisis goes through the same phases as the one before until eventually the slump is followed by another boom. That is the trade cycle – boom, slump, boom, slump – which goes on for ever (every five years) as far as English industry is concerned.

Engels describes the crisis of 1842 from the point of view of its effects upon the condition and growth of the "surplus population". He shows how – in Stockport for example – whole streets stood empty because the poor rates levied on the houses amounted to an addition of forty per cent to the rents paid by householders. In Bolton the rateable value sank from an average of £86,000 to £36,000 in 1842 while 14,000 persons – twenty per cent of the entire population – were on poor relief. Engels also draws attention to another aspect of the competition among the workers themselves in England. This is the "Irish immigration" which has had deleterious consequences for the English workers. Engels examines the social consequences of the commercial crisis from the evidence of official reports. He shows how they affect the physical and moral condition of the workers. This topic has been discussed so often that it will not be necessary for us to go over the same ground again here.

Having given a general account of the condition of the English workers Engels goes on to describe the particular branches of industry. In this section he again examines the factors which he regards as causes of distress among the industrial workers. We have seen that Engels has ascribed the social evils of modern industrial society to the invention of new machines and we have made clear our own view that it is only because of the existence of certain social and political circumstances in England that the new machines – and other factors – have had the results which they have had. But in this part of his book Engels himself has to admit that "the improvement of machinery would have had happy results if an orderly state of society had existed". But he immediately adds that at present "owing to the war of all against all it is particular individuals who secure for themselves the advantages of new machinery and at the same time deprive the vast majority of the people of the opportunity to maintain a decent standard of living." Here Engels appears to imply that the capitalists – those who possess property – have quite deliberately oppressed the workers. He assumes that only the fall of the capitalists can release the workers from their servitude. If Engels had examined the facts calmly he would surely have seen that fundamental social and political factors have inevitably led to the distress of the workers – and not the personal desires and deliberate policy of a particular group of individuals. This neglect of a wider point of view is in fact the most serious criticism to be made of Engels's book. It is a weakness which has led Engels to attack the whole English bourgeoisie class with unrestrained violence. Since Engels is blind to the real causes of the present state of affairs, he is even more blind to the developments that are likely to occur in the future. Engels is dealing in pure fantasy when he paints a grim picture of the none too distant future and dreams of a frightful revolution of the English workers. We refrain from discussing this matter in detail. It is not given to man to look into the future and in any case Engels's prophecies rest upon an insecure foundation. We turn instead to Engels's detailed description of various branches of English industry.

The most important branches of manufacture which Engels examines are those which are organised on a factory basis and are covered by the Factory Acts. This law regulates the hours of work in all establishments in which wool, silk, cotton and flax are spun and woven by power – water or steam – machinery. This includes the most important parts of English industry. The textile workers have the longest history. They are the most numerous, the most intelligent, the most energetic – but also the most restless – of the English workers. They are at the head of the trade union movement while their employers are at the head of the "bourgeois agitation" – the Anti-Corn Law League. Owing to the growth of the factory system and the invention of new machines the textile workers have been torn from their former way of life. Of all the English workers they are the ones who have been most affected by the factory system. In Manchester, for example, in 35 factories only 1,060 additional mule spinners have secured jobs since 1841 although in the same period the number of spindles has increased by 99,239. In five factories there are no more spinners because so-called self-actors have been introduced. The improvements in machinery which have occurred since 1841 – particularly the doubling of the rows of spindles – have reduced the number of spinners in employment by half and even more than half. In one factory, which until recently employed 80 spinners, there are now only 20 at work. The others have either lost their jobs or have to perform children's tasks at children's pay. In Stockport the number of spinners has declined from 800 in 1835 to 140 in 1843 although in this period there was a considerable expansion in cotton spinning in this town. Engels exaggerates somewhat the evil consequences for the workers of this expansion of industry. It should be remembered that improvements in the factories lead to reduced prices and increased consumption – followed by new opportunities for employment by the workers. Nevertheless some of Engels's conclusions are correct as when he draws attention to a general decline in conditions of work in the factories and to the very serious condition of the female operatives. In the spinning mills the throstles are operated only by women and children while the mules have only one adult male spinner – and even he is not needed if self actors are installed. The tying up of the threads is done by piecers who are generally women and children, occasionally by youths aged between eighteen and twenty, and very occasionally by an old spinner who has lost his former job. Here improvements in machinery has made it possible to replace men by women and children. The wage structure has completely changed. According to Horner, a Factory Inspector, there are hundreds of young men aged from twenty to thirty years who are employed as piecers (or who do other work) and who earn no more than eight or nine shillings a week. In the same factory children aged 13 earn 5s and young girls aged between 16 and 20 earn from 10s to 12s a week. The power looms are generally operated by weavers aged between 15 and 20 and a few older men are also employed. In general, however, these weavers lose their jobs when they reach the age of 21. In 1839 there were 419,560 factory workers in Britain and 129,887 – or nearly half of them – were under the age of 18. There were 242,296 female workers of whom 112,191 were under the age of 18. Adult males therefore represented only 23 per cent – or less than one quarter – of the total labour force.

The drawbacks of such a system are to be seen in the dissolution of the family, the degradation of the female sex, and the physical weakening of children owing to overwork. Engels produces ample evidence to prove these three aspects of industrialisation in England. With regard to the first point – the dissolution of the family – Engels shows that factory work gives a married woman no time to look after her children or to attend to her household duties. The children grow up like wild creatures. They may be looked after by other women who get a shilling or sixpence a week for doing so or they may be left in an empty house and suffer the most grievous harm from accidents. The records of the Manchester coroners show that in nine months there were 69 fatal accidents from burning, 56 cases of drowning, 23 deaths from falls, and 77 other fatal accidents in the home. It is obvious that the high infantile mortality rate is due to the fact that mothers of infants and young children go out to work. It often happens that a woman returns to work only three or four days after giving birth to a child and of course the baby is left at home. Engels rightly indicates the cause of this evil but he does not show that there is a remedy for this state of affairs. He argues that female labour necessarily causes the family to break up. And in the present state of society – which is based upon family life – this dissolution of the family demoralises both the parents and the children. A woman who has no time to look after her child, a woman who does not give her infant the normal loving attention that one expects from a mother, a woman who hardly ever sees her child – such a woman cannot be a real mother to her child. Inevitably she adopts an attitude of indifference towards the child; she does not look after the child or treat it with affection; she treats it as if it were a strange child. And children who are brought up in this way are later incapable of appreciating family life. When they themselves have children they cannot bring them up properly because they have known only an isolated sort of existence. All this leads to a universal decline in family life among the workers. Another factor influencing the decline of the family is child labour, especially when children earn more than is required to keep them. In such cases the children feel emancipated at an early age and treat their parent's home as if it were a lodging house which – and this is no infrequent occurrence – they can exchange for another if they feel like it. Female labour frequently not merely destroys family life but it turns family life upside down. The wife supports the family while the husband stays at home to look after the children and to do the cooking and cleaning. In Manchester alone there are several hundred men who are condemned to domestic duties.

The second disadvantage of this system of work is that it ruins the female sex. The next generation of women is ignorant of domestic work but soon learns all sorts of undesirable accomplishments. A witness from Leicester stated that he would rather see his daughters begging in the streets than working in a factory. Most Leicester prostitutes have learned their trade in a factory. A witness from Manchester went so far as to allege that three quarters of the factory girls aged between 14 and 20 were not virgins.

By overworking children in factories the physical condition of the next generation of workers is being endangered. This has been shown in various official enquiries. The Apprentices Bill of 1802 was the first of various enactments which have somewhat curbed the worst abuses of child labour. Children now do not start to work until they are 8 or 9 years of age but a day's work of 14 to 16 hours is a scandalous cruelty to inflict upon children of such tender years. The great parliamentary enquiry of 1833 showed that children who had worked long hours in factories were physically weakened and suffered from injuries to the spine and limbs. Factory workers are considered to be old men when they reach the age of 40 or – at the most – 45 and they are then not considered to be capable of doing a normal day's work. They look 10 or 15 years older than they really are. Engels states that women who work in factories suffer from many maladies and find child-bearing very difficult. He examines various factory occupations – and the illnesses associated with them – and he shows that very little has been done to remedy the situation. The author ends this chapter with a bitter attack upon the English factory owners.

The facts that Engels gives are taken from the official report of 1834 – an enquiry set up by the factory owners themselves. Long before this date the evils of the factory system had been enumerated and discussed. But the factory owners and their supporters had denied the existence of these evils. Then in 1831 Michael Sadler, supported by the Tories, secured the appointment of a parliamentary committee to look into the factory system. Its report in the following year led to a great public outcry. In view of this report the factory owners themselves pressed for a more thorough enquiry and this led to the production of a new report in 1834 which was followed by the passing of a new Factory Act in the same year. This Act forbade the employment of children under the age of nine in factories. Children aged between 9 and 13 were not allowed to work for more than 9 hours per day and 48 hours per week. Young persons aged between 14 and 18 were not allowed to work for more than 12 hours per day or 68 hours per week. A minimum break for meals – one and a half hours per day – was laid down. Night work was again forbidden for all young people under the age of 18. At the same time it was laid down that all factory children under the age of 14 were to attend school for two hours a day. A factory owner was liable to be punished if he employed children without a certificate of age from the factory doctor or without a school attendance certificate from a schoolteacher. Factory doctors or factory inspectors were appointed who had the right to enter a factory at any time. They could take evidence from workers on oath and could enforce the law by applying to the magistrates. This legislation led to the virtual disappearance of at any rate some of the worst social evils in the factories. Only weak workers were now likely to be crippled by factory work and there was less obvious evidence of the evil physical effects of factory labour. But later factory reports show that some evils remain – swollen foot-joints, weaknesses in the legs, hips and spine, varicose veins, ulcers, sickness, loss of appetite, digestive complaints, hypochondria and so forth. To some extent the factory owners have evaded the law. As early as 1839 an agitation in favour of a Ten Hour Day was started among the factory workers and since 1841 the present Tory government has again turned its attention to the question of factory legislation. But the middle classes who are in a very strong position from a political point of view, have (with the support of the Church) checked any further factory legislation. Sir James Graham's Bill of 1843 attempted to improve the situation with regard to the education of factory children. But his Bill had to be dropped owing to opposition from the Whigs (the factory owners' party) and from the Dissenters who were jealous of the influence of the Established Church and launched a great campaign against the Bill. On March 19, 1844 a ten hours clause was accepted by the House of Commons but this decision was reversed when the ministry threatened to resign. As Engels observes, this has led the workers to criticise the existing system of parliamentary representation.

It would take too long for us to examine the other branches of manufacture and to follow Engels in his description of the evils from which many workers suffer – such as stocking knitters, lace workers, calico printers, velvet cutters, silk weavers, metal workers, machine builders, glass makers, artisans and finally the London milliners and seamstresses. We refer our readers to Engels's description of the condition of these workers. Engels also discusses two other evils – the truck system and the cottage system both of which have led to discontent among the workers. The truck system forces the worker to accept wages in the form of goods instead of cash while the cottage system forces him to rent a house from his employer. Engels next examines the trade union and the Chartist movements, the conditions under which miners and farm labourers work, and – finally – the relations between the middle classes and the proletariat. These topics are discussed less thoroughly and his examination of them is marred by his peculiar socialist views. This part of the book is less interesting than the earlier chapters. So we will pass them by. We conclude by quoting an interesting – if biased – comparison which the author makes between the English proletariat of the present day and the English serf of 1145:

> "Let us compare the situation of the free-born Englishman in 1845 with that of the Saxon serf under the whip of the Norman baron in 1145. The serf was *adscriptus gebae*, that is, he was bound to the soil. The free factory worker is tied in the same way by the cottage system. The medieval lord of the manor exacted the *jus primae noctis* from his serfs. The modern factory owner goes much further and demands the right on any night. The serf was unable to acquire any property of his own. His lord could seize anything which he had acquired. The free factory worker also owns no property. He is not in a position to acquire property owing to the pressure of competition. The factory owner goes further than the Norman baron. By means of the truck system, he actually controls so personal a part of the life of the worker as his daily housekeeping. In medieval times the relations between lord and serf were regulated by traditions and by laws which were observed because they conformed with the customs of the time. Today, on the other hand, although the relations between master and man are on a legal basis, the law is in fact not carried out because it does not conform either to the interests or the traditions of the masters. In medieval times the lord of the manor could not eject the serf from his holding. Serf and land were indissolubly linked. The lord could not sell the serf because in practice he could not sell the land, since he held his land not in freehold tenure, but as a fief from the Crown. Today the middle classes force the worker to sell himself. The medieval serf was tied to the land on which he was born, while the modern worker is tied to the money that he must have to acquire the necessaries of life. Both are the slaves of material objects. The serf's livelihood was guaranteed by the existence of feudalism, in which everyone had his allotted place in society. The modern free worker has no similar guarantee because he is only certain of a place in society when the middle classes require his services. On the other hand, when the bourgeoisie has no use for the worker they simply ignore him and pretend that he does not exist. The serf risked his life in the service of his master in time of war, while the modern factory worker risks his life for his master in times of peace. The feudal lord was a barbarian who treated his serfs as beasts of burden. The modern civilised factory owner treats his workers as

if they were machines. In short there is little to choose between the position of the medieval serf and the free worker of the present day. If anything, the situation of the factory operative is less enviable than that of the medieval serf. Slavery has been the lot of both the serf and the factory worker. While in medieval times serfdom was an honourable status, undisguised and openly admitted, the slavery of the working classes today is hypocritically and cunningly disguised from themselves and the public. It is a far worse type of slavery than medieval serfdom. The Tory humanitarians were justified in referring to the factory operatives as 'white slaves'."[4]

[4] F. Engels, *The Condition of the Working Class in England* (translated and edited by W. O. Henderson and W. H. Chaloner, 1958), pp. 207–8.

III

INTRODUCTION TO THE COMMUNIST CIRCULAR AGAINST HERMANN KRIEGE, MAY 11, 1846[1]

A meeting was held which was attended by the communists Engels, Gigot, Heilberg, Marx, Seiler, Weitling, von Westphalen and Wolf. The policy of the *Volkstribun*, a German language newspaper edited in New York by Hermann Kriege was discussed and certain resolutions were passed, only Weitling voting against their adoption. The reasons why the resolutions were passed are given in the Circular. The resolutions are as follows:

1. The policy advocated by editor Hermann Kriege in the *Volkstribun* is not a communist policy.
2. The childish and pompous way in which Kriege advocates this policy seriously compromises the communist party not only in the United States but in Europe as well inasmuch as Kriege is regarded as the literary representative of German communism in New York.
3. If the fantastic soulful raptures in which Kriege indulges in New York and calls "communism" were accepted by the workers there it would lead to their complete demoralisation.
4. These resolutions and the justification for them will be circularised among communists in Germany, France and England.
5. A copy of the resolutions and the justification for them will be sent to the *Volkstribun* with the demand that they should be published in the next number of the journal.

Brussels — Engels, Philippe Gigot, Louis Heilberg,
May 11, 1846 — K. Marx, Seiler, von Westphalen, Wolf

[1] G. Winkler (ed.), *Dokumente zur Geschichte des Bundes der Kommunisten* (1957), p. 70.

IV

LETTER TO G. A. KÖTTGEN OF ELBERFELD[1]

Brussels, June 15, 1846

To G. A. Köttgen for wider circulation.

We hasten to reply to your letter which we received a few days ago.

We entirely agree with your opinion that the German communists should emerge from isolation and should be united by a regular mutual exchange of ideas. We too appreciate the value of reading circles and discussion groups. The communists should clearly understand that their progress will be limited unless they meet regularly to discuss communist principles. We also agree that cheap, readable leaflets and pamphlets putting forward the communist point of view should be published. The organisation of study groups and the printing of pamphlets should be regarded as matters of immediate urgency. You will also appreciate the need to secure regular financial contributions from supporters of the communist movement. But we do not agree with your suggestion that your contributions should be used to finance communist writers and enable them to enjoy lives of easy comfort. We think that the contributions should be used only to print cheap communist leaflets and pamphlets and to defray the cost of correspondence within Germany and abroad. It will be necessary to fix a minimum monthly contribution so that the organisers will always know exactly how much money they can afford to spend in promoting the objects of the communist movement. Please send us a list of the names of the members of your communist group so that we may know – as you know from us – with whom we are dealing. Please let us know the rate of your monthly subscriptions (designated for general expenditure) since it is desirable to decide speedily on the publication of some popular pamphlets.

You really have some odd ideas about the Bundestag, the King of Prussia, the estates and so on. A memorandum would achieve

[1] G. Winkler (ed.), *Dokumente zur Geschichte des Bundes der Kommunisten* (1957), pp. 67–9.

its purpose only if Germany had a strong, well organised communist party but this is not the case. A petition would be effective only if it were a threat supported by a mass of compact organised public support. All that you can do – provided that the circumstances in your district are favourable – is to organise an imposing petition signed by *a great many* workers.

We do not think that the time is ripe for holding a communist conference. Only when Germany is covered with a network of communist groups with adequate financial reserves would it be possible for representatives from these groups to hold a congress with any chance of success. This will not be possible before next year. Until it is possible to hold a conference the only means by which communists can keep in touch with each other will be by regular correspondence.

We are already in correspondence from time to time with communists in England and France and also with German communists living abroad. Whenever we receive any news about the communists movements in England and France we will pass on the information to you. All other news will also be forwarded to you.

Please give us a *safe* address to which we can write. Do not put the full name (G. A. Köttgen for example) on the seal. Indicate both the writer and the recipient. When you write to us please use the following absolutely safe address – Monsieur Philippe Gigot, 8 rue de Bodembroek, Brussels.

K. Marx, F. Engels, Philippe Gigot, F. Wolf(f)

Postscript

Weerth sends his greetings. He is in Amiens just now.

If you do go ahead with your proposed petition it would simply mean that the communist party would openly proclaim how weak it is at the moment. And it would let the government know the names of the people whom it should keep an eye on in the future. Unless you can get up a workers' petition with at least 500 signatures it would be better to follow the example of the middle classes in Trier and petition in favour of a graduated tax on property. If the bourgeoisie in your district refuse to support you then you should support them – for the time being – in their public demonstrations. You should act like jesuits and give up your ideas of German honour, candour and respectability. You should support the middle class petitions in favour of freedom of the press, a constitution and so on. When these middle class aims have been achieved the ground will have been prepared for communist propaganda. Then we shall have greater opportunities to advance our cause since the antagonism between the middle classes and the workers will have been accentuated. From a party point of view you should support anything which will be to our advantage eventually and you must not be deterred by any boring moral scruples.

In addition you should appoint a permanent committee to carry out your correspondence. This committee should meet regularly and should draft and discuss all letters to be sent to us. You should choose the person whom you consider best fitted for the task to draft the letters. Avoid personal considerations when doing this for that would ruin everything. You must of course let us know the names of the members of the committee responsible for your correspondence.

Greetings from the signatories overleaf.

V

ADDRESS OF THE GERMAN DEMOCRATIC COMMUNISTS OF BRUSSELS TO MR FEARGUS O'CONNOR, 1846[1]

Sir,

We embrace the occasion of your splendid success at the Nottingham election to congratulate you and through you the English Chartists on this signal victory. We consider that the defeat of a Free Trade minister at the show of hands by an enormous Chartist majority, and at the very time, too, when Free Trade principles are triumphant in the Legislature, we consider this, Sir, as a sign that the working classes in England are very well aware of the position they have to take after the triumph of Free Trade. We conclude from this fact that they know very well that now, when the middle classes have carried their chief measure, when they have only to replace the present weak go-between ministry, in order to be the acknowledged ruling class of your country, that now the great struggle of capital and labour, of bourgeois and proletarian, must come to a decision. The ground is now cleared by the retreat of the landed aristocracy from the contest; middle class and working class are the only classes betwixt whom there can be a possible struggle. The contending parties have their respective battle cries forced upon them by their interests and mutual position – the middle classes: "extension of commerce by any means whatsoever, and a ministry of Lancashire cotton lords to carry this out"; the working class: "a democratic reconstruction of the Constitution upon the basis of the People's Charter" by which the working class will become the ruling class of England. We rejoice to see the English working men fully aware of this altered state of affairs; of the new period Chartist agitation has entered of late; with the final defeat of the third party (the aristocracy); of the prominent position which Chartism henceforth will and must occupy, in spite of the "conspiracy of silence" of the middle class press; and finally of the new task, which by these new circumstances has

[1] *Northern Star*, July 25, 1846.

devolved upon them. That they are quite aware of this task is proved by their intention to go to the poll at the next general election.

We have to congratulate you, Sir, in particular upon your brilliant speech at the Nottingham election, and the striking delineation given in it of the contrast between working class democracy and middle class liberalism.

We congratulate you besides on the unanimous vote of confidence in you, spontaneously passed by the whole Chartist body on the occasion of Thomas Cooper, the would-be respectable's calumnies. The Chartist party cannot but profit by the exclusion of such disguised bourgeois, who, while they show off with the name of Chartist for popularity's sake, strive to insinuate themselves into the favour of the middle classes by personal flattery of their literary representatives (such as the Countess of Blessington, Charles Dickens, D. Jerrold and other "friends" of Cooper) and by propounding such base and infamous old women's doctrines as that of "non-resistance".

Lastly, Sir, we have to thank you and your coadjutors for the noble and enlightened manner in which the *Northern Star* is conducted. We hesitate not a moment in declaring that the *Star* is the only English newspaper (save perhaps the *People's Journal* which we know from the *Star* only) which knows the real state of parties in England; which is really and essentially democratic; which is free from national and religious prejudices; which sympathises with the democrats and working men (now-a-days the two are about the same) all over the world; which in all these points speaks the mind of the English working class, and therefore is the only English paper worth reading for the continental democrats. We hereby declare that we shall do everything in our power to extend the circulation of the *Northern Star* on the Continent and to have extracts from it translated in as many continental papers as possible.

We beg to express these sentiments, Sir, as the acknowledged representatives of many of the German communists in Germany, for all their relations with foreign democrats.

For the German Democratic Communists of Brussels
The Committee
Engels, Ph. Gigot, Marx

VI

THE *STATUS QUO* IN GERMANY, 1847[1]

Month by month there is a decline in the standard of socialist writing in Germany. It is becoming more and more restricted to the pathetic effusions of those so-called "true socialists" the sum of whose knowledge is simply a mixture of German philosophy and German bourgeois sentimentality served up with a few poor communist catch-phrases. These scribblers flaunt their ineffectual policy in so obvious a manner that they are able to spout forth their innermost thoughts in spite of the censorship. The fact that the German censor finds virtually nothing objectionable in their effusions is proof enough that the authors belong to the stolid reactionary wing of German literature and have no connection with the progressive and revolutionary wing. These "true Socialists" include not only those who call themselves "socialists" but also most German writers who have adopted the "communist" party label. The latter are, if anything, more miserable specimens than the former.

In these circumstances it goes without saying that these so-called "communists" in no way represent the German Communist Party and do not further its aims. And of course they are not recognised by the Communist Party as its literary representatives. On the contrary these literary hacks represent quite different interests. They defend quite different principles and those are principles to which the Communist Party is utterly opposed.

The "true socialists" – to whom must be added most so-called German "communist" writers – have learned from the French communists that the transition from absolute monarchy to a modern parliamentary system in no way ameliorates the misery of the masses but merely brings to power a new social class – the middle class. Our "true socialists" have also learned from the French communists that this very middle class – because of its control over

[1] Translation from an incomplete manuscript (written in March–April 1847) printed in Karl Marx-Friedrich Engels, Vol. 4, *Geschichte und Politik*, 2 (Fischer Bücherei, 1966), pp. 17–33 and in *Marx-Engels Gesamtausgabe*, Part I, Vol. VI, 1932.

capital – is mainly responsible for the oppression of the workers and is therefore naturally regarded by genuine communists and socialists – the true representatives of the masses – as their deadliest enemy. But the "true socialists" have not taken the trouble to compare the political development of Germany with that of France. Nor have they studied the conditions that actually exist in Germany today – conditions which must influence all future developments in the country. They have simply transferred their very limited knowledge (of France) to Germany without giving the matter very serious consideration. If they had been genuine party members they would have aimed at achieving real practical results and they would have represented the common interest of a definite and united social class. In those circumstances they would at least have seen – as the French opponents of the bourgeoisie from the editors of the *Réforme* newspaper to the ultra-communists have seen – how old Cabet, the acknowledged spokesman of the vast mass of the French workers, attacked the middle classes. And they would have observed that real party members are not content to spend their time writing for the newspapers but actively support political reforms – like proposals for a wider franchise – which are often of *immediate* direct interest to the workers. Real communists do not disdain such political activity. But our "true socialists" are not active party members: they are merely German doctrinaires. They are not interested in practical affairs and real achievements; they only seek eternal truths. The interests which they try to represent are those of "humanity" while the aims which they pursue are limited to the discovery of profound philosophical "truths". Consequently all that they have to do is to bring their new enlightenment into line with their own philosophical consciences and then announce at the top of their voices to all Germany that political progress – that all political activity – is to be condemned. They argue that the middle classes – the most dangerous enemies of society as a whole – should be allowed no respite and that to allow them to have representative parliamentary government would simply permit them to achieve a position of supremacy in society.

For the last seventeen years[2] the French middle class has enjoyed greater power than the bourgeoisie of any other country. Consequently the attacks of the French workers – and of their party leaders and writers – on the bourgeoisie have been attacks upon the ruling class in society. They have been definitely revolutionary attacks upon the existing political system. The extent to which the

[2] Since the July revolution of 1830 when Louis Philippe came to the throne of France.

French middle class realised what was happening has been proved by the countless prosecutions against the press and against all combinations. It has been proved by the banning of meetings and banquets and by the hundreds of shameful actions of the police directed against reformers and communists.

In Germany the situation is quite different. There the middle class, far from having attained power, is the most dangerous enemy of the existing governments. The diversion mounted by the "true socialists" has come at just the right moment for the German governments. Our "true socialists" have not followed the example of the French communists who have suffered imprisonment and exile for fighting the middle classes. In the lukewarm breasts of our German doctrinaires the revolutionary fervour of the French attacks upon the middle classes has dwindled into puny criticisms written in such a way as actually to pass the scrutiny of the censor. So long as our "true socialists" pursue so harmless and lifeless a policy they receive a positive welcome from the German governments as allies against the importunate bourgeoisie. The "true socialists" have actually managed to adapt their revolutionary war-cries so that they can be used to defend the political morass of modern Germany.

The middle classes have long been aware of this reactionary policy of our "true socialists". They have pretended that the attitude of "true socialist" writers reflects the views of German communists as well. Publicly and privately the middle classes have actually accused communists of working hand in glove with governments, civil servants and nobles because the "true socialists" have criticised representative institutions, trial by jury and freedom of the press and have lost no opportunity of denouncing the bourgeoisie.

It is high time that the German communists at long last should repudiate decisively any sort of responsibility for the reactionary policy and activities of the "true socialists". It is high time that the German communists – who clearly support the true aims of the German proletariat – should in no uncertain manner break off relations with this literary clique (for the "true socialists" are no more than a literary clique) which does not know whom it represents. And since they do not know this the "true socialists" are being embraced by the German governments. The "true socialists" aspire to serve "humanity" but actually they glorify the miserable German bourgeoisie. In fact we communists have nothing in common with the "true socialists". We are not concerned with the conscientious scruples of their disordered minds. Our attacks upon the bourgeoisie are quite different from those of the "true socialists" just as they are quite different from those of the reactionary nobles such as the Legitimists in France and Young England in Britain. The supporters of the *status quo* in Germany cannot exploit our attacks which are directed much more against them than against the bourgeoisie. It is true that the bourgeoisie is our *natural* enemy and the fall of the bourgeoisie will eventually bring us to power. But it is still more true that the German *status quo* is at this moment a much greater enemy from our point of view. This is because the *status quo* stands between us and the middle classes and prevents us from throwing off the shackles of the middle class. Consequently we are not prepared to give up our place among the great mass of the opponents of the *status quo* in Germany. We are simply the advance guard of the opposition. And because of our genuine detestation of everything that the middle class stands for we are able to take up a very special position among the opponents of the middle class.

The struggle against the German *status quo* has now entered a new phase with the calling of the Prussian United Diet. The question of the survival or fall of the *status quo* depends upon the decisions which it takes. At the moment the German political groups are divided by uncertain policies and ideological trivialities. Now they must make up their minds what interests they represent and what tactics they propose to adopt. They must sort themselves out into definite parties each supporting a practical policy. And the Communist Party – the newest of them all – faces the same problem. This party, too, must make up its mind and adopt a definite policy and a definite plan of campaign. This party, like the others, must assess the actual means at its disposal to achieve its aims. And its first decision must surely be to wash its hands of any connection with the reactionary "true socialists". This will be a simple matter for the Communist Party because it is quite strong enough to stand on its own feet without the help of associates who might compromise the future success of its policy.

II. The *Status Quo* and the Middle Classes

The present situation in Germany is as follows. In England and France the middle classes have gained sufficient power to overthrow the nobility and to become the ruling class in society. In Germany, on the other hand, the middle classes have not secured power. They have indeed gained some influence over the various governments but they always have to give way if their interests clash with those of the noble landlords. In England and France the towns rule the countryside but in Germany the countryside rules the towns while the agrarian interests are more powerful than those of industry or commerce. And this applies not only to German states which are ruled by absolute monarchs – such as Austria and Prussia – but also to states ruled by constitutional monarchs such as Saxony, Württemberg and Baden.

The explanation for this state of affairs lies in the fact that Germany is a backward country compared with England or France. In those countries the needs of the vast majority of the inhabitants are supplied by industry and commerce while in Germany agriculture is still of paramount importance. England exports no agricultural products whatever and in fact always has to import foodstuffs. France imports at least as much agricultural produce as she exports. Germany on the other hand exports few manufactured goods but she does export large quantities of grain, wool, cattle and so forth. The overwhelming importance in our economy was even greater than it is today at the time when Germany's constitutional affairs were settled. And it should be remembered that in 1815 the significance of agriculture was increased by the fact that the agrarian parts of Germany had contributed most to bring about the fall of Napoleon.

In Germany, as in most European states, the nobles – the owners of great estates – are representatives of agrarian interests from a political point of view. When the nobles completely dominate society their interests are reflected in the nature of the political institutions known as the feudal system. And this system has fallen into decay to the same extent that agriculture has ceased to be the dominant sector of a country's economy. As an industrial class has begun to rival the farming community and as the towns have expanded at the expense of the villages, so feudalism has declined.

Thus a new social class is in the process of formation in Germany and it is beginning to threaten the power of the owners of great feudal estates and the peasants who are more or less dependent upon the nobility. But this new class is by no means the equivalent of the middle class which exercises power today in advanced countries like England and France. This new German social class is the *petty* bourgeoisie, not the fully fledged bourgeoisie.

Germany's present constitution is simply a compromise which has handed over administration to a third social group – the bureaucracy. Both the nobles and the petty bourgeoisie have contributed to the formation of this third group. Since the nobles represent the agricultural interest which is the most powerful economic force in the country it is they who hold the highest posts in the civil service while the petty bourgeoisie has to be satisfied with the lower posts. It is only in exceptional circumstances that a member of the petty bourgeoisie secures a senior post in the administration. In the German states which have constitutions civil servants come under a measure of direct parliamentary control. Here, too, the landed aristocracy and the petty bourgeoisie share the real power. It is easy to appreciate that the nobles enjoy the lion's share of influence in the affairs of state. The petty bourgeoisie will never be able to share power on an equal basis with the nobles. And the petty bourgeoisie will certainly never be able to overthrow the landed aristocracy. To do this the petty bourgeoisie will need the help of the fully fledged bourgeoisie which is a different social class. The fully fledged bourgeoisie have wider interests, more property and greater courage than the petty bourgeoisie.

The fully fledged bourgeoisie have evolved from the petty bourgeoisie in all countries which share in world trade and in which modern industries have developed with the introduction of free competition and the concentration of property in fewer hands. The petty bourgeoisie represent internal and coastal trade as well as handicraft industry. These sectors of the economy operate in a restricted area and with a limited turnover. They require only a relatively modest amount of capital and have to face only insignificant local competition. The fully fledged bourgeoisie, on the other hand, are concerned with universal commerce, a well developed money economy, the exchange of products between all parts of the world, and the factory system of making manufactured goods. This type of industrial economy operates over the largest possible area, requires really large amounts of capital, depends upon a very rapid turnover, and generates a universal and violent competition. The petty bourgeoisie may be identified with local interests. The fully fledged bourgeoisie with universal interests. A member of the petty bourgeoisie considers that his future is fully safeguarded if he has an *indirect* influence upon the parliament of his country and if he has a *direct* influence upon the provincial government, and if he can *control* the local municipal authorities. On the other hand a member of the fully fledged bourgeoisie feels that his interests are fully safeguarded only if he is able to exercise a *direct* and continuous control over the central administration and parliament and the foreign policy of his country. The old Imperial Cities of Germany represent the classical creation of the petty bourgeoisie while parliamentary democracy in France represents the classical achievement of the fully fledged bourgeoisie. The petty bourgeoisie are conservative as soon as they have secured a few concessions from the ruling class in society. But the fully fledged bourgeoisie follow revolutionary aims until they themselves have siezed power.

What are the relations today between the German middle classes – the nobles and the petty bourgeoisie – who now share effective power in the country?

The seventeenth century in England and the eighteenth century in France saw the origin of the middle class which has subsequently grown in importance. In Germany, however, it was not until the nineteenth century that this class began to develop. There had previously existed in Germany a few great shipowners in the Hansa towns and a few wealthy financiers in the commercial centres in the interior of the country. But no class of powerful capitalists, and there were certainly no great *industrial* capitalists in existence in Germany. The German middle class was created by Napoleon. He introduced the continental system which fostered the growth of industry and mining in Germany. The introduction of industrial freedom into Prussia, for which Napoleon was indirectly responsible, also stimulated Germany's industrial expansion. The new – or expanding – industries developed with great rapidity and within a few years a middle class had begun to appear as a result of this extension of modern manufactures. As early as 1818 the new middle class was sufficiently powerful to force the Prussian government to grant it a measure of protection in the new (Maassen) tariff. The enactment of this tariff was the first occasion on which the Prussian government publicly recognised the existence of the middle class. Prussia – with a heavy heart and with much hesitation – accepted the fact that a fully fledged bourgeoisie had become a class which was essential for the economic welfare of the country. It is true that only fiscal and political considerations originally brought about the adhesion of most other German states to the Prussian customs system. But in the long run it was only the German – and above all the Prussian – middle class which profited from the existence of the *Zollverein*. Of course the nobles and the petty bourgeoisie have, from time to time, derived some minor benefits from the customs union but, on the whole, the interests of these two groups have suffered from the founding of the customs union. They have suffered because the *Zollverein* has fostered the continued growth of a fully fledged bourgeoisie, has promoted competition on a much greater scale than before, and has stimulated the introduction of modern techniques for producing manufactured goods. Since those days the middle class has grown fairly quickly in Germany, particularly in Prussia. Although the middle classes have not grown as rapidly in Germany as in England and France in the last thirty years, they have introduced most branches of modern industry into the country. In some parts of Germany the middle classes have made an end of the patriarchal structure of society associated with either the petty or the fully fledged bourgeoisie. They have concentrated capital to some extent, they have created a proletariat, and they have built a network of railways. The extent of their achievements may be judged from the fact that a situation has now arisen in which the middle class must either go ahead and become the dominant class in society or it must retreat and surrender its former conquests. Moreover the middle class is at the moment the only class in Germany which is making political progress and which could, if necessary, rule the country for a time. The future existence of the middle class depends upon its ability to establish not only actual power but also legal authority over the whole country.

The rise of the middle class and the extension of its power goes hand in hand with the decline of those classes which have wielded political authority in the past. Ever since the Napoleonic wars the economic position of the nobles has declined and they have sunk deeper and deeper in debt. They have lost the feudal services rendered by the serfs and this has increased the cost of producing grain. At the same time they have had to face unwelcome competition from a new class of free smallholders. These circumstances were not appreciated by the nobles when the serfs were emancipated. When their grain comes on the market it has to compete with Russian and American grain. The wool produced by the nobles has to compete with wool from Australia and – in certain years – from southern Russia. The more the costs of production rise and the effects of foreign competition become more serious the more obvious does it become that the German nobles are no longer capable of farming their estates at a profit. They have failed to make use of the most modern farming techniques. The German nobles of the present day – like the English and French nobles a hundred years ago – are simply squandering their capital in the great cities and are enjoying a higher standard of living than ever before. Nobles and bourgeoisie are competing for social status, for intellectual leadership, for material wealth. And they compete in the outward display of wealth. Such rivalry always occurs just before the bourgeoisie gains political power and – like any other kind of rivalry – it is the wealthier class which gains the victory. By becoming mere flunkies at court the owners of great estates have paved the way for their own rapid and certain downfall. The three per cent incomes of the nobles have been defeated by the five per cent profit of the bourgeoisie. The capital of the nobles has taken flight to land mortgage banks in the hope of securing the funds necessary to maintain an ever increasing standard of living but this policy only has the effect of hastening the doom of the nobility. The few owners of great estates who have had the sense to avoid bankruptcy are amalgamating with the rising class of townsmen who have purchased estates in the country. In this way a new class of *industrial landed gentry* has been created. This class is engaged in farming on a business footing and it uses bourgeois capital, technical knowledge and standards of efficiency. This class has no feudal illusions about agriculture and these new farmers do not regard their business as a leisurely occupation suited to gentlemen farmers. In France this class of industrial landed gentry has placed no obstacles in the advance of the middle class to power. Indeed the industrial landed gentry and the urban bourgeoisie exist peacefully side by side. And – in proportion to its wealth – the industrial landed gentry is able to share power with the urban middle class. The industrial landed gentry may be regarded as that section of the bourgeoisie which lives in the country and is engaged in farming on strictly commercial lines. In this way the power of the nobles has declined and they have to some extent already been absorbed by the middle class.

The petty bourgeoisie – always weak in relation to the feudal nobility – has been even less able to resist the rise of the new middle class. The petty bourgeoisie is, next to the peasants, the most miserable social class that has ever tried to act a part on the stage of history. Its finest hour was in the later middle ages. Even then it was interested only in petty local affairs, in petty local struggles, and in petty local advances towards improved conditions. It survived *on sufferance* side by side with the nobility and it never aspired to exercise any wider political influence. Once the fully fledged bourgeoisie began to develop, the petty bourgeoisie lost even the *outward appearance* of a class with a historic mission in world affairs. The petty bourgeoisie is being ground between the nobles on the one hand and the fully fledged bourgeoisie on the other. It has been overwhelmed by the political power of the nobles and the economic power of the large capital controlled by the middle class. Under the impact of these pressures the petty bourgeoisie has split into two sections. The richer urban petty bourgeoisie has – with some hesitation – thrown in its lot with the revolutionary fully fledged bourgeoisie. The poor petty bourgeoisie – especially those living in small towns – tend to cling to the existing social order and to support the feudal nobles. But every step forward taken by the middle class denotes a decline in the power of the petty bourgeoisie. Eventually the poorer section of the petty bourgeoisie must recognise that it will certainly be ruined if it persists in supporting the *status quo*. It can see that once the middle class gains political power there is a bare *possibility* that the poorer members of the petty bourgeois class may become rich enough to attain middle class status. Yet it is very *probable* that the poorer section of the petty bourgeois class will be ruined. When their destruction becomes inevitable the members of the petty bourgeois class must fall under the domination of the powerful middle class. As soon as the fully fledged bourgeoisie has gained a position of supremacy in the state, the petty bourgeoisie again splits into two sections. One provides recruits for the middle class while the other acts as a link between the middle class and the proletariat which now emerges as a class which has demands of its own to make. This link includes several more or less radical and socialist groups. They can be seen in action in the lower houses of both the French and the English parliaments and their activities are chronicled in the daily press. The middle class with its heavy cannon of capital and its closed ranks of joint stock companies can bring overwhelming pressure to bear upon the ill armed and undisciplined ranks of the petty bourgeoisie. As the middle class steps up its pressure so the petty bourgeoisie loses heart and retreats in disorderly flight. In the end the members of the petty bourgeois class have the choice of being absorbed in the mass of the proletariat or of surrendering unconditionally to the middle class. This edifying drama is unfolded in England every time that a slump occurs. And in France it is being enacted at this very moment. In Germany we have so far only reached the point at which the petty bourgeoisie – now in a desperate state of financial difficulty – has taken the heroic decision to abandon its support of the nobility and to throw in its lot with the middle class.

It is obvious that the German petty bourgeoisie is in a less favourable position than the owners of great landed estates to become the leading social class in the country. It is equally obvious that the petty bourgeoisie is falling every day more and more under the thumb of the middle class.

Finally we shall consider the position of the peasants and the social class which owns no property.

The "peasants" with whom we are concerned may be owners of farms or tenants but they all have quite small plots of land. Our definition excludes farm labourers who are wage earners. The peasants are just as helpless a social class as the petty bourgeoisie but differ from them by being more courageous. But they have no historical tradition behind them. Even their emancipation from the status of serfdom was achieved only under the aegis of the middle class. In the alpine cantons of Switzerland and in Norway the peasants have been able to hold power because of the absence of either an aristocracy or a middle class. Peasants are honest and reliable but they have a narrow-minded mentality and when they are the dominant social class in society conditions of barbaric feudalism and fanatical bigotry prevail. In Germany the peasants and the nobility exist side by side and the peasants – like the petty bourgeoisie – are caught between the nobles and the middle class. From one point of view – in order to safeguard their farming interests – one would expect them to throw in their lot with the feudal nobility. From another point of view – to protect themselves from the overwhelming competition of the nobles, particularly the new industrial estate owners – one would expect them to support the middle class. The size of the smallholding is the decisive factor in the peasant's decision which of these two classes to support. In eastern Germany some peasants have large farms and they exercise feudal rights over their labourers. These peasants have interests similar to those of the nobles and they tend to ally themselves with the nobles. In western Germany, on the other hand, where large estates have been split into very small farms, the peasants support the middle class because their interests clash with those of the nobles. Similarly the smallholders of the east who are under the jurisdiction of their manorial lords – and sometimes render feudal services to them – are oppressed by the nobles and they too support the middle class. Evidence for this can be found by examining the proceedings of the Prussian provincial diets.

Fortunately there can be no question of the German peasants ever becoming the dominant class in our society. Such a thing has never occurred to them and most of them are already allied to the middle classes.

And what about the class that has no property, the group which is called the "working class"? We propose to discuss the position of the workers at greater length later on. For the present it is sufficient to point out that this class is split into several groups. The "workers" include farm labourers, day labourers, apprentices to a craft, factory workers, and unskilled casual labourers. These workers are scattered over a large thinly populated region which has only a few focal points of urban settlement. In the circumstances it is impossible for the workers to realise that they have interests in common. It is not possible for them to organise themselves into a coherent social class. All that they can do is to fight for things that affect their daily lives. The struggle for higher wages is the limit of their ambitions. The workers believe that their interests coincide with those of their employers. And so each section of the workers becomes a tool in the hands of the middle class. The farm labourers and the day labourers support the nobles or farmers for whom they work. The factory workers support the manufacturers when they demand the imposition of protective tariffs. Gangs of casual labourers and tramps can be hired for a few shillings to fight the battles between the middle class, the nobles and the police. And when the interests of two rival groups of employers clash, the struggle between them is reflected in another struggle between their workers. in the circumstances it would be ridiculous to suppose that the proletariat would be capable of playing a leading rôle in public affairs in Germany.

We may sum up the present situation by saying that the nobles, the petty bourgeoisie, the peasants, and the workers cannot hope to dominate German society. The nobles are too impoverished, the petty bourgeoisie and the peasants are too humble, and the workers are not ready to aspire to such a position. Only the middle class remains.

The main cause of Germany's wretched condition today is that so far no social class has been strong enough to raise its economic activity to one of such overwhelming national importance that it can come forward as the undisputed leader of the whole country. All classes that have arisen in Germany since the tenth century have existed side by side and not one of them has attained a position of leadership. This applies equally to nobles, serfs, free peasants, petty bourgeoisie, apprentices, craftsmen, middle classes and the proletariat. Some of these classes – the nobles, the free peasants, the middle class – have owned sufficient property to dominate particular sectors of the economy. They have had a share of political power in proportion to their numbers, their property and their share of the national wealth. The division of power has been such that the lion's share has fallen to the nobles, and a much smaller share to the petty bourgeoisie. The middle class and the peasants have *officially* enjoyed no power at all though in practice the middle class has had a certain influence through the nobles. The fact that at present effective authority is wielded by the civil servants is a reflection of the shocking decline of political life in Germany. German society has sunk to such a position of weakness, insensibility and degradation that it is universally despised. Germany is a mere ragbag of thirty-eight states which are no more than regions and localities except for Prussia and Austria and they are divided into independent provinces. It is a disgrace that Germany should be so weak that she can be exploited and trampled upon by foreign countries. The cause of this wretched state of affairs is poverty – that is to say lack of capital. Every single social class in poverty-stricken Germany has, from the very first, carried the mark of bourgeois mediocrity and pauperism in comparison with similar classes in other countries. Since the twelfth century both the upper and the lower sections of the German nobility have been but pale shadows of the wealthy, carefree and imperious English and French nobles. Similarly the middle classes of the Imperial Cities and the Hansa towns have been but a poor reflection of the turbulent citizens of Paris in the fourteenth and fifteenth centuries and the Puritans of London of the seventeenth century. What minnows are our leading industrialists, financiers and shipowners when compared with the merchant princes who frequent the stock exchanges of Paris, Lyons, London, Liverpool and Manchester. Even the German workers behave like members of the petty bourgeois class. The petty bourgeoisie may be oppressed both from a social and a political point of view but at least it has the consolation of knowing that it is the typical German social class and that it has impressed upon all other classes its own brand of mediocrity.

How are we to get out of this wretched state of affairs? There is only one remedy. One class must become strong enough so that its progress will lead to the progress of the whole country. And the growth of the economic strength of all other classes must be a reflection of the growth of the wealth of this dominant class. The interests of this single class must be the national interest and – for the time being – this class must become truly representative of the country as a whole. As soon as this happens the new dominant class – and indeed the majority of the population – must clash with the existing *status quo*. At present the *status quo* is appropriate to circumstances which no longer exist. It is appropriate to a state of affairs in which there is a balance of power as between different social classes. The new economic interests find that their style is cramped and even some sections of the class for whose benefit the *status quo* was established find that the present state of affairs does not reflect their economic needs. The abolition of the *status quo* whether by peaceful means or by force must inevitably follow from this state of affairs. The *status quo* will be replaced by the domination of a social class which – for the moment – can represent the interests of the entire nation. And from that point a new phase in the development of the nation can begin.

It has been seen that the present situation in Germany – the poverty and the weakness of the country – has been brought about by lack of adequate capital. That situation can be ended only when capital is concentrated in the hands of *one* class which by that means achieves a dominant position in the country.

Does such a class – capable of ending the *status quo* – exist in Germany? It does exist although in a somewhat miniature form when compared with the corresponding classes in England and France. It exists in the form of the middle class.

The bourgeoisie is the class which has taken over authority wherever a bureaucratic monarchy has existed and has represented a balance of power between the nobles and the petty bourgeoisie.

This is the only class in Germany whose interests can be shared by a substantial part of the "industrial" owners of landed estates, the petty bourgeoisie, the peasants, the workers and even a minority of the nobles. These classes already march – for practical purposes – under the banner of the middle class.

The middle class party is the only one in Germany which knows exactly what it wants to put in the place of the *status quo*. It is the only party which does not have a policy based upon abstract principles and historical deductions. Its platform has definite and clearly formulated aims capable of immediate realisation. It is the only party which – at any rate on a local or provincial basis – has some sort of organisation and some sort of plan of action. In short it is the party which has taken the lead in fighting the *status quo* and is directly concerned with bringing it to a speedy end. The middle class party is therefore the only party which has any serious chance of success in the struggle against the *status quo*.

The next question to be answered is this. Has the middle class been put in a position in which it must take over power if the *status quo* is brought to an end? Is the middle class strong enough to overthrow the *status quo* by its own resources and because of the weakness of its opponents?

Let us examine this question. The most powerful members of the German middle class are the factory owners. The manufacturers are running an expanding industry which is responsible for the growth of internal trade, for the overseas commerce of Hamburg, Bremen and (to some extent) Stettin, for the activities of the banks and the railways, and also for the most significant aspects of the activities of the stock exchanges. The only economic activities that are independent of industry are the export trades in grain and wool of the Baltic ports and the relatively unimportant commerce in imported manufactured goods. So the interests of the factory owners represent the interests of the whole middle class and of those classes which – for the moment – are dependent upon the middle class.

The factory owners may be divided into two sections. There are those manufacturers who turn raw materials into semi-manufactured products and there are those who turn semi-manufactured products into finished goods. The owners of spinning mills belong to the first group and the owners of weaving sheds belong to the second group. In Germany the ironmasters belong to the first group.

[There is a gap in the manuscript at this point.]

The existence of a fully developed industrial system implies the use of new inventions and modern techniques, good transport facilities, cheap machinery and raw materials, and the presence of a skilled labour force. It is necessary that the activities of all branches of industry should be completely co-ordinated. It is also necessary to have ports which dominate the industrial hinterland and are engaged in a flourishing overseas commerce. All this has been laid down by economists long ago. A fully developed industrial society also requires a comprehensive tariff to protect all those branches of industry which are threatened by foreign competition. And the tariff should always be adjusted to meet changing circumstances. At present only England has no reason to fear competition from abroad. Neither the existing *Zollverein* states nor the present government is capable of giving German industry this protection. Such a tariff can be introduced and carried through only by governments controlled by the middle class. This is why the middle class cannot do without political power any longer.

A protective tariff is particularly necessary in Germany because domestic industry is dying. Unless its interests are safeguarded it will be overwhelmed by the competition of English machines and this will lead to the collapse of all sections of the community whose livelihood depends upon domestic industry. The middle class might as well kill off what is left of the domestic industries with German rather than with English machines! The German middle class therefore needs protective duties and no one can introduce them except the middle class itself. For that reason alone the middle class must secure control of political authority.

The factory owners suffer not only from lack of adequate fiscal protection but also from the effects of bureaucratic administration. In the matter of protection against foreign competition the factory owners face government indifference but as far as bureaucratic administration is concerned they face active government hostility.

The bureaucracy has been created to wield authority over the petty bourgeoisie and the peasants. These social classes are scattered in little towns and villages and their interests are entirely local in character. Their attitude to life is correspondingly limited in outlook. They are quite incapable of running the government of a great state themselves. They have neither the knowledge nor the breadth of vision to co-ordinate the diverse rival interests that exist in a modern state. And this class has just reached the level of culture that corresponds to a flourishing petty bourgeois society. In such a society conflicting interests are most complex. This has been shown in the past by the internecine conflicts of the various gilds. Consequently the affairs of the petty bourgeoisie and the peasants must be administered by an efficient and numerous bureaucracy. They have to accept civil service tutelage in order to prevent social confusion and a great spate of lawsuits.

The bureaucracy which is a necessity for the petty bourgeoisie soon becomes an insupportable burden for the middle class. In the age of domestic industry official inspection and meddling was bad enough but a fully fledged factory system really cannot operate under such official oversight. In the past German manufacturers have bribed officials to keep the bureaucratic wolf at bay and they can hardly be blamed for doing so. But the use of bribery has only shifted a small part of the burden from the backs of the factory owners. It is obviously impossible to bribe *all* the officials with whom a manufacturer may come into contact. And bribery does not help the factory owner to pay fees to lawyers, architects, engineers, and other consultants who have to be engaged because of the existence of a system of bureaucratic control. It may be added that officialdom also imposes much extra work upon the manufacturers and this consumes a great deal of time. As industry expands the more active do the "conscientious officials" become. They plague the unfortunate factory owner either out of sheer cussedness or because they detest the manufacturers.

The middle class has therefore been put into a position which makes it imperative for the pompous dishonest civil servants to be overthrown. The power of the bureaucracy will collapse as soon as the middle class has gained control over the legislature and the machinery of government. When that happens the civil servants who have plagued the middle class in the past will become the humble servants of the middle class in the future. The rules and regulations which have been devised by civil servants to lighten their own labours at the expense of the factory owners will be replaced by new enactments which will lighten the work of the manufacturers at the expense of the bureaucracy.

It is urgently necessary for the middle class to take such action promptly because, as we have seen, all sections of the bourgeoisie are directly involved in the rapid expansion of the factory system and this type of economy cannot develop if it is hamstrung by the bureaucracy.

The middle class is most directly interested in securing two major reforms. They are to gain control over the tariff and over the bureaucracy. But this by no means exhausts the legitimate demands of the middle class. In nearly all German states the middle class will have to undertake a drastic reform of the legislature, the administration, and the legal system. At present our parliaments, civil servants, and judicial systems operate within a social structure which the middle class is pledged to overthrow. The circumstances which make it possible for nobility and petty bourgeoisie to exist side by side are radically different from the circumstances under which the middle class can exercise real power. At present the German states officially recognise only the *status quo* which operates entirely to the advantage of the nobles and the petty bourgeoisie. Let us take the present situation in Prussia as an example. A sleepy "independent" group of magistrates and judges hold in their hands the personal liberty and the property rights of the petty bourgeoisie and both the administrative and the legal bureaucracy. In return the petty bourgeoisie have received some protection from the arbitrary actions of the feudal nobles and sometimes also from the civil servants. The middle class cannot allow this state of affairs to continue. In disputes concerning property which come before the courts the middle class must insist that the hearings are held in public. In criminal cases the middle class also demand the introduction of the jury system and the permanent control of judicial procedure by an independent, impartial, middle class commission.

The petty bourgeois can accept the fact that nobles and civil servants are exempt from ordinary processes of law because this is a natural consequence of the low social status of the petty bourgeoisie. The middle class cannot accept this state of affairs. It must either gain control over society and the state or face the complete collapse of all its ambitions. The petty bourgeoisie, living a peaceful life in some rural backwater, can accept the fact that the nobles dispense justice on their own estates. The petty bourgeoisie can hardly do otherwise since it is fully occupied in defending its own parochial interests in little urban communities from the encroachments of the landed aristocracy. The middle class, on the other hand, cannot allow the nobles to enjoy complete power in the countryside. In its own interests the middle class must press forward with plans to "industrialise" farming, to put all agricultural land to effective use, and to introduce a system whereby land can be freely bought and sold. The great landowners require mortgages and this has given the middle class an opportunity to play a part in the development of agriculture. The nobles have had to give the middle class some say in the passing of laws concerning mortgages and landed property.

The wretched old commercial code has not greatly inconvenienced the petty bourgeoisie for they trade on only a limited scale; they have only a very modest turnover; and their customers are concentrated in a small region. Indeed they might be thankful that their interests have enjoyed some trifling protection under the law. The middle class on the other hand cannot be expected to put up with the commercial code. The business transactions of the petty bourgeoisie are of the simplest kind. These transactions are not between wholesalers and merchants but between retailers and the general public. One seldom hears of bankruptcies among the petty bourgeoisie and consequently there are few complaints about the bankruptcy laws. Under these laws bills of exchange take priority over other debts – though generally the lawyers devour all the assets while the creditors get little or nothing. The bankruptcy laws have been divised for the benefit of the judicial bureaucrats and for all social classes other than the middle class. The nobles benefit the most from the bankruptcy laws because bills of exchange on the purchaser or his agent are used in their dealings in grain. In fact the law favours those whose business activities are limited to one transaction in the year which is accomplished by means of a bill of exchange. Among those whose business transactions are on a large scale it is the wholesalers and the bankers who receive most protection under the law while the interests of the factory owners are neglected. The commercial transactions of the middle classes are entirely transactions between one merchant and another. Their bills of exchange come from all over the world and their transactions are of a highly complex nature. They can find themselves involved in somebody's bankruptcy at any time. In the circumstances the middle classes can easily be ruined by these absurd laws.

The only interest that the petty bourgeoisie has in politics is the preservation of peace. The restricted circle within which he moves makes it impossible for him to take a serious interest in international affairs. The middle classes are engaged in trade with the most distant foreign countries and compete with manufacturers in far off lands. They cannot make progress unless they have a direct say in foreign policy. The petty bourgeoisie accept taxes imposed upon them by the bureaucracy and the nobles for the same reason that it accepts the leadership of the civil servants. The middle classes are directly interested in securing the establishment of a system of taxation which places as light a burden as possible upon *their* businesses.

In short the petty bourgeoisie is prepared to achieve a measure of political influence simply by massing its stolid members in opposition to the nobles and the bureaucracy. The middle class cannot do this. It must become the ruling class. Its interests must take priority in the making of laws, in the administration, in the functioning of the judiciary, in the fixing of taxes, and in the conduct of foreign policy. The middle class must expand, must put its capital to full use, must extend its commercial contacts and markets every day, and must improve its transport facilities. And it must do these things in order to avoid annihilation itself. It is forced to do so by fierce competition in world markets. In order to be able to expand its interests without hindrance to the fullest extent the middle class must strive for political supremacy and must make all other interests subordinate to its own interests.

At this very moment it is essential that the middle class should gain political supremacy in Germany if it is not to be destroyed. We have already shown why the middle class must do this in our discussions of the tariff question and of the relationship between the middle class and the bureaucracy. The proof of this statement lies in the present position of the market both with regard to money and to commodities.

During the year 1845 there was a trade boom in England accompanied by speculation in railway shares. This boom has had greater repercussions upon France and Germany than any previous period of prosperity. German manufacturers did good business and the German economy as a whole was in a flourishing state. The German agricultural districts did good business by exporting their wheat to England. Universal prosperity promoted great activity in the money market and made it easier to obtain credit. Small savings, which are normally half dormant in Germany, appeared on the market. In Germany – as in England and France, only a little later and in. . .[3]

[3] The manuscript breaks off at this point

VII

THE FREE TRADE CONGRESS IN BRUSSELS[1]

On the 16th, 17th and 18th of September there was held here [Brussels] a congress of political economists, manufacturers, tradesmen etc. to discuss the question of Free Trade. There were present about 100 members of all nations. There assisted on the part of the English Free Traders Dr Bowring M.P., Colonel Thompson M.P., Mr Ewart M.P., Mr Brown M.P., James Wilson Esq., editor of the *Economist* etc.; from France had arrived M. Wolowski, professor of jurisprudence, M. Blanqui, deputy professor of political economy, author of a history of that science and other works, M. Horace Say, son of the celebrated economist, M. Charles Dunoyer, member of the Privy Council, author of several works upon politics and economy, and others. From Germany there was no Free Trader present[2] but Holland, Denmark, Italy etc. had sent representatives. Senor Ramon de la Sagra of Madrid intended to come but came too late. The assistance of a whole host of Belgian Free Traders need hardly be mentioned as being a matter of course.

Thus the celebrities of the science had met to discuss the important question – whether Free Trade would benefit the world? You will think the discussions of such a splendid assembly – discussions carried on by economical stars of the first magnitude – must have been interesting to the highest degree. You will say that men like Dr Bowring, Colonel Thompson, Blanqui and Dunoyer must have pronounced speeches the most striking, must have produced arguments the most convincing, must have represented all questions under a light the most novel and surprising imaginable. Alas, Sir, if you had been present you would have been piteously undeceived. Your glorious expectations, your fond illusions, would have vanished within less than an hour. I have assisted at innumerable public meetings and discussions. I have heard the

[1] *Northern Star*, No. 520, October 9, 1847 (by F. Engels).

[2] Nine German delegates, led by Prince Smith and Dr C. W. Asher attended the congress. Only one of them (Rittinghausen) was a protectionist. See Julius Becker, *Das Deutsche Manchestertum* (1907), p. 31.

League pour forth their Anti-Corn Law arguments more than a hundred times, while I was in England but never, I can assure you, did I hear such dull tedious trivial stuff, brought forward with such a degree of self complacency. I was never before so disappointed. What was carried on did not merit the name of a discussion – it was mere pot house talk. The great scientific luminaries never ventured themselves upon the field of political economy in the strict sense of the word. I shall not repeat to you all the worn-out stuff which was brought forward on the first two days. Read two or three numbers of the *League* or the *Manchester Guardian*, and you will find all that was said, except perhaps a few specious sentences brought forward by M. Wolowski, which he, however, had stolen from M. Bastiat's (chief of the French Free Traders) pamphlet of *Sophismes Economiques*. Free Traders did not expect to meet with any opposition but that of M. Rittinghausen, a German Protectionist, and generally an insipid fellow. But up got M. Duchateau, a French manufacturer and Protectionist – a man who spoke for his purse, just as Mr Ewart or Mr Brown spoke for theirs, and gave them such a terrible opposition, that on the second day of the discussion a great number, even of Free Traders, avowed that they had been beaten in argument. They took, however, their revenge at the vote – the resolutions passed, of course, almost unanimously.

On the third day a question was discussed which interests your readers. It was this: "Will the carrying out of universal Free Trade benefit the working classes?" The affirmative was supported by Mr Brown, the South Lancashire Free Trader, in a lengthy speech in English; he and Mr Wilson were the only ones to speak that language, the remainder all spoke French – Dr Bowring very well, Colonel Thompson tolerable, Mr Ewart dreadfully. He repeated a part of the old League documents, in a whining tone, very much like a Church of England parson. After him got up Mr Weerth of Rhenish Prussia. You know, I believe, this gentleman – a young tradesman whose poetry is well known and very much liked throughout Germany, and who during several years' stay in Yorkshire, was an eye-witness to the condition of the working people. He has a great many friends among them there, who will be glad to see that he has not forgotten them. As his speech will be to your readers the most interesting feature of the whole Congress I shall report it at some length. He spoke as follows –

"Gentlemen – You are discussing the influence of Free Trade upon the condition of the working classes. You profess the greatest possible sympathy for those classes. I am very glad of it, but yet I am astonished not to see a representative of the working classes amongst you! The monied classes of France are represented by a peer – those of England by several M.P.s – those of Belgium by an ex-Minister – and even those of Germany by a gentleman who gave us a faithful description of the state of that country. But where, I ask you, are the representatives of the working men? I see them nowhere; therefore gentlemen, allow me to take up the defence of their interests. I beg to speak to you on behalf of the working people, and principally on behalf of those five millions of English working men, amongst whom I spent several of the most pleasant years of my life, whom I know and whom I cherish [cheers]. Indeed, gentlemen, the working people stand in need of some generosity. Hitherto they have not been treated like men, but like beasts of burden, nay – like merchandise, like machines; the English manufacturers know this so well, that they never say we employ so many workmen, but so many hands. The monied classes, acting upon this principle have never hesitated a moment to profit by their services and then turn them out upon the streets as soon as there is no longer any profit to be squeezed out of them. Thus the condition of these outcasts of modern society has become such that it cannot be made worse. Look wherever you like – to the banks of the Rhône, into the dirty and pestilential lanes of Manchester, Leeds and Birmingham, or the hills of Saxony and Silesia, or the plains of Westphalia – everywhere you will meet with the same pale starvation, the same gloomy despair, in the eyes of men who in vain claim their rights and their position in civilised society" [great sensation].

Mr Weerth then declared his opinion to be, that the protective system in reality did not protect the working people, but that Free Trade – and he told them plainly and distinctly although he himself was a Free Trader – that Free Trade would never change their miserable condition. He did not at all join in the delusions of the Free Traders as to the beneficial effects of the carrying out of their system upon the working classes. On the contrary, Free Trade, the full realisation of free competition, would force the working people as much into a keener competition amongst themselves as it would make capitalists compete selfishly against each other. The perfect freedom of competition would inevitably give an enormous impulse to the invention of new machinery, and thus supersede more workmen than even now were daily superseded. It would stimulate production in every way, but for this very reason it would stimulate overproduction, overstocking of markets and commercial revulsions, just in the same measure. The Free Traders pretended that these terrible revulsions would cease under a system of commercial freedom; why just the contrary would be the case, they would increase and multiply more than ever. Possibly, nay certainly, it was that at first the greater cheapness of provisions would benefit the work people – that a lessened cost of production would increase consumption and the demand for labour, but that advantage would very soon be turned into misery. The competition of the workpeople amongst themselves would soon reduce them to the former level of misery and starvation.

After these and other arguments (which appeared to be quite novel to the meeting for they were listened to with the greatest attention, although *The Times* reporter deigns to rid himself of them with the impudent but significant sneer – "Chartist common-place"), Mr Weerth concluded as follows:

> And do not think gentlemen that these are but my individual opinions; they are the opinions too of the English working men, a class whom I cherish and respect, because they are intelligent and energetic men [cheers]. Indeed I shall prove that by a few facts. During full six years the gentlemen of the League whom we see here, courted the support of the working people, but in vain. The working men never forgot that the capitalists were their natural enemies; they recollected the League riots of 1842, and the masters opposition against the Ten Hours Bill. It was only towards the end of 1843, that the Chartists, the elite of the working classes, associated for a moment with the League, in order to crush their common enemy, the landed aristocracy. But it was for a moment only and never were they deceived by the delusive promises of Cobden, Bright & Co, nor did they hope the fulfilment of cheap bread, high wages, and plenty to do. No, not for a moment did they cease to trust in their own exertions only; to form a distinct party, led on by distinct chiefs, by the indefatigable Duncombe, and by Feargus O'Connor who, in spite of all calumnies [here Mr Weerth looked at Dr Bowring who made a quick convulsive movement] within a few weeks will sit upon the same bench with you in the House of Commons. In the name then of those millions who do not believe that Free Trade will do wonders for them, I call upon you to seek for some other means to effectively better their condition. Gentlemen, I call upon you for your own interests. You have no longer to fear the Emperor of all the Russians; you dread not an invasion of Cossacks; but if you do not take care you will have to fear an irruption of your own workmen, and they will be more terrible to you than all the Cossacks in the world. Gentlemen, the work-people want no more words from you, they want deeds. And you have no reason to be astonished at that. They recollect very well that in 1830 and 1831 when they conquered the Reform Bill for you in London, when they fought for you in the streets of Paris and Brussels, that then they were courted, shaken hands with, and highly praised; but that when a few years after they demanded bread, then they were received with grapeshot and the bayonet [Oh!

> No, no! Yes, yes, Bazançais, Lyons]. I repeat therefore to you, carry your Free Trade. It will be well, but think at the same time about other measures for the working classes or you will regret it [loud cheers].

Immediately after Mr Weerth, up got Dr Bowring to reply. "Gentlemen", said he, "I can tell you that the hon. member who has just sat down has not been elected by the English working people to represent them in this Congress. On the contrary, the English people generally have given us their suffrages for this purpose, and, we claim our places as their true representatives." He then went on to show the beneficial effects of Free Trade, as proved by the increased importation of articles of food into England since the introduction of last year's tariff. So many eggs, so many cwt of butter, cheese, ham, bacon, as many heads of cattle etc. etc.; who could have eaten that if not the working people of England? He quite forgot, however, telling us what quantities of the same articles have been produced less in England since foreign competition has been admitted. He took it for granted that increased importation was a decisive proof of increased consumption. He never mentioned wherefrom the working people of Manchester, Bradford and Leeds, who now walk the streets and cannot get work, wherefrom these men get the money to pay for this supposed increase of consumption and Free Trade comforts – for we never heard of the masters making them presents of eggs, butter, cheese, ham and meat, for not working at all! He never said a word about the present depressed state of the trade, which in every public paper is represented as really unexampled. He seemed not to know that all the predictions of the Free Traders since the carrying of the measures have proved just the reverse of reality. He had not a word of sympathy for the sufferings of the working classes but, on the contrary, represented their present gloomy condition as the brightest happiest and most comfortable they could reasonably desire.

The English working people, now, may choose betwixt their two representatives. A host of others followed, who spoke about every imaginable subject upon earth, except upon the one under discussion. Mr McAdam, M.P. for Belfast spun an eternally long yarn upon flax spinning in Ireland, and almost killed the meeting with statistics. Mr Ackersdijk, a Dutch professor, spoke about Old Holland and Young Holland, the University of Liège, Walpole and De Witt. M. van de Casteele spoke about France, Belgium and the ministry, M. Asher of Berlin about German patriotism and some new article he called spiritual manufacture. M. den Tex a Dutchman about God knows what. At last, the whole meeting being half asleep, was awakened by M. Wolowski, who returned to the question and replied to M. Weerth. His speech, like all speeches delivered by Frenchmen, proved how much the French capitalists dread the fulfilment of Mr Weerth's prophecies. They speak with such pretended sympathy, such canting and whining of the sufferings of the working classes, that one might take it all for good earnest, were it not too flagrantly contradicted by the roundness of their bellies, by the stamp of hypocrisy deeply imprinted upon their faces, by the pitiful remedies they propose, and by the unmistakeably striking contrast between their words and their deeds. Nor have they ever succeeded in deceiving one single working man. Then up got the Duc d'Harcourt, peer of France, and claimed, too, for the French capitalists, deputies etc. present the right of representing the French working people. They do so in the same way as Dr Bowring represent(s) the English Chartists. Then spoke Mr James Wilson repeating most brazenfacedly the most worn out League argument, in the drowsy tone of a Philadelphia Quaker.

You will see from this what a nice discussion it was. Dr Marx of Brussels, whom you know as by far the most talented representative of German Democracy, had also claimed his turn to speak. He had prepared a speech, which, if it had been delivered would have made it impossible for the congressional "gents" to vote upon the question. But Mr Weerth's opposition had made them shy. They resolved to let none speak of whose orthodoxy they were not quite sure. Thus Messrs Wolowski, Wilson and the whole precious lot spoke against time, and when it was four o'clock, there were still six or seven gentlemen who wanted to speak, but the chairman closed the discussion abruptly, and the whole set of fools, ignorants, and knaves called a Congress of Political Economists, voted all votes against one (the poor German fool of a Protectionist aforementioned) – the Democrats did not vote at all – that Free Trade is extremely beneficial to the working people, and will free them from all misery and distress.

As Dr Marx's speech, although not delivered, contains the very best and most striking reputation of this barefaced lie, which can be imagined, and as its contents – in spite of so many hundred pages having been written pro and con the subject – will yet read quite novel in England, I enclose you some extracts from it.[3]

[3] Engels's article on "The Free Trade Congress at Brussels" was followed by the "Speech of Dr Marx on Protection, Free Trade and the Working Classes" (*Northern Star*, October 9, 1847).

VIII

PRINCIPLES OF COMMUNISM, NOVEMBER 1847[1]

1. What is Communism?

   Communism is the doctrine which explains how the proletariat can throw off its chains and gain its freedom.

2. What is the proletariat?

   The proletariat is the social group which exists simply by selling its labour and which draws no profit from any kind of capital. The entire existence of the proletariat – its prosperity and hardships, its living and dying – depends upon the existence of a demand for its labour, and the demand for the labour of the proletariat is influenced by the booms and slumps in the economy and by trade fluctuations which are brought about by the existence of unrestricted competition. In a word the proletariat is the working class of the nineteenth century.

3. But has there not always been a proletariat?

   No. It is true that both the poor and the workers have always existed. It is true also that the workers have generally been poor. What is new is the sort of poverty and the type of workers which are typical of the economic system that we have described. Moreover competition has by no means always been free and unrestricted in earlier periods of history.

4. How has the modern proletariat arisen?

   The proletariat has been created by the industrial revolution which began in England in the second half of the eighteenth century and has subsequently spread to all civilised parts of the world. The industrial revolution was brought about by the invention of the steam engine, various spinning machines, the power loom, and many other mechanical appliances. Since

[1] Written by Engels in 1847 and submitted to Marx. Translated from *Karl Marx – Friedrich Engels*, Band III, *Geschichte und Politik* I (Fischer Bücherei, 1966), pp. 42–58.

these machines were very expensive they were monopolised by rich capitalists. The new machines completely revolutionised the old methods of producing goods and put the domestic workers out of business. Manufactured articles could now be made more efficiently and more cheaply by the new machines than by the relatively inefficient spinning wheels and hand-looms used by domestic craftsmen. The new machines delivered industrial production into the hands of wealthy capitalists and rendered quite valueless the modest property of the craftsmen – their tools, looms and so forth. Before long the capitalists owned everything and the workers owned nothing. In this way the factory system was introduced in the textile industries to produce various types of cloth.

Although the system of production in factories by machinery began in the textile trades it soon spread to all other branches of manufacture, particularly to printing, pottery and metal-working. Industrial processes became more specialised than before so that a worker who formerly made an article by himself now made only a part of an article. By means of this division of labour it became possible to manufacture products more quickly and more cheaply than before. Under the new system of organising industrial production the worker performed only simple repetitive actions which could eventually be performed more efficiently by the machines themselves. One after another of the industries that we have mentioned came – like spinning and weaving – to be dominated by factories and power-driven machinery. And when this happened, these industries too fell into the hands of big capitalists and the workers lost the last vestiges of their independence. Gradually even those industries which had not been mechanised fell under the domination of the factory system and big capitalists established large workshops to employ formerly independent craftsmen. Once more substantial reductions in costs of production were achieved and the master craftsmen were ruthlessly pushed on one side. These developments have now gone so far that in all civilised countries nearly all manufactured articles are made in factories. Everywhere the domestic system of production has been replaced by the capitalist method of production in large factories. The former middle classes, especially the master craftsmen who operated on a large scale, have been ruined and the former position of the workers has been entirely changed. Two new classes have developed in society and they have swallowed up all the other classes.

(*a*) The class of large capitalists which in all civilised

countries already monopolises all the necessities of life and all the raw materials, factories and machinery required to produce them. This is the bourgeois class.

(*b*) The class which has no property at all and is forced to sell its labour to the bourgeoisie in order to secure the necessities of life. This class is called the proletariat.

5. Under what circumstances does the proletariat sell its labour to the bourgeoisie?

Human labour is a commodity and the price at which it is bought and sold obeys exactly the same laws as those governing the price of any other commodity. In a society dominated by capitalist industry and free competition – and we shall see that these two amount to the same thing – the average price of an article always equals the cost of producing it. The cost of labour amounts to the minimum quantity of the necessities of life that are needed to keep the worker alive and to prevent the working class from dying out. The worker, therefore, receives wages which are just sufficient for this purpose. The price of labour – or the rate of wages – is the absolute minimum necessary to maintain life. Since periods of prosperity alternate with periods of depression the wages of the workers fluctuate just as the income which the capitalist derives from the sale of his goods fluctuates. And just as the manufacturer on the average – taking both good times and bad times into consideration – secures for his goods no more and no less than his costs of production so the worker secures for his labour no more than the minimum required for the purchase of the necessities of life. This law of wages is applied with greater strictness as large-scale capitalist methods of production dominate an ever increasing number of branches of manufacture.

6. What types of workers existed before the industrial revolution?

In the past the relation of the workers to the ruling class and to the owners of property has varied according to the stage of development reached by society at any particular time. In the ancient world the workers were the slaves of the property owners. Slavery survives today in many backward countries and even in the southern parts of the United States. In the middle ages the workers were the serfs of the landowning aristocracy and this system of serfdom still survives in Russia, Hungary, and Poland. In addition – from the middle ages to the industrial revolution – the urban workers were in the service of bourgeois master craftsmen. And as large-scale manufactures developed (even without power-driven machinery) some workers came to be employed by large capitalists.

7. What is the difference between proletariat and slaves?

The slave is sold once and for all. The member of the proletariat has to sell himself daily – even hourly. The individual slave, however wretched his condition may be, belongs to a single master who has an interest in keeping him alive and fit. But the individual member of the proletariat belongs, as it were, to the whole bourgeois class. He can sell his labour only if someone wants to buy it and consequently he enjoys no security whatever. Only the proletariat as a whole enjoys a certain measure of security. While the slave stands outside the world of competition, the member of the proletariat is inside the world of competition and feels the effects of its fluctuations. The slave is regarded as a piece of property and is not accepted as a member of society. The member of the proletariat is recognised as a member of society. Slaves can enjoy a better standard of life than the proletariat. But the proletariat is part of a more highly developed form of society. The slave can secure his freedom if his property relationship with his master is ended. But all other rights of property in society survive and the status of the slave is changed into that of a member of the proletariat. On the other hand the proletariat can gain its freedom only if the whole conception of private property comes to an end.

8. What is the difference between proletariat and serfs?

The serf owns and uses an instrument of production – namely a piece of land – in return either for giving up part of the produce or for working for his lord. The member of the proletariat works with instruments of production that belong to somebody else and receives a part of the product in return. The serf gives up something but the worker has something taken off him. The serg enjoys security. The worker does not. The serf stands outside the competitive system while the member of the proletariat is part of this system. The serf can secure his freedom in various ways. He can escape to a town and become a craft worker. He can become a tenant by paying his lord a cash rent instead of rendering labour services or handing over farm produce. He can drive his lord away and become a freeholder. Whichever method the serf uses he secures his freedom by entering the property owning class and by entering the system of competition. The member of the proletariat can free himself only by ending all private property and all class distinctions.

9. What is the difference between the proletariat and the craft workers?

[There is a gap in the manuscript here.]

10. What is the difference between the modern proletariat and the craft workers (of the sixteenth, seventeenth and eighteenth centuries)?

From the sixteenth to the eighteenth centuries virtually all the craft workers owned some instrument of production such as a loom and some spinning wheels for his family as well as an allotment or garden that he could cultivate in his spare time. The member of the proletariat has none of these things. The craft worker nearly always lived in the country and enjoyed a more or less patriarchal relationship with his lord of the manor or his employer. A member of the proletariat generally lives in a big city and has a purely monetary relationship with his employer. The coming of large-scale capitalist industry has deprived the craft worker of his former patriarchal relationship with his employer. It has deprived him of his property. It has turned him into a member of the proletariat.

11. What were the immediate consequences of the industrial revolution and of the division of society into the bourgeoisie and the proletariat?

First, the domestic system of manufacture in its various forms was everywhere totally destroyed by the ever cheaper industrial products turned out by machinery. Underdeveloped countries more or less untouched by this great historical process and still in the age of domestic industry, were dramatically forced out of their backward state. They bought cheap English manufactured goods and allowed their own domestic industries to disappear. Countries like India which have made no progress for thousands of years have been revolutionised from top to bottom. Even China faces a revolution. Things have gone so far that a new machine, invented in England today, can deprive thousands of Chinese of their daily bread within a year. In this way modern machine industry has linked all the countries of the world together. All little local markets have been thrown together into a single world market and the way has been paved for civilisation and progress. Everything that happens in the civilised countries must have its consequences upon all other countries. If the workers in England or France secure their freedom then revolutions will occur in all other countries and the workers there too will gain their liberty.

Secondly, wherever modern machine industry has replaced the former domestic system the bourgeoisie has enormously increased its wealth and power and has become the dominant class in society. Consequently whenever this happened the bourgeoisie gained political power and pushed on one side the former ruling classes – the aristocracy on the land, the gild masters in the towns, and the absolute monarchy which represented the interests of those two sections of society. The bourgeoisie crushed the power of the nobility by abolishing all the former legal privileges of the landed aristocracy. The bourgeoisie also destroyed the master craftsmen by abolishing the privileges of the gilds. The former rights of the aristocrats and the gild masters were replaced by the system of free competition – that is to say the state of society in which every individual has the right to engage in any branch of industry that he pleases so long as he possesses the necessary capital. The introduction of free competition is a public declaration that in future the only inequalities in society will be those brought about by lack of capital. And since capital has now become the decisive force it is the capitalists – i.e. the bourgeoisie – who have become the foremost class in society. Free competition is essential when great industries start to develop because this is the only system within which modern manufactures can grow. Having crushed the social domination of the landed aristocracy and the gild masters the bourgeoisie proceeded to abolish their political power. And so the bourgeoisie became the leading class both socially and politically. Political power was gained through the introduction of the parliamentary system, equality before the law and the legal recognition of free competition. In Europe this has been done by the introduction of constitutional monarchies. In such monarchical states the franchise is limited to voters who have a certain amount of capital. In practice only the bourgeois class has the right to vote. The bourgeois voters elect the deputies and these bourgeois deputies have the power to fix the taxes and consequently are in a position to appoint a bourgeois government.

Thirdly, the proletariat develops in proportion to the

bourgeoisie. The growth in the number of the proletariat bears a direct relationship to the growth of the wealth of the bourgeoisie. The proletariat can be set to work only if adequate capital is available. Capital can increase only through the employment of labour. Consequently the expansion of the working class goes precisely hand in hand with the extension of capital. Both the bourgeoisie and the proletariat congregate simultaneously in great cities for it is there that large-scale industry can most successfully operate. Because they are concentrated together in large cities the working classes recognise their own strength. Moreover as this process continues – as more new machines are invented which drive the domestic craftsmen out of business – so the wages of the industrial workers are reduced. It has been seen that wages tend to sink to a minimum so that the situation of the proletariat becomes more and more unbearable. Social revolution is brought closer by the growing misery and by the growing sense of power of the industrial workers.

12. What were the further consequences of the industrial revolution?

The steam engine and the other new machines have provided modern industry with the means to achieve a limitless increase in the volume of production in a very short time. Free competition, an inevitable consequence of the new industrial system, has been greatly intensified because of this rapid expansion of production. A number of capitalists threw themselves into industry with the result that in a short time more goods were produced than could be consumed. The inability to dispose of manufactured products led to a so-called commercial crisis. The factories had to cease production, the manufacturers went bankrupt, and the workers had nothing to eat. There was universal distress. After a time the surplus goods were sold, the factories started to work again, and wages went up. Gradually business was better than ever. But before long too many goods were again produced and there was a new crisis which took exactly the same course as the previous crisis. In fact since the beginning of the nineteenth century the fortunes of industry have continually fluctuated between periods of prosperity and periods of slump. There has been a crisis every five or seven years and every time this state of affairs has been marked by great distress among the workers, by a general revolutionary fever, and by the most serious threat to the existing social order.

13. What are the consequences of these regularly recurring commercial crises?

First, although modern industry itself originally gave birth to free competition it has now developed to a stage when it no longer needs free competition. The position now is that competition – indeed the whole conception of rivalry between individual manufacturing firms – has become a restriction from which industry must and will free itself. So long as industry continues as it is at present it faces a new universal crisis every seven years which not only threatens the whole social structure but plunges the workers into deep distress and ruins a number of the bourgeoisie. Either modern industry must be given up – and that is utterly impossible – or society must be organised in a new way so that instead of individual manufacturers competing against each other, society as a whole becomes responsible for all industrial production in accordance with a predetermined plan.

Secondly, modern industry – and the illimitable expansion of output which it can achieve – has made possible the emergence of an economy in which such a volume of the necessities of life can be produced that every member of society could develop his potentialities to the full. The very feature of modern industry which at present results in commercial crises and social distress – under a different organisation of society – cause panics and distress to disappear. So it has been clearly proved

(i) that all these evils are due to the fact that the present organisation of society is no longer suited to the modern industrial economy,

(ii) that the means are at hand to abolish these evils completely through the creation of a new organisation of society.

14. How will society have to be organised in the future?

In the new society it will be essential to take the control of all branches of manufacture out of the hands of competing individuals. Industry will have to be run by society as a whole for everybody's benefit. It must be operated by all members of society in accordance with a common plan. Co-operation must take the place of competition. It has been seen that the present system of private property follows logically from the control of industry by private individuals. Again competition is simply the way in which industry is run under a system of private ownership of the means of production. Consequently the private ownership of individual industrial plants and the system of competition cannot logically be separated. So private property will also have to be abolished and it must be replaced by the sharing of all products in accordance with an agreed plan. This is the so-called "community of goods". Indeed the "abolition of private property" is the shortest and most striking way of summing up the way in which society as a whole will have to be recast in view of recent developments in the organisation of industry. Communists have every justification in making the abolition of private property the main demand on their political platform.

15. Is it true that the abolition of private property was formerly impossible?

All changes in the structure of society and all revolutions in the control over property are the necessary consequence of the creation of new forces of production to which the old system of property ownership cannot adapt themselves. Private property itself grew up in this way. Private property did not always exist. Towards the end of the middle ages a new method of producing goods developed which could not fit in with the existing system of feudalism and gilds. Private property replaced feudalism as the social organisation best adapted to the needs of the new type of economy. The domestic system and the early stages of modern industrialisation could survive only under a social system of private property. At that time it was impossible to produce, not merely a sufficient quantity of goods for everybody to be supplied, but also enough goods to provide a surplus that could be used to expand the social capital and to increase further the means of production. In those circumstances there were always bound to be two classes in society – a ruling class which controlled the means of production and a poor, oppressed class of wage-earners. The structure of these two classes depends upon the stage of economic development that has been attained. In the agrarian economy of the middle ages we had the baron and his serfs. In the cities of the later middle ages we had the gild master and his journeymen and apprentices. In the seventeenth century we had the early "factories" and their craftsmen. In the nineteenth century we have the large industrial establishments and the proletariat. It is clear that in the past the economy has not had the power to produce enough goods to satisfy everybody's demands. And the system of private property checked the expansion of the productive forces of society. But now three things have happened as the result of the development of modern large scale industries –

(i) Capital and productive powers have enormously increased and there is every prospect that this expansion will continue quickly and indefinitely.

(ii) These productive powers are concentrated in the hands of a small number of the bourgeoisie. At the same time the vast mass of the population is sinking to the level of the proletariat. The wealth of the bourgeoisie increases in exact proportion to the poverty of the working classes.

(iii) The enormously increased powers of production – which are capable of still further rapid expansion – can no longer be controlled by private property and by the bourgeoisie. They have led to serious disturbances in the structure of society. Consequently the abolition of private property is now not only possible but absolutely necessary.

16. Will it be possible to abolish private property by peaceful means?

It is highly desirable that private property should be abolished by peaceful means and the communists are the strongest advocates of this course of action. Communists are all too well aware of the fact that revolutions are both useless and harmful. They know very well that revolutions are not made on purpose but that they have always inevitably been brought about by circumstances which are quite beyond the control of particular political parties or social classes. Communists are also aware of the fact that in almost all civilised countries the growth of the proletariat has been followed by the forcible suppression of the proletariat and that it is the opponents of communism who have been evoking with all their might and main to bring about a revolution. If the oppressed proletariat is driven to revolt we communists will support the workers with deeds as vigorously as we now support them with words.

17. Will it be possible to abolish private property with one blow?

No, this will not be possible – just as it would not be possible *immediately* to expand the existing forces of production to such an extent that enough goods could be made to satisfy all the needs of the community. Consequently it is very likely that – after the revolution of the proletariat – the present structure of society will only change gradually. Private property can be abolished only when the economy is capable of producing the volume of goods needed to satisfy everybody's requirements.

18. How will this revolution progress?

Above all the revolution will lead to the promulgation of a democratic constitution and so – directly or indirectly – the political supremacy of the proletariat will be established. In England the power of the proletariat will be established directly because the majority of the population already consists of the working classes. In France and Germany the supremacy of the proletariat will be established indirectly because there the majority of the people is composed not only of workers but of peasants and the urban bourgeoisie – groups which are only now becoming part of the proletariat – and will, from a political point of view, become more and more dependent upon the proletariat whose demands they will have to accept.

Democracy is quite useless to the proletariat unless it can immediately be used as a means by which the proletariat can secure the adoption of laws which attack private property and ensure the future prosperity of the workers. The most important of such measures – already clearly necessary in the light of existing circumstances – are:

(i) Restriction of private property through progressive taxation, high death duties, abolition of the right of brothers and nephews to inherit property, and forced loans.

(ii) Gradual expropriation of landowners, factory owners and owners of railways and shipping lines – partly by the competition of nationalised industries and partly by expropriation (with compensation in the form of government bonds).

(iii) Confiscation of the property of all emigrés and all those who fight against the majority of the people.

(iv) The organisation of work – that is the employment of workers on state farms and nationalised factories and workshops. This would remove competition as between workers. In so far as private factory owners were allowed to survive they would be forced to pay the higher wages earned by workers in nationalised enterprises.

(v) All members of society to be under an equal obligation to work – until private property is completely abolished. Establishment of industrial armies, especially for agriculture.

(vi) Centralisation of the system of credit and of dealing in money in the hands of the state through the establishment of a nationalised bank with state capital and the abolition of all private banks and bankers.

(vii) Increase in the number of nationalised factories, workshops, railways and ships. All farm land to be cultivated. Land already under cultivation to be further improved as the capital and manpower available for the purpose increases.

(viii) Education of all children (as soon as they can leave their mothers) in state schools at public expense. Education and factory work to go hand in hand.

(ix) Erection of large buildings on state farms as common dwelling houses for groups of citizens who would be engaged both in agriculture and industry. In this way the advantages of town life and country life could be united without having to put up with the drawbacks of either.

(x) Destruction of all unhealthy and badly built dwellings and parts of towns.

(xi) Legitimate and illegitimate children to have equal rights of inheritance.

(xii) Concentration of all means of communication in the hands of the state.

All these measures cannot of course be introduced at once. But every one of these measures that is introduced will automatically lead to the introduction of another. Once the first radical attack has been made upon the institution of private property the proletariat will be forced to go further and to concentrate in the hands of the state all capital, all land, all industry, all transport, and all commerce. The measures that have been mentioned will all tend to achieve this object. They can be carried out – and they bring about the centralised control of all the means of production – in direct proportion to the extent to which the productivity of the country expands through the labours of the workers. Finally when all capital, all industrial and agricultural production, and all the means of exchange are concentrated in the hands of the state, then private property will automatically disappear, money will become superfluous, production will have increased to such an extent and human beings will have changed so much that the old society will have disappeared.

19. Will it be possible for this revolution to take place in a single country?

No, this will not be possible. Modern industry has already created a world market. All countries in the world – certainly the civilised ones – are so closely linked together that every country is influenced by what happens elsewhere. Moreover all civilised states now have the same social structure. In all of them the bourgeoisie and the proletariat have become the two main classes in society and in all of them the struggle between them has become the decisive struggle of our time. Consequently the communist revolution will not be a national revolution in one country. It will take place simultaneously in all the civilised countries – certainly in England, America, France and Germany. The speed with which the revolution will take place in these countries will depend upon which state has the most developed industry, the greatest wealth, and the largest forces of production. So in Germany the revolution will take place more slowly and will be achieved with the greatest difficulty while in England it will take place most rapidly and with the greatest ease. The revolution will have significant repercussions in the other countries in the world and will change and speed up developments that have occurred so far. It will be a universal revolution and its effects will be felt everywhere.

20. What will be the consequences of the final abolition of private property?

Society will take all means of production, all transport facilities, and all means of exchange out of private hands. The distribution of the available output will be planned by society in accordance with the needs of the community. In this way the evil consequences of modern industrial expansion will be removed and commercial crises will disappear. The expansion of output – which in society as it is now constructed leads to overproduction and is a major cause of social distress – will in future be insufficient for the needs of the community and will have to be still further increased. Overproduction will no longer lead to social distress. It will not only meet immediate needs but will give a new impetus to further progress. And this progress will not, as in the past, bring the social order into a state of confusion. Modern industry, freed from the incubus of private property, will expand at such a rate that the present rate of expansion will appear as insignificant as the output of the old domestic system appeared to be in relation to the output of industry today. The new rate of industrial growth will produce enough goods to satisfy all the demands of society. At present farming is restricted by the pressure of private property and the system of dividing land into very small holdings. In future farming will be able to make full use of new scientific methods and will expand to such an extent that its output will be sufficient to meet all the requirements of society. By these means society will achieve an output which will be sufficient for the needs of all its members and will be fairly divided among them. The division of society into rival classes opposed to each other will be superfluous. It will not only be superfluous but it will not be possible in the new society of the future. It is the division of labour which has split society into classes and in future the division of labour as we now know it will disappear completely. Mechanical and chemical aids are not in themselves sufficient to achieve the volume of output that is needed. It will be necessary to secure an appropriate increase in the skill of the people who will use these machines and chemical processes. Just as the peasants and craftsmen of the eighteenth century had to alter their way of life and actually became quite different people when they were swallowed up by modern industry so the new method of production and society as a whole will require the services of a new type of person and will in fact itself be responsible for creating such a new type. Production by society as a whole cannot be accomplished by people as they are today. At present every individual is subordinated to a particular branch of industry to which he is chained and by which he is exploited. At present every individual has developed one skill at the expense of all others. He is familiar with only one branch – or a part of a branch – of production. Even now modern industry has less and less use for such people. A society which plans and operates all industries requires people with a variety of skills who are in a position to appreciate the whole manufacturing process. At present machinery has led to the division of labour and has turned one man into a peasant, a second into a shoemaker, a third into a factory worker, and a fourth into a speculator on the stock exchange. All this will be swept away. Education in the future will enable young people to appreciate the whole process of production and will give them the training necessary to exercise one skill after another according to the varying needs of society and their own inclinations. They will not be one-sided human beings of the type now created by the division of labour. In this way society organised on communist lines will give its members the opportunity to use to the full all the varied skills of which they are capable. The existing social class will of course disappear. Social classes cannot in principle exist side by side with a communist society. And the creation of a communist society provides the means by which class rivalry can be abolished.

Similarly in a communist society there can be no clash of interests between town and country. It is an elementary principle of communism that farming and industrial work should be carried out by the same people and not by two different classes. The contrast between the scattering of the rural population over the countryside and the concentration of the urban population in the towns represents the existence of both an undeveloped system of agriculture and an underdeveloped system of industry. This is a barrier to progress the effects of which are already very much in evidence.

The main results of the abolition of private property will be the joint and planned exploitation of the forces of production by society as a whole; the expansion of output to such an extent that it will satisfy everybody's needs; the ending of the system by which one man's requirements can be satisfied only at the expense of someone else; the complete destruction of social classes and the conflicts to which they give rise; and the universal development of the skills of all members of society by industrial training, by periodic changing of jobs, by the universal sharing of all products, and by the union of town and countryside.

21. What influence will a communist society have upon family life?

Under communism the relationship between the two sexes will be a purely private matter which affects only the persons concerned and with which society has nothing to do. This will be possible because communism will abolish private property and will bring up all children together and by these means the foundations of marriage as it now exists – the dependence of wives upon their husbands and the dependence of children upon their parents – will be abolished. This is the answer to the outcry of highly moral members of the bourgeoisie against the communist "community of women". In fact the 'community of women' is a feature of bourgeois society and can be seen clearly in operation today in the institution of prostitution. Prostitution depends upon private property and will disappear when private property disappears. Far from introducing the "community of women" communism will abolish it.

22. What will be the relationship between communism and existing nationalities?

No change.

23. What will be the relationship between communism and the existing religions?

No change.

24. What is the difference between communism and socialism?

The so-called socialists may be divided into three groups.

The *first* group consists of members of the old feudal and patriarchal society which is in the process of being destroyed by modern industry, by world trade and by the bourgeois society which has arisen as a result of these developments. This group believes that the evils of modern society can be abolished by re-establishing the feudal and patriarchal society in which such evils did not exist. In one way or another all their suggestions really have this end in view. Communists will always attack these reactionary socialists however many tears they shed over the sorrows of the proletariat. This is because

(i) They are supporting a policy which is absolutely impossible to carry out.

(ii) They are trying to restore the authority of the nobles, the gild masters and the owners of great workshops – with their associated absolute or feudal monarchs, officials, soldiers and priests. Their society it is true was free from the evils of the present society. On the other hand their society had plenty of evils of its own and the oppressed workers of those days did not have a communist organisation to work for their freedom.

(iii) They show themselves in their true colours by immediately uniting with the bourgeoisie against the proletariat whenever the proletariat shows signs of adopting communist or revolutionary principles.

The *second* group consists of members of the existing society who are afraid that this society will collapse if nothing is done about the evils for which society is responsible. So they advocate the maintainance of the existing society while endeavouring to remove the evils associated with it. To achieve this some of them recommend the adoption of more welfare schemes while others advocate schemes which pretend to re-organise society but in fact would retain the fundamental principles upon which society is organised. Communists will always attack these *bourgeois* socialists because they are the allies of the enemies of communism and they defend a society which communists wish to overthrow.

The *third* group consists of *democratic* socialists who advocate some of the changes that communists advocate. But they advocate these changes not as a means of establishing a communist society but simply as measures which they regard as adequate to cope with the evils that exist in modern society. Some of these democratic socialists are working men who have not yet fully understood what has to be done to free the proletariat. Others are craftsmen and shopkeepers – a class which in many ways has the same interests as the proletariat, particularly during the period when democracy is being achieved and the first socialist measures are being introduced. The communists will be prepared to come to an understanding with these socialists and to make common cause with them – in so far as these socialists do not serve the ends of the ruling bourgeoisie class and attack the communists. It is clear that communists must be prepared to enter into discussions with those socialists so as to try to remove differences that may divide them.

25. What is the relationship between the communists and the other political parties of our time?

The relationship differs in various countries. In England, France and Belgium, where the bourgeoisie is in power, the communists have an interest in co-operating with the various democratic parties that exist in those states. The co-operation will become closer the more the democratic parties advocate socialist measures which approach the goal to which the communists are striving. The communist co-operation with the democratic parties will become closer the more clearly and the more definitely those parties represent the interests of the working classes and seek support from the working classes. In England, for example, the working class Chartists are much closer to the communists than the democratic bourgeoisie or so-called radicals.

In America, where a democratic constitution is in force, the communists must work with the party that is prepared to use this constitution against the bourgeois in the interests of the workers. This party is the agrarian National Reform Party.

In Switzerland the Radicals – though a very mixed party – are the only people with whom the communists could co-operate. The Radicals of Waadtland and Geneva are the most progressive.

Finally, in Germany the decisive struggle between the bourgeoisie and the absolute monarchy has only just begun. The decisive struggle between the communists and the bourgeoisie cannot be undertaken until the bourgeoisie is the ruling class in society. In the circumstances it is in the interest of the communists that the bourgeoisie should be helped to attain power as quickly as possible – so that the communists can then turn them out again. Consequently the communists must support the liberal bourgeois party against the governments. But the communists must be careful that they do not deceive themselves in the way that the bourgeois party deceives itself. The communists must not be under any illusions concerning the promises of the bourgeoisie that a victory of the bourgeoisie would be followed by reforms which would benefit the proletariat. The only advantages that the communist would derive from a victory of the bourgeoisie would be

(i) the granting of various concessions which would make it easier for the communists to defend, discuss and propogate their principles and so unite the proletariat into a single, well organised, militant class,

(ii) the knowledge that on the day when the absolute governments fall, the struggle between the bourgeoisie and the working classes can begin. From that day onwards in Germany the policy of the communists will be exactly the same as it now is in those countries in which the bourgeoisie has already achieved power.

IX

STATUTES OF THE COMMUNIST LEAGUE, 1847[1]

WORKERS OF THE WORLD, UNITE!

Part I

The League (*Bund*)

Article 1

The purpose of the League is to destroy the power of the middle classes and to secure power for the proletariat. The League aims at abolishing the existing bourgeois society which is based upon the opposition of one class to another and at establishing a new classless society in which private property will cease to exist.

Article 2

The conditions of membership are

(*a*) to adopt a way of life in conformity with the aims of the League and to work for the achievement of those aims.

(*b*) to engage in communist propaganda with revolutionary energy and zeal.

(*c*) to accept the doctrines of communism.

(*d*) to refuse to support any political or national party which opposes communism; to refuse to belong to any association registered with the local authorities and opposed to communism.

(*e*) to accept the decisions of the League.

(*f*) to keep secret the existence and the decisions of the League.

(*g*) to be admitted into a communist cell by unanimous vote.

Anyone who fails to meet the conditions of membership will be excluded from membership (see Part VIII).

Article 3

All members are equal and are brothers and as such should be helped in every way.

[1] See Wermuth and Stieber, *Die Communisten-Verschwörungen im neunzehnten Jahrhundert* (two volumes, 1853–4; new edition 1969), Vol. 1, Appendix 10, pp. 239–43; G. Winkler, *Dokumente zur Geschichte des Bundes der Kommunisten* (1957), pp. 106–11.

Article 4
All members will be given special names.

Article 5
The League is organised in cells, groups, senior groups, the executive committee, and the congress.

Part II

The Cell (*die Gemeinde*)

Article 6
The minimum membership of a cell is three and the maximum is twenty.

Article 7
Every cell elects a chairman and a vice-chairman. The chairman presides over meetings. The vice-chairman acts as treasurer and presides over meetings in the absence of the chairman.

Article 8
New members are admitted by the chairman if the cell has previously given its approval.

Article 9
Cells are unknown to each other and do not correspond with each other.

Article 10
Cells are named so that they can be distinguished from one another.

Article 11
Any member who changes his residence must notify the chairman of his cell.

Part III

The Group (*der Kreis*)

Article 12
A group includes at least two and not more than ten cells.

Article 13
The chairmen and vice-chairmen of the cells together form the committee to administer the affairs of the group. The group com-

mittee elects one of its members to act as group chairman. The group corresponds with its constituent cells and with the senior group.

Article 14

The administration of the group is responsible for all cells within the group.

Article 15

New cells must either join an existing group or link up with established cells to form a new group.

Part IV

The Senior Group (*der leitende Kreis*)

Article 16

The various groups in a country or province come under the oversight of a senior group.

Article 17

The congress of the League, on the recommendation of the executive committee of the League, is responsible for organising the groups and for deciding which of them shall be the senior group.

Article 18

The senior group has authority over all its constituent groups. It corresponds with its constituent groups and with the central executive committee of the League.

Article 19

Newly established groups are allocated to the nearest senior group.

Article 20

Senior groups are responsible in the first instance to the executive committee but they are ultimately responsible to the congress of the League.

Part V

The Central Executive Committee

Article 21

The central executive committee administers the affairs of the League and is responsible to the congress.

Article 22

The central executive committee consists of at least five members and is elected by the group committee of the place at which the congress is held.

Article 23

The central executive committee corresponds with the committees of senior groups. It makes a report every three months on the affairs of the whole League.

Part VI
Common Regulations

Article 24

The cells, committees of the groups, and the central executive committee meet at least once a fortnight.

Article 25

The members of the central executive committee and the group committees serve for one year and are eligible for re-election. But they can be dismissed at any time by those who elected them.

Article 26

Elections take place in the month of September.

Article 27

The group committees are responsible for arranging discussions in the cells concerning the policy and the aims of the League. If the executive committee considers that certain matters are of immediate interest it should urge all groups and cells to organise discussions on these questions.

Article 28

Individual members of the League should submit a written report to their group committee at least once every three months. Each cell should report to the committee of its group at least once a month. Each group must send a report to its senior group every two months. Every senior group should submit a report on the activities of its constituent groups to the central executive committee once every three months.

Article 29

Every committee should take steps to ensure the security and the effective working of the League. It is responsible for taking all necessary measures – within the authority given to it by the Statutes of the League – to bring this about. It should report immediately to the next higher authority when it has been necessary to take such measures.

Part VII
The Congress

Article 30

The congress is the legislative organ of the whole League. All suggestions for the alteration or amendment of the Statutes should be sent to the central executive committee through a senior group. Such suggestions will be submitted to the congress of the League by the central executive committee.

Article 31

Every group may send one representative to the congress.

Article 32

Every group with a membership of under thirty is entitled to send one representative to the congress. For each further thirty members an additional representative may be sent to the congress. A group may be represented by a member of the League who is a member of another group. In such a case, however, the representative must bring with him to the congress a certificate which proves that he is entitled to represent the group in question.

Article 33

The congress will meet every year in the month of August. In exceptional circumstances the central executive committee may call an extraordinary meeting of the congress.

Article 34

At each meeting the congress will decide at which place the central executive committee will sit for the next year. The congress will also decide where the next annual meeting of the congress will be held.

Article 35

Members of the central executive committee are entitled to attend the congress of the League but their votes will carry the same weight as those of normal representatives.

Article 36

At the conclusion of each of its meetings the congress will issue in the name of the party a circular to its groups and a manifesto to the public.

Part VIII
Activities Harmful to the League

Article 37

Anyone who fails to observe the conditions of membership (Article 2) will – according to circumstances – be given an opportunity to resign or will be expelled. Anyone who has resigned may be readmitted to the League but anyone who has been expelled is not eligible for readmission.

Article 38

Only the congress of the League has the authority to expel members.

Article 39

A group or a cell which is not attached to a group has the power to ask a member to resign. Such action must be immediately reported to higher authority. The final decision will be taken by the congress of the League.

Article 40

The readmission of a member who has been asked to resign is in the hands of the central executive committee acting on the recommendation of the former member's group.

Article 41

A group committee is responsible for dealing with offences against the League and for carrying out the sentence.

Article 42

The conduct of persons who have been asked to resign or who have been expelled should – in the interests of the League – be watched so as to render them harmless. Any action taken by such individuals (which appears likely to harm the League) should be reported to the cell which is likely to be affected by such conduct.

Part IX
Finance

Article 43

The congress fixes a minimum individual subscription for each country.

Article 44

Half of this subscription is allocated to the central executive committee and half is allocated to the group or to the cell (if the cell is not attached to a group).

Article 45

The funds of the central executive committee will be used

(i) to cover the cost of administration and correspondence

(ii) to print and distribute propaganda leaflets

(iii) to defray the travelling expenses of emisaries appointed by the central executive committee for specific purposes.

Article 46

The funds of local groups or cells will be used

(i) to defray the cost of correspondence

(ii) to print and distribute propaganda leaflets

(iii) to defray the expenses of appropriate emisaries.

Article 47

Groups or cells which are six months in arrears with their subscriptions to the central executive committee will be recommended by the executive committee for expulsion from the League.

Article 48

Group committees will lay their accounts before their cells for audit at least every three months. The central executive committee will inform the congress of the financial position of the League giving information concerning income, expenditure and the balance in hand. Any misappropriation of funds belonging to the League will be severely punished.

Article 49

Extraordinary expenses and the cost of running the congress will be covered by special levies.

Part X

Admission

Article 50

The chairman of the cell will read Articles 1 to 49 of the Statutes to the candidate for admission. He will explain their meaning and he will make a brief speech emphasising the responsibilities which the candidate will accept as a member of the League. Then the chairman will ask the candidate: "Do you now wish to join the League?" If the candidate answers "Yes" the chairman will accept his word of honour that he will faithfully carry out his obligations as a member of the League. Then the chairman will declare that the candidate is now a member of the League and he will introduce him to the next meeting of the cell.

London, December 8, 1847
In the name of the second congress held in the autumn of 1847
(signed): Engels (secretary) Karl Schapper (president).

X

DEMANDS OF THE GERMAN COMMUNIST PARTY, 1848[1]

WORKERS OF THE WORLD, UNITE!

1. The whole of Germany is declared to be a united indivisible republic.
2. Every German over the age of twenty-one is entitled to the vote and may stand for election provided that he does not have a criminal record.
3. Deputies will be paid so that workers can sit in the German parliament.
4. Popular militia. The armies of the future will be armies of workers (as well as armies of soldiers) so that they can earn their keep instead of being a burden on the taxpayer. This will also serve as a method by which work can be planned and organised.
5. Justice is free.
6. All feudal dues and services with which people living in country districts are at present burdened will be abolished. No compensation will be paid to the owners.
7. Landed estates and mines, owned by royalty and feudal nobles, will be nationalised. Such estates will in future be operated on a large scale with the aid of the most modern technical knowledge for the benefit of the whole community.
8. Farm mortgages will be nationalised. In future farmers and peasants will pay interest on mortgages to the state.
9. In those districts where farms are leased to tenants the ground rent will in future be paid to the state.

The measures listed in paragraphs 6, 7, 8 and 9 are aimed at reducing the public and private financial burdens of farmers and smallholders without reducing the revenues required by the state and without endangering agricultural output.

The landowner who is neither a tenant farmer nor a smallholder

[1] Wermuth and Stieber, *Die Communisten-Verschwörungen des neunzehnten Jahrhunderts* (two volumes, 1853–4, new edition, 1969), Vol. 1, pp. 68–9.

takes no part whatever in the output of agricultural products. What he consumes, therefore, is wasted and is to be condemned.

10. A single state bank – with notes of legal tender – will replace all private banks.

This measure will make it possible to regulate credit in the interest of the *whole* community and will undermine the power of the great financiers. The state bank will gradually replace gold and silver by paper money and will thereby cheapen the essential means by which citizens exchange goods and service. The expansion of the universal means of exchange at home will enable gold and silver to be used for foreign transactions. This measure is also necessary to secure the support of the conservative middle classes for the revolution.

11. All communications – railways, canals, steamships, highways, post office etc. – will be taken over by the state and nationalised. Transport service will be made available without charge to poor people.
12. The salaries of all civil servants will be equalised except that those with families – and therefore with heavier responsibilities – will draw higher salaries than the others.
13. Church and state will be completely separated. Priests of all churches will be paid by their congregations.
14. Restriction of the right to inherit property.
15. Introduction of highly progressive system of direct taxation and abolition of indirect taxes.
16. Erection of national workshops. The state guarantees full employment and takes responsibility for looking after workers who are incapable of earning a living.
17. Universal free education.

It is in the interest of the German proletariat, the peasants and the lower middle classes to work energetically for the adoption of these measures. Only if this programme is achieved will it be possible to save the millions of people in Germany who are exploited by a handful of oppressors and who will continue to be held in subjection. Only if this programme is achieved will the oppressed receive justice and enjoy the power that they ought to have since they are the people who generate all the wealth that society enjoys.

The Committee: Karl Marx, Karl Schapper, H. Bauer, F. Engels, J. Moll, W. Wolff.

Index

(Marx and Engels omitted)